DANCE
OF DIVINE
LOVE

DANCE OF DIVINE LOVE

The Rāsa Līlā of Krishna from
the *Bhāgavata Purāṇa*,
India's Classic Sacred Love Story
Introduced, Translated, and Illuminated

GRAHAM M. SCHWEIG

PRINCETON UNIVERSITY PRESS
PRINCETON AND OXFORD

Published by Princeton University Press,
41 William Street, Princeton, New Jersey 08540
In the United Kingdom: Princeton University Press,
3 Market Place, Woodstock, Oxfordshire OX20 1 SY

Library of Congress Cataloging-in-Publication Data

Puranas. Bhāgavatapurāṇa. Selections.
Dance of divine love : the Rasa Lila of Krishna from the
Bhagavata Purana, India's classic sacred love story /
introduced, translated and illuminated [by]
Graham M. Schweig.
p. cm.
Includes bibliographical references and index.
ISBN 0-691-11446-3 (cloth : alk. paper)
1. Puranas. Bhāgavatapurāṇa—Criticism, interpretation, etc.
2. Rādhā (Hindu deity) 3. Krishna (Hindu deity) 4. Rāsa
Līlā (Dance) I. Schweig, Graham M., 1953–
BL1140.4.B436P87 2005
294.5'925—dc22 2004045788

British Library Cataloging-in-Publication Data is available

This book has been composed in Minion
and Hindi Sanskrit

Printed on acid-free paper. ∞

Frontispiece. "The Wondrous Circle of the Rāsa Dance: Rāsa Maṇḍala" (illustrates the *Bhāgavata Purāṇa,* book ten, chapter 33, verses 2 and 3, or Rāsa Līlā 5.2 and 5.3). Painting by Krishna Priya in Jaipur, State of Rajasthan, India (2001). Opaque watercolor, silver, and gold on handmade jute and cotton board (31½ inches by 23½ inches). Commissioned by and located in the private collection of the author.

pup.princeton.edu

Printed in the United States of America

1 3 5 7 9 10 8 6 4 2

To the cowherd maidens of Vraja,
and to all lovers of the divine.

Contents

Part III Notes and Comments

Part IV The Sanskrit Text

List of Figures and Tables

FIGURES

TABLES

Foreword

This book will give you access to a poem that has been loved in India for over a thousand years. It is the long lyric poem called the Rāsa-Pāñcādhyāyī, "The Five Chapters on the Rāsa," the word Rāsa referring to Krishna's dance with his female devotees. A long and distinctive poem preserved in the tenth book of the beautifully written *Bhāgavata Purāṇa,* its present form was completed, at the latest, by the ninth century. Very early the entire Purāṇa, with its precious insert, received all-India fame, as attested by the great number of manuscript copies that are found even today in the old libraries of every region. It was a best-seller. It is known that these copies were much read and well remembered. The proof lies in the unanimity and correctness of the surviving texts, compared with the spoiled texts of most Purāṇas, which have suffered from careless copying and have been bloated with graceless interpolations. Not so for the *Bhāgavata.* It was defended from corruptions by its ardent, vigilant, and well-versed audiences. As early as 1030 A.D. the name of the *Bhāgavata* was given to al-Biruni in a list of the eighteen authentic and orthodox Purāṇas. Today that is still its status among Hindus—a sacred scripture.

In contrast with India's resonant appreciation of the *Bhāgavata Purāṇa,* the outside world has ventured little appraisal of it until recently. There were reasons for this taciturnity. Some Western writers were stunned and repelled by the erotic factor in its contents. Others were silenced by the difficulty of its language, which made confident judgments risky. Well-considered literary discussions were also discouraged by a lack of any but perfunctory translations into English. About other Purāṇas—cruder in their language and their thought—scholars' comments were frank and full and seldom complimentary. But the *Bhāgavata Purāṇa* was perceived to be different and not easy to judge. Generations of scholars dealt with *this* Purāṇa in a few positive words, and passed on quietly to discuss other Indian writings that were easier to assess.

Today, Sanskrit studies are no longer in their infancy in the extra-Indian world. Students of Sanskrit now know and pay the price for competence in that language, and have become skilled workers in many new fields, including the *Bhāgavata Purāṇa.* The metric science of the Purāṇa's poetry is understood. The poet's language is perceived now to be a cultivated diction, often using courtly figures of speech such as the bards of Indian kings were wont to use. Touches of the revered language of the Vedas are noticed in it, and the mellifluous flow of the poet's sound effects are appreciated. The personal genius of its legendary author, known as Vyāsa, is now recognized and acclaimed. Connoisseurs increasingly acknowledge that we have here a poem that is entitled to world esteem. A notable evaluation is that of Professor Daniel H. H. Ingalls of Harvard: "For all its traditional lore and traditional piety, and despite its frequent archaisms, the *Bhāgavata* remains, especially in its tenth book, the most enchanting poem ever written."[1] This rating is high, but it comes from an authority with long experience as teacher of the *Bhāgavata Purāṇa* to university students—including our translator, Dr. Schweig.

Even students of modern competence face the ancient and ever-present difficulty in producing from a great poem a great literary translation. Help is not available, as in the case of some classic texts, from a long succession of respectable English translators of good if not great talent. The only older translation that is praiseworthy for its literary quality is M. Hauvette-Besnault's translation into French done in 1865 and published in the fifth volume of Eugene Burnouf's *Le Bhagavata Purana* (Paris, 1898, 1981ff.). Dr. Schweig's sensitive literal translation into English now takes the lead. It is up-to-date, expert, and exceptionally lucid.

With the appearance of this major translation, a milestone will be passed in the world's acquaintance with the Sanskrit poetry of Krishna-centered Vaishnavism. In a thousand years, Krishna-worshiping communities produced in Sanskrit two lyric poems of supreme quality: the *Gītagovinda* of Jayadeva, and the Rāsa-Pañcādhyāyī that we have at hand. The unsatisfying nature of the early translations of both caused critics to doubt that the difficulties of translating either of them would ever be met. But, twenty-five years ago, Barbara Stoler Miller produced the *Love Song of the Dark Lord: Jayadeva's Gītagovinda* (New York: Columbia University Press, 1977) to such acclaim that experts declared that the way to Jayadeva had been opened. This should be the year of a proclamation of like importance: that the world has access now to both of the masterpieces of an entire poetic tradition.

Beyond the literary excellence that it shares with the *Gītagovinda,* our "Five Chapters on the Rāsa" has a great additional role as shaper of the course of Hindu religion. Born out of the life of a strong sect that

1. Foreword in *Krishna: Myths, Rites, and Attitudes,* edited by Milton Singer (Honolulu: East-West Center, 1996), p. vi.

in the ninth century was already more than a millennium old, this poem, during the next thousand years, was itself the mother of many new religious movements. Once all the persons of this Purāṇa's faith could be identified effectively by calling them Bhāgavatas. But these Gopāla-worshipers grew in various lines, and now precise reference requires the names of their denominations. Yet a usefulness remains in the single vague term Krishnaism, which recognizes a certain unity in them all. Today the faith has a significant following outside of India as well. The prominence within Hinduism of the worship of Krishna as Gopāla, the cowherd youth, has not yet received due recognition. In the world's awareness it was long overshadowed by India's *advaita* monism that has commonly been presented in the past as the mainstream of religious India. We know well the *advaita* teaching that individual persons, human or divine, are unreal as such, and that all such illusory persons, when they know the truth, will vanish in the impersonal divine Absolute. The worshipers of Krishna as Bhagavān or personal Lord are now that powerful monism's strongest modern competitors. The immensity of their movement—never measured by any census—is suggested only in police estimates of the number of pilgrims that in a given year flood their holy city of Mathurā. Two million devotees, they say, come within a year, on a monsoon day to celebrate Krishna's birth or on a full-moon night of autumn to hear or tell or see rehearsals of the story of Krishna's dancing of the Rāsa. That story's power, as paradigm, is beyond calculation.

Worldwide, old religious communities remember quite selectively the various ages of their history. They retrace in memory, again and again, those special experiences, real or imagined, that shaped their people. These famous narratives become their catechetical schools, their mental dwelling places, and the workshops of their collective thought. Jews remember above all the Exodus. Christians of New Testament times and all later times ponder the story of the passion of Jesus. In their thought about *this* history, marked by the cross, much of their thought about *all* history evolves. Buddhists never forget the night of the enlightenment of the Buddha and the emergence of the prime Buddhist truths. Small images of the Buddha, serene under the Bodhi tree, betoken everywhere the Buddhist identity of the displayer. The painting at the front of this book, of Krishna leading the dancers of the Rāsa, is such a paradigmatic presentation of a faith, a shaper of the faith, and a token of the presence of a believer.

The *Bhāgavata Purāṇa* was, by the love and use that it received, the reformulator of the ancient Bhāgavata faith. "The Five Chapters on the

Rāsa" in particular provided a new mental world, and new ideas that became very potent. The one word that most refreshed a jaded community was the old but unexploited word *līlā* or "sport" (see the word in *The Encyclopedia of Religion,* New York: Macmillan, 1987). The idea was that any act done by the one Lord of all the universes was, by reason of His already possessing all, an act done without self-interest, sinless, and an act of grace. Such joyful and spontaneous sportiveness impelled God's creation of the world. In time this idea of divine sport had many impacts: in encouraging a new spirit in social ethics, for instance. Here we shall discuss only its effect on thought about sexuality, a matter on which the "Five Chapters" will compel all readers to reflect. Any possible sex-like act of God, the thinkers held, would necessarily be as free of self-interest as his creation of worlds. God, who already has all and enjoys all, could not possibly in love be motivated by lust, or commit the offense of seduction or rape. God's erotic sports are gracious acts of shared joy, granted out of love for his devotees.

The developers of this thought are of course deep readers of "The Five Chapters on the Rāsa" and defenders of the purity of the Rāsa dance. Justification of human promiscuity was far from their intentions. Not desireless but rather lustful, such behavior was deemed to be sinful, and anyone even dreaming of imitating the acts of Krishna should expect ruination (BhP10:33.30). What ordinary believers in Krishna were entitled to do was to contemplate and celebrate the blameless and beautiful acts of Krishna. Celebration of all of Krishna's deeds had in fact been required long ago, in *Bhagavad Gītā* 4:9 and 10:9, verses that command devotees to enlighten each other with joyous narration of Krishna's marvelous acts. This duty and pleasure the devotees of the new age now took up, with "The Five Chapters on the Rāsa" in hand or in mind. They brought about a revolution, for instance, in the content of the meditational disciplines of Krishna worshipers. Even the theistic bhakti traditions had their yogic practices, and directors of the inner life. But the content of Krishnaite introspection became, now, something extraordinary. In the older and central yoga, one of the very first demands, asked of any beginner, was to root out every vestige of erotic thought. With the meditators on Krishna, to the contrary, the queen of all the moods of meditation became the *madhura,* the romantic mood, that hopes for experience of the deity in an erotic relationship. The revered saints of these spiritual seekers were not ascetics but the very nubile Gopīs, the cowherd women of Vraja. The story of Krishna and the cowherd women became the prime literature of meditation. Writers fulfilled a great demand for the story, told in innumerable Sanskrit manuscripts, in vernacular translations and retellings. The erotic aspects of the stories were no longer resisted but deliberately evoked and dwelt on in the mind. Even devotees' conception of salvation was eroticized: the ancient paradises—Kailāsa, even Vaikuṇṭha—lost their charm. Devotees aspired now to reach the cow-world Goloka, highest heaven of all, the heaven of Krishna, where the blessed Gopīs are assembled, and Krishna in his eternal sporting-place calls departed devotees to savor eternally the blameless deeds described in scripture.

It is not surprising that the flood of eroticism in Krishnaite literature and life has caused some outsiders to see these worshipers as a libertine community, praising and probably practicing promiscuity in sexual matters. It is indeed to be observed that the orthodox Hindu society was, after the triumph of caste in the Gupta age, one of the most restrictive in the world in sexual matters, and that, by the time of the *Bhāgavata Purāṇa,* tantric groups had arisen that were in rebellion against the severe moral codes. In secluded places they were said to hold lawless congress in meetings comparable in some ways to the gathering for the Rāsa. Were these Bhāgavatas not social rebels of the same kind?

Not at all, according to our best records. No report is known, made by either friend or foe, that Bhāgavatas ever performed the Rāsa as carnal act, either as holy rite or in folk festivals. The *Bhāgavata*'s prohibition appears to have been observed. Even in the gossip of outsiders these believers are never connected with the tantrics. From the time of the *Bhagavad Gītā,* civic concern had been prominent in their literature. Their relationships with the dominant brahmins and kshatriyas, arbiters of Hindu society, were not hostile. The Bhāgavata community was part of the establishment, we would say, and through the thousand years following the writing of the *Bhāgavata Purāṇa,* they were clearly supporters rather than opponents of the orthodox morality. When a prurient literature did appear—the Ratī school of Hindi poetry that throve for several centuries and starred even Krishna as roué—it had to find its patrons in the very secular and worldly royal courts of north India, not among devotees. At the end of a millennium of the ever-increasing influence of Krishna worship, Hindu society retains its puritan character, more because of than in spite of Krishna worship.

The community's intention to support the established morality is in fact stated clearly in the *Bhāgavata Purāṇa* itself. In the very last verse of "The Five Chapters on the Rāsa," we are at that point in Sanskrit writings when authors address their faithful readers in a sentimental conclusion. Commonly they celebrate the greatness of the book just written, then give assurance regarding the magnificent rewards that will inevitably come to patient readers or hearers. It is an effusive moment and the promises are great: expiation of all sins, vast spiritual merit, ascent to heavenly realms, in the end final liberation, and commonly, in the meantime, diverse material benefits of no mean dimension. In striking contrast is the simplicity of the promise uttered by the author of this work. Read *Bhāgavata*'s verse 10.33.40 (herein as act 5 verse 40) for yourself. Only one assurance is given: the person who has heard this story will attain high devotion to the Lord, and then, sobered, he will quickly throw off lust, the disease of the heart.

In no other work have I seen this conclusion. It is not a thoughtless formula but a personal utterance for a special occasion. Its simplicity bespeaks sincerity. The intention that sustained the author in writing the entire poem is before us. Just how hearing this story will throw off lust may not be clear to everybody. There is some mystery here. But no culture on earth is not compelled by human nature to face in some degree the tensions that the *Bhāgavata* addresses. For all, there is something here to learn. At very least, we have in this lyric poem the literary wellspring of a major faith. For study of it, there is no better starting point than this.

The verses are eloquently expressive, but they are not simple, and even a mastery of Sanskrit grammar does not solve all of the riddles that they present to outsiders. To lay forth the meanings of these lines is not an easy task for anybody. By reason of the many uncertainties, even scholars who know Sanskrit well have shrunk from publishing their translations. Professor Schweig, who has had a personal interest in the devotional Vaishnava tradition, has pondered the Rāsa-Pañcādhyāyī for eight years. As an academic student of Indian culture and religion, his search has been for the original meanings of the author. He has contemplated the insights of Western experts and traditional Indian interpreters as well. He has paid the price of certainty, and he puts before you, boldly, to the best of his ability and maybe to the limit of possibility, what the poet intended to say.

The story is before you. Know this poem, and you will know something of the spirit of Indian civilization.

Norvin Hein
Professor Emeritus of Comparative Religion
Yale University

Acknowledgments

The idea for this book began during my doctoral studies at Harvard University. For years, my intention for a dissertation topic had been to compare theological ideas from sixteenth-century Spanish Catholic mysticism to the theistic mysticism of Caitanya Vaishnavism—it was never my plan to focus on the Rāsa Līlā of the *Bhāgavata Purāṇa.* Under the guidance of Professor John B. Carman, however, I discovered how little scholarly attention had been given to the highest vision of the Vaishnava side of the comparison, and thus I began to concentrate on the Caitanya school's vision of the Rāsa Līlā in order to pave the way for further comparative work. My gratitude, therefore, first goes to John Carman for his direction that ultimately led to the writing of this volume.

A book that presents one of the world's greatest pieces of sacred literature can hardly be the quiet or private academic project of an isolated scholar. A work like this quickly becomes dependent on many friends, teachers, and guides within the academic, publishing, and religious arenas, as well as on family members. Although it would be impossible to acknowledge everyone who has contributed knowingly or unknowingly to this work, I will attempt here to recognize those who have contributed most significantly.

Traditional Indian scholarship emerging over the centuries, along with Western academic research from the past three decades on Vaishnava literature and religion, have produced a treasure trove of knowledge from which I have steadily drawn. Many of these scholars and their works are acknowledged and referenced throughout the book.

My academic background has prepared me well for this task, and several key teachers deserve special mention. While attending Harvard, I received invaluable training from Daniel H. H. Ingalls, Gary Tubb, Sheldon Pollock, Wilfred Cantwell Smith, Diana L. Eck, and Ninian Smart. Additionally, I had the privilege of studying under several fine scholars at the University of Chicago, specifically J.A.B. van Buitenen, Edward C. Dimock, Jr., A. K. Ramanujan, Paul Ricoeur, and David Tracy. I am also obliged to Charles S. J. White and David Rodier of American University, my first professors in Sanskrit and Indian religious traditions.

For their feedback and encouragement, special thanks goes to David L. Haberman, Barbara Holdrege, Klaus K. Klostermaier, June

McDaniel, Miranda Shaw, and Mekhala Natavar. I am especially indebted to the late Edward C. Dimock, Jr., and Edwin F. Bryant for the priceless attention they have given to this work. My deepest gratitude goes to the contributor of the Foreword, Norvin Hein, from whom I have received ongoing counsel on the translation, and with whom I have had a series of inspiring and enlightening conversations on the subject.

The continual encouragement from my colleagues at Christopher Newport University has been enthusing and supportive. I would like to thank them all, and especially acknowledge Ken Rose, George Teschner, Ashby Kinch, and Terry Lee. I am very grateful to Dean Douglas Gordon and his office for the support of two grants for completing this book and a reduced teaching load. Additionally, my students from the university, as well as former students at Duke University and Guilford College, have studied my translations and provided insightful reactions to the material.

Special thanks goes to all who helped at Princeton University Press, for their great interest and involvement in this work, especially to Brigitta van Rheinberg, Senior Editor, whose enthusiasm and guidance along the way has been essential. Brigitta challenged me to write this volume in a way that would speak to the reader who is unfamiliar with the subject matter, as well as the specialist and student of Indic traditions. Thanks go to Margaret Case for her conscientious editorial review and for her sensitivity to this work. Sara Lerner and Alison Kalett were also very helpful, patient, and informative during the production process.

Many friends and teachers within the Vaishnava community have been a motivating force behind this work, and I am deeply grateful to all of them. I especially owe an inestimable debt to A. C. Bhaktivedanta Swami Prabhupāda who, through his deep faith and undaunted determination, was able to spread Vaishnava teachings worldwide for the first time in history. Without his achievements, I never would have entered the academic study of Vaishnavism, and his life and work continue to inspire me in both my scholarly and spiritual pursuits. Shrivatsa Goswami, Steven J. Rosen, and Hridayananda Das Goswami have offered friendship and guidance at different points along the way, and Lalita Madhava and Krishna Kanta have given their valuable assistance. I also extend my heartfelt thanks to Krishna Priya, the Vaishnava artist with whom I worked on the compositional design of the beautiful Rāsa Maṇḍala painting that she rendered for the frontispiece and the book's cover.

In many ways, the support of my family members has been amazingly energizing. My gratitude goes first to our caring and supportive parents, Cecil and Lucy Fritz, Ed and Nannette Hoffman, and Noel Schweig. Lucy and Nannette have been especially accommodating, and their astute editorial suggestions directly influenced the outcome of the work. Thanks goes to each of our children who have exercised much patience all these years, and especially to Rohini, with whom I spent many hours reviewing the verses. Finally, the deepest gratitude goes to my wife and spiritual partner, Susan. Her tireless editing and organizing of the manuscript and loving suggestions offered throughout the whole project are not possible to describe here. Without her steadfast support, poetic sensitivity, and creative energy, this book would simply not be what it is.

Pronunciation

The standardized transliteration system for the Sanskrit alphabet is utilized in this book. Listed below are the vowels and consonants that require clarification with regard to pronunciation. Transliterated consonants not listed below are pronounced exactly as in English pronunciations. It is important to note that Sanskrit vowels and consonants have only one consistent sound in pronunciation, and unlike English, do not vary.

Transliterated vowels and consonants are listed below in English alphabetical sequence in order to provide easy reference for the English-speaking reader.

VOWELS

a	is pronounced like "a" in "around"
ā	like "a" in "yacht"
ai	like "ai" in "aisle" ("ai" represents a single transliterated vowel)
au	like "ow" in "cow" ("au" represents a single transliterated vowel)
e	like "e" in "prey"
i	like "i" in "bit"
ī	like "i" in "magazine"
ḷ	like "lree" (this vowel is rare and is pronounced by combining the English "l" and "r" with an "ee" sound following)
o	like "o" in "home"
ṛ	like "ri" in "rich"
ṝ	like "rea" in "reach" (this vowel is rarely found)
u	like "u" in "put"
ū	like "u" in "rude"

CONSONANTS

c	like "ch" in "chart" (never pronounced like the English "k" or "s")
d	like "d" in "lude"
ḍ	like "d" in "red"; in the West, we don't hear the subtle distinctions between the two "d's", nor are we used to making these distinctive sounds with the tongue in English
g	like "g" in "gate" (the soft "g" as pronounced in the word "germane" is never represented by this consonant; the soft "g" sound is found only in the Sanskrit letter "j")
h	like "h" in "hot" (standing alone or followed by a vowel, without following a consonant)
_+h	any consonant followed by "h" is merely aspirated, like the subtle aspirated breath sound naturally occurring in the word "pot" (whereas aspiration is naturally absent from "dot"); thus "ph" sounds like the letter in the word "loophole" (not an "f" sound); and the "h" placed after the "t" as "th" in Sanskrit is *not* a "th" sound as in "thorn," as is typically the case in English
ḥ	is the silent consonant often found at the end of words; when located at the end of a word at the end of a sentence, it reduplicates the last syllable: for example, the "ḥ" in "rāmaḥ" sounds like "rāma*ha*," and "śaktiḥ" sounds like "śakti*hee*" (the underlining indicates an accented syllable)
j	like "j" in "joy"
ṁ	like "n" in the French word "bon"
n	like "n" in "soon"
ṅ	like "n" in "song"
ñ	like "n" in "staunch"
ṇ	like "n" in "sand"
ph	like "p" in "pan" (with aspirated breath; it never makes the sound of "f" as it often does in English, for example, the "ph" in the word "elephant")
ṛ	is a vowel; see "ṛ" in the section above entitled "Vowels"
s	like "s" in "suit"
ś	like "sh" in "shoot" (this sibilant and the following are commonly pronounced by English speakers without any discernable distinction)

ṣ	like "sh" in "shout"
t	like "t" in "tool" (with tip of tongue near where the teeth meet roof of mouth)
ṭ	like "t" in "lute" (with tip of tongue toward the middle of the roof of the mouth)

In most compounded consonants, each consonant retains its original sound in combination with the others. The one exception to this, although optional, is the combination "jñ" as found in the word "jñāna." These combined letters in this sequence are often pronounced like the "gy" in the English words "dog yard."

List of Abbreviations

Translations from foreign language texts presented throughout this work are the author's unless otherwise credited to others.

BB	Śrīdhara Svāmī *Bhāvārthabodhinī*
BG	*Bhagavad Gītā*
BhP	*Bhāgavata Purāṇa*
CC	Krishnadāsa Kavirāja, *Caitanya Caritāmṛta* (Gauḍīya Mission ed.)
GG	Jayadeva Gosvāmin, *Gīta Govinda*
HV	*Harivaṁśa*
KK	Līlaśuka Bilvamaṅgala, *Kṛṣṇa Karnāmṛta*
KrS	Jīva Gosvāmin, *Krama Sandarbha*
KS	Jīva Gosvāmin, *Kṛṣṇa Sandarbha* (in *Bhāgavata Sandarbha*)
MW	*Sanskṛit-English Dictionary* by Sir M. Monier-Williams
NBS	*Nārada Bhakti Sūtra*
PrS	Jīva Gosvāmin, *Prīti Sandarbha* (in *Bhāgavata Sandarbha*)
RL	Rāsa Līlā
SD	Viśvanātha Cakravartin, *Sārārtha Darśinī*
TS	Jīva Gosvāmin, *Tattva Sandarbha* (in *Bhāgavata Sandarbha*)
UNM	Rūpa Gosvāmin, *Ujjvala Nīlamaṇi*
VA	*The Practical Sanskrit-English Dictionary* by Vaman Shivaram Apte
VP	*Viṣṇu Purāṇa*
WEB	*Webster's Third New International Dictionary*
YS	*Yoga Sūtra* of Patañjali

DANCE
OF DIVINE
LOVE

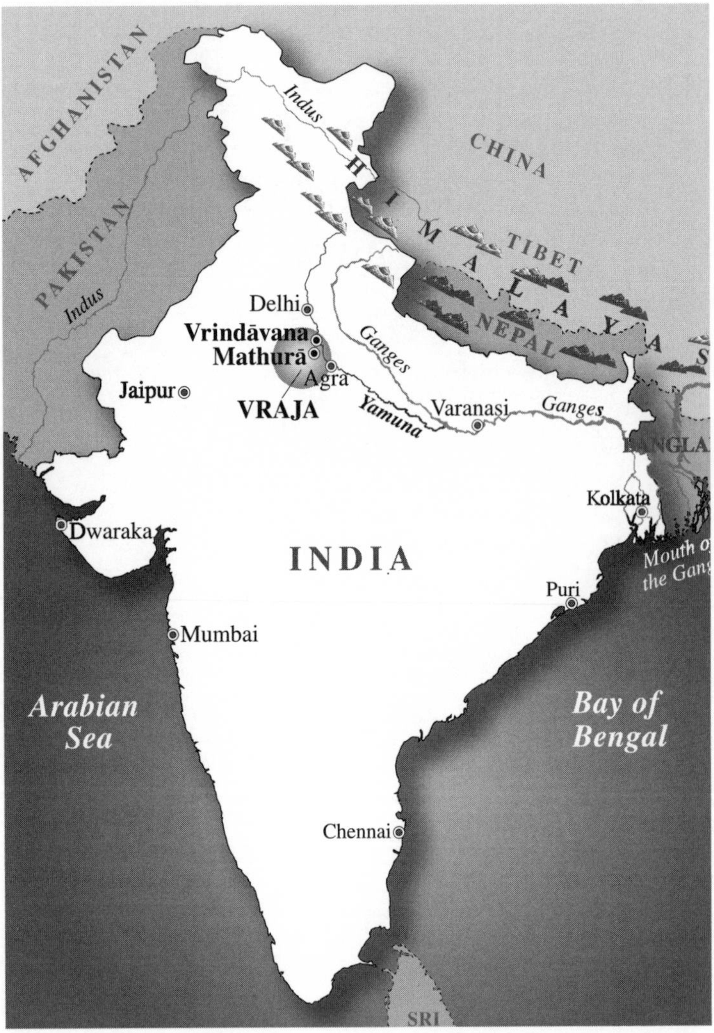

Figure 1. Location of the Vraja region in India. Map art by Gregory Golem.

The Sacred Love Story

Dance of Divine Love presents India's classical sacred love story known as the Rāsa Līlā.[1] It is a dramatic poem about young maidens joining with their ideal beloved to perform the wondrous "circle dance of love," or Rāsa. Its story is an expression of the eternal soul's loving union with the supreme deity in "divine play," or Līlā. The Rāsa Līlā is considered the ultimate message of one of India's most treasured scriptures, the *Bhāgavata Purāṇa.*[2]

The narrator of this story tells us that the highest devotional love for God is attained when hearing or reciting the Rāsa Līlā. Undeniably, its charming poetic imagery, combined with deeply resonating devotional motifs, expresses to any reader much about the nature of love. Narrated in eloquently rich and flowing Sanskrit verse, it has been recognized as one of the most beautiful love poems ever written.

A DRAMA OF LOVE

The Rāsa Līlā is set in a sacred realm of enchantment in the land known as Vraja, far beyond the universe, within the highest domain of the heavenly world. This sacred realm also imprints itself onto part of our world as the earthly Vraja, a rural area known as Vraja Maṇḍala ("the circular area of Vraja") in northern India, about eighty miles

1. The four-syllable phrase *Rāsa Līlā* (abbreviated as RL throughout this book) consists of two Sanskrit words pronounced phonetically "Rah–suh Lee–lah" ("ah" as "a" in "father," "uh" as "u" in "sun," and "ee" as in "see"). Definitions of key Sanskrit terms are listed in the glossary. In Hindi, the second short syllable is dropped, resulting in the three-syllable phrase "Rah-s Lee–lah." In Bengali, the second syllable is also dropped, but pronounced "Rah-sh Lee–lah." The specific sacred text known as "Rāsa Līlā" is to be distinguished from the name used for the pilgrimage dramas of Vraja, known in Hindi as *rās līlā.* Note that the distinction is made clear in this work through the presentation of the latter term in lowercase italic letters, with the Hindi spelling. For proper pronunciation of transliterated words from the Sanskrit language used throughout this book, please see the pronunciation table.

2. The words *Bhāgavata Purāṇa* mean "the timeless stories (Purāṇa) about God (Bhāgavata)." The title for this most popular sacred text of India has two variations: *Śrīmad Bhāgavatam* and *Bhāgavata Mahāpurāṇam.* It is often called simply the *Bhāgavata.* Among the eighteen famous Purāṇas, it is considered the most important, as will be discussed below.

south of the modern capital city of Delhi.[3] Vraja is described as a land of idyllic natural beauty, filled with abundant foliage heavy with fruit and bloom, roaming cows, and brightly colored birds singing melodiously. The Rāsa Līlā takes place in the earthly Vraja during the bountiful autumn season, when evenings abound with soothing scents and gentle river breezes. The following is a summary of the five chapters of the Rāsa Līlā story from the *Bhāgavata*'s tenth book.

One special evening, the rising moon reached its fullness with a resplendent glow. Its reddish rays lit up the forest as night-blooming lotus flowers began to unfold. The forest during those nights was decorated profusely with delicate starlike jasmine flowers, resembling the flowing dark hair of goddesses adorned with flower blossoms. So rapturous was this setting that the supreme Lord himself, as Krishna, the eternally youthful cowherd, was compelled to play captivating music on his flute. Moved by this beauteous scene, Krishna was inspired toward love.

Upon hearing the alluring flute music, the cowherd maidens, known as the Gopīs,[4] who were already in love with Krishna, abruptly left their homes, families, and domestic duties. They ran off to join him in the moonlit forest. Krishna and the Gopīs met and played on the banks of the Yamunā River. When the maidens became proud of his loving attention, however, their beloved Lord suddenly vanished from their sight. The Gopīs searched everywhere for Krishna. Discovering that he had run off with one special maiden, they soon found that she too had been deserted by him. As darkness engulfed the forest, the cowherd maidens gave up their search, singing sweet songs of hope and despair, longing for his return. Then Krishna cleverly reappeared and spoke to them on the nature of love.

The story culminates in the commencement of the Rāsa dance. The Gopīs link arms together, forming a great circle. By divine arrangement, Krishna dances with every cowherd maiden at once, yet each one thinks she is dancing with him alone. Supreme love has now reached its perfect fulfillment and expression through joyous dancing and singing long into the night, in the divine circle of the Rāsa. Retir-

3. Vraja (commonly spelled and pronounced as the Hindi "Braj") is a region covering approximately 1,450 square miles. At the heart of Vraja is the forest village of Vrindāvana, the home of Krishna, and the city of Mathurā, Krishna's birthplace. Vrindāvana is located between Delhi and the city of Agra (the home of the Taj Mahal, about 34 miles to the south). Throughout the Rāsa Līlā passage, Vraja is interchangeable with and often refers to Vrindāvana; see RL 1.18–19.

4. *Gopīs* is the plural of *Gopī,* "a female cowherd," pronounced as the English word "go," and "-pī," as the English word "pea."

ing from the vigorous dancing, Krishna and the Gopīs refresh themselves by bathing in the river. Then, reluctantly, the cowherd maidens return to their homes.

A FIRST READING of the story might lead one to believe that an obsessive love and passion for Krishna consumed the cowherd maidens. Their love could appear selfish and irresponsible, perhaps even unethical, as they abandoned their children, husbands, families, and homes. A closer reading, however, reveals the idealized vision of the story intended by its author and embraced and expounded upon by various traditions, in which the passionate love of the Gopīs becomes the model, even the veritable symbol, of the highest, most intense devotion to God.

Contrary interpretations may arise because the vision of God presented herein is intimate, esoteric, and complex, containing elements that are familiar to both Western and Indic religious traditions, as well as those that are unfamiliar. Certainly, one can observe how Krishna is acknowledged within the text as being a sovereign deity—a God of grace who teaches and redeems devoted souls, and who possesses other mighty and divine attributes, characteristics one would expect to find in the divinity of Semitic traditions. But there is a unique vision presented in this dramatic poem—a vision of the inner life of the deity. Here, God is celebrated as an adorable, eternally youthful cowherd boy who plays the flute and delights in amorous dalliance with his dearest devotees.

In Indic traditions, the attainment of God is commonly believed to be achieved through asceticism and renunciation. Yet such an unyielding, self-imposed renunciation for personal spiritual gain is not favored in the *Bhāgavata Purāṇa,* thus contrasting with the greater tradition out of which it arises. Rather, the text promotes renunciation that is naturally occurring and selflessly generated, spontaneously arising out of love. The cowherd maidens are considered to have achieved the perfection of all asceticism and to have attained the highest transcendence simply through their love and passionate devotion to God. This method of attainment is clearly distinct from the rigorous asceticism and ceaseless search for world-denying transcendence for which much of religious India is known.

Even though the divinely erotic tenor of the Rāsa Līlā story has delighted many, it has confused others. Some Western and even Indian interpreters have assumed that the love exhibited between the cowherd women and their beloved Krishna is nothing more than a display of worldly lust.[5] The author's intention expressed in the text, however, is quite the contrary—the hearing or reciting of this story, he proclaims, will *free* souls from lust, the "disease of the heart." Therefore saintly voices from particular traditions within the Hindu complex of religion claim that its erotic imagery is an expression of the intensity and intimacy of divine love, rather than a portrayal of worldly passion. It is only a lack of enculturation and purity of heart on the part of the reader that prevents one from appreciating the Rāsa Līlā as the greatest revelation of love.[6]

Such traditions tell us that the true interpretation of the story requires a certain type of vision, the "eye of pure love," *premā-netra,* which sees a world permeated by supreme love constantly celebrated by all beings and all of life.[7] This eye beholds a realm of consummate beauty and bliss, in which both the soul and intimate deity lose themselves in the eternal play of love. *Premā-netra* is said to be attained when the "eye of devotion" is anointed with the "mystical ointment of love," an ointment that grants a specific vision of the "incomprehensible qualities of the essential form of Krishna."[8] These traditions claim that such qualities are revealed through the Rāsa Līlā text, which, with

5. The various interpretations of the Rāsa Līlā story in the West as well as the East have a long and interesting history, not within the scope of this study. My interest here is to prepare the reader for appreciating the rich literary and religious dimensions of the text, and for understanding aspects of the esoteric vision of its drama.

6. The modern exponent of Vaishnavism who spread the tradition worldwide, Bhaktivedanta Swami Prabhupāda (1896–1977), cautioned outsiders or nonpractitioners in their reading of the stories of Krishna and the Gopīs presented in his volume entitled, *KṚṢṆA: The Supreme Personality of Godhead* (Los Angeles: Bhaktivedanta Book Trust, 1970), p. 188ff., a retelling of the *Bhāgavata*'s tenth book, interpolated with his own grave warnings against misinterpretation. It is important to point out that the Swami presented these stories of the *Bhāgavata* to the modern Western world, a world he encountered as having far more promiscuity than the traditional Indian culture out of which he came. However, he also battled the dark side, within his own culture, of radical heterodox Sahajiyā traditions arising out of Bengal Vaishnavism. Such traditions had been influenced by tantric Buddhist practices, in which practitioners, according to the Swami, lacked "requisite practice and spiritual discipline in devotional love," *sādhana-bhakti,* and thus the humility for truly understanding the *Bhāgavata*'s stories. At worst, some Sahajiyā sects have attempted, to this day, to reenact the divine acts of Krishna with the Gopīs through sexual rituals. The perception of orthodox Vaishnavas is that Sahajiyā practitioners dwell on the intimate divine acts of God prematurely, taking the teachings cheaply or sentimentally.

7. The phrase *premā-netra* is taken from Krishnadāsa Kavirāja's great biographical and theological exposition, *Caitanya Caritāmṛta* [CC] 1.5.21, in which he describes how the eye of love can comprehend "the manifestations of divine essence," or *svarūpa-prakāśa.*

8. These phrases and ideas are taken from a verse of the *Shri Brahma-Samhita* (Madras: Sree Gaudiya Math, 1958), v. 5.38. Translations are mine. The *Brahmā Saṁhitā* (BrS) was discovered in south India and canonized by the bhakti saint Caitanya in the sixteenth century. Caitanya's discovery of the BrS is related in CC 2.9.237–241.

Figure 2. The village of Barsānā surrounded by beautiful Vraja landscape. Photograph courtesy of Helmut Kappel.

its sensuous spirituality and innocent playfulness set in alluring poetic verse, ever beckons and attracts souls to enter into its drama.

This is the vision of saints, which I myself do not claim to possess. As one who is Western-born and trained in the academic study of religion, having had the privilege of living in India among saintly practitioners and participating with them in devotional practices, however, I am perhaps in a position to present this work to those both outside and within these traditions. My intention is to illuminate a particular tradition's special vision of such an important text, thereby facilitating further dialogue with other world traditions of theistic mysticism.

This work, then, explores a vision of intimacy with the supreme deity as presented by the Rāsa Līlā text and elaborated upon by recognized sages possessing this eye of love. The translation of the story, found at the heart of the book, is intended to be literal and faithful, striving to capture some of the exquisite poetic beauty and profound theological expression of the original. Within the introductory and commentarial sections that frame the translation, deeper or more hidden meanings of its verses are presented through general discussion and specific verse comments. It is hoped that these key teachings and traditional commentaries, from one of the most influential traditions interpreting the text, will enrich the reading of this masterpiece of world literature and enhance its appreciation.

SACRED LOVE STORIES

Among all love stories of the world, only a few are considered divine revelation. Certain mystical traditions honor a particular love story as their ultimate vision of supreme love. These stories exhibit erotic longings, often in the feminine voice, as can be observed in the following similar expressions of passion presented in two very different scriptural texts, the first biblical and the second purāṇic: "Let him kiss me with the kisses of his mouth!" (Song of Solomon 1.2), and "Please bestow upon us the nectar of your lips!" (Rāsa Līlā 3.14). These explicitly romantic expressions have been perceived as the voice of the soul in its passionate yearning for the divine. Devout mystics and saintly persons have shown, through their own elaborate worship and interpretation of these stories, that the desire to love God intimately and passionately lies deeply within the human heart. These special stories can thus be called sacred love stories.

God as the divine lover is not as foreign to us in the West as perhaps we might assume. According to a sociological study conducted several years ago, a surprising 45 percent of Americans can "imagine God as a lover."[9] Intimate love of the deity, therefore, is apparently neither remote nor uncommon, nor is it seen as existing only in the past among people of different cultures and distant places. That its presence is concealed may be due to the confidential nature of the experience of intimacy in relation to the sacred; perhaps the phenomenon is preserved at an understated and private level of human religious experience. Though it would be impossible to determine the pervasiveness of this religious phenomenon, or the type and depth of experience, it is clear that humans throughout the ages have desired intimacy with the divine.

Sacred love stories, in many ways, appear to present the passionate love shared between a lover and a beloved. They disclose explicit conceptions or allegorical depictions of a transcendent realm of love, in which a supreme deity and affectionate counterpart—either a devout soul or divine personage—join together in various phases of amor-

9. See Wade Clark Roof and Jennifer L. Roof, "Images of God among Americans," *Journal for the Scientific Study of Religion* 23, no. 2 (June 1984): 201–205. The summarized results of this study received attention from the popular magazine *Psychology Today* (June 1985): 12, and the nationwide newspaper *USA Today* (May 30, 1985). The latter focused specifically on the content of "God as a lover" from *Psychology Today,* which was highlighted in its section called "Life," under "Lifeline: A Quick Read on What People Are Talking About."

ous, even erotic intimacy. The purest and highest attainable love associated with these stories occurs only when the recipient of the soul's exclusive devotion is the supreme Beloved. Such stories have inspired the human heart to reach for superlative and pure expressions of love. It is not surprising that generations of religious writers, in numerous works, have developed and embellished essential themes drawn directly from these sacred stories.

In the Western world, the biblical book Song of Solomon, also known as the Song of Songs, relating the passionate love between a king and queen, has been regarded by many as a sacred love story.[10] This story has become foundational for various forms of Jewish mysticism, such as the Kabbalah. The rich and erotic words of the Song reveal the union of lover and beloved who symbolize, for these traditions, the divine "queen" and "king" within the godhead. Additionally, the Song of Solomon has been a profound source of inspiration for Catholic love mysticism and Christian piety in general. The feminine and masculine voices of the text have represented the loving relationship between the soul and God, respectively, in which the soul becomes the "bride" and Christ the divine "bridegroom."

Similarly, traditions of Islamic love mysticism have drawn upon an ancient Arabic tale that allegorizes the soul's capacity to be utterly intoxicated with love for God. The story of Layla and Majnun describes Majnun's uncontainable madness of affection for his beloved Layla, from early boyhood throughout his life, and even beyond life.[11] Although there has never been complete agreement on the sacred value or degree of holiness of these particular love stories, often because of the explicit sensuality and erotic imagery of their content, there is no doubt that powerful traditions of love mysticism have based their religious visions on such texts. Sacred love stories are indeed stories of romance and passion, but they are often seen as much more than that. They are regarded by many as sacred expressions of the innermost self that can lift the human spirit into the highest realms of intimacy with the deity.

10. The Song of Songs is readily accessible in any complete translation of the Hebrew Bible. It has also received scholarly attention as a text apart from its biblical context, and one finds, to this day, attempts to translate its especially rich poetry into English. For example, see *The Song of Songs: A New Translation,* by Ariel Bloch and Chana Bloch (Berkeley: University of California Press, 1995) with elaborate introduction and commentary to the text; and *The Song of Songs: A New Translation,* by Marcia Falk (San Francisco: Harper, 1990) with illustrations and introduction to the translation. Both editions present the original text in Hebrew script.

11. See Nizami's *The Story of Layla and Majnun,* translated from the Persian and edited by Dr. Rudolf Gelpke (New Lebanon, N.Y.: Omega Publications, 1997).

INDIA'S SONG OF SONGS

The love poem of the Rāsa Līlā could easily be regarded as the "Song of Songs" of ancient India. Several Vaishnava sects—those traditions within the Hindu complex of religion whose worship is centered upon the supreme deity Vishnu, also known as Krishna—single out the story of the Rāsa Līlā, claiming it to be the essence of all *līlās.*[12] As the Song of Solomon has been elevated to the highest status above all other biblical books by many Jewish and Christian mystics, and thus has become known as the "Song of Songs," the Rāsa Līlā also has been honored as the "essence of all *līlās*" and the "crown-jewel of all acts of God" by several Vaishnava traditions, for which it functions as the ultimate revelation of divine love.[13]

The enchanting Rāsa Līlā has had great influence on the culture and religion of India, perhaps even more than the Song of Songs has had on the Western world. For over a thousand years, poets and dramatists have continually told its story, often creating new stories that expand upon particular themes of the Rāsa Līlā. Artists and dancers from a variety of classical Indian schools have attempted to capture the beauty and excitement of various events within the story through pictorial renderings and interpretative dance performances. In modern times, in the West and in India, literary and artistic creations continue to be generated directly from this great work. The passionate love of the Gopīs for their beloved Lord Krishna has epitomized sacred love in Indian civilization, and to this day provides the richest source of poetic and religious inspiration for Hindu love mysticism.

Another Sanskrit love poem, the *Gīta Govinda* or "Song of Govinda," by Jayadeva, has been referred to as the song of songs of India by some Indian and Western scholars.[14] This twelfth-century work concerning Govinda, who is Krishna, and his most beloved Gopī,

12. The Vaishnava sects of Vallabha, Caitanya, and Rādhāvallabha celebrate the Rāsa Līlā as the greatest *līlā.*

13. Krishnadāsa Kavirāja uses the words *līlā-sāra* ("essence of *lilās*") to describe the RL in C 2.21.44. Viśvanātha Cakravartin describes the Rāsa Līlā as *sarva-līlā-cūḍa-mani* in his commentary to the first verse of the RL.

14. The first translation of Jayadeva's work was by the nineteenth-century British scholar Sir Edwin Arnold, and its title clearly makes the claim: *The Indian Song of Songs* (London, 1875). Indian scholars have echoed Arnold's claim and accepted this work's association with the biblical text; see *Kangra Paintings of the Gīta Govinda,* by M. S. Randhawa (Delhi: National Museum, 1963), p. 13. Western scholars of the Song of Solomon have also drawn parallels between the two works. See *Song of Songs: A New Translation with Introduction and Commentary,* by Marvin H. Pope (New York: Doubleday, 1977), especially the section entitled "Gita-Govinda, the So-Called 'Indian Song of Songs,'" pp. 85–89.

Rādhā, presents a tempting parallel to the Song because of the singular hero and heroine between whom a passionate love tale ensues. By contrast, the Rāsa Līlā portrays a group of heroines, though there is special attention given in one chapter to a favored Gopī, who is assumed by some Vaishnava sects to be Rādhā.[15] Furthermore, the Rāsa Līlā does not reach the erotic intensity of the *Gīta Govinda* and the Song of Songs. Whereas the general tone of the Rāsa Līlā is more amorous or romantic, the overall tone of both the Song and Jayadeva's work is considerably more sensuous, if not explicitly or metaphorically sexual.

Despite these similarities of Jayadeva's work to the biblical song, the Rāsa Līlā deserves recognition as India's song of songs in light of its literary-historical and scriptural parallels. Historically, the *Gīta Govinda* appears centuries later than the *Bhāgavata.* In fact, the Rāsa Līlā is referred to repeatedly in a refrain within the second part of Jayadeva's story (vv. 2–9). Similarly, the Song of Solomon functions as the source of much literary activity, as we find with the Spanish mystic poet, John of the Cross, who himself derived direct inspiration from the Song for his poetry describing the spiritual marriage of the soul and Christ.

The Song of Solomon has had significant influence on Western religious traditions, especially on Jewish and Catholic forms of mysticism, in which it has received unmatched attention. The Rāsa Līlā has also had widespread cultural and religious recognition, particularly within certain bhakti or devotional traditions of Vaishnavism. Whereas appreciation of the *Gīta Govinda* has been primarily concentrated in eastern regions of India such as the states of Bengal and Orissa, the Rāsa Līlā has had a pan-Indian presence.

Perhaps the most compelling argument for claiming the Rāsa Līlā to be India's song of songs would be the powerfully supportive scriptural contexts in which each text is found. Although Jayadeva's poem is directly inspired by the *Bhāgavata,* it is an independent poem, lacking the greater literary and scriptural context that the *Bhāgavata* and the Hebrew Bible provide for the Rāsa Līlā and the Song of Solomon, respectively.[16] One could argue that the biblical Song is perhaps even more dependent upon its context than the Rāsa Līlā is on its scriptural setting, because of the absence of any explicit religious statements in

15. The *Gīta Govinda* is the first text to powerfully establish the name, identity, and role of Rādhā as Krishna's favorite Gopī, stimulating a great deal of later poetic activity, as well as influencing the way viewers and readers perceive Rādhā's role in the RL text itself.

16. The *Gīta Govinda* compensates for a lack of scriptural context or authority by providing a theological introduction: the first chapter is devoted primarily to singing the praises of the various "divine descents," or *avatāra* forms, of Krishna and Vishnu.

Figure 3. Ivory miniature painting of Rādhā and Krishna. Artist unknown; from the private collection of the author.

the Song. The story line of the Rāsa Līlā, on the other hand, is a continuation of earlier events from within the greater *Bhāgavata* story, and there is notable material prior and subsequent to the Rāsa Līlā that anticipates or reflects upon its story. Moreover, much of the theological content of the *Bhāgavata* and references to many of its surrounding stories are engaged within the Rāsa Līlā itself.

It is on the basis of this dependence on context that the poetic love story of the Rāsa Līlā gains, as does the Song of Songs, its sacred aura and religious authority. Furthermore, each text, as a rarified sacred love story, has become the jewel in the center of its own scriptural setting. In light of these significant parallels, the Rāsa Līlā may truly be considered the song of songs of India.

BHĀGAVATA AS THE ULTIMATE SCRIPTURE

There are eighteen Purāṇas, or collections of "ancient stories," and Indian and Western scholars alike have recognized that among them, the *Bhāgavata* stands out. Dozens of traditional commentaries have been written on the *Bhāgavata,* whereas other Purāṇas have received just one or two, if any.[17] The *Bhāgavata Purāṇa* (BhP) itself declares that it is "the Purāṇa without imperfection" (*amala purāṇa*) and the most excellent of all Purāṇas.[18]

Modern Indian scholars acknowledge the greatness of the text. S. K. De writes that "The *Bhāgavata* is thus one of the most remarkable mediaeval documents of mystical and passionate religious devotion, its eroticism and poetry bringing back warmth and colour into religious life."[19] Specifically referring to the tenth book of the *Bhāgavata,* A. K. Majumdar states: "the most distinguishing feature of the *Bh.P.* is the tenth canto which deals with the life of Kṛṣṇa, and includes the *rāsa-līlā,* which is unique in our religious literature."[20] Western scholars have also identified the synthetic nature of the text. Daniel H. H. Ingalls writes: "The *Bhāgavata* draws from all classes, as it does from all of India's intellectual traditions. It does this without being at all

17. Edwin F. Bryant, in his introduction to his translation of the tenth book of the *Bhāgavata,* has counted as many as eighty-one currently available commentaries on this part of the text. See his work *Krishna: The Beautiful Legend of God* (New York: Penguin, 2004), p. xii.

18. See BhP 12.13.17–18.

19. S. K. De, *Early History of the Vaiṣṇava Faith and Movement in Bengal* (Calcutta: Firma K. L. Mukhopadhya, 1961), p. 7.

20. A. K. Majumdar, *Caitanya: His Life and Doctrine* (Bombay: Bharatiya Vidya Bhavan, 1969), p. 35.

interested in social questions and interested in intellectual questions only so far as they may illustrate or fortify its doctrine of love. What is important to the *Bhāgavata* is to feel God, to be moved by Him."[21]

The compelling text of this Purāṇa presents a rich tapestry of diverse forms of ancient Indian theological discourse, social thought, and literature, all of which support its evolved doctrine of devotion. More than any other Purāṇa, it engages much that comes before it by elaborating upon philosophical themes and stories of religious India, drawing from both northern and southern traditional cultures, as well as from great scriptures dated as early as the Vedas (circa 3000–1200 B.C.E.), India's oldest and foundational scriptures.[22] Indeed, the *Bhāgavata* has been regarded as the quintessential scripture: "The very essential core (*sāraṁ sāram*) of all of the Vedas and all of the histories has been collected [in the *Bhāgavata*]" (CC 2.25.145).

The challenge of dating the *Bhāgavata* brings out some of the text's literary characteristics. The precise date of its complete formation has been difficult to ascertain, since the *Bhāgavata* re-presents much of what has already come before it.[23] Whereas scholars have often pointed to the seventh or ninth century C.E. as periods during which either portions of the text or the complete work appeared in its present written form, the text has also been dated to as early as the fourth century. Moreover, the *Bhāgavata* records layers of narrations that were initially orally transmitted. This is not surprising, since India is known for its rich oral literary traditions, beginning with the Vedas themselves, which were preserved and handed down by priestly families for many generations.

Devout Hindus see the *Bhāgavata Purāṇa* as an eternal revelation; yet the text itself presents a description of how it came into exis-

21. Daniel H. H. Ingalls in his foreword to *The Divinity of Krishna*, by Noel Sheth, S.J. (New Delhi: Munshiram Manoharlal, 1984), p. xii.

22. See BhP 1.1.3. Friedhelm Hardy considers the *Bhāgavata* "an opus universale," a special purāṇic text that blends the poetic sense and intense devotional expression from southern Tamil culture with philosophical themes of the Upanishads and Vedanta, and the dharmic social system of the north. See his work *Viraha Bhakti: The Early History of Kṛṣṇa Devotion in South India* (Delhi: Oxford University Press, 1983), pp. 489ff.

23. It is interesting to note that as early as the second century C.E., the Rāsa dance of Krishna has been described in the South Indian text known as the *Cilappatikāram* by Iḷaṅkō Aṭikaḷ. See canto 17 entitled, "The Round Dance of the Herdswomen" in *The Cilappatikāram of Iḷaṅko Aṭikaḷ, An Epic of South India,* translated, with an introduction and postscript, by R. Parthasarathy (New York: Columbia University Press, 1993), pp. 170–178. For a recent study critically reviewing the complex issues surrounding the dating of the *Bhāgavata Purāṇa,* see Edwin F. Bryant's lucid article, "The Date and Provenance of the *Bhāgavata Purāṇa* and the Vaikuṇṭha Perumāl Temple," *Journal of Vaishnava Studies* 11, no. 1 (Fall 2002): 51–80.

tence.[24] The sage Vyāsa, whose name means "compiler," became despondent due to a lack of fulfillment, even after compiling the great literatures of India such as the Vedas, the *Mahābhārata,* and others.[25] He turned to his teacher, the renowned sage Nārada, and expressed his utter dissatisfaction. Nārada addressed his disciple's frustration by explaining to Vyāsa that although he had delineated the "ultimate purposes of human life" (*puruṣārtha*), he had yet to describe the greatness of Krishna. Thus the *Bhāgavata* is a text that is thought of as completing the task of compiling the scriptures, by crowning them with the full theology of Vishnu or Krishna. Certainly there is no other scriptural text that presents this theology so comprehensively. The teachers of the sixteenth-century bhakti school founded by the mystic and revivalist Caitanya express the superiority of the text over that of all other sacred Indian texts, collectively referred to in the following as the Vedas: "The *Bhāgavata* describes the essential nature of Krishna, bhakti, and the relationship to God (*rasa*). Therefore its greatness is supreme among Vedic scriptures" (CC 2.25.150).

Much of the *Bhāgavata* is a "compilation" of earlier texts, but not merely that. The works engaged by the *Bhāgavata* are refined versions of previous materials, incorporating the highly evolved theology of Vishnu, and this is certainly the case with the Rāsa Līlā story. This act of literary refinement and re-vision is expressed toward the very beginning of the *Bhāgavata,* in a verse that depicts the text as the "ripened fruit" of the wish-granting tree of all Vedic literature.[26] The name of the primary narrator of the text, Śuka, meaning "parrot," holds special significance here. Vyāsa's compiled stories are narrated by Śuka, his son, which causes them to become especially refined and sweet, just as it is believed that a parrot makes the juice of a mango sweeter, once it has sliced the fruit with its beak. Also, parrots are known to repeat faithfully what they hear, and similarly, Śuka faithfully retells the stories he has heard.[27]

24. For the *Bhāgavata*'s account of why it was written, see BhP 1.5.2–9.

25. Vyāsa is known for compiling sacred texts, especially the Vedas, the oldest and most authoritative scripture of India, perhaps the oldest scriptural text in the world. Among the four parts of the Vedas, the *Ṛg Veda* is the best known, appreciated for its Sanskrit hymns praising sacrificial practices, philosophical musings, and devotional expression.

26. "The ripened fruit (*galitaṁ phalam*) of / the wish-granting tree of the Vedas / Has perfectly culminated in the flow / of nectar (*amṛta-druva*) from the mouth of Śuka. / You drink the juice (*rasa*) of this fruit constantly, / which is the *Bhāgavata,* the ultimate abode—/ Ah, for you appreciate what is tasteful (*rasikāḥ*) / and possess a sense for what is beautiful (*bhāvukāḥ*) in this world" (BhP 1.1.3).

27. For more information on the significance of Śuka as a transmitter within Hindu traditions, see Wendy Doniger's "Echoes of the Mahābhārata: Why Is a Parrot the Narrator

This finer, more pleasing result produced by the parrotlike effect of Śuka's narrations is readily observable when comparing other purāṇic versions of Krishna's dalliance with the cowherd women to the *Bhāgavata*'s presentation. Śuka's vision combines some essential Krishna-Gopī themes found in three other versions: the *Viṣṇu Purāṇa, Brahma Purāṇa,* and *Harivaṁśa* texts. The verses in the *Viṣṇu* and *Brahma* Purāṇas that parallel the *Bhāgavata*'s Rāsa Līlā actually include the event of the Rāsa dance, whereas the *Harivaṁśa* does not, although it clearly shares other scenes and motifs of the story. All three versions are similar to the *Bhāgavata* in dramatic content and utilize, in places, similar and even the same vocabulary. But the story's finest imagery and poetic rendition are found in the *Bhāgavata* version.[28]

As mentioned above, the *Bhāgavata*'s Rāsa Līlā reflects several of the literary and theological features of the greater *Bhāgavata,* a context that is lacking in the three counterpart versions. It is no wonder that this text has been preferred by later Vaishnava sects (those following Vallabha, Caitanya, and Rādhāvallabha). The dramatic tone and content of the *Bhāgavata* story embellish the erotic presentation of the *Harivaṁśa* and further develop the theological apologia of the *Viṣṇu Purāṇa,* thus combining and engaging aspects from both, resulting in a far richer text. The effect, then, of Śuka's parrotlike narration on the *Bhāgavata*'s Rāsa Līlā is a substantially more developed story that is the most eloquent, dramatic, and theologically sophisticated of the four versions.

We have seen that the Vaishnava teachers regarded the Rāsa Līlā as their "song of songs," the most important and elevated passage of the *Bhāgavata.* We may ask, does the *Bhāgavata* text itself enthrone the Rāsa Līlā passage as the *līlā* of all *līlās*? Are the Vaishnava interpreters of the text correct in thinking that the *Bhāgavata* regards the Rāsa Līlā in this way, or is their appreciation doctrinally driven? I will present, in the "Textual Illuminations" and "Notes and Comments" sections of

---

of the Bhāgavata Purāṇa and the Devī Bhāgavata?" in *Purāṇa Perennis: Reciprocity and Transformation in Hindu and Jaina Texts,* edited by Wendy Doniger (Albany: State University of New York Press, 1993).

28. See treatment of first verse in Notes and Comments to RL 1.1 for a comparison of the first verse of the *Bhāgavata* to the *Viṣṇu Purāṇa* and *Harivaṁśa* versions. Clearly, a measure of vocabulary and imagery is shared by all three. A synoptic analysis of these versions brings out much of what is unique about the *Bhāgavata*'s presentation (see appendix 3, "Synoptic Analysis of Rāsa Līlā").

this work, compelling indications, both literary and theological, that the *Bhāgavata* indeed elevates the Rāsa Līlā to an ultimate status within its vast text.

Let us consider the major literary indications pointing to the Rāsa Līlā's special status. First, the poetic language and style of the text are distinctive. Second, no other story within the *Bhāgavata* resembles a drama as does the Rāsa story, and though its drama clearly fits into the greater text of which it is a part, it also has the ability to stand independently, as one would expect of a Sanskrit romantic drama. Furthermore, the tight dramatic structure stretching over an unusually lengthy five contiguous chapters is, again, a unique feature among all *līlās* of the *Bhāgavata.* Third, as has been mentioned, "framing" passages placed before the story anticipate and lead up to the text, and those that follow remember and invoke the significance of the *līlā.* These passages may be a single verse (inside and outside of the tenth book), or partial and even whole chapters (within the tenth book), prior to or following the five-chapter story. No other episode in the *Bhāgavata* has received this type of elaborate framing. Moreover, the characters of the hero and heroines are developed prior to the story, and their interactions within the episode reach heights not achieved prior to or following the Rāsa event. Finally, throughout the passage as many as eighteen other *līlās* from within the *Bhāgavata* are recalled, a rare occurrence in any *līlā.*

Unique theological features also indicate the special status of the Rāsa Līlā. The first and last verses of the piece launch and cap off its story with dramatic indications. Krishna takes full refuge in the Goddess in the first verse, which is unprecedented in the greater *Bhāgavata* text, and the author states in the final benedictory verse that the "highest devotion" is achieved by hearing or reciting this story, a benediction that is not offered anywhere else. Additionally, the *Bhāgavata* presents many great devotees of Krishna, but none receives the same level of recognition and praise in the text as the cowherd maidens of Vraja, whose love and sacrifice even amaze Krishna himself. They are depicted as master *yoginīs* who are capable of embracing God within their hearts, their devotion excelled by no one. Furthermore, among all the Gopī passages of the *Bhāgavata*'s tenth book, the Rāsa Līlā drama introduces and tells the tale of the special singular Gopī, identified by the Caitanya school as Rādhā, Krishna's dearest consort. This favored cowherd maiden is revisited only once more, seventeen chapters later (BhP 10.47), where her soliloquy to the black bee is presented. Clearly, the *Bhāgavata,* through these and other theological and literary features of the text, deliberately establishes the Rāsa Līlā as the very center of its work, celebrated as such by many Vaishnava traditions.

SACRED CONTEXT OF THE RĀSA LĪLĀ

The *Bhāgavata*'s Sanskrit text contains 335 chapters, consisting of sacred stories, philosophical discourse, and epic poetry that all respond to the essential question of what one is to do to prepare for death.[29] Of the twelve books forming the *Bhāgavata,* the tenth and longest book comprises ninety chapters, including the five chapters of the Rāsa Līlā (chapters 29–33). This is the most famous and widely read of the books, particularly known for its descriptions of Krishna's youthful *līlās* in Vraja.

The *Bhāgavata Purāṇa* presents a dialogue between the sage Śuka and a king named Parīkṣit, which addresses the question of how to prepare for death. The text possesses a complex narrative structure consisting of three layers. The authorial first voice, as we have seen, is understood to be that of Vyāsa. The work opens by introducing the voice of the general narrator, the sage Sūta, as he addresses a gathering of holy men in the Naimiṣa forest, delivering the outer narrative shell. Sūta in turn narrates the vision of the narrator of the *Bhāgavata* stories themselves, the sage Śuka. Thus, the first narrative is by Vyāsa, who reveals the dialogue between Sūta and the sages assembled at Naimiśa. And the second narrative is by Sūta, who reveals the dialogue between Śuka and King Parīkṣit. Within this second narrative frame, we learn about the king, whose death is imminent due to a curse from a small boy. The story goes as follows:

The renowned king Parīkṣit, while searching for water in the forest, came across a great sage deeply immersed in meditation. The king requested water from the sage, but received no response. Feeling resentful, he picked up a nearby dead snake with his bow, and angrily draped the snake over the shoulder of the sage. The son of the sage, infuriated upon hearing how the king had insulted his father, cursed the king to die in just seven days from the poisonous bite of a fanciful snake-bird.

29. For a scholarly treatment on the theme of death in the *Bhāgavata,* see E. H. Rick Jarow's book *Tales for the Dying: The Death Narrative of the Bhāgavata-Purāṇa* (Albany: State University of New York Press, 2003).

The king, feeling remorseful, accepted the curse as his fate and seated himself on the bank of a holy river. Soon, many renowned sages arrived, for he was a much-loved king. After greeting them, the king said, "Let the snake-bird bite me at once. I desire only that all of you continue reciting the glorious divine acts of Lord Vishnu."[30] Inquiring from the sages about the highest perfection of life, he asked, "What is the duty of one who is about to die?"[31] The beautiful young sage known as Śuka, son of Vyāsa, praised the king for his inquiry, and offered an explanation that points to an essential message of the *Bhāgavata:* a long life wasted in ignorant activity is useless compared to a short life utilized in achieving the ultimate spiritual goal.[32]

The third narrative, then, constitutes the greater part of the *Bhāgavata* text. Here, Śuka responds to the seminal question of the king concerning how to prepare for death. Throughout the *Bhāgavata,* Śuka narrates stories to and converses with Parīkṣit, the king, who is in the submissive role of Śuka's student. The Rāsa Līlā also opens with Śuka as the narrator, and his voice is heard in each act of the drama.

Most of the stories or narrations of the *Bhāgavata* begin with an introductory line preceding the opening verse (that is, just before the first quarter line of the poetically metered verses), and the Rāsa Līlā is no exception. Directly preceding the first verse of the drama are the words, *śrī-bādarāyaṇir uvāca,* "the illustrious Bādarāyani spoke."[33] Here, Śuka is introduced by the name Bādarāyani, which appears only once, to inform the reader that Śuka is the son of Badarāyana, another name for Vyāsa.[34] Therefore, Śuka is not only a sage recognized by the king and assembly of sages accompanying him; he is also the son of the divinely empowered Vyāsa, the compiler of the *Bhāgavata,* granting even greater authority to his narration.

The vision that Śuka shares with his student, King Parīkṣit, is not only what he sees but also his interpretation of what he sees. When Śuka reveals the poetic narrative and descriptions of the Rāsa Līlā, he acts as a bard and sage, whereas when he discusses and reflects upon the stories, he acts as the interpreting theologian. The conversation

30. BhP 1.19.15.

31. BhP 1.19.37.

32. BhP 2.1.12.

33. The reader may consult the complete transliterated text of the Rāsa Līlā in the section titled "The Sanskrit Text," toward the end of this book.

34. Only some editions of the *Bhāgavata Purāṇa* introduce Śuka as Bādarāyani in the Rāsa Līlā passage. Other editions simply introduce him as Śuka.

Figure 4. Wall painting of Śuka narrating the *Bhāgavata*'s Rāsa Līlā to the King and Gathered Sages. From Gopīnāthjī Temple, Jaipur. Photograph by the author.

between Śuka and the king is in turn being narrated by Sūta to an audience consisting of Śaunaka and his group of sages. Sūta and Śaunaka's conversation is obviously narrated, as well, by the original narrator and author, Vyāsa. Effectively, then, the Rāsa Līlā is delivered to the reader through telescoping narratives; it is a multilayered conversation within which narrations of other conversations are taking place.

Before exploring the many other remarkable features of this literary masterpiece in greater detail, I will introduce the translation of the dramatic poem itself, so that the reader may experience a fresh encounter of its plot and imagery. Following the translation, further mediation or guidance will be offered in the "Textual Illuminations," as well as the "Notes and Comments" portions of this book. The translation is presented as a freestanding drama, with chapters 29 through 33 from the tenth book of the *Bhāgavata* now appearing as acts 1 through 5 within the drama, each act containing various scenes.

Following the Rāsa Līlā translation are translations of two famous passages concerning the cowherd maidens. These episodes frame the Rāsa story, one prior to and the other following it. The first is the chapter known as "Song of the Flute" (Veṇu Gīta), in which the Gopīs describe the power and beauty of Krishna's divine flute music. It is appropriate that this passage should appear before the Rāsa Līlā in the *Bhāgavata,* since it is the flute music that awakens the maidens' loving self-surrender at the beginning of the story, initiating the unfolding of the plot. The second translation is called "Song of the Black Bee" (Bhramara Gīta), a portion of a chapter that expresses loss and love in separation from Krishna. It is famous for its description of the special Gopī, identified as Rādhā, who speaks to a black bee in loving madness.

Figure 5. Decorative stencil of Krishna with flute.
Courtesy of S. S. Rangoli Art, Mathura, India.

Part I

POEMS FROM THE *BHĀGAVATA PURĀṆA*

Dance of Divine Love: Rāsa Līlā

DRAMATIS PERSONAE

(in order of appearance)

Son of Vyāsa/Śuka, *the narrator*

The Beloved Lord/Krishna, *the protagonist of the story*

Other personal names used for Krishna (in order of appearance): Govinda, Acyuta, Hṛṣīkeśa, Adhokṣaja, Hari, Keśava, Mādhava, Urukrama, Varāha, Śauri, Mukunda, Vāsudeva, and Vishnu

The Gopīs, *married and unmarried cowherd maidens, the heroines of the story*
as all of the Gopīs
as a partial group of Gopīs
as individual Gopīs (often speaking on behalf of other Gopīs)

Parīkṣit, *the king for whom the story is narrated and from whom questions arise*

Special Gopī *(most often identified as Rādhā), the maiden with whom Krishna runs off*

Non-Speaking

Yogamāyā (or Māyā), *the manifestation of the Great Goddess who directs her illusive power to arrange for divine loving union*

Cowherd men, *husbands of the Gopīs*

Families or relatives *of the Gopīs*

Cows *milked by the Gopīs*

Trees, plants, flowers, and vines *spoken to by the Gopīs in the Vraja forest*

Tulasī, *most sacred plant of Krishna flourishing in the Vraja forest*

The Earth, *consulted by the Gopīs in their search for Krishna*

Wife of the deer, *consulted by the Gopīs in their search for Krishna*

Bees *around Krishna's garland and as a chorus for Rāsa dance*

DENIZENS OF THE HEAVENS AND THEIR WIVES, *from their celestial chariots in the sky*

GANDHARVA SINGERS AND THEIR WIVES, *from their celestial chariots in the sky*

SCENES

The region of Vraja: a rural area located in central northern India
about eighty miles south of Delhi, near Agra (home of the Taj Mahal);
a paradisal natural countryside with many forests
and the Yamunā River running through it

The village of Vraja: also known as Vrindāvana,
located within the region of Vraja,
bordering the Yamunā River;
home of Krishna, the Gopīs, and their families

Act One

KRISHNA ATTRACTS THE GOPĪS AND DISAPPEARS

Bhāgavata Purāṇa Book 10 Chapter 29

Scene I
Narrative: Beauty Arouses Love in God Attracting Souls to Him

The illustrious son of Vyāsa spoke:

Even the Beloved Lord,
  seeing those nights
  in autumn filled with
  blooming jasmine flowers,
Turned his mind toward
  love's delights,
  fully taking refuge in
  Yogamāyā's illusive powers.[1] 1

Then the moon,
  king among stars, arose,
Spreading soothing reddish rays
  over the face of the eastern horizon;
Dispelling the sorrow
  from those who looked on,
As a lover caresses his beloved's blushed face,
  consoling her after long separation. 2

1. son of Vyāsa: Śuka, the sage who narrates this story.

the Beloved Lord: God, as Krishna, the intimate persona and ultimate deity of the godhead, the divine hero of this story. The various names and epithets for Krishna throughout this text will be briefly explained in these notes, with greater explanation in the "Verse Illuminations" and glossary sections of the book.

Those nights in autumn filled with blooming jasmine flowers: jasmine amazingly blossoms here during "those nights in autumn," even though the flower only blossoms in the spring and summer in India. "Those nights" metaphorically introduces the cowherd maidens of Vraja, or the Gopīs, who are explicitly introduced for the first time two verses later. See "Textual Illuminations" and "Notes and Comments" for a fuller discussion.

Yogamāyā: divine feminine power or Great Goddess who arranges loving exchanges between God and his devotee.

Seeing lotus flowers bloom
 and the perfect circle of the moon
Beaming like the face of Ramā,
 reddish as fresh *kuṅkuma*;
Seeing the forest colored
 by the moon's gentle rays,
He began to make sweet music,
 melting the hearts of
 fair maidens with beautiful eyes.[2] 3

Upon hearing that sweet music,
 their passion for him swelling,
The young women of Vraja whose
 minds were captured by Krishna,
Unaware of one another,
 ran off toward the place
Where their beloved was waiting,
 with their earrings swinging wildly.[3] 4

Some left abruptly
 while milking the cows—
 due to excitement
 the milking had ceased.
Some left the milk
 as it boiled over;
 others departed
 leaving cakes on the hearth. 5

2. Ramā: the Goddess Lakṣmī, consort of Vishnu (Krishna's cosmic persona and form of four arms), not to be confused with Rāma (note the macron over the first "a" rather than the second), the brother of Krishna or the consort of Sītā as the avatāra or divine descent of Vishnu.

kuṅkuma: vermilion; a brilliant deep reddish colored powder.

fair maidens with beautiful eyes: the cowherd heroines of the story, known as the Gopīs.

3. Vraja: the beautiful village and surrounding rural area in central northern India, considered a divine manifestation of the highest heaven in this world.

Krishna: "the dark-complexioned one" or "the divinely attractive one"; primary name of the Beloved Lord, who is both supremely powerful and supremely intimate.

Some suddenly stopped
dressing themselves;
others no longer
fed children their milk.
Some left their husbands
who had not yet been served;
others while eating
abandoned their meals. 6

Some were massaging
their bodies with oils
or cleansing themselves;
others applying
ointment to their eyes.
Their garments
and ornaments
in utter disarray,
they hastened
to be with Krishna. 7

Their husbands,
fathers, brothers—
all relatives endeavored
to detain them.
Since their hearts
had been stolen by Govinda,
they who were entranced
did not turn back.[4] 8

Some Gopīs,
unable to leave,
had gone inside their homes.
With eyes closed,
fully absorbed in love,
they meditated upon Krishna.[5] 9

4. Govinda: Krishna, "one who tends the cows."

5. Gopīs: "cowherd maidens"; the fair young women of Vraja; the collective heroines of the story.

The intense burning
of unbearable separation
from their dearest beloved
disrupted all inauspiciousness;
Due to the joy
of embracing Acyuta
attained through meditation,
even their worldly happiness was lost.[6] 10

Certainly, he is the supreme Soul,
though they knew him
intimately as their lover.
They relinquished their bodies
composed of material elements,
and any worldly bondage
was instantly destroyed. 11

Scene II
Theological Discourse: Lovers of God Offer All Emotions to the Divine

The celebrated king Parīkṣit spoke:

They knew Krishna, however,
as the greatest lover and
not as the source of Brahman.
O sage, how did the underlying
current of natural forces
stop affecting their minds
controlled by such forces?[7] 12

6. Acyuta: Krishna, "the infallible one."

7. Parīkṣit: the king to whom the sage Śuka narrates this story.

Brahman: the word used to indicate the "ultimate reality" or "supreme being" in the Upanishads and Vedanta philosophical texts.

underlying current of natural forces: the three constituent *guṇas* or qualities underlying the natural world as well as human consciousness and qualities of human interactions. These forces refer to the three *guṇas*: *sattva* (light, clarity, or goodness), *rajas* (haziness, mixture of goodness and ignorance), and *tamas* (darkness or ignorance). In verse 14, the same word is translated as "forces of nature."

The sage Śuka spoke:

This was explained to you previously:
if the king of Cedi could
achieve perfection
Even while despising Hṛṣīkeśa,
why would not they,
so dear to Adhokṣaja,
be much more likely to do so?[8] 13

For the purpose of
benefiting all, O king,
the Beloved Lord
manifests himself.
He is imperishable, immeasurable,
unbound by the forces of nature—
the Soul from whom
such powerful forces arise.[9] 14

Desire, anger, fear, and
certainly loving attachment,
intimacy and affection
Should always be directed toward Hari;
by so doing, persons become
fully absorbed in God.[10] 15

Surely this should not surprise you;
the Beloved Lord exists without birth.
He is Krishna, the supreme Lord of yoga;
by him this entire world is liberated.[11] 16

8. king of Cedi: Śīśupāla, who insulted Krishna; Krishna granted liberation to Śīśupāla by killing him. See BhP 10.74.30–46.

Hṛṣīkeśa: Krishna, "the Lord of the senses."

Adhokṣaja: Krishna, "the Lord who is beyond the perception of the senses."

9. forces of nature: the *guṇas*. Krishna as Lord is the original source of these basic forces of nature and therefore is not bound by them. These same forces are called "underlying current of natural forces" in verse 12.

10. Hari: Krishna, "one who steals the heart" or "one who takes away suffering."

11. supreme Lord of yoga: Krishna; yoga refers here to the divine supernatural powers that unite the soul with the supreme reality.

Scene III
Dialogue: Souls Renounce the World in Passionate Attraction to God

Seeing they had arrived nearby,
  the Beloved Lord then approached
  the young women of Vraja.
He, most eloquent of all speakers,
  began to converse with them,
  bewildering them with playful words. 17

The Beloved Lord spoke:

Welcome, most fortunate ladies!
  What can I do to please you?
Is all going well in Vraja?
  Please explain the purpose of your arrival. 18

Night has a frightening appearance;
  inhabiting this place are
  fearsome creatures!
Please return to Vraja—
  women should not remain here,
  O ones with beautiful waists.[12] 19

12. This verse and several following verses have double-entendre meanings, cleverly expressing Krishna's ethical and trans-ethical intentions. Traditional commentators recognize the opposite meanings that are simultaneously expressed in these verses (see "Notes and Comments" for further explanation of how this is possible in Sanskrit). An opposite meaning for this verse can read as follows:

Night is without a frightening appearance;
  inhabiting this place are
  creatures that are not fearsome.
Please do not return to Vraja—
  women should remain here,
  O ones with beautiful waists.

Your mothers, fathers, sons,
  brothers and husbands cannot find you.
They are searching for you—
  do not create anxiety for your families.[13] 20

You have seen the forest
  filled with flowers,
  glowing with the rays
  of the full moon;
Made beautiful by leaves of trees,
  playfully shimmering
  from the gentle breeze
  off the river Yamunā.[14] 21

Please go to the village without delay!
  O chaste ladies, attend your husbands.
Your calves and children are crying for you—
  you must go feed and nurse them.[15] 22

Or perhaps your hearts are bound
  out of deep affection for me.
Since all living beings are dear to me;
  you also must have come to be near me. 23

13. A clever alternative reading of this verse is the following:

Your mothers, fathers, sons,
  brothers and husbands cannot find you.
Even though they are searching for you,
  you must not be anxious for your families.

14. Yamunā: the river that runs through Vraja that is dearest to Krishna, and therefore most sacred.

15. An alternative reading of this verse is the following:

Please do not go back right away
  to attend your husbands, O chaste ladies.
Your calves and children are crying for others [not for you!];
  you need not feed and nurse them.

For every woman the highest dharma
  is to serve her husband without falsity,
Be agreeable toward his family members,
  and nourish the children.[16] 24

Even if unpleasant, unfortunate,
  old, decrepit, sickly or poor,
  if not morally fallen,
The husband should not be deserted
  by women desiring a better
  position in the next world. 25

For this does not lead to heaven
  nor to good reputation;
  instead it brings undesirable,
  painful, fearful results.
Certainly adultery
  is condemned everywhere
  by women from good families.[17] 26

By hearing about me,
  seeing me,
  meditating on me,
  and praising me,
  you feel love for me—
Not by being in my presence.
  Therefore you
  should return
  to your homes. 27

16. An alternative reading of this verse is the following:

> For the dharma of all other women
>   is to serve false husbands,
> Be agreeable toward their family members,
>   and nourish the children.

dharma: one's essential purpose in life; one's "duty" in this world that also links one to the divine; a sense of one's place in the cosmic scheme of things that is intimately related to one's place in the total social order; the ultimate matrix of divine and social law combined that places the individual perfectly within the universe.

17. The second half of this verse can also be read as the following:

> Women from good families know
>   adultery is found everywhere [with their own husbands],
>   and it should be condemned.

The sage Śuka spoke:

Having heard these unpleasant
words of Govinda,
the Gopīs felt great sadness.
Their expectations broken,
they felt unbearable anxiety
too difficult to overcome. 28

Bowing their heads in sorrow,
with reddened lips dried
by heavy breathing,
Scratching the ground with their feet,
they were burdened
with intense distress;
With streaming tears
washing away
the *kuṅkuma* on their breasts,
And *kajjala* running
down from their eyes,
they stood there in silence.[18] 29

Having discarded all desires for the sake
of their most beloved Krishna,
Who had addressed them
as if disinterested in love,
Wiping their eyes while
trying to stop crying,
Those impassioned ones, choked up,
spoke with faltering voices. 30

18. *kajjala:* a black ointment eyeliner used by Indian women and sometimes men.

The beautiful Gopīs said:

O all-pervading one,
you should not speak
so cruelly to us!
We have fully abandoned
all objects of desire
for the soles of your feet.
O unattainable one,
do not reject us—
accept us as your devotees
Just as you, the Lord,
the original Person,
accept those who desire liberation. 31

O dear one, as you
who knows dharma
have stated,
The proper duty for women
is to be loyal to husbands,
children and close friends.
Let this dharma of ours be for you,
O Lord, since you are
the true object of such teachings.
Truly you are the dearest
beloved of all living beings,
the most intimate relation,
for you are the supreme Soul. 32

O Soul, the spiritually advanced
certainly feel attraction to you
as their eternal beloved.
With these husbands, children, and
others causing much trouble,
what is to be done?
O supreme Lord,
please be merciful unto us.
O one with eyes like lotus flowers,
do not destroy our hopes
that we have held for so long. 33

While in our homes, our minds
were easily stolen by you;
So also were our hands
engaged in housework.
Our feet will not move even one step
from the soles of your feet.
How shall we return to Vraja—
what would we do there? 34

O dear one,
with the flood of nectar
coming from your lips,
Extinguish the fire
burning within our hearts
born of your sweet music,
your glances and laughter.
For if you don't,
we shall place
our bodies in the fire
born of separation from you.
Then, O friend,
by means of meditation
we shall go to the abode of your feet. 35

O lotus-eyed one,
so dear to sages
residing in the forest,
From the moment we touched
the soles of your feet,
a moment rarely granted
even to the Goddess Ramā,
From that time on,
we have been unable to stand
directly in the presence
of any other man;
Indeed, we have become
filled with joy
because of you. 36

The Goddess Śrī,
   though having obtained
   a place on your chest,
And for whose very glance
   the gods ultimately aspire,
Desires, along with
   the sacred *tulasī* plant,
   the dust of your lotus feet.
It is the same way for us—
   our shelter is the dust of your feet.[19] 37

O destroyer of affliction,
   please have mercy on us.
Having found the soles of your feet,
   we have abandoned our homes
   with the hope of worshiping you.
O jewel among men,
   please grant unto us
Whose hearts are burning
   with intense desire,
   inspired by your beautiful
   glances and smiles,
   the chance to serve you. 38

Upon seeing your face encircled
   by curling locks of hair,
   your lips of sweet nectar,
The earrings on your beautiful cheeks,
   and your glances and smiles;
Seeing your strong arms
   which award fearlessness,
And your chest, the only
   pleasure for the Goddess Śrī—
   we must become your maidservants! 39

19. The Goddess Śrī: Lakṣmī, the consort of Vishnu.
tulasī: name of the aromatic flowering plant dearest to Krishna; the most sacred of all plants.

O dear one, what woman
in the three worlds
would not abandon
her noble character,
After being overcome
by the sweet melodious
music of your flute?
Seeing your beauty,
the most magnificent
in all the three worlds,
The animals, trees,
birds and cows are elated
with bodily ripplings of bliss.[20] 40

Clearly, you are the one who removes
the suffering of the people of Vraja,
As you, the Lord, the original Person,
protect the celestial world of the gods.
O friend of the distressed,
place your hand, beautiful like the lotus,
On the heads and impassioned breasts
of your maidservants. 41

Scene IV
Narrative: God Disappears from Prideful Souls

The sage Śuka said:

Thus the supreme Lord
among masters of yoga
heard their despondent words.
Laughing, yet with compassion,
he, possessing all
pleasure within himself,
still arranged for
the pleasure of the Gopīs. 42

20. elated with bodily ripplings of bliss: the positive experience of bodily hairs standing on end; see "Notes and Comments" for this verse and "Textual Illuminations" for a discussion of the special sense of this translated phrase.

Acyuta, whose actions are exalted,
whose jasmine-like teeth
Shone forth from his eloquent smile,
joined together with all of them,
Whose faces were blossoming
with loving glances;
He was glowing like the full moon
surrounded by stars. 43

Being praised through song,
then singing in response,
he was the leader of
hundreds of young women.
Wearing the garland Vaijayantī
while moving among them,
he was decorating the forest.[21] 44

Upon reaching the river bank
with its cool sands,
accompanied by the Gopīs,
He delighted in breezes
that carried the fragrance of
white lotuses, joyfully dancing
in the waves of that river. 45

Embracing them with wandering arms;
playfully touching their hands
with the tips of his fingernails
Which then fell upon their breasts,
belts, thighs, and hair;
Conversing coyly
with glances and laughter,
He joyfully awakened the god of love
in those beautiful young women from Vraja. 46

21. Vaijayantī: "victory," name of Krishna's garland consisting of five differently colored flowers strung together.

Thus those who received honor
  from the Beloved Lord,
  Krishna, the great Soul,
Thought themselves the best
  among all women in the world—
  they then became filled with pride. 47

Keśava could see how they
  had become intoxicated
  with their good fortune;
Bestowing upon them his grace,
  in order to quell their pride,
  suddenly, right before them,
  he disappeared.[22] 48

Act Two

THE GOPĪS SEARCH FOR KRISHNA

Bhāgavata Purāṇa Book 10 Chapter 30

Scene I
Narrative: Loving Madness in the Fervent Search for God

The sage Śuka spoke:

When the Beloved Lord
  disappeared so suddenly
  the young women of Vraja
  could no longer see him.
They felt greatly tormented,
  like female elephants
  who have lost
  their male leader. 1

22. Keśava: Krishna, "one with beautiful long hair."

By his movements,
affectionate smiles,
passionate glances,
His attractive speaking
and the passion of
his playfulness,
Their hearts were captivated;
those crazed women
began to imitate various
Actions of the Lord of Ramā,
losing themselves,
fully absorbed in him.[1] 2

Through their movements,
smiles, glances, speech,
and other gestures,
The bodily forms of his lovers
became similar
to those of their beloved.
The young women,
their selves fully absorbed in him,
thus declared, "I am he!"
Their amorous,
playful gestures
were those of Krishna. 3

Singing out loud about him
like deranged persons,
Together they searched
from forest to forest.
They inquired from trees,
the lords of the forest,
about the supreme Person
Who is present internally and
externally for all living beings,
as heavenly air pervades all beings,
within and without. 4

1. Lord of Ramā: Vishnu, Lord of the Goddess Lakṣmī, whom the Gopīs also identify as Krishna.

[The Gopīs spoke:]

O Aśvattha fig tree,
Plakṣa and Nyagrodha trees,
have you seen the son of Nanda?
He has stolen our minds
with his loving smiles
and glances.[2] 5

O Kurabaka tree,
Aśoka and Nāga trees,
O Punnāga and Campaka plants,
Has the younger brother of Rāma
passed this way?
His smile steals the conceit
of all proud women.[3] 6

O most fortunate Tulasī
to whom the feet
of Govinda are so dear,
Have you seen Acyuta, our beloved,
wandering about in this forest
followed by a swarm of bees? 7

O Mālati, Mallikā, Jāti, and
Yūthikā jasmine flowers,
have you seen him?
When Mādhava was passing by,
did he cause you great delight
with the gentle touch of his hand?[4] 8

2. son of Nanda: Krishna; the foster father of Krishna is Nanda.

3. younger brother of Rāma: Krishna; the older brother of Krishna is Rāma, or Balarāma. Not to be confused with Ramā, a name for the Goddess.

4. Mādhava: Krishna; a name derived from the word madhu, meaning "honey" or "sweet."

O Cūta mango and Priyāla trees,
Panasa jackfruit tree,
Āsana and Kovidāra trees;
O Jambu rose-apple tree, small Arka plant,
Bilva wood-apple tree, Bakula mimosa,
Āmra mango and Nīpa trees;
O all other plants and trees
growing by the banks
of the Yamunā
Whose lives are devoted
to the service of others—
please show us the path to Krishna,
for we are losing our minds! 9

O Earth,
what severe austerity
have you performed?
Ah, you appear resplendent
with the grass hairs of your body
blissfully standing erect, elated
from the touch of Keśava's feet.
Is this perhaps
the result of footsteps coming
from his earlier descent
as Urukrama?
Or, even before that, is it
coming from the embrace
of his divine form of Varāha?[5] 10

5. Urukrama: "the wide-striding one," also known as Vāmana, the divine form of Krishna whose two steps spanned the whole universe. See BhP 8.17–23.

Varāha: Krishna who takes the form of a "divine boar," lifting the earth with his tusks to protect it. See BhP 3.13.

O wife of the deer,
  have you encountered Acyuta
  in this place with his beloved?
O friend, have your widened eyes
  received great pleasure from
  the sight of his beautiful limbs?
The garland of jasmine worn
  by the Lord of this group is tinged
  with reddish *kuṅkuma* powder
Coming from the breasts of his lover
  whom he has embraced;
  its scent is blowing in our direction.[6] 11

Perhaps the younger brother of Rāma,
  holding a lotus flower in one hand
  and resting his other arm
  on the shoulder of his beloved,
Was followed here by a swarm of bees
  hovering around his garland of *tulasī*,
  all of them blinded by madness.
O trees,
  when walking by,
Did he graciously accept
  your respectful bowing
  with his affectionate glances?[7] 12

Let us inquire from these vines,
  even though they are embracing
  the branch-like arms
  of their tree-husband.
Certainly they must have been
  touched by his fingernails—
  just see how they are elated
  with bodily ripplings of bliss! 13

6. wife of the deer: a doe, with whom the Gopīs identify.
7. younger brother of Rāma: Krishna.

[Śuka spoke:]

Thus the Gopīs, discouraged
by their search for Krishna,
uttered these irrational words.
They began to act out
the *līlā* of their Beloved Lord,
for they were wholly absorbed in him.[8] 14

One of them mimicked Pūtanā,
while another imitated Krishna
who drank from her breast.
Yet another acted like a crying infant;
with her foot she kicked one
who pretended to be a cart.[9] 15

One imitated a demon carrying away another
who pretended to be Krishna as an infant.
Another crawled around, dragging her two feet
with the tinkling of ankle bells.[10] 16

Some performed like Krishna and Rāma,
others acted like their cowherd friends.
One mimicked the slaying of the calf demon,
another the slaying of the crane.[11] 17

8. *līlā*: the divine play or drama of God.

9. Pūtanā: the demonness who tried to kill Krishna as a baby by nursing him from her poisoned breast. See BhP 10.6.

one who pretended to be a cart: imitation of the "cart demon," Śakaṭa, whom Krishna kicked over as an infant. See BhP 10.7.4–10.

10. a demon carrying away another: refers to the "whirlwind demon" Tṛṇāvarta, who carried away Krishna. See BhP 10.7.20–33.

tinkling of ankle bells: Krishna is loved as an infant whose feet are adorned with this sounding jewelry.

11. Rāma: short for Balarāma; the older brother of Krishna (distinguished from Ramā, the Goddess Lakṣmī).

calf demon: Vatsāsura, whom Krishna slays. See BhP 10.11.41–44.

crane: the demon Baka, whom Krishna slays. See BhP 10.11.45–53.

One of them called for the cows
who had wandered off,
just as Krishna would;
then, imitating him,
She pretended to sport about
while making music with a flute.
Others praised her,
saying "Well done!" 18

One of them, placing her arm on another girl,
sauntered about and declared,
"I am Krishna! Look at my graceful gait."
Their minds were absorbed in him. 19

"Don't be afraid of the wind and rain—
I have arranged for your protection,"
Another said, lifting her upper garment
with her hand as if to shield them.[12] 20

One of them rose,
climbed up and placed
her foot on the other's head,
saying, "O wicked snake, go away!
Indeed, I have been
born as the one
who gives punishment
to those who are evil."[13] 21

Then another one declared,
"O cowherd boys,
look at the raging forest fire—
Quickly close your eyes!
I shall easily arrange
for your protection."[14] 22

12. lifting her upper garment with her hand: imitating Krishna, who lifted Govardhana hill with his finger to protect the residents of Vraja from Indra's wrath in the form of great rain storms and thunderbolts. See BhP 10.25.

13. "O wicked snake": refers to the multi-hooded poisonous serpent Kāliya, whom Krishna as a young boy subdues and conquers; Krishna then performs a dance on Kāliya's hoods. See BhP 10.16.

14. raging forest fire: a great fire that Krishna extinguishes by swallowing it in order to protect his cowherd friends. See BhP 10.17.20–25 and 10.19.

One of them, with a garland,
was tied to a grinding mortar
by a slender maiden
Who said, "I am binding
the one who has
broken the butter pots
and stolen the butter!"
Another covered her
face and beautiful eyes,
pretending to be afraid.[15] 23

Scene II
Narrative: Selfish Love and Pride as Downfall for the Soul

Just then, as they inquired about Krishna
from the trees and vines of Vrindāvana,
They saw, in an area of the forest,
the footprints of the supreme Soul.[16] 24

[The Gopīs spoke:]

Clearly these are footprints
of the great Soul,
the son of Nanda.
Here they can be identified by
the flag, lotus, thunderbolt,
elephant goad and barley seed,
along with other signs.[17] 25

15. the butter pots: the Gopīs imitate Krishna as a mischievous butter thief and his mother, Yaśodā, who attempts to control him. See BhP 10.9.

16. Vrindāvana: the village within the greater region of Vraja, sometimes interchangeable with Vraja; "the forest of tulasī."

supreme Soul: Krishna.

17. flag, lotus, thunderbolt, elephant goad and barley seed: symbols found on the soles of the feet of various avatar ("divine descent") manifestations of Vishnu or Krishna.

[Śuka spoke:]

Those maidens went forward by
tracing various footprints
along his path.
Discovering in the pattern of footprints
those of a young woman,
they became distressed
and spoke these words:[18] 26

[The Gopīs spoke:]

Whose footprints are these?
Someone was walking
with the son of Nanda!
He must have placed
his arm on her shoulder,
just as an elephant
rests his trunk on a mate. 27

The Beloved Lord,
the supreme Lord Hari,
was worshiped by her perfectly.
Having abandoned us,
being so pleased with her,
Govinda led her to a secret place.[19] 28

Ah, this dust
from the lotus feet
of Govinda
is sanctified, O friends!
Even Brahmā, Śiva, and
the Goddess Ramā
place this dust
upon their heads,
in order to dispel their sins.[20] 29

18. young woman: commonly identified as Rādhā, the Gopī who is Krishna's supreme beloved. This verse and the following verses through verse 41 describe this special Gopī, or Rādhā.

19. Hari: Krishna.

20. Brahmā: the deity of cosmic creation, most often associated with the cosmic deities Vishnu and Śiva.

These footprints of hers
cause great pain for us
since she alone,
Among all the Gopīs,
was taken to a secret place
and now enjoys the lips of Acyuta. 30

Her footprints are not visible over here;
the soles of her soft feet certainly were
Hurting from the sprouting blades of grass;
the lover must have lifted up his beloved. 31–1

These footprints
are sunken from
carrying this maiden.
O Gopīs, look! Krishna,
the amorous one, became
heavy from bearing her weight.
There, the great Soul
must have set her down
to gather flowers. 31–2

Here, flowers were gathered
by the lover for his beloved.
Just see these incomplete footprints,
leaving impressions only of his toes. 32

Then, this impassioned lover
decorated the hair
of his beloved over here.
He undoubtedly was seated
while making for his dearest
a crown of flowers. 33

Śiva: the deity of cosmic dissolution.
The Goddess Ramā: the Goddess Lakṣmī, consort of Vishnu.

[Śuka spoke:]

He delighted in loving her,
  yet he delights in the self
  and takes pleasure in the self,
  for he is complete.
By contrast, then, he revealed
  the abased condition
  of lustful men with
  bad-hearted women. 34

Thus, showing each other
  patterns of footprints
  while wandering about,
  the Gopīs became bewildered.
They concluded that
  Krishna had departed
  with one special Gopī,
  leaving behind the other
  young women in the forest. 35

She believed herself to be
  best among all women
  and she considered,
"Abandoning the other Gopīs,
  struck by passionate love,
  he adores me as his only beloved." 36

Then, reaching a certain place in the forest,
  she became proud and said to Keśava:
"I am unable to walk any further—
  please take me wherever you desire." 37

Thus addressed by his beloved,
  he replied, "Please climb on my shoulder."
Then Krishna suddenly disappeared;
  the young woman was devastated. 38

[The Gopī spoke:]

O my Lord! My pleasure!
My dearest! Where are you?
Where are you,
mighty-armed Lord?
O Friend!
I am your miserable
maidservant—
please show me
that you are near! 39

The sage Śuka spoke:

As the Gopīs were
following the path
of their Beloved Lord,
not far away,
They caught a glimpse
of their grieving friend,
overwhelmed by separation
from her beloved. 40

They intently listened to her story;
how she first received
honor from Mādhava,
Then, due to self-indulgence,
how she was dishonored;
they were completely amazed. 41

Upon entering the forest,
they continued their search
until they no longer could see
by the light of the moon.
Then, finding themselves
surrounded by darkness,
the young women
turned back. 42

Their minds were
filled with thoughts of him;
they spoke about him constantly;
their movements
were no longer their own
for they were fully absorbed in him.
While praising
his qualities in song
they forgot their homes;
indeed, they even forgot themselves. 43

They again returned
to the banks of the Kālindī,
immersed in their feelings for Krishna.
Sitting together,
singing about Krishna,
they ardently longed for his return.[21] 44

Act Three

THE SONG OF THE GOPĪS: GOPĪ GĪTA

Bhāgavata Purāṇa Book 10 Chapter 31

Monologue: Longing for God's Presence with Humility and Passion

The Gopīs spoke:

Glorious is Vraja, surpassing all,
for it is the land of your birth.
Indeed, the Goddess Indirā
resides in this place forever.
O beloved, please allow
your maidservants to see you!
Their very life-breath is sustained in you,
and they search for you everywhere.[1] 1

21. Kālindī: the Yamunā River.

1. Indirā: name for the Goddess Lakṣmī, goddess of prosperity, consort of Nārāyaṇa or Vishnu.

With your eyes,
you steal the beauty
of the center
Of an exquisite fully bloomed
lotus flower, rising out
of a serene autumn pond,
O Lord of love,
and it is killing us,
your voluntary maidservants—
O bestower of benedictions,
in this world,
is this not murder? 2

Whether it be
from poisonous waters
or a fearsome demon;
From torrential rains,
wind storms, and
fiery thunderbolts;
From the bull demon,
the son of Maya, or from
any other fearful predicament;
O almighty one,
you have been our protector
time and time again.[2] 3

2. poisonous waters: caused by the demon serpent Kāliya, on whose multiple heads Krishna dances.

fearsome demon: commonly understood as the gigantic wicked snake Agha, whom Krishna slays. See BhP 10.12.

torrential rains: alluding to Indra in the Govardhana *līlā,* or the demonic activities of Tṛṇāvarta.

fiery thunderbolts: could again be referring to the god Indra in the Govardhana *līlā*.

the bull demon: referring to the demon Ariṣṭa, whom Krishna slays. See BhP 10.36.1–15.

son of Maya: the demon Vyomāsura, whom Krishna slays. See BhP 10.37.27–34.

Clearly you are not the son of a Gopī;
you are the Witness
Residing in the hearts
of all embodied beings.
When Vikhanas prayed to you
for protection of the universe,
O friend, you appeared
in the dynasty of the Sātvatas.[3] 4

O leader of the Vṛṣṇis,
those who fear the cycle
of endless suffering
Approach your feet,
which grant fearlessness.
O beloved,
please place on our heads
Your hand, beautiful as a lotus,
that fulfills all wishes
and holds the hand of Śrī.[4] 5

O destroyer of suffering
for the residents of Vraja;
O hero of all women
whose smile crushes
the pride of your devotees;
O friend, please accept us
as your maidservants—
Show us the beauty
of your lotus-like face! 6

3. Witness: Krishna as the indwelling Lord within the heart of all beings.
Vikhanas: the cosmic creator deity, Brahmā.
dynasty of the Sātvatas: name for the Yādava Dynasty, in which the Yadus worship Krishna.
4. Vṛṣnis: the dynasty in which Krishna appears.

Your lotus feet
remove all sins of
those surrendered unto you.
Your feet, the resting place
of the Goddess Śrī,
follow cows out to graze.
May your lotus feet,
once placed on
the hoods of a serpent,
Be placed upon our breasts—
please crush this passion
lying within our hearts![5] 7

By your sweet voice
and charming words
So attractive to the wise,
O one with lotus eyes,
These maidservants
are becoming delirious—
O hero, please revive us
with your intoxicating lips! 8

Your words of nectar
described by sages and poets
Are life for the suffering,
destroy all sins, and
are auspicious to hear.
Those who extol your praises
throughout the world
Are the most generous persons,
bestowing the greatest riches. 9

5. the hoods of a serpent: refers to the serpent demon Kāliya.

Your smiles,
loving glances
for your beloved ones,
And your intimate
playful ways
are auspicious meditations;
Also the promises
you made to us in secret—
all have touched our hearts.
O cunning one,
indeed, these things
agitate our minds. 10

When you leave Vraja
while herding the cows,
Your feet, O Lord,
beautiful as a lotus,
May be hurt by stones,
grasses and grains;
O beloved, our hearts
become disturbed.[6] 11

At the close of each day,
your face, encircled by
Dark blue locks of hair,
like the lotus enveloped
by forest foliage,
Displays thickly smeared
dust from cows.
O hero, you constantly place
this loving memory
within our hearts. 12

6. Vraja: the village within the Vraja region.

Your lotus feet fulfill
the desires of all
who humbly submit to them.
Worshiped by the one
born from the lotus flower,
they are the ornament of the earth.
They are to be meditated upon
during times of distress, for
they grant the highest satisfaction.
O charming lover,
please place upon our breasts
your lotus feet, O slayer of misery.[7] 13

The nectar that
strengthens our love
and vanquishes our grief;
The nectar that
is abundantly kissed
by the flute you play,
Making everyone forget
all other attachments;
O hero, please bestow
upon us this nectar
of your lips! 14

During the day when
you go off to the forest,
we cannot see you.
The smallest fraction
of a moment seems
like thousands of years.
When we eagerly behold
again your beautiful face
with curling locks of hair,
It seems the creator was mindless,
making eyelids to cover our eyes. 15

7. the one born from the lotus flower: Brahmā, the god of creation, who is born from the navel of Vishnu.

Our husbands, sons, brothers,
ancestors and all others
Have been completely forsaken, O Acyuta,
so we could be in your presence.
You know why we have come here—
we were captured by your alluring song.
O deceiver, who would abandon
such women in the middle of the night?[8] 16

The promises you made
to us in secret and
the passionate feelings
rising in our hearts;
Your smiling face and
glances of pure love;
Your broad chest,
the abode of Śrī;
Recalling all this,
we feel constant,
unbearable longing for you
and our minds become bewildered. 17

O dearest one,
by manifesting yourself,
You remove the distress
of the inhabitants
of the forest of Vraja.
Please give to us, whose
hearts are longing for you,
That medicine which brings relief
to our tormented hearts,
fully devoted to you. 18

8. alluring song: the sound of Krishna's flute.

Your fine feet,
delicate like the lotus,
we gently place upon our breasts
Which we fear, O dear one,
may be too rough for you.
When you roam the forest,
we wonder, are your feet not hurt
By small stones and other harsh objects?
Our minds are turning and reeling—
our very lives are only for you. 19

Act Four

KRISHNA REAPPEARS AND SPEAKS OF LOVE

Bhāgavata Purāṇa Book 10 Chapter 32

Scene I
Narrative: God Appears before Souls Possessing Unconditional Love

The sage Śuka said:

Thus after the Gopīs sang out for him,
lamenting in these wondrous ways,
They burst into tears, O king,
longing for the vision of Krishna. 1

Then, right before them,
the heroic Śauri appeared,
his face blossoming like a lotus
and beaming with a smile.
Wearing yellow garments and
adorned with a flower garland,
the supreme God of love
stood directly before them,
alluring even the love-god
who himself charms all others.[1] 2

With eyes opening wide,
the maidens became
filled with love
upon seeing their
dearest beloved return.
All of them stood up at once,
as if the breath of life
had just returned
to their bodies. 3

One of them reverently held
in her joined palms
the hand of Śauri,
beautiful as the lotus;
Another placed his arm,
covered with the balm
of sandalwood,
on her shoulder. 4

One slender maiden held
his chewed betel nut
in her joined palms;
Another, burning with desire,
placed his lotus feet
on her breasts. 5

1. Śauri: Krishna, appearing very powerful as a descendent of the Śura Dynasty.
the love-god: known as Kāmadeva, the "Cupid" of India who functions much like the Greek god.

One of them,
 straining her eyebrows,
 was beside herself
 with loving fury.
With accusing glances
 as if to injure him,
 she glared at him,
 biting her lip. 6

Still another,
 though greatly delighted
 as she gazed with unblinking eyes
 at the beauty of his lotus-like face,
Could not be satisfied,
 just as saintly persons who
 meditate upon his feet
 remain insatiable. 7

One of them took him
 into her heart through
 the aperture of her eyes;
 then closing her eyes,
 she embraced him within.
She became elated with
 bodily ripplings of joy,
 as the body of a yogi
 is overcome with bliss.[2] 8

All of them,
 as their tranquillity
 fully blossomed
 by fixing their gaze upon Keśava,
Put aside their sorrow
 born of separation,
 as persons who are blessed
 with the presence of a wise sage. 9

2. yogi: one who practices the arduous physical, mental, and spiritual disciplines of yoga.

The Beloved Lord, Acyuta,
was surrounded by those
whose sorrow had dispersed.
O dear king,
he appeared radiant,
like the supreme Person
with his splendorous powers. 10

Having taken them
to the river Kālindī,
the almighty one
approached the sandy shore,
Where a light breeze
carried fragrances of blooming
jasmine and coral trees,
attracting many bees. 11

The darkness of the night
was graciously dispelled
by an abundance of rays
from the autumn moon,
While the water
of the Kṛṣṇā River
gathered soft sands
with her rippling hands.[3] 12

3. Kṛṣṇā River: another name for the Yamunā River.

The pain in their hearts
   was driven away
   by the delight of seeing him;
Their hearts' bliss
   reached its limits as if
   the goal of the revealed scriptures
   had been attained.
Using their delicate shawls,
   colored by reddish *kuṅkuma*
   from their breasts,
They arranged a seat
   for the true companion
   of all souls.[4] 13

The Beloved Lord was seated
   there among them
   as the supreme Lord,
Who arranges for himself
   a seat within the hearts of all,
   as the supreme Lord of yoga.
Appearing resplendent,
   he was worshiped in
   that assembly of Gopīs;
He exhibited his form as
   the only source of beauty
   pervading all the three worlds. 14

4. shawls: the light-weight "upper coverings" of the Gopīs used not so much for warmth as for modesty.

Scene II
Dialogue: The Purity of Love Is Its Own Reward

Honoring the one who ignited
the passion of their love
With their sporting eyebrows,
playful glances and smiles;
Placing his limbs on their laps
while gently touching both
his feet and hands;
Offering effusive praises,
though mildly angered they spoke. 15

The Gopīs spoke:

Some love only
those who love in return;
some, however, love those
who may not return their love;
Some do not love
in either of these ways;
please explain this
clearly to us, O dear one. 16

The Beloved Lord spoke:

Friends who love each other,
yet ultimately strive
for their own self-interest,
Do not find endearment
nor fulfill dharma;
indeed, such friends have
no purpose other than self-interest. 17

Those who love others who
may not offer love in return
are either parents
or persons of compassion.
O ladies with beautiful waists,
they are persons of dharma
who are without fault
and are truly endearing. 18

Some do not love even
those who offer them love,
let alone those who are
not loving toward them.
Such persons may be
satisfied by the self
and fulfilled in all desires,
or they may be ungrateful,
even hateful toward the venerable. 19

Now, O friends, in order
to strengthen their love,
I may not return even the love
of those who love me;
Like a poor man who obtains
a treasure and then loses it,
Such a person knows nothing else,
filled with no other thought
than regaining that treasure. 20

Dear ladies,
indeed, for my sake alone
You have abandoned the world,
the Vedas, and
even your relatives,
out of love for me.
It was out of love for you
that I became invisible,
though you were never
removed from my sight.
Therefore, you should not be
discontented with me—
O dearest ones,
I am your beloved![5] 21

5. the Vedas: the foundational Sanskrit sacred texts of India, the texts symbolizing complete knowledge.

I am unable to reciprocate,
your faultless love for me,
your own purity,
And all that you have
sacrificed for me,
even over the lifetime
of a great divinity.
Severing strong ties
to your homes so difficult
to overcome, you have
lovingly worshiped me.
May your reward be
your own purity. 22

Act Five

THE RĀSA DANCE

Bhāgavata Purāṇa Book 10 Chapter 33

Scene I
Narrative: God Dances with Souls in the Eternal Celebration of Love

The sage Śuka spoke:

Thus having heard
the enchanting words
of their Beloved Lord,
The Gopīs forgot the agony
caused by separation from him;
their desires were fulfilled
simply by touching his limbs. 1

Then Govinda commenced
the play of the Rāsa dance
with his devoted ones;
Those jewel-like maidens,
joined together by love,
linked their arms with one another.[1] 2

The festival of the Rāsa dance commenced
with a circular formation of Gopīs.
The supreme Lord of yoga, Krishna,
entered among them between each pair—
Each thought she alone was at his side
as he placed his arms around
the necks of those young women. 3

Then hundreds
of celestial chariots
crowded the sky,
Carrying the captivated denizens
of the heavens along with their wives,
their souls anxious to behold that scene.[2] 4

Kettledrums resounded
while showers of blossoms
fell to the ground.
The leading Gandharvas
and their wives sang
about his perfect glory.[3] 5

The bracelets, ankle bells, and
bells decorating the waists
of those young women,
Each with her own beloved,
created a tumultuous sound
in the circle of the Rāsa dance. 6

1. Rāsa dance: the word *rāsa* is the name of a special kind of ancient circular dance, which also includes singing on the part of the participants.

2. celestial chariots: heavenly beings ride in *vimānas,* or chariots that navigate through the heavens.

3. Gandharvas: celestial singers who produce exquisite instrumental music.

There, glowing brilliantly among them,
was the Beloved Lord, son of Devakī—
In a setting of golden ornaments,
he appeared like a magnificent emerald![4] 7

With their feet
stepping to the dance;
with gestures of their hands,
loving smiles and sporting eyebrows;
With waists bending
and the rhythmic movements
of garments covering their breasts;
with earrings swinging
on their cheeks;
The spiritual wives of Krishna,
with moistened faces
and braids and belts
tied tightly,
sang his praises—
They appeared
like lustrous flashes
of radiant lightning
engulfed by a ring of dark clouds. 8

While dancing,
they sang out loud
and the throats of those
so delighted by love
became reddened.
They were overjoyed
by the touch of Krishna,
and the whole universe
became filled
with their song. 9

4. Devakī: Krishna's original birth mother and the wife of Vāsudeva.

One of them, together with Mukunda,
sang out in pure embellished tones,
freely improvising on a melody.
Pleased by her performance,
he honored her, saying
"Well done!" "Well done!"
Another one sang out that melody
in a stylized rhythmic pattern,
and he offered her much praise.[5] 10

Another, weary from
the Rāsa dance,
stood beside the one
who carried a baton;
Placing her arm
around his shoulder,
her jasmine flowers
and bracelets slackened. 11

Then one of them placed
on her shoulder
the arm of Krishna,
with the fragrance
of a blue lotus.
Upon smelling this scent,
blended with the balm
of sandalwood,
she became elated
with bodily ripplings of bliss
and kissed his arm tenderly. 12

5. Mukunda: Krishna, "one who grants liberation, or mukti."
in a stylized rhythmic pattern: a particular measure of music known as *dhruvam*.

One, decorated with
shimmering earrings
that swayed to the dance,
placed her cheek next to his.
With his cheek
touching hers,
he gave her
the betel nut he was chewing. 13

Another, whose ankle bells
and bells of her belt
were accompanying
the singing and dancing,
stood by his side.
Becoming weary,
she tenderly brought
the lotus-like hand of Acyuta
to her breasts. 14

The Gopīs had obtained Acyuta,
the exlusive beloved of Śrī,
as their lover.
With their necks
embraced by his arms,
they delighted in singing about him. 15

The beauty of their faces was enhanced
by droplets of perspiration
decorating their cheeks, and
By lotus flowers in their hair
and behind their ears.
With music resounding from
their bracelets and ankle bells,
and garlands falling from their hair,
The Gopīs danced
together with their Beloved Lord;
bees became a chorus of singers
in that assembly of the Rāsa dance. 16

Thus with his hands
touching them in embraces,
With broad playful smiles
and affectionate glances,
The Lord of Ramā delighted in
loving the fair maidens of Vraja,
Just as a small child plays
with his own reflection. 17

From their contact with his limbs,
their senses were filled with joy.
The young women of Vraja
could hardly keep their hair,
Skirts, and upper garments
that covered their breasts
From becoming disheveled, and
their garlands and ornaments
from scattering, O leader of the Kurus.[6] 18

Observing the play of Krishna,
celestial ladies
moving in the sky
became enchanted and
Passion arose in them—
even the moon
with its constellations
became amazed. 19

Having multiplied himself
in as many forms as there
were cowherd women,
He, the Beloved Lord, knowing
all pleasure within himself,
delighted in loving them
in this divine play. 20

6. leader of the Kurus: the king Parīkṣit to whom the Rāsa Līlā is being narrated.

Scene II
Narrative: Intimate Encounters with God in Playful Acts of Love

When he saw how they
   had become weary
   from their amorous play,
The compassionate one
   lovingly wiped their faces,
   O king, with his soothing hand. 21

The Gopīs were beautiful
   with shining cheeks,
Locks of hair, brilliant gold earrings,
   and glances enhanced by sweet smiles.
They honored their hero
   and sang of his auspicious acts,
Delighted by the touch
   of his fingernails. 22

His garland,
   crushed by their limbs
   joined together with his,
Was colored with
   the reddish *kuṅkuma*
   that covered their breasts.
Followed by a chorus of bees
   who sang as though they
   were the best of Gandharvas,
He swiftly entered the water to dispel
   the maidens' fatigue and relax with them,
   like a roused elephant along
   with his female elephant companions,
   breaking down any boundaries in his way. 23

In the water,
 being splashed by the girls,
He gazed upon them with pure love
 as they laughed all around him,
 dear king.
He was worshiped by those
 traveling in celestial vehicles who
 showered lotus flowers upon that scene.
He, who himself possesses all pleasure,
 took pleasure in amorous love,
 playing like the king of elephants. 24

Then he moved along the banks
 of the Kṛṣṇā River
 into a small forest grove,
In the direction of a gentle breeze
 carrying fragrances of flowers
 over land and water.
Surrounded by
 that group of maidens
 who gathered around him like bees,
He was just like a large elephant
 reeling with excitement
 in the company of female elephants. 25

Thus he allowed himself to be
subdued by those nights
made so brilliant
by the rays of the moon—
He was perfectly
fulfilled in all desires
and pure within himself;
While with that group of maidens
so passionately attached to him,
sexual enjoyment was of no issue—
Inspiring the narrations
and poetry of autumn,
all those moonlit nights
found their refuge in *rasa.*[7] 26

Scene III
Theological Discourse: God's Love Transcends and Satisfies Ethical Concerns

The king Parīkṣit spoke:

For the purpose of
establishing dharma and
subduing all that opposes it,
The Beloved Lord, accordingly,
descends with his counterpart
as Lord of the universe.[8] 27

How could he—the teacher,
executor and protector
of the limits of dharma—
O knower of Brahman,
act in contrary ways
by touching others' wives? 28

7. *rasa:* "taste," aesthetic experience or poetic delight. The word also connotes a "divine relationship of affection and tenderness." Note that this word is different from *Rāsa,* Krishna's "wondrous circle dance" with the Gopīs.

8. counterpart: Krishna's complementary divine associate(s) and/or divine abode.

With what intention
would the Lord of the Yadus,
whose desires are supremely fulfilled,
Perform such acts that
would usually be condemned?
Please destroy our doubt, O strict sage.[9] 29

The sage Śuka spoke:

Apparent transgressions of *dharma*
in the acts of the most exalted souls
can appear bold or reckless.
Among such powerful beings
there is no adverse effect,
just as fire can devour anything
without being affected. 30

If one, unlike the exalted soul,
is not powerful,
one should never perform
any transgressions,
even within one's mind.
Such a person
who acts foolishly would perish,
as anyone other than Rudra
would be destroyed by poison
generated from the sea.[10] 31

Words from exalted souls,
meant for us, are always true,
though their actions
only sometimes can be followed.
Therefore one who
possesses intelligence
should act in agreement
with their teachings. 32

9. Lord of the Yadus: Krishna.

10. Rudra: name for the deity of cosmic dissolution, Śiva.

poison generated from the sea: Śiva saves the universe by drinking the *kālakūṭa* poison that was produced from the churning of the ocean. See BhP 8.7.

Selfishness in this world
is not found in the behavior
of virtuous persons.
Actions appearing at times
to be contrary, which are
without any false sense of self,
are not without true purpose,
O dear king. 33

Thus, for the Lord, how could
there be good or bad effects
arising from the piety
or impiety of creatures,
Whether they be animals,
human beings,
or inhabitants of heaven,
who are themselves controlled by him? 34

Those whose bondage to karma
has been shaken off
by the power of yoga
Are fully satisfied
by humble service to the dust
of the lotus feet of the Lord.
Such sages act freely
without becoming
materially bound.
The supreme Lord, who accepts
various revealed forms according
to his own supreme desire,
also acts freely—
how then, for him,
could there possibly be bondage?[11] 35

11. karma: the soul's ties to actions and reactions of this world. Karma keeps a soul bound to this world, to the cycle of birth and death, without allowing its final release into the eternal world of Spirit in which the highest abode is Krishna's blissful world of Vraja.

Scene IV
Narrative: Divine Drama Inspires Highest Devotional Love

He who dwells within the Gopīs
and within their husbands,
indeed, within all embodied beings
As the internal Witness,
also acts in this world
through his divine dramas,
by assuming various forms.[12] 36

In order to show
special favor to his devotees,
he reveals his personal
human-like form.
Upon hearing
how he affectionately
enacts his divine plays
in this manner,
one becomes fully devoted to him. 37

The husband cowherds of Vraja
felt no jealousy whatsoever
toward Krishna.
Deluded by his power of Māyā,
each husband thought his wife
had remained all the while by his side.[13] 38

12. the internal Witness: manifestation of Krishna within the heart of living beings. assuming various forms: refers to the avatāra forms, or "divine descents" of the supreme deity or Vishnu.

13. his power of Māyā: the divine illusory power of God causing forgetfulness (see Yogamāyā in verse 1.1).

During the sacred hour before dawn,
  at the end of the night of Brahmā,
  and with the consent of Vāsudeva,
The Gopīs returned to their homes,
  though reluctantly—
  for they so loved the Beloved Lord
  and they were so loved by him.[14] 39

This is the divine play of Vishnu
  with the fair maidens of Vraja.
One who is filled with faith,
  who hears or describes this play,
Having regained the highest
  devotion for the Beloved Lord,
Has lust, the disease of the heart,
  quickly removed without delay—
  such a person is peaceful and wise.[15] 40

14. night of Brahmā: a night of the creator god, Brahmā, is a night in cosmic or heavenly terms, an extraordinary length of time, the equivalent of 4.32 billion human years.

Vāsudeva: Krishna; son of Vasudeva, Krishna's father and husband of Devakī.

15. Vishnu: Krishna in his persona as a cosmic deity, sustainer of all the universes.

Song of the Flute: Veṇu Gīta

Bhāgavata Purāṇa Book 10 Chapter 21

The sage Śuka spoke:

Thus, the forest was filled
with clear autumn waters
and gentle breezes carrying
the sweet scent of lotus flowers.
Entering that scene
together with cows
and cowherd friends,
Acyuta, the infallible one, appeared.[1] 1

Among groves of flowering trees,
and lakes, rivers, and hills
Resounding with flocks of birds
and swarming maddened bees,
Madhupati arrived, accompanied by
Balarāma and the cowherd boys.
While tending the cows
he began to play his flute.[2] 2

1. Song of the Flute: the word "song" here has two possible meanings. It can mean the "song about Krishna's flute," and the "song-like music produced by Krishna's flute."
Śuka: the sage-narrator of this passage.
Acyuta: a name of Krishna.
2. Madhupati: a name for Krishna, meaning "chief of the Madhu dynasty."
Balarāma: the older brother of Krishna.

Those young women of Vraja
were aroused by Passion
after hearing
the song of his flute.
Some of them, in his absence,
were moved to describe
the qualities of Krishna
to their intimate friends.[3] 3

As they began to describe him,
they remembered
the playful activities of Krishna.
Their minds again became
disturbed by the force of Passion
and they could no longer speak, O king.[4] 4

Adorned with a crown
of peacock feathers
and blue *karṇikāra* flowers
ornamenting his ears,
He, most excellent of dancers,
wearing the Vaijayantī garland
and yellow garments brilliant as gold,
Filled the holes of his flute
with the nectar of his lips
while his praises were
being sung by cowherd friends.
He then entered
the Vrindāvana forest,
made beautiful by his footprints.[5] 5

3. Vraja: the rural region in which Krishna and the Gopīs reside.
4. Passion: amorous love personified, intimating the god of love.
king: Parīkṣit, the listener to whom this passage is being narrated.
5. *karṇikāra* flowers: the pericarp portion of lotus flowers.
Vaijayantī: the name of Krishna's garland consisting of flowers of five colors.
Vrindāvana: the village and surrounding forests in which Krishna and the Gopīs reside.

Thus hearing, O king,
  the sound of the flute
  that captivates
  the hearts of all beings,
The young women of Vraja
  began describing
  that alluring sound yet again,
  embracing him within their minds. 6

The beautiful Gopīs spoke:

O friends,
  for those who have eyes,
  we know of no greater
  reward than this—
Entering the forest
  with their companions and
  herding the cows before them,
The two sons of the ruler of Vraja,
  whose faces are adorned
  by the flutes they play,
Cast loving glances
  all around them—
  it is this vision that
  is constantly imbibed. 7

Dressed in a splendid array
  of garments; decorated
  with tender mango leaves,
Peacock feathers and bunches
  of flowers; and wearing
  garlands of lotuses and lilies;
The two of them
  are exceedingly beautiful,
  sometimes singing
Among their cowherd friends,
  and appearing like the most
  excellent of dancers on a stage. 8

O Gopīs, what auspicious acts
must have been performed
by this flute,
For it enjoys the nectar flowing
from the lips of Dāmodara,
leaving only a taste for us cowherd girls
to whom this nectar truly belongs.
The rivers, themselves
mothers of the bamboo
from which the flute is made,
feel jubilant with blooming lotuses;
And the forefathers of the flute,
the bamboo trees, shed tears
of joy with their flowing sap.[6] 9

O friend,
Vrindāvana enhances
the beauty of the earth
With treasure obtained
from the lotus feet
of the son of Devakī.
Upon hearing
the flute of Govinda,
peacocks dance in rapture—
Observing their dancing from hilltops,
all other creatures
become stunned.[7] 10

6. Dāmodara: Krishna, the "one whose waist is bound," referring to the *līlā* in BhP 10.9.
7. O friend: a form of address of one Gopī to another.
Devakī: Krishna's birth mother.
Govinda: Krishna, the protector of the cows.

Blessed, surely,
  in spite of their ignorance,
Are these female deer
  who have taken birth as animals.
Upon hearing the exquisitely dressed
  son of Nanda sound his divine flute,
They offer him worship
  through affectionate glances,
  along with their black deer mates.[8] 11

Gazing at Krishna whose
  pleasing form and behavior
  are utterly elating for all women,
And hearing
  the enchanting music
  emanating from his flute,
The hearts of the gods' wives
  are agitated by Passion while
  they move in heavenly chariots;
They become bewildered
  and their belts loosen,
  as flowers fall from their hair. 12

Cows, too, drink the nectar
  of the song of the flute
Coming forth from Krishna's mouth
  into the vessels of their up-raised ears.
Indeed, calves stand still,
  their mouths filled with milk
  flowing from their mothers' teats.
Watching with tearful eyes,
  they embrace Govinda
  within their hearts. 13

8. Nanda: Krishna's foster father, husband of Yaśodā.

In this forest, O mother, the birds
are most certainly great sages.
Beholding Krishna playing
the melodious song of his flute,
They rise to branches of trees
covered with beautiful foliage.
With unblinking eyes they listen,
while all other sounds cease.[9] 14

When rivers hear
the music of Mukunda,
their flowing currents are broken
And their waters swirl
out of intense love for him.
The two feet of Murāri
are made stationary,
seized by the embrace of
Arm-like waves that present
offerings of lotus flowers.[10] 15

Seeing how he tends
the animals of Vraja
in the heat of the sun,
Along with Balarāma
and the cowherd boys;
and how he follows the cows
while playing his flute;
The rain-cloud,
rising high in the sky
with love overflowing,
Creates from its own form
an umbrella for its friend,
showering flower-like raindrops. 16

9. mother: a form of address of certain Gopīs for other Gopīs.
10. Mukunda: Krishna, the giver of liberation.
Murāri: Krishna, the killer of the Mura demon.

The native women of Pulinda
  are fully satisfied by contact with
The *kuṅkuma* powder that decorates
  the breasts of his beloveds,
  released from the beautiful
  reddish lotus feet
  of the greatly praised Lord.
Even though they feel
  tormented by the sight
  of reddened blades of grass,
They also experience relief from
  the pangs of that vision of Passion
  when they spread the powder upon
  their own faces and breasts.[11] 17

Ah! This hill is best among all
  the servants of Hari, O friends.
It delights in the touch of the feet
  of Krishna and Balarāma,
Offering respects to them both,
  along with their cows
  and cowherd friends,
By supplying fresh water,
  pastures of soft grass,
  sheltering caves and edible roots.[12] 18

11. women of Pulinda: a local indigenous people.
kuṅkuma: a deep reddish powder.

12. This hill: refers to Govardhana, the hill on which Krishna and Balarāma play with the cows, which was effortlessly lifted by Krishna to protect the residents of Vraja from the wrath of the god Indra.
Hari: Krishna, the one who steals the hearts of all.

The cows are led through
the forest by the two boys
and their cowherd friends.
They are accompanied by
sweet sounds of melodious notes flowing
from the enchanting flute, O friends,
That cause moving beings not to move,
and non-moving beings like trees
to be elated with ripplings of bliss.
The two boys can be recognized
by the ropes they carry to bind
milking and rambunctious cows—
all of this is wonderful![13] 19

[The sage Śuka spoke:]

Thus, the various divine acts
of their Beloved Lord as he
wandered about Vrindāvana
Were being described
by each one of them,
for the Gopīs had attained
complete absorption in him.[14] 20

13. elated with ripplings of bliss: see "Notes and Comments" for RL 1.40.
14. Beloved Lord: Krishna; translates *bhāgavat.*

Song of the Black Bee: Bhramara Gīta

Bhāgavata Purāṇa Book 10 Chapter 47 Verses 1 through 21

The sage Śuka spoke:

The women of Vraja were gazing
upon one companion of Krishna,
Whose arms were long
and eyes like young lotus flowers.
Wearing a yellow garment
and a garland of lotuses,
His face, beautiful as a lotus,
was glowing with shining earrings.[1] 1

They were astonished
by his charming appearance:
"Who is this? From where does he come?
And just whom does he serve?
His ornaments and clothing
are like those of Acyuta!"
Speaking these words and
very excited indeed,
all of them surrounded him,
Whose shelter was the lotus feet of
the most excellent and famous one.[2] 2

1. one companion of Krishna: Uddhava, Krishna's messenger, whose name is revealed in verse 9.

2. Acyuta: Krishna, "the infallible one."

the most excellent and famous one: name for Krishna or Vishnu; translates the compound Uttamaśloka, more literally meaning, "The one whose hymns of praise (*śloka*) are the greatest or highest (*uttama*)." This epithetical name is also found in verses 13 and 15 below.

They bowed down to him
  and honored him properly
With modesty, shyness, smiling,
  glances and pleasing words.
In confidence, they inquired from him
  as he was seated comfortably before them,
For they knew he was carrying a message
  from the Lord of the Goddess Ramā.[3] 3

[The Gopīs spoke:]

We know that you have arrived
  as a companion
  of the Lord of the Yadus,
And that you, good sir,
  have been sent here by him
  who desires to give pleasure to his parents.[4] 4

Otherwise, in these cow pastures of Vraja,
  for him, we see nothing else
  worth remembering.
Certainly the bonds of affection
  in family relations are difficult
  to give up, even for a sage. 5

Friendliness toward others
  is displayed for a purpose,
  until one's purpose is achieved.
This is the case with men
  in relation to women,
  and black bees in relation to flowers. 6

3. Lord of the Goddess Ramā: Krishna.
4. Lord of the Yadus: Krishna.

Prostitutes abandon men
  who have no money;
  citizens abandon
  incompetent kings;
Students, their teachers
  after completing their education;
  and sacrificial priests, their patrons
  after receiving their compensation. 7

Birds abandon trees
  when their fruits are gone;
  guests abandon houses
  after they have eaten;
Similarly, animals abandon
  burnt-down forests;
  and lovers abandon women
  after having enjoyed love with them. 8

[The sage Śuka spoke:]

These were the words of the Gopīs
  whose minds, bodies, and speech
  were completely devoted to Govinda.
They turned to Uddhava who had just arrived,
  for he was a messenger from Krishna,
  and they dropped all worldly concerns.[5] 9

They sang about
  the various times
  they spent with him, their beloved;
  giving up their shyness
  they began to cry.
Over and over,
  they remembered all the events
  of his childhood and youth. 10

5. Govinda: name for Krishna.

Uddhava: the name of Krishna's companion-messenger to whom the Gopīs have been speaking.

One of them, contemplating
her closeness with Krishna,
observed a black bee.
Imagining it to be a messenger
sent to her by her beloved,
she thus began to speak. 11

The Gopī spoke:

O black bee,
friend of a cheater—
please do not touch my feet
with your whiskers,
Which are clearly tinged
by reddish *kuṅkuma* powder
that has fallen onto his garland
from the breasts of rival lovers.
Let the Lord of the Madhu Dynasty,
for whom you are the messenger,
bear the marks of favor
from these proud women—
Such behavior would be the object of
ridicule in the assembly of the Yadus![6] 12

After having us drink just once
the enchanting nectar
of his own lips,
He suddenly abandoned us,
just as you might abandon
blossoming flowers.
So how is it that the Goddess Padmā
continues to serve his feet,
beautiful as the lotus?
Oh! Her mind has certainly been stolen
by the deceitful speech of the most
excellent and famous one.[7] 13

6. The group of verses known as the Bhramara Gīta, "The Song of the Bee," begins with this verse and ends with verse 21 as presented below.

reddish *kuṅkuma* powder: saffron or vermilion.

the Madhu Dynasty: the dynasty in which Krishna appears.

the Yadus: the great and powerful dynasty to which Krishna belonged.

7. the Goddess Padmā: another name for Lakṣmī, the divine consort of the cosmic Vishnu.

O six-legged creature,
  why are you singing
About the ancient one,
  Lord of the Yadus,
  here before us homeless girls?
Let the singing about him,
  the friend of the victorious one,
  be instead for all his lady friends
Whose breasts he now relieves
  of their intense agony—
  those beloved ones of his
  will provide what it is that you desire.[8] 14

Are there any women
  in the celestial, earthly,
  or lower worlds
Who would not be available to him,
  with his playful arching eyebrows
  and deceptive, charming smiles?
After all, what are we to him,
  the dust of whose feet is worshiped
  by the Goddess Lakṣmī herself?
Nevertheless, those who are destitute
  are favored by the words of
  the most excellent and famous one.[9] 15

8. friend: refers to Krishna.
the victorious one: refers to Arjuna, the warrior hero of the Mahābhārata.
9. the Goddess Lakṣmī: the consort of Krishna's cosmic form of Vishnu.

Please keep your head
away from my foot!
I understand you very well—
You know how to offer flattering words
while acting as his messenger
because you have been trained by Mukunda.
Now he has abandoned us,
who have given up our children, husbands,
and all others in the world for his sake—
Therefore, why, since he is ungrateful,
should we make up with him?[10] 16

Behaving like
a cruel-hearted hunter,
he shot arrows
at the king of monkeys;
While dominated by one woman,
he disfigured another
who approached him
with passionate desires;
Even after accepting the worship of Bali,
he tied him up with ropes like a crow
who, after devouring its prey,
hovers over it.
So enough of this friendship
with that dark-complexioned one,
even if the treasure of such stories
about him is impossible to give up![11] 17

10. Mukunda: Krishna, the one who grants liberation.

11. a cruel-hearted hunter: refers to Rāma, a divine manifestation of Krishna, presented fully in the great Sanskrit epic *Rāmāyaṇa,* and presented briefly in Book 9 of the *Bhāgavata Purāṇa.*

the king of monkeys: Vāli. See BhP 9.10.12.

one woman: Sītā, the wife of Rāma. See BhP 9.10 and 9.13.18.

disfigured another who approached him: refers to Śūrpanakā. See BhP 9.10.4.

accepting the worship of Bali: refers to Vāmana. See BhP 8.17–23.

For one who constantly seeks
   to hear of his divine acts,
   the ears are filled with nectar,
A drop of which, if relished even once,
   destroys all attachment to worldly duties
   filled with conflict and duality.
Such irresponsible persons promptly
   give up their families and homes,
   leaving them in a wretched condition.
Here, many of them wander about
   acting as mendicants,
   begging for their livelihood
   like so many birds. 18

We had faith
   that his deceptive speech was true,
Just as the foolish female companion
   of the black deer is deceived
   by mimicking sounds of a hunter.
We, the maidservants of Krishna,
   have experienced repeatedly
   the pain of his amorous love
Created by the ardent touch of his nails—
   O messenger, please speak of other things! 19

O friend of my dear one,
have you been sent here
once again by my beloved?
You ought to be honored
by me, my friend—
so what do you wish from me?
How will you lead us who
remain here to his side,
he with whom togetherness
is too difficult to give up?
After all, O gentle one,
the Goddess Śrī, his consort,
is forever present with him
resting upon his chest.[12] 20

Oh, indeed! Is it not regrettable
that the son of a highly esteemed man
now resides in the city of Mathurā?
O gentle one, does he remember
his father's house, his family relations
and his cowherd friends?
Does he ever relate to you
any words about us,
his maidservants?
When might he place his hand,
with the fragrant scent of
soothing aloe-wood balm,
on our heads?[13] 21

12. the Goddess Śrī: another name for the consort of Krishna's cosmic form of Vishnu.
13. the city of Mathurā: the large city about twenty miles from Vrindāvana village.

Figure 6. Marble sacred image of Krishna elaborately worshiped. International Society for Krishna Consciousness, London. Photograph by the author.

Part II

TEXTUAL ILLUMINATIONS

1

Background of the Text

DEVOTIONAL LOVE AS "RASA"

Literature describing the soul's passionate love for the deity is extensive in India, spanning the course of at least one millennium prior to and following the common era. Consequently, the *Bhāgavata Purāṇa*'s portraits of intimacy with the divinity come out of a colorful and extensive literary past, a heritage reflected in the devotional and aesthetic achievements of the Rāsa Līlā. Sources of such amorous devotion are scriptural, dramatic, and poetic.

Love between the soul and the deity has taken a variety of forms that have been articulated in depth by the theistic Vaishnava tradition that arose in the eastern province of Bengal, and is referred to here as Caitanya Vaishnavism.[1] The tradition spread throughout regions of Bengal, Orissa, and the northern areas of India, initiated and inspired by the charismatic figure known as Krishna Caitanya (1486–1533 C.E.). This ecstatic mystic and devotional revivalist of the sixteenth century, along with his close disciples, established a theological school of thought and religious practice centered upon devotion, or bhakti, to the supreme Lord Krishna. The scholar Klaus Klostermaier states that, among the plethora of religious traditions in India, "perhaps the most subtle and detailed system of gradual ascent to God by means of love has been developed in the Caitanya school of Vaishnavism."[2] Scholars have observed that the Caitanya school makes a particularly valuable contribution in examining the nature of human religious emotion.

Caitanya left no written works, with the exception of his famed *Śikṣāṣṭakam*, or "Eight Instructive Verses."[3] He instead chose to inaugurate

1. This tradition is often known as Bengal or Gauḍīya Vaishnavism. These names, however, are limiting because they fail to indicate the full extent of the spread of the tradition. Moreover, the other Vaishnava traditions are named after their founders. For these reasons, I use the name of the founder to identify this Vaishnava school.

2. Klaus Klostermaier, "*Hṛdayavidā:* A Sketch of a Hindu-Christian Theology of Love," *Journal of Ecumenical Studies* (1972): 765.

3. These verses are woven into Krishnadāsa Kavirāja's *Caitanya Caritāmṛta;* see CC 3.20.

his devotional movement through direct instruction to key disciples known as the Six Gosvāmins of Vrindāvana, along with others, who established the doctrine of the school, built temples, and formed communities of worship in Vrindāvana.[4] Caitanya's school was developed in part by his own exemplary and ecstatic behavior in bhakti, observed and recorded by these early writers of the school. Of these recordings, the most famous and loved text is the *Caitanya Caritāmṛta* of Krishnadāsa Kavirāja Gosvāmin. This extensive work, considered to be an unequalled theological synthesis of the school's thought, presents a comprehensive blend of Caitanya's theology and hagiography.[5] Written a half century after the passing away of Caitanya in 1533, the author describes the mystic leader as imparting essential teachings of the school to the two leading Gosvāmins, Rūpa and Sanātana. Of these two, Rūpa is perhaps the more important, as it was he who developed, under the direct guidance of Caitanya, the articulated and formulated theology of *bhakti-rasa*—"the soul's particular relationship with the divinity in devotional love," within the realm of *līlā* or "divine play."

Rūpa Gosvāmin (sixteenth century C.E.), along with other disciples of Caitanya, derived his principles of divine aesthetics from Indian dramaturgy and adapted these to his systematic psychology of divine love. In Sanskrit poetics (*kāvya*) and Indian dramaturgy (*nāṭya*), the word *rasa* (not to be confused with *Rāsa*, as in the dance) refers to the pervasive mood or emotion experienced by an audience as aesthetic delight. Based on the concept that God manifests in his *līlā*, or "divine drama," the Gosvāmin applied Indian dramatic theory to the devotional process of reentering God's eternal drama. In his important work *Bhakti Rasāmṛta Sindhu*, "The Ocean of Eternal Rasa in Devotional Love," Rūpa further developed the understanding of *rasa* as the pervasive emotion of relationships found solely within devotional love, *bhakti-rasa*. David L. Haberman observes that the Caitanya school believes that "love itself is identified as an aspect of the essential nature of God," and notes that it became the task of

4. The Six Gosvāmins are six renunciates famous for having assisted Caitanya in his mission. Their names are Rūpa, Sanātana, Jīva, Gopāla Bhaṭṭa, Raghunātha, and Raghunātha Baṭṭa.

5. S. K. De states that the CC is "by far the most authoritative biography of Caitanya," and that it "at once took its place among the most authoritative texts of the sect. . . . It is a remarkable mediaeval document of mature theological scholarship." See De, *Vaishnava Faith and Movement*, pp. 53–57.

Caitanya's disciples, therefore, to elaborate on the love of the divinity.[6] Rūpa's text draws largely from the foundational theory of *rasa* formed by Bharata Muni, the originator of Sanskrit dramaturgy, or Nāṭya Śāstra (perhaps as early as the second century B.C.E.) and, further, from theorists such as Bhoja (eleventh century), Abhinavagupta (twelfth century), and Viśvanātha (fourteenth century).[7]

The teachers of the Caitanya school, specifically Rūpa, and following him, Jīva Gosvāmin and Krishnadāsa Kavirāja Gosvāmin, broadly define and describe the relationship with God as *rasa.* The word *rasa* has several meanings worth mentioning here because, collectively, they give us a feel for the word's power and depth in its religious context. It has the sense of "essence" or "taste." It can also mean "the sap of a plant," "the juice of fruit," or more broadly, "the best or finest or prime part of anything," or the "vital essence" of a thing.[8] The word can mean connotatively and more generally "spiritual experience," or more specifically a particular relationship with God.

The Caitanya Vaishnavas apply the sense of "the prevailing feeling," "religious sentiment," or even "disposition of the heart or mind" to the term *rasa.* Their general connotative meaning is the directly experienced intimate relationship with the divinity. According to the bhakti school, God is *rasa,* God supremely enjoys *rasa,* and God is the ultimate object of *rasa.* The theological use of the word can be found very early, about two thousand years before the Caitanya school, in a phrase that the tradition frequently quotes: "Truly, the Lord is *rasa*" (*raso vai saḥ*).[9] This statement expresses the view that God is the one who is the sole object of *rasa.* God is "the greatest connoisseur of *rasa,* or divine loving relation" (*rasika śekhara*).

Devotion to God as conceived by the Caitanya school consists of five primary types of loving relations with the deity. The soul's particular

6. David Haberman has done much to show how Rūpa's conception of *rasa* has drawn from previous theorists, yet makes its own unique contribution to *rasa* theory. See Haberman's chapters "Religion and Drama in South Asia" and "The Aesthetics of Bhakti" in *Acting as a Way of Salvation: A Study of Rāgānugā Bhakti Sādhana* (New York: Oxford University Press, 1988) for a detailed overview of the history and development of *rasa* theory as it establishes itself in the thought of Rūpa Goswāmin. Another valuable discussion can be found in the Introduction to Haberman's *The Bhaktirasāmṛtasindhu of Rūpa Gosvāmin* (New Delhi: Indira Gandhi National Centre for the Arts; and Delhi: Motilal Banarsidass, 2003).

7. This Viśvanātha of poetics should not be confused with the bhakti commentator Viśvanātha Cakravartin of the eighteenth century, whose commentary on the *Bhāgavata* has been invaluable for this study.

8. The word can also mean "flavor," or even "love," "affection," or "desire."

9. *Taittirīya Upaniṣad* 2.7.1.

relationship with the divinity in devotional love, *rasa,* can closely resemble the variety of loving feelings that humans experience for one another.[10] These types of *rasa* between the soul and God can be described as follows:

1. *Reverential Love (śānta-rasa).* The soul loves the Beloved from a distance, as a great and powerful emperor is loved by subjects who are not personally serving him. Here the soul is removed from the direct presence of the Beloved, due to the soul's awareness of his or her finite existence in relation to the overwhelming majesty and omnipresence of the Lord. This love is characterized as quiet veneration and admiration; reverential love is passive and contemplative, unlike the dynamic and more intimate forms of love that follow.

2. *Subservient Love (dāsya-rasa).* The soul loves the Beloved actively and more closely, as personal servants love and directly serve their king. Here the soul is in a submissive position to the Beloved, who is in a superior position. This love is characterized as obedient service. The distance between the soul and God in reverential love is replaced by dynamic service in subservient love, although the relationship here remains formal.

3. *Mutual Love (sākhya-rasa).* The soul loves the Beloved more intimately in mutuality and equality, as a friend loves a companion. The endearing love of close friendship is now experienced with the supreme Beloved, who places himself on an equal level with the soul. This love is characterized by confidential, even playful and affectionate exchanges. Mutual love constitutes a greater level of intimacy with the divine, since the superior position of the Beloved is no longer acknowledged.

4. *Nurturing Love (vātsalya-rasa).* The soul loves the Beloved even more deeply and tenderly, as a parent loves a child. The soul's love for the Beloved is from a higher or superior "parental" position as the soul cares for and protects the Beloved, who in turn exhibits dependency upon the soul. This love is characterized by adoration and nurturing affection; here, the carefree and casual familiarity of mutual love is replaced by a constant mindfulness and sense of responsibility for the well-being of the Beloved.

10. It has even been suggested that the types of experiences within the various *rasas* with Krishna parallel those experiences that Christains can have in particular relationships with Christ. See Sudhindra Chandra Cakravarti's discussion on "Christianity and Bengal Vaiṣṇavism" (ch. 14) in his work *Philosophical Foundation of Bengal Vaiṣṇavism* (Delhi: Academic Publishers, 1969), especially p. 382.

5. *Passionate Love (śṛṅgāra-rasa).* The soul loves the Beloved in the most intimate way, as a lover loves a beloved in a conjugal, premarital, or extramarital relationship. It is the most confidential form of love, and the intensity of amorous feelings exchanged represents the greatest attainable intimacy in *rasa.* This love is characterized by total self-surrender of the lover in an exclusive passionate union with the divine, often heightened by periods of intense separation. Essential elements of all four previous *rasas* are present within this highest *rasa.*

The school views these five types of intimacy with the deity collectively, as hierarchically arranged stages of love. Each *rasa,* beginning with the first and proceeding to the fifth, represents a higher intensity of love and progressively greater level of intimacy. Yet each *rasa,* in and of itself, is also recognized as a perfection of love for the divine. Even so, the *rasa* of passionate love is regarded as the ultimate perfection among all perfect *rasas.* It should be noted that these *rasas* are not categories in the strictest sense, because each higher *rasa* incorporates selective aspects from the lower *rasas.*[11]

ANCIENT SOURCES OF DEVOTIONAL LOVE

Many characteristics of all five *rasas* are found in the Vedic devotional hymns, which display strikingly intimate expressions of love for the divine. Although the formal categorization of these *rasas* in bhakti was not developed until the sixteenth century, it could be asserted that the religious experience presented as early as the ancient *Ṛg Veda* anticipates dimensions of the formal practice of bhakti, or devotional love, in the Caitanya school.[12]

The divinity of the Vedas enters into a variety of love relations with the Vedic worshiper, who relates to the deity as a father, mother, or father and mother together; as a brother, son, or friend; or as a beloved, even as a bride.[13] The "passionate love" of this last worshiper is expressed in these prayerful words: "As yearning wives cleave to their yearning husband, so cleave our hymns to thee, O Lord most potent"

11. It is explained that certain elements within each *rasa* are unique, and others are transferred or carried over into the higher *rasas* in more intensified forms. See CC 2.19.

12. The paradigmatic examples of the various *rasas* and the ideal personalities associated with them are elaborated upon by the close disciple of Caitanya, Rūpa Gosvāmin, in *Bhakti Rasāmṛta Sindhu.* See note 6 above.

13. Mrinal Das Gupta, "Śraddhā and Bhakti in Vedic Literature," *Indian Historical Quarterly* 6, no. 2 (June 1930): 325.

(*Ṛg Veda* 1.62.11), and "As wives embrace their lord, the comely bridegroom" (*Ṛg Veda* 10.43.1–2).[14] In other examples the soul "strives to win the heart" of the divinity (*Ṛg Veda* 8.31.18), a sentiment found throughout the *Ṛg Veda.* Note that the worshiper in the first two instances above is feminine in gender. At other times the worshiper is masculine, as in the following: "I, like a bridegroom thinking of his consort" (*Ṛg Veda* 4.20.5). Moreover, the divine spouse of the deity himself is also acknowledged in the Vedas: "Vishnu, together with his Spouse" (*Ṛg Veda* 1.156.2). The soul's passionate love for the deity can therefore be seen to mirror the love found directly within divine conjugal relations.

The other higher *rasas* of nurturing and mutual love are also expressed in Vedic hymns. Nurturing love can be observed in the words, "Thou art a Son to him who duly worships thee" (*Ṛg Veda* 2.1.9), and in the passage, "Be to us easy of approach, even as a father to his son" (*Ṛg Veda* 1.1.9).[15] Mutual love between the soul and the divinity is evidenced in the words, "Friend among men" (*Ṛg Veda* 1.67.1), and "Him, him we seek for friendship" (*Ṛg Veda* 1.10.6). Much of the Vedic literature is permeated with such heartfelt emotion expressed by the soul to the deity, or about the deity.

The Upanishads, recorded after the Vedas yet hundreds of years before the common era, at times will engage the theme of devotional love. These texts record intimate dialogues between a teacher and student, addressing philosophical and metaphysical questions on the relationship of the soul to "the supreme Self" (the supreme Lord as the soul within the soul) or to "ultimate reality," Brahman. The Upanishadic teacher stresses that the supreme Self is the source of love in human relationships, as demonstrated in this passage:

14. *The Hymns of the Ṛgveda,* translated by Ralph T. H. Griffith (Delhi: Motilal Banarsidass, 1973). The excerpted quotations that follow are taken from this work.

15. In this example of nurturing love, the father is the deity and the son is the dependent soul. Generally, the nurturing *rasa* designates the worshiper as the parental figure, and God as the dependent child. Even when the reverse is found, the *rasa* is considered to be that of nurturing love. Other examples of nurturing love can be found in *Ṛg Veda* 1.66.1 and 6.2.7.

Truly, it is not due to the love of a husband
that a husband becomes dear,
but due to the love of God
that a husband becomes dear;
Truly, it is not due to the love of a wife
that a wife becomes dear,
but due to the love of God
that a wife becomes dear; . . .
Truly, it is not due to the love of all things
that all things become dear,
but due to the love of God
that all things become dear.
(*Bṛhadāraṇyaka Upaniṣad* 2.4.5)

In the following quote, a simile drawn from the human experience of conjugal love is engaged, in order to convey the soul's experience of union with the supreme:

As a husband knows nothing within or without
when embraced by his beloved wife,
a person knows nothing within or without
when embraced by the Intelligent Soul.
(*Bṛhadāraṇyaka Upaniṣad* 4.3.21)

Here, when the soul "embraces" the supreme Soul, an erotic union occurs, characterized by a nondistinction between what is external and what is internal. These examples of passionate devotion of the soul for the divine clearly demonstrate the fervent emotion that filled the heart of the worshiper in post-Vedic times.

The use of the term *bhakti* as the practice of "devotional love for the deity" first appears in the Upanishads (*Śvetāśvatara Up.* 6.23).[16] It is in the epic literature following the Upanishads, however, that we find the developed philosophical and doctrinal presentation of bhakti. In the *Bhagavad Gītā,* the famous passage within the great *Mahābhārata* epic, "mutual love" is predominantly exhibited between Krishna and Arjuna. In fact, Krishna declares that he is the "dear friend of all beings" (BG 5.29). The other intimate forms of love are

16. Other Upanishads present a doctrine of grace (*Katha Up.* 1.2.23 and *Mundaka Up.* 3.2.3).

indicated, as well, and "intimacy" with the divinity (*mādhurya*) is emphasized over reverence for the "majesty" of the divine (*aiśvarya*).

The *Bhagavad Gītā* (or simply *Gītā*) thus firmly and comprehensively establishes the concept of intimacy with the deity. When Krishna gives Arjuna a private vision of his unlimited greatness manifest in his "universal form" (*virāṭa-rūpa*), Arjuna yearns to experience once again his more loving relationship with Krishna. He does not desire to serve the Lord in awe and with reverential devotion; rather, he prays to be with Krishna in a personal, affectionate way:

> Even as a father loves a son,
> a friend loves a friend
> or a lover loves a beloved,
> O Lord, please be loving to me.
> (BG 11.44)

Clearly, the three higher *rasas* are acknowledged and preferred by Arjuna. Although the narrative line of the *Gītā* places Arjuna and Krishna together as close companions, and their *rasa* is undoubtedly that of mutual love, still some of Krishna's devotional prescriptions resonate with motifs of a more intense love:

> Be absorbed in thinking of me,
> be devoted to me,
> sacrifice everything for me
> and bow down to me.
> Indeed, you will come to me,
> for you have completely
> engaged yourself
> in devotion to me.
> (BG 9.34)

These words do not sound like those coming from a friend; rather, the total self-surrender that characterizes passionate love is depicted here, and there are many more such expressions throughout the *Gītā* text. The Gopīs, in the Rāsa Līlā, as we shall see, exemplify such passionate devotion for the deity. Indeed, the drama represents a culmination of the history of intimacy with the divine in India. Let us now consider the path of devotional love as it relates to other paths leading to God.

DEVOTIONAL LOVE AS THE PATH TO GOD

The religious complex that arises from and finds its foundational scriptural authority in the Vedas is commonly known as Hinduism. The word "Hindu," oddly enough, is not derived from either the ancient or the many vernacular languages of India.[17] Instead, the word was created by Persian-speaking persons who invaded the northwest corner of India, specifically the area of the Sindhu (Indus) River, around the ninth century of the common era. This nomenclature was adopted at least two millennia after the birth of much Indic religious activity to which we refer when using the name; yet, the word "Hindu" has been firmly integrated into the religious identity of persons within Indic traditions. It is perhaps more accurate to speak of a "Hindu complex" of religion rather than Hindu-*ism*, given the great number and variety of Indic religious traditions that consider the Vedas as their foundation.

The primary Hindu traditions, those that focus upon a particular divinity such as the masculine deity Śiva, the Great Goddess Devī, or the cosmic form of Krishna as Vishnu, regard the Vedas as the original revelation of all knowledge, even if they have no active relationship with the Vedic literature or practices. In some ways, the situation parallels that which is found among the Semitic traditions: Christianity and Islam are traditions in their own right, and not merely sects of Judaism; yet both Christian and Islamic traditions rely upon the Jewish Bible at least as a foundation for their faiths, despite their newer, independent revelations and differing forms of worship.

As we can say that Judaism, Christianity, and Islam are the major traditions within the Semitic complex, we can also point to three major South Asian traditions that include the majority of Hindus in India and its northern neighboring country, Nepal. These three traditions—Śaivism, Śaktism, and Vaishnavism—are each named after the ultimate deity upon whom practitioners center their worship. Thus Śaivism focuses on worship of the deity Śiva, known for his universal role in cosmic dissolution; Śaktism involves worship of Śakti, the supreme feminine power of Devī, or the Goddess; and Vaishnavism is centered on worship of Vishnu, known for his universal role in cosmic sustenance, or Krishna, the intimate and playful deity.

17. It is telling that almost every scholar of "Hinduism" is obliged to discuss elaborately the awkward and unself-explanatory nomenclature of this religious complex when writing introductory texts on the subject.

Even though these traditions within the Hindu family of religion do not focus upon the same ultimate deity, they do share the same understanding of the soul's various paths for attaining salvation. Vedic hymns reveal practices that later became formalized as "paths of the soul" (*margas*), which have persisted throughout Indian religious history. Traditions of India may emphasize one of these methods of salvation over the others, or prescribe a combination of the three, which are as follows: the path of "action" (*karma*), in which one "works" for his or her salvation; the path of "knowledge" (*jñāna*), in which one undergoes a process of study, meditation, and introspection; and the path of "devotional love" (*bhakti*), in which one is actively dedicated to the deity in loving service and experiences the reciprocal "grace" of the deity.

Although a pan-Indian phenomenon, bhakti is particularly associated with Vaishnava traditions and the *Bhāgavata* text, emphasizing deep devotional love and affectionate self-surrender offered to a singular personal supreme deity, along with God's transforming grace for the worshiper. It is primarily the Vaishnava sects across India that developed bhakti into sophisticated theologies and practices, especially during the bhakti renaissance of the medieval period (eleventh through seventeenth centuries).

Philosophers of bhakti are quick to point out that the paths of action and knowledge, along with all other paths apart from bhakti, are egocentric and self-interested, and therefore lack the purity of heart found in bhakti. Although they acknowledge that other paths lead to transcendence and are effective spiritual achievements for the soul, they insist that such religious endeavors are intrinsically self-centered and are not ultimately carried out for the pleasure of God; whereas in bhakti, self-sacrifice and lack of self-concern are both conducive to complete theocentrism, or god-centeredness. Thus the *Bhāgavata* and Vaishnava traditions extol devotional love in bhakti as the superior path to salvation, while also recognizing the presence of the other two paths, *jñāna* and *karma.* Such paths are considered valid, however, only if they lead to or are naturally incorporated in bhakti; they are not regarded as valuable paths independent of bhakti.

For all practitioners within the Hindu complex, the ultimate truth and reality is known as Brahman. The goal of Hindu religion has consistently been the union of the individual soul (*ātman*) with the supreme reality, Brahman. Although some traditions understand Brahman to be the supreme *personal* being, others regard Brahman as the supreme state of *impersonal* being.[18] Many accept that the supreme reality contains both personal and impersonal dimensions, but the question remains as to the priority and superiority of one over the other. If a tradition asserts that Brahman at its highest is a supreme personal being from whom all living beings and realities originate, and the very source from which the impersonal Brahman emanates, then it presents a theism. On the other hand, if a tradition asserts that Brahman at its highest is a supreme state of impersonal being in which there are no longer any distinctions between souls, divinity, and Brahman, then such a tradition presents a monism. In theistic Brahman, the soul and divinity remain distinct and eternally related entities between whom a supreme love is forever sustained. By contrast, in monistic Brahman, there is no scope for love since the relationship between soul and divinity is ultimately dissolved.

Vaishnava traditions from the Hindu complex of religion are theistic in that they consider the process of devotion to the supreme deity to be salvation itself, and not merely a means to salvation. In other words, they accept the means and the end of devotion to be the same. Rudolf Otto, the famous twentieth-century German comparative theologian, recognized Vaishnavism as possessing a profound sense of theism. After searching the religions of the world for Christianity's greatest "competitor," he found that the Vaishnava tradition was worthy of being compared to Christianity precisely because of its theological sophistication.[19] Other traditions, such as the Śaiva and Śakta sects, typically retain a curtain of monism behind their devotional and theistic practices. Such non-Vaishnava traditions can exhibit the appearance of a theism, since bhakti is engaged. However, their ultimate goal is to go beyond a relationship with the deity to attain an eternal state of impersonal oneness. Vaishnavism could thus be considered the most strictly theistic among traditions within the Hindu complex, for it sustains theism in the fullest sense.

18. In Christian theology, these types of distinctions are made with the terms *via positiva* (or *via affirmativa*) and *via negativa,* or cataphatic and apophatic distinctions, respectively.

19. In this matter, Rudolf Otto states, "the special problems of the doctrine of grace have been developed more acutely and in greater detail among the Vishnu-*bhaktas* than among those of Śiva"; *India's Religion of Grace and Christianity Compared and Contrasted,* translated by Frank Hugh Foster (New York: Macmillan, 1930), p. 27. In spite of the evolved forms of bhakti in the Śaivaite tradition, especially in the Śaiva Siddhānta of south India, an ultimate veil of monism, in my estimation, seems to eclipse a fully developed bhakti theism of the sort found in Vaishnava sects.

FORMS OF THE DEITY VISHNU

Vaishnava practitioners understand the name Vishnu to be identical to the supreme personal Brahman to whom all worshipers return. Vishnu is also regarded as the supreme personal being who is the very source of Brahman, and who fills the cosmos with a stratified government of minor divinities working under his divine direction. Moreover, Vishnu plays a role in the triune cosmic godly functions, with Brahmā serving as the god of creation, Vishnu as the god of sustenance, and Śiva as the god of destruction. From the Vaishnava theological perspective, Brahmā and Śiva, though extraordinarily powerful minor divinities within the complex cosmic government, do not have the supreme divine status of Vishnu.

Vishnu exhibits various cosmic or divine forms in his transcendent spiritual realms, and simultaneously appears in this world in varying manifestations, each known as an *avatāra* or "divine descent." Although the word *avatāra* is often translated by both Western and Indian scholars as "incarnation," Vishnu is not technically in-carnate; rather, he manifests a divine descent of his own form.[20] Thus when he condescends to this world, it is understood that Vishnu comes in his very own form, spiritual and omnipotent.

Commonly held Hindu belief recognizes that when Krishna comes to this world as the manifest divinity, he does so as an *avatāra* of Vishnu. In fact, Krishna is listed in the *Bhāgavata* as the twentieth *avatāra* manifestation (BhP 1.3.23). Within those Vaishnava traditions for whom the form of Krishna is the ultimate form of the divinity, however, he is both a "divine descent" and "the original person of the godhead" (*ādipuruṣa-devatā*). He is the very source of even Vishnu, who is in turn the source of Brahman. Krishna is understood, then, as the supremely intimate deity from whom all-powerful and cosmic forms of the divinity emanate.

Krishna is also known as *pūrṇāvatāra,* the "full descent of the deity." Thus, the Vaishnavas regard Krishna as descending to earth through the power of his Vishnu form. These three levels of divinity are schematized in figure 7. The most intimate form of God is also the ultimate form of the deity, which I have termed "The Intimate

20. The English word "incarnation" unavoidably possesses certain Christian senses that are not present in the word it attempts to translate. Etymologically, "incarnation" and *avatāra* have very different senses. The word "incarnation" means "the act of coming into a carnal body," and *avatāra* means a "con-descent" of a divine body (literally, *ava-* = "down" and *-tāra* = "a crossing over").

Supreme Deity of the Godhead." From this foundational level comes "The Omnipotent Cosmic Deity," who is Vishnu, "the manifestation of God's sustaining power and almightiness," along with Brahmā (as the Creator) and Śiva (as the Annihilator). Vishnu, then, is the immediate source of the divinity of this world, the manifest deity Krishna, as well as other *avatāra* manifestations.

(1)
KRISHNA
The Intimate Supreme Deity
of the Godhead
Along with Divine Associates
such as Rādhā and the Gopīs

(2)
Brahmā —— VISHNU —— Śiva
(Sub-divinity of Creation) (All-pervading Sustaining Deity) (Sub-divinity of Dissolution)
The Omnipotent Cosmic Deity

(3)
KRISHNA
The Manifest Deity
of this World
The divine descent of the *purnāvatāra,*
the intimate form of the deity

Figure 7. Intimate, cosmic, and compassionate manifestations of Krishna.

Furthermore, inasmuch as the identities of Krishna and Vishnu are distinctive, they are also identical and interchangeable. One observes an interesting twist in the last verse of the Rāsa Līlā, the only instance of the drama in which the name Vishnu occurs: "This is the divine play of Vishnu with the young women of Vraja" (RL 5.40). Here, Krishna, who has been the hero all along, unexpectedly is named Vishnu as the narrator concludes the story, identifying Vishnu rather than Krishna as the hero of the drama.

Although there are many *avatāra* forms of Vishnu honored and celebrated by Hindus, the most famous are those of Rāma and Krishna. The scholar A. L. Basham characterizes the *avatāra* Rāma as a deity of loyalty and righteousness: "Rāma and his faithful wife Sītā combine the ideals of heroism, long suffering, righteousness, loyalty, and justice in a story so full of exciting incident that it has become part of the tradition not only of India, but also of most of South-East Asia."[21] The *Rāmāyaṇa* by Vālmīki, which describes the deeds of Rāma, is without question one of the most loved sacred texts for Hindus.

By comparison, the deity Krishna shares more personal and loving relationships with his worshipers. Basham confirms this in the following portrait of Krishna's personality:

> Krishna, probably even more popular than Rāma, is a divinity of a rare completeness and catholicity, meeting almost every human need. As the divine child he satisfies the warm maternal drives of Indian womanhood. As the divine lover, he provides romantic wish fulfillment in a society still tightly controlled by ancient norms of behaviour which give little scope for freedom of expression in sexual relations. As charioteer of the hero Arjuna on the battlefield of Kurukshetra, he is the helper of all those who turn to him, even saving the sinner from evil rebirths, if he has sufficient faith in the Lord.[22]

While Basham observes correctly Krishna's popularity and completeness as a divinity, his explanation of Krishna's role as "the divine lover" seems shortsighted. After all, the famed *Kāma Sūtra,* a veritable manual of passionate love and sexuality, has arisen out of Indian culture, which certainly could lead one to believe that India possesses a great deal of "freedom of expression in sexual relations."

Basham describes what I have termed the "intimate deity" of Krishna. This more personal form of the divinity is elaborately presented in the great classical texts of India, the *Mahābhārata* and the *Bhāgavata Purāna.* Intimate *līlās* of the deity are not associated exclusively with the *avatāra* form; rather, they are a manifestation, according to certain Vaishnava sects, of the ultimate deity and his activities from within the very center of the godhead. In other words, the deity's activities are taking place eternally in the spiritual realm and are simultaneously manifest by the deity in this world at special times in the revolution of the cosmos.

21. A. L. Basham, ed., *A Cultural History of India,* (Oxford: Oxford University Press, 1975), pp. 80–81.

22. Ibid., p. 81.

2

Aspects of the Story

FRAMING PASSAGES OF THE RĀSA LĪLĀ

The tenth book of the *Bhāgavata,* significant not only because of its length but also because of the *līlās* it presents, contains stories of Krishna's birth, his childhood, and his youth, including his friendships with village boys and cowherd girls. Also described are his later activities in which he assumes the role of royalty in distant places. The first nine books leading up to the tenth, along with the eleventh and twelfth books that follow, are filled with narrations, stories, discourses, prayers, and poetry about the powerful manifestations of God and souls who are devoted to him. The literary content of these chapters acts as a frame around the more intimate stories of the tenth book.

The Rāsa Līlā drama is colorfully anticipated as early as the *Bhāgavata*'s third book, in the final verse of the second chapter. The first two lines of the verse invoke imagery drawn from the opening verse of the story, and the second two allude to the climactic event of the Rāsa dance in the final act:

> Regarding the mood of those nights
> brightened by the rays of the autumn moon,
> He enjoyed singing sweet songs
> as the ornament in the circle of women.
> (BhP 3.2.34)

This verse reveals essential themes of the Rāsa Līlā, not again referred to until the tenth book in which, approximately one-third of the way through, the five chapters of the story are presented. Preceding the Rāsa Līlā chapters (BhP 10.29–33), as well as following them, are short references within verses, whole verses, sections of chapters, and even complete chapters concerning the Gopīs. The overall effect created by these surrounding passages is a complex composition that supports the innermost focal point of the *Bhāgavata,* the story of the Rāsa Līlā. Moreover, the episodes relating to the Gopīs, along with other intimate or *mādhurya līlās* from within the tenth book, contain elements of amorous devotion to God, making the text of the Rāsa Līlā inseparable from and continuous with the whole of the tenth book. Thus, the related surrounding passages effectively provide a rich frame within which the Rāsa Līlā is established as the most honored *līlā* among all the divine dramas of Krishna.[1]

Chapters 21 and 22 from the tenth book constitute the two major "Gopī" chapters prior to the presentation of the Rāsa Līlā. In chapter 21, the Gopīs sing praises of the power of Krishna's flute music and how it affects all the residents of Vraja, even all of creation. The first six verses of chapter 21 constitute a narrative description of the cowherd maidens who, inspired by the sounds of Krishna's flute, have achieved a state of remembering him constantly.

The narrator explains that when the Gopīs hear Krishna's flute music from afar, they converse about his acts and become overwhelmed with intense love, to the point of becoming speechless. Thus stunned and quieted by their love for Krishna, they again are able to hear his flute, which causes them to again react to the divine music, further perpetuating a blissful unending cycle of remembrance for the cowherd maidens.[2] Chapter 21 clearly prepares the reader for the Gopīs' irresistible attraction to the sounds of Krishna's flute, to which they are helplessly drawn at the beginning of the Rāsa Līlā. This powerful force of the divine flute is also anticipated in earlier passages of the tenth book.

The Gopīs' attraction to Krishna becomes heightened to such a point, in chapter 22, that each one desperately prays to the Goddess to make a conjugal arrangement for her:

1. The first partial-verse presentation of the Gopīs within the tenth book prior to the RL story is BhP 10.15.7–8. The first full verse presentation is BhP 10.19.16: "The greatest bliss for the Gopīs was the vision of Govinda. Each moment without him became like hundreds of ages." In chapter 20, two verses express how the Gopīs cannot be relieved of the scorching late afternoon heat, due to the intense heat arising from love's separation (BhP 10.20.42, 45). The more significant passages following the RL, in addition to chapters 35 and 47, are the twelve verses of a chapter in which the Gopīs speak prayerful words of separation (BhP 10.39.19–30). There are many other dispersed Gopī-related verses following the RL, up to a verse in the final chapter of the tenth book, expressing how Krishna's smiling face increases the passion of the Gopīs (BhP 10.90.48).

2. See BhP 10.21.6 in the Veṇu Gīta, the translation for which is provided within this volume.

O Kātyāyanī,
whose power
is very great (*mahā-māyā*),
O great *yoginī*,
supremely controlling Goddess,
O Devī, I offer my respects unto you.
Please make the cowherd son of Nanda my husband!
(BhP 10.22.4)

The Goddess is one, though her names are many. The Gopīs take refuge in the Goddess as Devī, also called Kātyāyanī and "great *yoginī*," in order to be united with Krishna, who himself also takes refuge in the Goddess as Yogamāyā, to arrange for his rendezvous with the Gopīs (RL 1.1). The significance of the role of the Goddess and her colorful nomenclature will be explored below.

The Gopīs' union with Krishna is anticipated through this prayer to the Goddess. Fulfilling their deepest desire, Krishna appears before them and playfully steals their garments while they are bathing in the Yamunā River, then carries their clothing as he climbs up a nearby tree. In order to retrieve their clothes, the cowherd maidens are convinced by Krishna to get out of the water. Their nakedness before him is taken as an expression of full self-surrender of love to the supreme Beloved. The Gopīs experience great joy in Krishna's presence, for their desire to serve him as their husband has now been fulfilled. He then promises, "With me you will enjoy the coming nights" (BhP 10.22.27), alluding to the nights that inspire Krishna toward love on the special evening of the Rāsa dance.

At least two chapters that follow the Rāsa Līlā drama depict almost exclusively the behavior of the Gopīs in Krishna's absence. In chapter 35, they sing songs about Krishna's *līlās* whenever he goes into the forest with his cowherd boyfriends. The Gopīs once again describe Krishna's flute playing and the effect it has on Vraja's cows, rivers, trees and vines, lake-dwelling birds, heavenly beings, and others, and finally on themselves. They also tell of his glorious return from the forest and how he is greeted by various gods on the way.

Chapter 47 is particularly important because it focuses on the theme of Krishna's prolonged separation from the Gopīs while he resides in Mathurā. In order to appease the Gopīs, Krishna sends his messenger, Uddhava, who is amazed as he witnesses the intense devotional love of the cowherd maidens. Especially well known is the passage popularly named the Bhramara Gīta, "The Song of the Black Bee," in which one Gopī, identified as Krishna's favorite, Rādhā, speaks in loving madness to a black bee, the translation of which is provided in this volume. Acknowledging the passionate devotion of the Gopīs, Uddhava desires to honor their superlative worship of Krishna, or "love of the whole heart" (*sarvātma-bhāva*). In verses 23–28, Uddhava's words praise the cowherd maidens for such exemplary devotion.

Uddhava then relates to the Gopīs a message coming from Krishna containing several essential points, his first point being: "You were never apart from me, for I am the Soul of all" (BhP 10.47.29). In verses 34 and 35, however, he appears to be more sensitive to the Gopīs' despair and carefully addresses the intention behind his separation from them:

> I, who am indeed
>   dear to your sight,
>   am now far away from you.
> However, for the purpose of
>   intensely attracting your minds,
>   this [departure] was my desire
>   in order to increase your meditation on me.
>
> The minds of women are not as fully absorbed
>   in their beloved when he is present before their eyes,
> For he is not as much in their thoughts
>   as when he is far away.
>
> (BhP 10.47.34–35)

The Rāsa Līlā is decorated by many such passages, prior to and following its story, which illuminate the prized devotion of the Gopīs and indicate the special status of the drama within the *Bhāgavata*.

POETIC AND DRAMATIC DIMENSIONS

What sets the language and tone of the Rāsa Līlā apart from most of the *Bhāgavata* text is the pronounced presence of poetic and dramatic elements, reflecting the highly developed classical schools of Indian poetics (*kāvya*) and dramaturgy (*nāṭya*). I will attempt to highlight some of these features that contribute to the aesthetic achievement of this dramatic poem.

Good Sanskrit drama typically consists of no fewer than five and no more than ten acts, and the Rāsa Līlā appears to meet this requirement. The five consecutive chapters of the Rāsa Līlā are not arbitrary divisions; rather, each chapter functions as a principal act (*aṅka*) within the dramatic story line. Thus, in my translation, I have designated each chapter of the Rāsa Līlā as an "act": act one corresponds to chapter 29 of the *Bhāgavata,* act two to chapter 30, and so on. For purposes of clarity and comprehensibility I have provided titles for each act, even though the chapters are untitled and only numbered in the original. Titles of the acts are worded to communicate the basic movement of the plot:

Act One: Krishna Attracts the Gopīs and Disappears

Act Two: The Gopīs Search for Krishna

Act Three: The Song of the Gopīs: Gopī Gīta

Act Four: Krishna Reappears and Speaks of Love

Act Five: The Rāsa Dance

These five acts represent a complete drama that can be appreciated in and of itself. Nevertheless, the deeper meanings of a text of this kind are fully understood only in relation to its greater literary and traditional contexts.

An act, in Sanskrit drama, generally consists of one or more "scene" (*sandhi*) subdivisions. In the Rāsa Līlā text, transitions from one scene to another naturally occur when there is a change in the situation of the drama, especially indicated by a shift in voice or activity. Furthermore, the subdivisions are often reinforced by visible changes in versification. Because these scenes are not determined in the original text, I have indicated scene changes with titles, along with sequential numbering. Although the story line is straightforward, titles for each scene are offered in order to provide the reader with general symbolic themes suggested in the various scenes.

There are essentially four types of voices in the Rāsa Līlā, simply described as narration, discourse, dialogue, and monologue. One of these types dominates each scene, although other types may also be present.[3] The majority of verses utilize the voice of narration—words of the narrator describing actions taking place within the story. In fact, there are eight distinctive narratives out of a total of thirteen scenes. The voice of discourse is employed twice, in the second and

3. For example, one can observe some monologue within the narration in scene 1 of act two. One also observes dialogue within the narration of scene 2 of act five, and some discourse-like verses in the dialogue of act four. There is also some narration woven into the two dialogue scenes in acts one and four.

TABLE 1. ACT AND SCENE SUBDIVISIONS WITHIN THE RĀSA LĪLĀ DRAMA

ACT ONE	ACT TWO	ACT THREE	ACT FOUR	ACT FIVE
Scene 1 Narrative 1 (vss. 1–11)	Scene 1 Narrative 3 (vss. 1–23)	Scene Monologue (vss. 1–19)	Scene 1 Narrative 5 (vss. 1–14)	Scene 1 Narrative 6 (vss. 1–22)
Scene 2 Discourse 1 (vss. 12–16)	Scene 2 Narrative 4 (vss. 24–44)		Scene 2 Dialogue 2 (vss. s15–22)	Scene 2 Narrative 7 (vss. 23–26)
Scene 3 Dialogue 1 (vss. 17–41)				Scene 3 Discourse 2 (vss. 27–36)
Scene 4 Narrative 2 (vss. 42–48)				Scene 4 Narrative 8 (vss. 37–40)

penultimate scenes. It consists of a didactic dialogue between the narrator Śuka and his audience, the king, guiding the listener's understanding of the drama. Scenes that engage the voice of dialogue also appear twice, once each in the first and fourth acts; they involve Krishna, the hero, and the Gopīs, the heroines. The middle act consists of only one scene, in which the monologue voice appears. Here, the Gopīs offer passionate and prayerful songs to Krishna in his absence.

In table 1, the primary voice associated with each scene within the five acts is displayed diagrammatically. A natural symmetry is immediately observable in the arrangement of scenes within the various acts of the drama. Theorists of classical Sanskrit dramaturgy explain that five types of scenes are employed in a drama, each one moving the action of the story forward to build toward its climactic event. These scene types are to be found throughout the Rāsa Līlā drama, and are as follows: the opening scene, progressive scene, developmental scene, pausing scene, and culmination scene. Within each of these scene types, certain dramatic elements can be found, which will be further discussed in the introductory remarks to each of the acts in the "Notes and Comments" section.

The opening narrative verse of the Rāsa Līlā presents a vivifying entrance into its drama. This simple metered verse paints an unexpectedly condensed picture of the drama as a whole:

Even the Beloved Lord, seeing those nights	*bhagavān api tā rātrīḥ*
in autumn filled with blooming jasmine flowers,	*śāradotphulla-mallikāḥ*
Turned his mind toward love's delights,	*vīkṣya rantuṁ manaś cakre*
fully taking refuge in Yogamāyā's illusive powers.	*yoga-māyām upāśritaḥ*

Much of Sanskrit drama focuses on the theme of romantic love (*śṛṅgāra-rasa*). Here, the romantic tone is created by the words "love's delights." Remarkably, all four constituent principals of the drama are introduced in the first verse: first, the leading male figure or divine hero, "the Beloved Lord," Krishna; second, the collective leading female figures or heroines, the young women of Vraja or the Gopīs, subtly revealed by way of a complex metaphor that is found in the following principal; third, the idyllic natural scenery of Vraja, described here as "nights in autumn filled with blooming jasmine flowers"; and fourth, the divine feminine power of loving union, Yogamāyā. The very "seed" or *bīja* of the plot, represented by the simple subject and predicate of the verse, is also sown, presenting the Beloved Lord who is inspired toward love by the beauty of the scene. The divine potency of Yogamāyā arranges for the seed of the plot to grow into the full drama of love.

Consideration of the ways in which the four principals participate in the Rāsa Līlā can enhance appreciation of the literary and theological expression of this work. Of these principals, we shall address the Gopīs last, as their role is the most complex.

KRISHNA: LORD OF LOVE AND BEAUTY

There is no other deity within the Hindu complex of religion, perhaps even among the religious traditions of the world, who is as amorous, personable, and playful as Krishna, and the tenth book celebrates this divine persona. Whereas in most of the *Bhāgavata* text, Krishna is presented as the cosmic Vishnu, the supremely powerful deity under whom all other partial divinities work, here in the tenth book he is especially portrayed as the supreme person who resides in his abode known as Goloka ("the divine world of the cows"), the highest of the heavenly worlds. Here, Krishna as a playful child and young boy is utterly adored by his devotees. The supreme Lord's intimate *līlās* are occurring eternally, and his "day" is divided into morning, afternoon, and evening types of play: in the morning, Krishna behaves just like a mischievous child with his parents; he frolics in the fields of Vraja with cows and cowherd friends in the afternoon; and in the evening he engages in sweet amorous play with the cowherd girls.

The beauty of Krishna's form is elaborately described throughout the *Bhāgavata* text and is depicted as "exquisitely brilliant"—the "exclusive reservoir of beauty in all the three worlds." The imagery of this intimate deity is consistently vivid, intricate, and naturalistic. He is known by his effulgent, dark bluish hue. His face, eyes, hands, and feet are often compared to the loveliness of the lotus flower. Always dressed and decorated in distinctive ways, he wears yellow silken garments, brilliant as gold. On his head of dark curling locks of hair, Krishna wears an ornament adorned with a peacock feather. Ornate earrings decorate either side of his soft glowing face, and he wears a garland made of various colored forest flowers and leaves. He is often found equipped with a herding stick and buffalo horn.

Perhaps the most prominent feature of the divine cowherd is that he carries a bamboo flute from which he produces enticing music. As compared with the numerous four-armed forms of Vishnu, which hold combinations of the disc, conch, club, and lotus, the special symbol of the intimate deity of Krishna is the flute held deftly to his mouth by his two lotus-like hands. He is clearly the Lord of love who captures the devotional heart with his flute music, playful movements, affectionate smiles, enticing glances, and eloquent speech.

The powerful effect of Krishna's flute music on all who hear it is extraordinary. In the *Bhāgavata* tradition, the Lord's flute enchants all the worlds and lovingly calls souls back to him. We learn that it is the music from his flute that calls out in love to the young women of Vraja, causing them to abandon their families and responsibilities. Thus the plot of the Rāsa Līlā drama begins with Krishna's intoxicating flute playing. A particular verse by a traditional Vaishnava poet expresses how the devotee appreciates this music not only in terms of the *mādhurya* or intimate activities of Krishna but also as it is connected to the *aiśvarya*, or cosmological and ontological dimensions of his lordship:

> All hail to the child's flute notes coming forth so
> that Om might sound.
> The flute notes cause the worlds to exult, the Vedas to
> sound, trees to rejoice,

mountains to fly, deer to be tame, cows blissful,
and cowherds bewildered, ascetics' flesh to
rise and the seven basic notes to sound.[4]

The mesmerizing music of Krishna's flute affects living and nonliving beings in various ways. Trees and vines exhibit bodily ecstasy and overflow with fruits and flowers upon hearing the divine flute. Clouds become generous, providing a gentle mist of rain and a percussive accompaniment of thunder. Flowing currents in the rivers are broken and begin to swirl, offering lotus flowers to the cowherd Lord. Birds close their eyes, listening intently to the music, and peacocks dance in madness. Nursing calves become still with wonder, their eyes filled with tears. All moving creatures become stunned and stationary beings begin to move. Even the wives of the heavenly denizens are entranced as their hair and clothing loosen. Such wondrous effects of hearing Krishna's divine flute playing are described in the *Bhāgavata*'s chapter known as the "Song of the Flute," the Veṇu Gīta (see the translation in this volume).

Just as all entities are affected by Krishna's flute music, all who are touched by him, including plant and animal life, experience blissful, rapturous feelings throughout their bodies. Krishna awakens amorous feelings in the cowherd maidens with his affectionate touch and enticing manner. He allows his feet to touch the breasts of the Gopīs, which represents their unique way of worshiping the feet of their beloved Lord (RL 3.13).

Krishna's feet are distinguishable by the signs appearing on their soles, such as the flag and thunderbolt (RL 2.25). Gods, goddesses, mystics, and lovers alike especially long for his feet because, along with other desired effects, they dispel sins. It is important to understand that in India, the feet of sages, and even more the feet of *avatāra* forms of the divinity (including sacred images of the deity Krishna) are considered holy and worthy of worship, and persons place the dust from such feet on their heads as an act of humility and devotion. At other times, persons worship the feet simply by bowing down to the ground near saintly souls or where their feet have tread. Thus, dust itself becomes sanctified when in contact, no matter how briefly, with holy feet. As for the dust

4. Līlāśuka Bilvamaṅgala, *The Love of Krishna: The Kṛṣṇakarṇāmṛta of Līlāśuka Bilvamaṅgala,* edited and translated by Frances Wilson (Philadelphia: University of Pennsylvania Press, 1975), II. p. 110.

from Krishna's feet, "Even Brahmā, Śiva, and the Goddess Ramā place this dust upon their heads, in order to dispel their sins" (RL 2.29).

Krishna is known by many names and epithets, and the Rāsa Līlā reflects his colorful nomenclature. Vaishnava worshipers honor "the thousand names of Vishnu" in the well-known traditional work *Viṣṇu Sahasra Nāma,* consisting exclusively of one thousand names of Krishna or Vishnu. Dozens of epithets and names of Krishna appear throughout the drama, and an overview of the most prominent ones reveals much about the protagonist's identity.

The specific name Krishna appears a total of twenty-seven times in the Rāsa Līlā text, more than any other name for the deity.[5] The meaning of the name is literally "dark blue" or "blackish," referring to Krishna's dark complexion, which is described poetically as the color of a beautiful new monsoon cloud. When he dances with the Gopīs in the circle of the Rāsa dance, his color is compared to that of "dark clouds" of a thunderstorm (RL 5.8). The name Krishna is derived from the verbal root *kṛṣ* (from which the precise transliterated form "Kṛṣṇa" comes), which means "to draw," or even more applicable here, "to draw into one's power," and hence the meaning "attractive." Theologians from the Caitanya school claim that the name means "supremely attractive." The divine cowherd certainly possesses this drawing power, dramatically expressed in the first scene of the text in which he allures the chaste cowherd maidens from their homes into the forest. Moreover, when Krishna's name first appears in the fourth verse of the text, this power is revealed:

> Upon hearing that sweet music,
> their passion for him swelling,
> The young women of Vraja whose
> minds were captured by Krishna,
> Unaware of one another,
> ran off toward the place
> Where their beloved was waiting,
> with their earrings swinging wildly.
> (RL 1.4)

5. The name Krishna appears in the following verses: 1.4, 1.7, 1.9, 1.12, 1.16, 1.30, 1.47 / 2.3, 2.9, 2.14, 2.15, 2.16, 2.17, 2.18, 2.19, 2.24, 2.31–2, 2.35, 2.38, 2.44 / 4.1 / 5.3, 5.8, 5.9, 5.12, 5.19, 5.38.

The name Krishna identifies the intimate deity of the godhead. Other names of Krishna found in the text are similarly associated with his more personal and affectionate nature, such as Govinda, or "one who tends the cows," referring to this pastoral deity in the rural region of Vraja;[6] Vāsudeva, "the son of Vasudeva";[7] Keśava, "the one with beautiful hair";[8] Mādhava, "the one who is sweet";[9] and Hari, or "one who steals our hearts."[10] Other names of Krishna express his grand or powerful nature, such as Mukunda, "the one who grants liberation."[11] These names appear far fewer times than his more intimate ones, clearly indicating the emphasis in the drama on the sweet and loving attributes of the deity.

The epithet Bhagavān is especially recognized as a name for Vishnu or Krishna.[12] The hero is immediately introduced in the first verse as Bhagavān, and with the exception of the name Krishna, Bhagavān is the most utilized name in the story, appearing a total of twenty times.[13] My translation of this significant epithet is "the Beloved Lord," intended to express both powerful and intimate aspects of the deity. The word *bhagavān* breaks down into two parts: the noun *bhaga* and the suffix *-vān* (*-vat*), meaning "one who possesses (*-vān*) all *bhaga*." The lexical senses of *bhaga* convey either the manifestation of supreme power or excellence (*aiśvarya*), expressed by the word "Lord" in the phrase; or the manifestation of supreme sweetness (*mādhurya*), expressed by the word "Beloved." The word *bhaga* carries both *aiśvarya*-related meanings such as "good fortune," "omnipotence," "virtue," "fame," or "excellence," and *mādhurya*-related meanings such as "love," "loveliness," "affection," "amorous dalliance," or even "sexual passion."

6. RL 1.8, 1.28 / 2.7, 2.28, 2.29, 2.30 / 5.2.

7. RL 5.39.

8. RL 1.48 / 2.10, 2.37 / 4.9.

9. RL 2.8 and 2.41.

10. RL 1.15 / 2.28.

11. RL 5.10. Other such names that appear are: Śauri, "the heroic descendent of the Śura dynasty" (RL 4.2, 4.4); Adhokṣaja, "one who is beyond the range of the senses" (RL 1.13); Hṛṣīkeśa, "the Lord of the senses" (1.13); and the avatāric manifestations of Varāha, "the divine boar" (RL 2.10), and Urukrama, "the great striding one" (2.10). In the benedictory last verse of the text, the narrator identifies Krishna with Vishnu as "the all-pervading one" (RL 5.40).

12. The word in other traditional contexts can also refer to the god Śiva or to the Buddha, or even to a Bodhisattva (MW).

13. "The Beloved Lord," or Bhagavān, is found in the following acts and verses: 1.1, 1.14, 1.16, 1.17, 1.18, 1.47, 2.1, 2.14, 2.28, 2.40, 4.10, 4.14, 4.17, 5.1, 5.7, 5.16, 5.20, 5.27, 5.39, and 5.40. References here to verses 1.18 and 4.17 refer to the introductory phrase "The Beloved Lord spoke." All other instances of Bhagavān are embedded within verse lines.

There are also other names in the narration that express Krishna's power, assuring the reader that this deity, typically known for his playful and intimate nature, is nonetheless the supreme divinity.[14] Although Krishna's identity is primarily that of an independent divinity, he places himself in a dependent position in order to enjoy love. This dependency, however, is itself an expression of his power and supremacy. After all, it is Krishna's *divine will* to submit himself fully to Yogamāyā, his potency for making loving arrangements.

Another name of Krishna, Acyuta, appearing nine times in the text, indicates Krishna's supremacy and invulnerability. Unlike any other name of the deity, including the name Krishna itself, Acyuta is the only name that is found at least once in each of the five acts.[15] The author of the text may have utilized the name throughout in order to emphasize that Krishna is not an ordinary soul, but rather the "supreme" soul. The name Acyuta means "the infallible one" or, literally, "the unshaken one" or "the one who is not fallen." The connotation is that he, as the supreme soul, does "not fall" to this world in which finite souls experience the endless cycles of birth and rebirth (*saṁsāra*).

The essential message behind the name Acyuta—that despite Krishna's erotic sports with the Gopīs, he does not fall into sexual relations with them—is a powerful and consistent theme running through the text. The narrator of the story carefully explains that Krishna's erotic play is due to the delight of *rasa* within the divine. In other words, when Krishna, who is full and complete in himself, engages in love's delights with the cowherd maidens, he is not conforming to the ways of this world. Rather, he is allowing his devotee and himself to love intimately and freely in a realm that transcends the everyday world—and transcends *even* himself.

A dramatic clue for appreciating this paradoxical theological theme can be found in the use of the word "even" in the first verse. As mentioned above, the epithetical nomenclature Bhagavān, "the Beloved Lord," expresses to the reader that Krishna is powerful as well as intimate, and full in all excellences. The adversative particle "even"

14. Krishna is referred to as the Supreme in verses 1.11, 1.32, and 2.24. A variety of names express his "supreme" status, such as "Soul" (*ātmā:* RL 1.14, 1.32, 1.33, 2.28, and 4.14); "supreme Soul" (*paramātmā:* RL 1.11, 2.24); "great Soul" (*mahatma:* RL 1.47, 2.31–2); "Person" (*puruṣa:* RL 2.4 and 4.10); "Lord" (*īśvara* or *parameśvara:* RL 1.33); "supreme Lord of Yoga" (RL 1.16, 1.42, 4.14, and 5.3); and "the supreme God of love" (literally, the "God of love among all love gods," RL 4.2).

15. The name Acyuta appears in the following verses: RL 1.10, 1.43 / 2.7, 2.11, 2.30 / 3.16 / 4.10 / 5.14, and 5.15. No other name of Krishna appears in the third act of the RL.

(*api*) subjoined to the subject noun of the verse, "the Beloved Lord," further heightens the extraordinary event that is occurring. Thus Krishna's supremacy is challenged and his intimate attributes augmented, expressing a theological paradox: all beauty and all loveliness is contained in Krishna, yet "those nights in autumn filled with blooming jasmine flowers" inspire *even* the supreme Lord. *Even* he is moved "toward love's delights"; though pleasure exists fully within himself, he succumbs to beauty and love. Moreover, *even* he takes full "refuge in Yogamāyā," desiring assistance from the Goddess for his intimate *līlā,* though he is unlimitedly powerful.

Other verses in the text express this paradox. In a verse depicting Krishna's dalliance with a special Gopī, it is stated, "He delighted in loving her, yet he delights in the self and takes pleasure in the self, for he is complete" (RL 2.34). Another verse describes Krishna's interactions with the collective Gopīs: "He, who himself possesses all pleasure, took pleasure in loving them, playing like the king of elephants" (RL 5.24).[16] Through these verses and others, it is clear that the supreme Lord is complete, without limitation or need, inexhaustible, and fully content, yet he is moved by the beauteous scene and submits himself to love. Krishna delights more in reciprocating the love of his devotees in *rasa* than he does in deriving pleasure from within his supreme self.

Although loving play occurs for the pleasure of his intimate devotees and his own delight, it also teaches those who read or hear about it, as expressed by the narrator who interprets these teachings in theological apologia throughout the story. Thus Krishna is a teacher to souls in this world through constituent phases of love play that take place in his own divine world. Such playfulness teaches souls that Krishna preserves the worldly ethical conventions and, at the same time, transcends them, as will be discussed further below.

While engaged in play with his most intimate female associates, Krishna teaches his reader that pride is the enemy of love and devotion. God disappears from the soul who exhibits pride. Even though such pride, as displayed in the Gopīs, is a component of their passionate devotion, the narrator uses the example of their "otherworldly" pride to teach an indispensable lesson about worldly pride. This lesson is indeed so important that he teaches it twice—first with the group of Gopīs at the end of the first act, then with the special Gopī in the second scene of the second act. After Krishna agrees to let the cowherd

16. See other similar expressions in RL 1.42 and 5.20.

maidens stay with him and then disappears due to their pride, he later reappears to join them in the Rāsa dance. This dialectical movement between divine absence and presence, between the hiddenness and revelation of the intimate divinity (perhaps the tradition's version of the Christian notions of *deus absconditus* and *deus revelatus*), creating a kind of "hide and seek" of love, is not only didactic but also part of Krishna's sportiveness. In the fourth act, the supreme Lord again exhibits his lesson-giving when he delivers to the maidens a discourse on the nature of love, which also imparts wisdom to the reader (RL 4.17–20). Thus, both the Gopīs and the reader benefit from Krishna's didactic words, often taught through his love play with his dearest devotees.

David Kinsley observes about the divinity of Krishna: "Play as divine activity in India is nowhere more fully illustrated."[17] As we have shown, this playfulness of Krishna often takes on a paradoxical character, appearing to be subversive, all the while demonstrating itself to be elevating and transcending. The author-narrator makes it tacitly clear that the pleasure Krishna experiences with his dearest cowherd maidens is not transgressive, nor is it limited or compromised by worldly interactions; rather, his pleasure takes place in a realm of pure poetry and divine aesthetics:

> Thus he allowed himself to be
> subdued by these nights
> made so brilliant
> by the rays of the moon—
> He was perfectly
> fulfilled in all desires
> and pure within himself;
> While with that group of maidens
> so passionately attached to him,
> sexual enjoyment was of no issue—
> Inspiring the narrations
> and poetry of autumn,
> all those moonlit nights
> found their refuge in *rasa*.
>
> (RL 5.26)

17. *The Divine Player: A Study of Kṛṣṇa Līlā,* by David R. Kinsley (Delhi: Motilal Banarsidass, 1979), p. 56. This book presents a comprehensive study of the idea of "play" in traditions surrounding the worship of Krishna and, additionally, throughout Indian religion in general.

The Beloved Lord's ultimate play manifests as dancing and singing with the Gopīs in the Rāsa dance. Afterward, they delight in sporting together in the forest and cooling river.

VRAJA: PASTORAL PARADISE

"Glorious is Vraja, surpassing all," the Gopīs extol. So wondrous is Vraja that the author of the *Bhāgavata* has devoted a full chapter to an elaborate description of its rainy and autumn seasons, often cleverly drawing parallels between characteristics of nature and the behavior of the spiritual aspirant (BhP 10.20.1–49). The sacredness and pastoral beauty of Vraja are engaged in essential ways throughout the Rāsa Līlā, and therefore it deserves treatment as one of the constituent principals of the drama.

The natural Vraja of this world is the geographic region of central northern India, in which the pilgrimage town of Vrindāvana—depicted in the Rāsa Līlā as a small agricultural village—is situated. The name Vrindāvana means "the forest of Vṛndā or Tulasī" (Krishna's favorite plant and the Goddess who embodies it). The setting of the Rāsa Līlā is in this world, but not exactly of this world. The divine realm of Vraja manifest in this world and known as Gokula is identical with its divine counterpart, the "heavenly Vraja," known as Goloka, though the practitioner must develop the proper vision to appreciate this phenomenon (CC 1.5.21). Vraja is a world in which every personality, including all plants, trees, and animals participate in and fully experience the love between Krishna and the cowherd maidens. The world of Vraja is devotionally alive as every object and soul exists only for the sake of the Beloved Lord. Every being and everything in this spiritual setting is full of knowledge and bliss, and gives off a splendor like the various luminaries of the sky.

The spiritual realm of Vraja is described as a place that clearly contrasts with the world as we know it. It is a mystical world of beauty; the ground in Vraja is covered with devotional jewels named *cintāmaṇi*, each "a fabulous gem supposed to yield to its possessor all desires." Even the trees are not ordinary, and are called *kalpa-taru*, or "wishing trees." Vraja is of extraordinary abundance: the trees produce fruit during every season, cows give milk unlimitedly, and the water is nectar. Here, all walking is dancing and all talking is singing, and time is only an eternal present within which unlimited varieties of divine events occur.[18]

18. These images of Vraja are taken from the *Brahma Saṁhitā* and the *Caitanya Caritāmṛta.*

Figure 8. Pilgrimage path and the Vraja countryside on the edge of Vrindāvana. Photograph courtesy of Nityatripta Devi Dasi.

The reader becomes acquainted with the landscape of the Rāsa Līlā in the first three verses, and it continues to play an indispensable role in the various phases of the story. In the second verse, the moon casts a reddish light above the horizon, contributing to the beauteous scene that inspires Krishna toward love. The light of the decorative stars and glowing full moon illuminate the sky and forest at night. Indeed, the narrator compares the beauty of Krishna and the Gopīs to the moon among the many stars. Images of the bountiful forest and plant life are described by both the narrator and the hero or heroines. Flowers in general are mentioned frequently, with special attention given to night-blooming varieties. The Gopīs, when separated from Krishna, talk to an array of forest plant life—from trees of all kinds to plants, vines, and other botanicals. Krishna also runs through the forest with the Gopīs. Enticed by its beauty early in the story, he shares his appreciation with the maidens:

> You have seen the forest
> filled with flowers,
> glowing with the rays
> of the full moon;
> Made beautiful by leaves of trees,
> playfully shimmering
> from the gentle breeze
> off the river Yamunā.
>
> (RL 1.21)

The Yamunā River, with its shores of cooling sands, is the place where Krishna and the Gopīs retreat in the first and final acts, in order to ei-

Figure 9. Nineteenth-century buildings along the Yamunā River in the area of Keshi Ghat, Vrindāvana. Photograph courtesy of Helmut Kappel.

ther play or refresh themselves after dancing. Gentle autumn breezes carve ripples in the waters of the Yamunā. In the second act, the wind becomes a messenger carrying news of which direction Krishna has gone, by sending scents from his garland to the Gopīs.

Essential to the story is the emphasis on flowers that bloom at night, since it is these flowers that inaugurate the Rāsa Līlā drama. Krishna, in the first act, suggests to the Gopīs that their coming to the forest at such a late hour is due to the alluring beauty of the flower-filled scene. He also gathers flowers for the special Gopī with whom he disappears, and the other Gopīs observe that "here, flowers were gathered by the lover for his beloved" (RL 2.32). At the conclusion of the drama, Krishna roams the banks of the Yamunā River "in the direction of the gentle breeze that was carrying the fragrances of flowers over the land and the water."

Jasmine flowers assume a diverse role throughout the drama, and appear in the very first verse in which the Beloved Lord is inspired toward love. Note that it is not merely one night that is strikingly beautiful, but many "nights." These autumn nights are curiously filled with "blooming jasmine flowers." This is surprising, since the plant typically does not produce blossoms in the harvest season, but only during spring and summer—an indication of the exceptional nature of these nights.

Jasmine is a delicate flower with a starlike formation, most often white, though sometimes light pink or yellow, which is particularly known for its intoxicating fragrance capable of arousing amorous and erotic feelings.[19] The scent of jasmine pervades the air of the Vraja forest. Krishna's teeth are compared to jasmine flowers, and some of the Gopīs wear the flower during the Rāsa dance. The cowherd maidens speak to varieties of jasmine when they are madly searching for Krishna (RL 2.8), and they are moved by the fragrance of the flowers coming from his garland (RL 2.11). The Beloved Lord is also delighted by both the sight and alluring fragrance of these pervasive jasmine flowers in full night bloom (RL 1.1).

The reader is informed that certain lotus flowers are night-blooming as well, and the narrator often refers to lotuses. The lotus flower is a frequently occurring symbol among Indian religious traditions.[20] In fact, the heavenly Vraja is in the shape of a lotus-flower blossom.[21] Within the Rāsa Līlā in particular, the image of the flower is used to convey beauty and passion a total of thirty times. The narrator begins the first scene by describing the autumn night that comes alive with the opening of lotus flowers, along with the rising moon. Krishna is pleased by their appearance (RL 1.3), and later by their scent: "He delighted in breezes that carried the fragrance of white lotuses, joyfully dancing in the waves of the river" (RL 1.45cd). While searching for Krishna, the Gopīs identify their beloved as the one who holds a lotus flower. Upon discovering his footprints, they are able to identify them easily because of the lotus emblem, along with other symbols, embellishing his prints. Krishna's arm is said to possess the fragrance of a lotus flower. The Gopīs themselves wear the flowers in their hair and behind their ears. Even the gods shower lotuses upon Krishna and the cowherd maidens as they perform the Rāsa dance.

Earlier in the tenth book of the *Bhāgavata,* the reader is informed that night-blooming lotuses are born from the water, and are not the same as varieties found in the forest. The special power of such night-blooming flowers is indicated in the following verse:

19. The powerful scent of jasmine is conveyed in RL 4.11.

20. See "Notes and Comments" on RL 1.3.

21. The lotus can represent cosmic evolution, since the creator god, Brahmā, is born from the lotus. Forms of the powerful Vishnu are found standing on lotus flowers, and the lotus is one of several possible items that a Vishnu form may be holding in one of his four hands.

When the sun rises
 water-born flowers blossom,
 except for night-blooming lotus flowers,
As subjects in the presence of their ruler
 are without fear, O king,
 except for the thieves.

(BhP 10.20.47)

This thief-like trait of the night-blooming lotuses is also a characteristic of the hero of the story, since Krishna, in his boyhood, is known for stealing butter from the women of Vraja in order to feed the monkeys. He is called Hari ("one who steals") because he "steals" the hearts of his devotees. And in the Rāsa Līlā, he steals the hearts of the Gopīs (RL 1.8). Yet these night-blooming flowers are able to steal even the mind and heart of Krishna!

The *tulasī* plant also plays a prominent role in the drama, as it does in the lives of Vaishnava practitioners. This plant is considered to be a great female devotee of Krishna, even a consort of Vishnu, who has taken the bodily form of a plant that is worshiped on a daily basis in Vaishnava temples and homes. Her minty leaves are used to garnish food preparations for sacred offerings, and are found decorating the feet of sacred images of Krishna. The wood of expired *tulasī* plants is carved into beads that are worn around the neck by Vaishnavas and also used as a rosary for the recitation of God's names. The special significance of the *tulasī* plant is recognized by the Gopīs when they speak of *tulasī* and Śrī (Lakṣmī): "The Goddess Śrī . . . desires, along with the sacred *tulasī* plant, the dust of your lotus feet" (RL 1.37). Krishna's garland is made up of the delicate and fragrant flowerets produced from the sacred plant and, in the second act, the Gopīs inquire from the *tulasī* plant concerning Krishna's whereabouts.

The natural surroundings of Vraja clearly assist in the loving rendezvous between Krishna and the Gopīs when they are apart from each other. In the absence of his beloved consorts, Krishna becomes inspired by the enchanting landscape and is compelled to produce melodious flute music, drawing the cowherd maidens to his side (RL 1.3). Following Krishna's sudden disappearance at the end of act one, the Gopīs remain apart from him in acts two and three. They sing like madwomen as they frantically question the trees in the forest for any indication of Krishna's whereabouts (RL 2.4). Commentators point out that the Gopīs first speak to the larger plant life in the Vraja forest, specifically the trees, but get no response. As they become more and more desperate they approach plants of all kinds and sizes, including the sacred *tulasī* and varieties of jasmine.

The maidens perceive these various plants and trees, in their selfless position, as beings "whose lives are devoted to the service of others," thereby indirectly expressing how they feel that their own existence is for the sake of Krishna (RL 2.9). Convinced that the vines on the trees must have had contact with their beloved Lord, the Gopīs feel that their textured bodily surfaces are actually "ecstatic eruptions" (*utpulakāni*) caused by his divine touch (RL 2.13). They envision the trees and plants, the branches of which are heavy with fruits and flowers during the harvest season, to be bowing before Krishna, whom they have just seen pass by (RL 2.12).

We have shown that both Krishna and the Gopīs relate intimately to or communicate personally with the beauteous Vraja setting, especially during periods of separation, as it serves to enhance their love play. In other words, the landscape is very much in the foreground when the hero and heroines are apart from one another. Conversely, when Krishna and the Gopīs come together in the first and final acts, the landscape assumes a background role. During these times, they roam the forest and use the shores of the Yamunā for play, then bathe in the river to cool off. Thus the forest provides an enchanting arena for the Rāsa dance itself, and becomes a place of recreation following the dance. Clearly, both hero and heroines are closely connected in various ways to the exquisite landscape of Vraja, when they are separated as well as when they unite. It is the power known as Yogamāyā that arranges for the divine cowherd and his maidens to come together in this paradisial landscape of love.

YOGAMĀYĀ: POTENCY FOR INTIMACY

Of the four principals of the Rāsa Līlā, Yogamāyā, a form of the Goddess, is the most subtle and elusive to comprehend. One finds that Yogamāyā, often called simply Māyā, is a mysterious power that escapes the understanding of souls and even of the divinity himself. Indeed, the *Bhāgavata* warns the reader: "If the supreme Soul himself does not understand the nature of Māyā, what to speak of others?" (BhP 3.6.39). Although the concept of Yogamāyā is enigmatic and complex, with a variety of functions and presentations in sacred texts and discourse, we shall nevertheless attempt to get a glimpse of her inscrutable potency.

The agency of Yogamāyā reveals God's identity to worthy souls and conceals his identity from unworthy souls. This potency constructs the perfect arrangement for the selfless love between God and devotee, or for the selfish conditioned love of this world. Thus, Māyā has a transforming function for souls in either divine consciousness or worldly consciousness. It is understandable that Daniel H. H. Ingalls states, "Māyā is one of the most beautiful concepts in the history of religion."[22]

The author of the *Bhāgavata* employs Māyā as an important theological idea in well over two hundred instances. Within the Rāsa Līlā itself, it is presented only a few times, each instance carrying a different sense.[23] The term *Yogamāyā* consists of two words, *yoga* and *Māyā,* and though it is often abbreviated as *Māyā,* it is the complete term that is especially significant here. Several uses of *Māyā* in the *Bhāgavata* indicate that this half of the compound phrase has the sense of "magic spell," "trick," "deceit," or in general "deception." The specific sense of the word *yoga* in *Yogamāyā* is "joining things together" or "making connections" for God's intimate *līlās.*[24] The compound could be translated literally as "the power of union" or "the power of illusion," whereas connotatively, Yogamāyā refers to the magical power that creates intimate arrangements.[25]

The word *Māyā* appears a total of three times in the five acts of the Rāsa Līlā; two of these instances are found within narration, in the beginning and toward the conclusion of the drama, and the third within dialogue. Among these three instances, the exact compound phrase *Yogamāyā* appears only once, in the very first verse, where it is spoken directly by the poet-narrator Śuka as theological explanation: "Even the Beloved Lord . . . turned his mind toward love's delights, fully taking refuge in Yogamāyā's illusive powers" (RL 1.1). The other instance of Māyā appearing in the narrative is the following: "The husband

22. *The Divinity of Krishna,* p. xii. In his foreword to this book, Ingalls defines the concept of *māyā,* then briefly observes interesting parallels to similar themes in Western literature. See pp. xii–xiii.

23. Most often throughout the *Bhāgavata* text, the concept of Māyā carries a metaphysical sense, specifically denoting the realm of "material nature" (*prakṛti*). Even more specifically, the phrase *māyā-guṇa* is used to refer to the illusory realm of the qualities of nature that originate in Sāṁkhya philosophy and also appear in the *Bhagavad Gītā* (*tri-guṇa*).

24. As with the word *māyā,* the word *yoga* carries independent senses. The literal meanings of the word from lexical sources are "union," "junction," "connection," "combination," or even "mixture." It is a derivative of the verb root *yuj,* which can be translated by the cognate "to yoke." The word can refer to "the eightfold path of mystic discipline," *aṣṭāṅga-yoga,* in which practitioners attempt to develop various mystical powers or "perfections," *siddhis.*

25. See discussion on Yogamāyā in "Notes and Comments" on RL 1.1.

Figure 10. Man and monkey at site of the Rāsa dance in Sevakunj, Vrindāvana. Photograph courtesy of Nityatripta Devi Dasi.

cowherds of Vraja . . . felt no jealousy whatsoever toward Krishna" because they were "deluded by his power of Māyā" (RL 5.38). Here, the function of "delusion" is demonstrated by the word *mohita,* a state caused by the power of Māyā. The single instance of Māyā found in dialogue is in Krishna's words to the Gopīs from the first act: "For every woman the highest dharma is to serve her husband without falsity [Māyā]" (RL 1.24). The Gopīs' relationship to dharma will be discussed below.

Yogamāyā has two major functions in the drama—creating arrangements for the various events, and causing forgetfulness in order to facilitate loving intimacy between God and the soul. The significant phrase constituting the fourth *pada* (quarter verse) of the opening verse is Yogamāyā *upāśritaḥ* ("fully taking refuge in Yogamāyā's illusive powers"). This phrase appositively modifies the simple subject "the Beloved Lord," or Bhagavān, immediately informing the reader that Bhagavān depends upon Yogamāyā to arrange this love-inspiring world of paradisial beauty, for achieving his goals of divine enjoyment.

Bhagavān, however, as the supreme person in whom the very power of Yogamāyā originates, is never subject to the control of Māyā the way a worldly soul is:

It is logically wrong to speak of Bhagavān,
who is the supreme controller and ever liberated,
As one who could be subject to Māyā,
not to speak of the weakness of bondage.
(BhP 3.7.9)

Therefore, it is an exceptional and unexpected event that the Lord should submit himself fully to Yogamāyā. The word *upāśritaḥ,* "fully taking refuge," is not engaged anywhere else in the entire *Bhāgavata* text to describe Bhagavān's dependency on anyone, including Yogamāyā, with the exception of this instance within the first verse of the Rāsa Līlā.[26]

Let us now turn to some of the amazing potencies of Māyā. In the *Bhagavad Gītā,* the word appears in six verses that introduce two essential dimensions of the concept. Krishna explains that his divinity is hidden from unqualified persons by this yogic power, as expressed in the *Gītā*'s single instance in which the full term Yogamāyā is found:

I, who am unborn and imperishable,
am not manifest to everyone
For I am covered by Yogamāyā—
one who is deluded does not know this.
(BG 7.25)

In addition to concealing reality from deluded souls, the power of Māyā reveals the Lord's divine nature to deserving souls: "By controlling material nature which belongs to me, I reveal myself through my own power, Māyā" (BG 4.6). These functions of Māyā in the *Bhagavad Gītā* anticipate other dimensions of her powers found in the *Bhāgavata.*

Repeatedly throughout the *Bhāgavata* text, the reader is reminded that Māyā is a power that belongs to God. One finds the word in compound phrases along with God's names, such as "the Māyā of

26. On the basis of the eight instances throughout the *Bhāgavata* text in which the word *upāśritaḥ* is found, two observations can be drawn. First, the word is never found in conjunction with the concept of *māyā* or *yoga-māyā* except in the case of the first verse of the Rāsa Līlā. The word stem *āśritaḥ,* without the prefix *upa-*, is found in only one other instance in conjunction with the word *māyā,* and here it is describing souls who are conditioned by the illusory power of Māyā, *māyāśritānām.* Second, in every instance other than the Rāsa Līlā's first verse, one finds the word *upāśrita* used to describe the dependency of the soul on God. This is also the case in the couple of instances found in the text of the *Bhagavad Gītā.*

Vishnu," or with epithets of God, such as "the Māyā of Bhagavān."[27] Yogamāyā is dependent on God, originates in God, and cannot exist without God or act without his sanction. Yet it is clear that Māyā is an independent potency, completely separate from his own personal manifestations. If this were not the case, Krishna would not be able to submit himself to it, as he does in the first verse of the Rāsa Līlā.

In his prayers to Krishna, Brahmā addresses the Lord as Yogeśvara, "O master of yogic power," and proclaims that all of Krishna's manifestations are made possible through the power of his Yogamāyā energy that extends into every universe (BhP 10.14.21). It is also said that Māyā is the agency of construction "of all the worlds," which includes Krishna's eternal abode of affectionate play (BhP 10.28.6). Thus Yogamāyā is an autonomous divine force intended for Krishna's direct use in his *līlā* of loving intimacy. One of the unusual characteristics of Māyā is its manifestation of multiple-personifications. Krishna explains to Yogamāyā herself that her personae will be identified by various names, such as Dūrgā and Vaiṣṇavī.[28] The author of the Bhāgavata acknowledges the femininity of Māyā through this nomenclature, clearly identifying this power as a *śakti* ("feminine power" or "energy") of God.

As has been shown, Māyā exhibits both concealing and revealing functions. She conceals the true nature of the self in relation to God through delusion: "This whole world is bewildered by such a power in which persons are constantly forgetful of their [true] selves" (BhP 10.14.44cd). And Māyā conceals the truth of the divinity from lovers of God through deception. In order to facilitate intimacy with such pure souls, it is said that God appears, by the arrangement of Māyā, to be just like an ordinary human (BhP 10.17.22). Therefore, Māyā conceals the identity of the deity not only from bewildered souls of this world but also from the most liberated and intimate souls of the heavenly world.

A classic example is that of the divine mother of the Lord from whom Krishna's divinity is concealed for the purpose of preserving their loving relationship (BhP 10.8). In this episode, Krishna's foster

27. These phrases include "the great power of Vishnu" (*viṣṇoḥ mahā-māyā*), "the *māyā* of Krishna" (*kṛṣṇa-māyā*), "the *māyā* of Bhagavān" (*māyā-bhagavataḥ*), "the *māyā* of God" (*deva-māyā*), "the Lord of *māyā*" (*māyeśa*), and "the *māyā* of the Lord" (*īśa-māyā*). The possessive suffix *sva-* and the reflexive use of *ātmā* are also found coupled with the word *māyā,* to indicate the divine source and possession of *māyā.* For example, phrases such as "his own *māyā*" (*sva-māyā* or *ātmā-māyā*), and "with the yoga of my own *māyā*" (*ātma-māyā-yogena*), as well as "my *māyā*" (*mat-māyā*) are found throughout the text.

28. "People from all over the earth will give you various names, such as Durgā, Bhadrakālī, Vijayā and Vaiṣṇavī, Kumudā, Caṇḍikā, Kṛṣṇā, Mādhavī, and Kanyakā; Māyā, Nārāyaṇī, Īśānī, Śāradā, and Ambikā" (BhP 10.2.11–12).

mother, Yaśodā, inspects her child's opened mouth for dirt particles. While she does so, an overwhelming and tremendous vision of the universe is revealed to her. The potency of Māyā thereafter conceals this *aiśvarya* manifestation of God, deceiving Yaśodā so that she will not be distracted from her maternal affection for Krishna, who is, after all, playing the role of her loving child (BhP 10.8.43–44).

Concealing the greatness, *aiśvarya,* in order for the sweetness, *mādhurya,* of the divinity to be revealed is a primary function of Māyā. The personal associates of God are "covered by a curtain of divine illusion," so that any awareness of his majesty is eclipsed, allowing for more affectionate exchanges with the deity. Throughout the tenth book one finds the phrase *māyā-mohita,* "bewildered by Māyā," in relation to Krishna's closest associates.[29] The word *mohita,* meaning "stupefied," "bewildered," "infatuated," or "deluded," is used to describe the state of mind in which such special souls find themselves:

> Thus both of them [Krishna's mother and father]
> who were bewildered (*mohita*)
> by the words of the Soul of all, who is Hari,
> Whose appearance in the human form
> was made possible by Māyā,
> joyfully placed him on their laps and embraced him.
> (BhP 10.45.10)

From this verse, it can be understood that the force of Māyā acts as a veritable catalyst for loving interaction with the divine. She allows the Lord to camouflage manifestations of his power and greatness by providing him with a form or "disguise" that his devotees can relate to affectionately and sweetly (BhP 10.84.16). The Lord also disguises himself from one who is bound to this world, as smoke covers the light of a fire (BhP 10.70.37). Thus, God's appearance in human form appears in an ordinary way to those attached to this temporary world, and at the same time appears intimately to those bound to him by devotion.[30]

At times, Māyā even allows the more formal aspect of God's *aiśvarya* to appear in the consciousness of intimate devotees, as in the following verse spoken by the Gopīs:

29. Instances of *māyā-mohita* can be found in BhP 10.13.42, 10.14.44, 10.23.50–51, and 10.63.40.

30. This type of human-like appearance by God is expressed in phrases such as *māyā-manuṣya,* "the appearance as a human"; *māyā-martya,* "appearance of an ordinary mortal"; and *māyā-manujam,* "appearance like a human being."

> Your lotus feet fulfill
> the desires of all
> who humbly submit to them.
> Worshiped by the one
> born from the lotus flower,
> they are the ornament of the earth.
> They are to be meditated upon
> during times of distress, for
> they grant the highest satisfaction.
> O charming lover,
> please place upon our breasts
> your lotus feet, O slayer of misery.
> (RL 3.13)

Note here that the cowherd maidens praise Krishna's feet as objects of worship for those who relate to him in his *aiśvarya* aspect, whereas the Gopīs themselves, who are immersed in the highest levels of *mādhurya-rasa,* look to his feet to satisfy their burning desire. It is common to find verses in the Rāsa Līlā that alternate between the Gopīs' appreciation of Krishna's greatness and their passion for him as his beloveds. For the devotees absorbed in the *mādhurya* aspect of the Lord, alternating shifts between feelings for the *aiśvarya* and the *mādhurya* are made possible by Yogamāyā. Often such acknowledgment of Krishna's *aiśvarya* attributes heightens their passion and deepens their feelings of separation. Thus, the *aiśvarya* can be seen as functioning positively to reinforce the intensity of the *mādhurya-rasa* between God and his dearest associates.

In the fifth act of the Rāsa Līlā, Māyā is the potency that produces a "double" for each of the Gopīs, in order to compensate for their absence in their homes. It is by means of Yogamāyā that the husbands and family members experience the full presence of those cowherd maidens, even though they have escaped into the forest and are completely involved with Krishna. Thus, the potential conflict of the Gopīs meeting another male in the middle of the night rather than dutifully remaining at home as chaste wives with their husbands has been avoided. It is also Yogamāyā who makes arrangements for the affectionate reciprocation between Krishna and the Gopīs, in which Krishna overcomes his own sense of divine power and the Gopīs, their sense of finitude. In these ways, Yogamāyā, magically, is able to create situations in which ethical and social reconciliation occurs.

As a final note, the *Bhāgavata* uses the metaphor of a dramatic play to explain Māyā.[31] God is not only the author of the play but also the creator and sustainer of the very stage on which the play is enacted, and simultaneously participates as one of the actors, completely losing himself in *līlā.* All of this occurs by the enabling power of Yogamāyā, who arranges the stage sets and directs the play. The spiritual actor and actresses, God and the pure souls, by virtue of the uniting force of Yogamāyā verily lose themselves in this divine aesthetic of *līlā,* in which all activities are executed for the purpose of increasing the intensity and intimacy of their love.

THE GOPĪS: BELOVEDS OF KRISHNA

South Asia has preserved a special and prominent place for the divine feminine, more than has any other civilization. Likewise, in the *Bhāgavata,* the feminine is exalted to the highest position. The Gopīs are portrayed as extraordinary souls who are the dearest beloveds of Krishna.

In the Rāsa Līlā story, the Gopīs' love for Krishna is in fact so exceptional that Krishna himself, as we have seen, explains that he does not feel he can reciprocate the purity of their love for him (RL 4.20–22). He reflects later, in the eleventh book, on the love of the Gopīs as being the only way that he can be attained, their path being superior to all other paths leading to the divinity (BhP 11.12.8–9). Krishna reminisces about their love during those autumn nights of the Rāsa, and compares the Gopīs in their devotion to sages who merge their spirits into the supreme reality, like rivers into the ocean.

In the latter part of the tenth book, Uddhava, the special friend sent by Krishna to console the cowherd maidens, is astonished by their unexcelled love and states that even great sages have difficulty attaining such a level of devotion (BhP 10.47.25). The Gopīs are declared to be the paradigms of devotion, which, in their case, is so powerful that it bestows grace upon anyone who observes it (BhP 10.47.27). Uddhava's effusive praise of the maidens for their exemplary love of Krishna continues to be expressed in several other verses (BhP 10.47.58–63).

The name Gopī, meaning "a cowherdess" or "cowherd maiden," appears in the plural form in the majority of instances within the Rāsa

31. "You [Krishna] are covered by a curtain of illusory power (*māyā*), and you who are imperishable are beyond the range of perception (*ajñādhokṣaja*) for ignorant persons. You are not perceived by the vision of deluded persons, just as an actor is not perceived when he is dressed for a drama" (BhP 1.8.19).

Līlā, since the maidens relate to Krishna as a group more often than not. It is by far the most utilized epithet for the consorts, appearing twenty-four times within the five acts.[32] No personal names are found for the cowherd maidens, who even refer to themselves as *gopīs* (RL 2.30, 2.31).

Many other colorful epithets appear in the drama, through which we learn about the identity of the maidens. They are called "fair maidens with beautiful eyes" (RL 1.3), "ones with beautiful waists" (RL 1.19, 4.18), and "jewel-like maidens" (RL 5.2). Names of servitude are presented throughout by the Gopīs themselves, such as "undemanding maidservants."[33] There are several epithets identifying the village of Vraja in relation to the maidens, who are called "the beautiful women of Vraja."[34] Epithets of affection are also found repeatedly. The cowherd maidens are referred to as "dear ones," "beloved ones," or "lovers," even "those who are dear to the Lord." In addition, the narrator calls the Gopīs "the delighted lovers." They are further described as "those who desire him," and the one special Gopī as "the girl desirous of love."

Some epithets of gender are indicators of the marital status of the maidens, who are called "women," "brides," and "young wives."[35] In the climactic verse of the drama they are referred to as *kṛṣṇa-vadhvaḥ*, which could easily be understood as "the wives of Krishna" (RL 5.8). Yet the inquiring king calls them "others' wives" (*para-dāra*, RL 5.28), while the narrator refers to them both as ones who are "faithful" to Krishna (RL 5.2) and as "cowherd women" (RL 5.20). Ironically, Krishna calls the Gopīs "chaste ladies" (RL 1.22), and even "friends" (RL 4.20). Clearly, the nomenclature used in the Rāsa Līlā leads to a complex portrait of the maidens, which indicates that they are wives of cowherd men as well as wives of Krishna, or simply unmarried girls who have become the young wives of Krishna. The question of the married or unmarried status of the Gopīs, which is addressed in "Ethical Bound-

32. There are twenty-two instances of the plural of *Gopī*, and two of the singular. Three of the plural instances are found in introductory lines external to the actual verses, as in "The beautiful Gopīs spoke."

33. For example, the words "of your maidservants" (*kiṅkarīṇām*, RL 1.41), "voluntary maidservants" (*aśulka-dāsikā*, RL 3.2), and "maidservants" (*vidhi-karīr*, RL 3.8) are found. The phrase "your miserable maidservant" (*dāsyās te kṛpaṇāyā*, RL 2.39) is cried out by the special Gopī when she is deserted by Krishna.

34. This phrase is a translation of *vraja-sundarī*, RL 1.46, 5.17. Other examples are *vraja-striyaḥ*, RL 1.4, 5.16; *vraja-yoṣitaḥ*, RL 1.17; *vrajāṅganāḥ*, RL 2.1; and *vraja-vadhūbhir*, RL 5.40.

35. Words meaning "women" are the following: *striyāḥ*, RL 1.19, 2.35, 2.42, and 5.2; *vadhū*, RL 1.26, 2.31–2, 2.38, 5.8, and 5.40; *abalāḥ*, RL 4.21, and *yuvatīḥ*, RL 5.24. The word *vadhū* can mean simply "woman," but the word's more essential meaning is "bride," "newly married woman," or "young wife" (MW).

aries and Boundless Love" below, as well as in the "Notes and Comments," has been a debated issue in the Caitanya school.

The presentation of the number of voices among the cowherd maidens is complex. The voice of the Gopīs shifts between plural (as the complete group or partial groups) and singular. At times it is difficult to discern whether one of the maidens is speaking on behalf of the group, or whether the Gopīs as a group are speaking in unison, like a Greek chorus. This shifting between singular and collective voices, as well as ambiguity in the number of voices, is intentional on the part of the *Bhāgavata*'s author. It conveys a deep sense of intimacy within the community of cowherd maidens and, at the same time, supports the various personalities of the individual Gopīs. Moreover, their collective and individual voices and actions are mutually interdependent; that is, the individual voice is expressive of the collective voice, which in turn is expressive of each of the individual voices.

This dialectical relationship between the collective and individual maidens is especially highlighted during the Rāsa dance, and becomes a major symbolic motif—all the Gopīs together form the Rāsa dance circle, yet, simultaneously, each one experiences Krishna's exclusive attention. Even as early as the first two verses, the introduction of the one and the many voices is conveyed by way of metaphor. The author establishes the cowherd maidens as a group in the first verse, then as a singular presence in the second verse. These two presentations anticipate the continuous movement in the story line between the Gopīs as a group and as individuals.

The Gopīs are presented by way of metaphor through the word "nights" (*rātrī*), found in the opening verse of the work. The term *rātrī,* a feminine noun stem in the plural, is one among many words in Sanskrit that have the meaning of "night," and is also the name of the Vedic goddess who is the personification of night.[36]

36. Words for "night" in Sanskrit are many, including *rātra, niśā, rajanī, kṣaṇadā, kṣapā,* and so on. The particular word chosen here by the author is the feminine form of *rātra,* the only word for "night" that is utilized to refer to the goddess of Night in the *Ṛg Veda.* The passages of the *Ṛg Veda* that focus on the goddess of Night are presented in the "Notes and Comments" for this verse.

The idea of *rātrī* functioning metaphorically as the goddess Nights, as the tenor of the metaphor, is supported by modern dramatic performance. In pilgrimage plays of the Rāsa Līlā story, the Goddess is not only personified as "Nights" but her role also includes a dialogue with Krishna! See "The Great Circle Dance," in *At Play with Krishna: Pilgrimage Dramas of Brindavan,* by John Stratton Hawley in association with Shrivatsa Goswami (Princeton: Princeton University Press, 1981), p. 184. How the tenor of this metaphor in turn becomes the vehicle for the deeper metaphor pointing to the Gopīs is also explored in the "Notes and Comments" section.

Figure 11. Sacred images of Rādhā and Krishna with eight principal Gopīs, worshiped in a major center of the International Society for Krishna Consciousness, Mayapur, India. Photograph courtesy of Nityatripta Devi Dasi.

The image here is of many "nights" adorned with beautiful jasmine, the scented flower commonly found ornamenting the hair of Indian women and girls of any social status, in order to attract the attention of a male. These "nights decorated with jasmine" can be seen as a metaphor for the many cowherd maidens, who also decorate themselves with jasmine in order to attract Krishna, the supreme male (RL 5.11). Just as this special jasmine blooms at night, the Gopīs' love for Krishna is to blossom that very night. And just as jasmine is "not supposed" to appear in the autumn season, the Gopīs are "not supposed" to appear in the forest after nightfall. Thus the forbidden and otherworldly quality of this *līlā* is conveyed through this complex metaphor.

The Night goddess presented in the plural clearly becomes the metaphorical vehicle for the collective heroines of the story. The features shared by the Vedic goddess and the Gopīs, the very grounds of the metaphor, are that both are enticingly beautiful, otherworldly, many in number, and both come alive at night. Thus, in this introductory verse, "those nights in autumn" represent the Night goddess, who reveals the collective heroines of the story, Krishna's night goddesses. The Gopīs, like the autumn nights, are beautiful and ripe for love in this festive and celebratory season, setting the scene for the Rāsa dance.

As the group of maidens is introduced through metaphor, the presence of a singular Gopī is anticipated through an implied metaphor found in the verse's simile. This feminine presence is conveyed in the second verse of the drama: "Then the moon, king among stars, arose, spreading soothing reddish rays over the face of the eastern horizon . . . as a lover caresses his beloved's blushed face, consoling her after long separation" (RL 1.2). Note that here a single lover and beloved are presented. This singular presence could be seen as anticipating the Gopī specially favored by Krishna, who is discovered by the group of maidens in the second scene of the second act. Thus, the first verse introduces the heroines as a group of Gopīs who are prominent in the first act, and the second verse subtly introduces the special maiden with whom Krishna departs in the second act. Her unique role will be examined in more depth below.

In the third verse, the cowherd maidens are presented explicitly as a group. Here, the Gopīs' love for Krishna has awakened, their eyes opening wide with affection and anticipation. The fourth verse describes how they are drawn to the flute music, their minds so enraptured by Krishna that they have no choice but to join him. Thus their presence effectively blossoms poetically in the four opening verses. In the first two verses, the petals begin to open, or the Gopīs' presence begins to unfold. In the third, their presence blossoms, and by the fourth they have almost fully bloomed, as the plot of the drama develops.

Verses five through eight briefly revisit the cowherd maidens in their homes, in order to present a description of the various activities in which they were engaged just before they fully blossomed forth into the forest. Here, the maidens are specifically described in terms of subgroups; some of them have abandoned the milking of cows, others the feeding of their children and husbands, and so on. In verses six and eight, we learn that some of the Gopīs are under the care of their husbands; others, of their fathers and brothers—yet they all abandon their caretakers to be with Krishna.[37] We then discover, in verses nine through eleven, that the particular Gopīs who could not abandon their homes instead enter into deep meditation, embracing their Beloved inside their hearts. In the last verse of this scene, it becomes clear that the Gopīs are not ordinary souls, since they have "relinquished their bodies composed of material elements" (RL 1.11).

37. In Indian society, women are traditionally under the care of a male—if not a father or husband, then a brother or other male in the family. However, the Gopīs abandoned any male caretaker for the purpose of being with Krishna.

The extraordinary nature of the cowherd maidens becomes the topic for discourse between the narrator and listener in the second didactic scene. The king observes that the maidens know Krishna as "the greatest lover," and not as "the source of Brahman." He inquires of the sage how it is that they are able to escape the influence of the underlying forces of nature, while remaining passionately in love with Krishna. The narrating sage provides two responses to his question: the Gopīs' deepest emotions are focused on Krishna, for they are "fully absorbed in God"; and the Lord liberates all, including persons who are hateful toward him, not to mention those who are in love with him.

After the Gopīs and Krishna meet, converse, and play in the forest, Krishna suddenly vanishes, ostensibly because of the pride of the maidens. Pride, though usually regarded as a negative quality for developing love of God—either as a self-indulgent or arrogant state of mind—in this instance is understood by the Caitanya school to be an expression of the purity and intensity of the Gopīs' love. Jīva Gosvāmin explains that their pride is that of "loving intimacy," and would only cause Krishna to favor them. Although it appears that he rejects the cowherd maidens in order to subdue their pride (RL 1.48), it is revealed by Krishna himself that he disappears in order to increase their love for him (RL 4.20–21).

There is ample evidence that the Gopīs "know" the various majestic and cosmic forms of Krishna, but it is his more intimate nature on which they focus, especially when their beloved is personally present before them. Theologians have observed, as mentioned above, that *aiśvarya* becomes prominent for the Gopīs when they are feeling some level of separation from Krishna, either anticipatory or actual. During periods of separation, they recall the formal, powerful aspect of Krishna, as in scene 1 of act two, and in act three. This is a matter taken up by Nārada in his *Bhakti Sūtra,* in which he recognizes the Gopīs as the foremost examples of bhakti (NBS 20). Nārada points out that they "know" Krishna's supreme greatness. However, it appears as if they do not recognize it at times, due to forgetfulness caused by their passionate devotion to him (NBS 21–24).

In the second act, the maidens desperately search for Krishna. Their madness, caused by intense love, is observable in their "deranged" behavior of speaking to the plants and vines of the forest:

Singing out loud about him
  like deranged persons,
Together they searched
  from forest to forest.
They inquired from trees,
  the lords of the forest,
  about the supreme Person
Who is present internally and
  externally for all living beings,
  as heavenly air pervades all beings,
  within and without.

(RL 2.4)

According to Jīva, this madness is an appreciation of God's presence based on pure love, allowing one to see God manifest in everything.

The Gopīs then begin to imitate the behavior of Krishna, due to identifying so deeply and dramatically with him:

Through their movements,
  smiles, glances, speech,
  and other gestures,
The bodily forms of his lovers
  became similar
  to those of their beloved.
The young women,
  their selves fully absorbed in him,
  thus declared, "I am he!"
Their amorous,
  playful gestures
  were those of Krishna.

(RL 2.3)

Viśvanātha Cakravartin, a prominent eighteenth-century commentator in the Caitanya school, explains that this state of divine madness, or *unmāda,* is characterized by taking on the bodily movements and behavioral qualities of the supreme beloved. The condition of the Gopīs is one in which the various movements of Krishna take over their minds and senses, and their very selves assume a likeness to their beloved. This madness of the cowherd maidens, as described in the

Bhāgavata, in turn becomes the model for Caitanya, whose life is famous for his ecstatic madness in devotion to Krishna.

While imitating Krishna, the Gopīs are a unified group of heroines who are collectively presented, but who exhibit individual activities. This interesting relation between the group and individual Gopīs is especially accentuated when the group finds a solitary Gopī abandoned in the forest. By the end of the first act, Krishna has left the collective maidens, and in the second act, the reader is informed that he has run off with one particular Gopī from whom he also disappears, ostensibly due to her pride. After this special maiden relates to the inquiring group of maidens what has happened to her, she rejoins them in their search for Krishna.

The third act consists of nineteen verses of song in which the Gopīs use their collective voice to pray, remember, and yearn for Krishna. By the time the drama reaches the fourth act, then, the primary portrait the reader has of the Gopīs is one of separation from their beloved, and longing for union with him. When Krishna suddenly reappears at the beginning of the act, the reactions and emotions of specific maidens are described in verses RL 4.4–7. The group of maidens "stood up at once, as if their very lives had just been returned to their bodies" (RL 4.3). By the middle of the act, the Gopīs collectively inquire from Krishna about the nature of love, and he responds in several verses (RL 4.17–22).

A certain phenomenon of psychosomatic bliss occuring in the Gopīs, as described in the fourth and fifth acts, is caused by their direct experience of the presence of Krishna, either through physical contact or through contemplation. A similar reaction occurs in other life forms found in Vraja, when they come in contact with Krishna: "Seeing your beauty, the most magnificent in all the three worlds, the animals, trees, birds and cows are elated with bodily ripplings of bliss" (RL 1.40). My translation of Sanskrit words that convey this experience of bliss attempts to uncover the essential meaning of these words, signifying a certain condition of ecstatic rapture caused by divine love. Since this condition clearly has no comparable English term, indicating an experience that is largely unacknowledged in Western culture, my translation of the Sanskrit warrants further discussion here.

We find this phenomenon depicted by the words *pulaka-aṅgī,* referring to the Gopīs, meaning literally "the [hairs] of the limbs standing," which I have translated as "elated with bodily ripplings of joy"

(RL 4.8).[38] Similarly, in the fifth act, the words *hṛṣṭa-romā,* meaning literally "having hairs that are thrilled," have been translated as "elated with bodily ripplings of bliss" (RL 5.12). Both these verses utilize one of two verbs that are characteristically used to describe this phenomenon; in fact, most of the words used throughout the complete *Bhāgavata* text to express this experience are derivative words from the verbs *hṛṣ-* "to excite" and *pul-* "to be high or stand."[39] In each of these instances, the meaning of the derivatives has the positive sense of delight and rarely carries the negative sense of fear typically found in English expressions that many translators employ to describe this phenomenon.[40]

The lexical definition of *pulaka* distinguishes between the positive and negative senses. The literal meaning of *pulaka* in its plural form, *pulakāni,* is "erection or bristling of the hairs of the body (considered to be occasioned by delight or rapture rather than by fear)" (MW). The word *pulakāni,* along with other similar terms, is intended to convey more than just the physical reactions—it clearly conveys that which causes such reactions, that is, the deeper stirrings of the soul that give rise to an experience of overwhelming joy and blissfulness, which in turn produces these physical signs. The rapturous sensation that is expressed here is described to a degree by the Rāsa Līlā story itself, when the narrator compares the Gopīs, in whom such a psychophysical state occurs, to the meditating yogi who becomes "flooded with bliss" (RL 4.8). This state of ecstasy, as observed by the cowherd maidens, is caused by contact with Krishna, either in his presence or absence.

The word "ripplings" within the phrase "elated with bodily ripplings of bliss," conveys the two ways in which this phenomenon is manifest in the Gopīs, either rising from within the body and moving to the bodily surface, or coming from an outside stimulus that affects the

38. Verse RL 2.10, however, is one instance in which I retain much of the literal translation of *pulaka.* My choice to do so was influenced by the imagery projected by the verse, which poetically engages imagery from the literal translation of the words. In addition, the surrounding supporting words lend themselves to this treatment.

39. See MW. Derivative words from *hṛṣ-* are *prahṛṣṭa-romā,* "with bristling or thrilling of hair"; *roma-harṣa,* "hairs thrilled or bristled"; *harṣa,* "bristling or erection (esp. of hair in a thrill of rapture or delight)" (MW); *prema-hṛṣṭa-tanu,* "a body with hairs standing out of love"; and *hṛṣyat tanū-ruhaḥ bhāva,* "due to loving emotion, the hair on the body was thrilled." Derivative words from *pul-* are: *utpulaka,* "hairs standing up"; *pulakācitāṅga,* "the body covered with raised hairs"; and *pulaka,* "raised hairs." Examples of less frequently used alternative expressions are *roma-utsava,* "standing up of hair" and *premṇā ūrdhva roma,* "with hairs standing due to love." Both of these phrases utilize the word for hair, *roma,* and another word indicating its upward direction, *utsava* or *ūrdhva.*

40. Only in the *Bhagavad Gītā* (from the greater text of the *Mahābhārata*) do we have a usage that conveys both the negative sense of fear before the universal form and, simulta-

surface of the body, in either case displaying eruptions of the skin. When the Gopīs meditate upon their beloved Lord, it is the former, and when they are physically touched by him, it is the latter. "Rippling" in the singular noun form is defined as "a shallow stretch of running water in a stream roughened or broken by rocky or uneven bottom" (WEB). This definition expresses how the "ripplings" of bliss come from within (since rippling, in this definition, is caused by the rough river bed, rather than something external to the river, such as wind, thrown or falling stones, and so on). Likewise, when "rippling" is defined as "the fretting or ruffling of the surface of water (as by wind)" (WEB), this corresponds to how such "ripplings" come from the outside, or from Krishna's touch.[41]

English lexical sources do not recognize the plural form of the word rippling, which I have created in order to illustrate the current of continuing joyfulness that constitutes this phenomenon, as opposed to a sudden, eruptive joy that might better fit the conception of "rippling" in the singular form. The plural word "ripplings" is indica-

---

neously, the positive sense of jubilation. The negative sense of fear, associated with a variety of English words or phrases, is often conveyed through translations of Sanskrit words or phrases originally intended by ancient authors to indicate a positive experience of joy or bliss. In other words, the negative English connotation conflicts with the positive intent behind the Sanskrit words. Therefore, I have avoided engaging such English expressions in a literal translation of the Sanskrit. Words or phrases such as "chills," "shivers," "goose flesh," or "goose pimples" generally convey reactions to the unpleasant emotions of fear or horror. Although these can indicate the more positive emotion of excitement, they still fail to communicate the full experience intended by the Sanskrit. "Horripilation," which would be a convenient one-word translation of the Sanskrit, is another unsuitable word choice. The word means, "a bristling of the hair of the head or body (as from disease, terror, or chilliness)" (WEB), and furthermore, is related etymologically to the word "horror," thereby carrying negative senses. The word "eruptions" also indicates negative qualities since one of its definitions is "the breaking out of an exanthem [eruptive disease] on the skin."

English words with more positive associations, on the other hand, are too often inadequate. The lexical meaning of the word "thrill" as "an instantaneous excitement: a tingling of or as if of the nerves produced by a sudden emotional reaction" (WEB) carries only a partial sense, failing to depict the full depth of this phenomenon, as described in the flood of bliss the yogi experiences (RL 4.8). Moreover, "thrill" can be associated with fear; thus a horror story is called a "thriller." And one cannot ignore the word's affiliation with negative colloquial connotations like "cheap thrill," which is clearly more fleeting and superficial than the experience conveyed through the Sanskrit terms. The phrase "sending chills up the spine" could be considered, but again, inadequately conveys the sustained intensity and superlative spiritual nature of the experience. Furthermore, the phrase can carry the sense of reaction to fear, which is certainly not the intended meaning.

41. The definitions of the word as a verb, "to ripple," further express the specific bodily condition related to this phenomenon. The experience described is not merely the "hairs standing on end," but it is the body as it "becomes fretted or lightly ruffled on the surface (as water)" (WEB). Also, the body may "become covered with or form in small waves or undulations" (WEB), or "move with an undulating motion or so as to cause ripples" (WEB).

tive of an ongoing, sustained sensation, rather than a short-lived, fleeting one. The complete phrase, "elated with bodily ripplings of bliss," possesses several senses that facilitate an understanding of this complex experience, including the joyful thrill and rapturous sensation, the resulting bumpy eruptions of the skin, and the sustaining waves or undulating movement of bliss that takes over the body. The bodily experience of the Gopīs, then, is a type of sustained yogic bliss arising from their direct and indirect contact with Krishna.

In the fifth and final act, the drama reaches its apex when Krishna joins the Gopīs in the dance known as the Rāsa (RL 5.2). The word "Rāsa" indicates a certain ancient dance form composed of a circular formation of many female dancers, whose hands or arms are interlocked with one another in a chainlike manner, and around whose necks the arms of their male dance partners are placed. In this particular Rāsa dance, however, it is Krishna who, by duplicating himself from the center of the divine circle through his mystic power, becomes the sole male partner for each maiden (RL 5.3). As the Gopīs begin to dance, each one experiences the exclusive attention of Krishna, and "each thought she alone was at his side." Together, they sing songs of love in chorus with their beloved Lord. This portrait of Krishna and the cowherd maidens is colorfully described a few verses later, just before the climactic verse of the story:

> There, glowing brilliantly among them,
>   was the Beloved Lord, son of Devakī—
> In a setting of golden ornaments,
>   he appeared like a magnificent emerald!
> (RL 5.7)

It is significant that Krishna, whose complexion is usually compared to a deep blue sapphire, appears like a brilliant green emerald as he mingles with all of the golden-complexioned Gopīs, in the wondrous ring of the Rāsa dance (to be discussed below).

THE SPECIAL GOPĪ: RĀDHĀ

The Caitanya school identifies the particular cowherd maiden who disappears with Krishna, leaving the other maidens behind, as Rādhā. In the second scene of the second act, the narrator describes how, while all the maidens are searching feverishly for Krishna, they find his footprints, along with a second set belonging to a young woman (RL 2.25–27). This Gopī has been selected by Krishna, among all others, to venture alone with him to a secret place; thus the *Bhāgavata* author presents her as the special Gopī.

The group of Gopīs gives the reason why this particular maiden must have been considered so attractive in Krishna's eyes: she must have worshiped him perfectly, and therefore he was pleased with her:

The Beloved Lord,
the supreme Lord Hari,
was worshiped by her perfectly.
Having abandoned us,
being so pleased with her,
Govinda led her to a secret place.
(RL 2.28)

Verses 30–38 in the second act proceed to present this favored cowherd maiden not merely as an individual Gopī who is mingling with the others, but as one who has been uniquely chosen by Krishna for his exclusive attention. This sequence of verses is the only place where the special Gopī is explicitly described.

The Caitanya school believes that the name and identity of Rādhā are both revealed and concealed in the verse quoted above, in the phrase, "the one who worships Krishna perfectly" (*anayārādhitaḥ*—note the letters *rādh* in the middle of this phrase, indicating Rādhā's name). The tradition gives Rādhā a very prominent position in the performance of the Rāsa dance itself, without any implicit or explicit indication of this in the narrative. In fact, the Caitanya school cannot envision the Rāsa Līlā without Rādhā in the center of the Rāsa *maṇḍala,* "the circle of the Rāsa dance," with Krishna (CC 2.8.109 and 3.14.19). Rāmānanda Rāya, speaking to Caitanya, reflects on the importance of Rādhā's place within the Rāsa Līlā:

The Rāsa Līlā is the full essence
of Krishna's desire.
Rādhā is the binding link
in his desire for the Rāsa Līlā.

Without her, the Rāsa Līlā
does not radiate in his heart.
Leaving the circle of the Rāsa,
he went to search for Rādhā.
(CC 2.8.113–114)

Note here Rāmānanda's words stating that Krishna leaves "the circle of the Rāsa" to search for Rādhā. In the *Bhāgavata* version of the story, Krishna deserts the group of Gopīs as they are frolicking in the forest at the end of the first act, yet there is no mention of him leaving them during the Rāsa dance, in the fifth act. This vision of Krishna departing from the circle of the Rāsa is an embellishment or variation on the theme of the story that is likely to have been taken from the vision of Jayadeva in his *Gītagovinda.* The capacity of the tradition's esoteric eye to interpolate will be further discussed below.

Although personal names of the Gopīs are absent from the Rāsa Līlā and the rest of the *Bhāgavata* text, many of their names, along with Rādhā's, appear in several other Purāṇas. With the aid of these Purāṇas and other sources, teachers of the Caitanya school have identified the names of various voices of cowherd maidens in the story, as well as elaborated upon intricate details concerning the maidens (see "Notes and Comments" on act five). Their esoteric teaching is that each of the Gopīs is a partial manifestation of the unique Gopī, Rādhā.

As a major theologian of the school, Krishnadāsa further explains that not only are all the Gopīs found in Rādhā but all other goddesses are as well; indeed, Rādhā is the supreme Goddess, the embodiment of all divine women. He identifies her as the particular Gopī who appears in the second act of the Rāsa Līlā (CC 1.4.87–88), and she is also understood to be the supreme *śakti* ("energy") of Krishṇa, who is the *śaktimat* ("the possessor of that energy"). Furthermore, we learn that Rādhā and Krishna are one and different from each other:

> Rādhā and Krishna are of one Soul,
> although they bear two bodies
> So they can enjoy the experience
> of *rasa* with one another.
> (CC 1.4.56)

The ultimate focal point of worship for the Caitanya school is this divine couple, Rādhā and Krishna. Their *līlā* is at the core of the tradition's devotion, bhakti. In order to appreciate the full esoteric significance of the Rāsa Līlā, we need to understand more about the supreme position of Rādhā in Caitanya theology.

Just as Krishna manifests in various *avatāra* forms, or divine forms of descent, so also, the tradition holds, does Rādhā appear in various forms (CC 1.4.76). Three types of manifestation coming from Rādhā are described: the forms of Lakṣmī, the consort goddess of the cosmic

Vishnu; the queens of Dvāraka and Mathurā, who are married to the regal form of Krishna; and the Gopī consorts of Vraja. Of these, the Gopīs are presented as superior to the other two types of feminine counterparts, not only because Rādhā herself is a cowherd maiden and the origin of all Gopīs but also because they are the consorts who participate in the Rāsa Līlā, the most significant of all *līlās*. The theologians of the school delight in the supremacy of Rādhā, who excels all other goddesses, since it is explicated that all such goddesses are but manifestations of her divinity:

> The Goddess filled with Krishna
> is known as Rādhikā,
> the supreme divinity.
> She is the one in whom all Lakṣmīs
> and all loveliness are found.
> She is utterly confounding
> and she is beyond all others.
> (CC 1.4.83)

Remarkably, then, Rādhā manifests in various multiple forms (CC 2.8.165), paralleling the way Krishna multiplies himself in the Rāsa dance.

Thus the Gopīs, according to the esoteric vision of the school, are truly parts of Rādhā, who accommodates Krishna with various manifestations of her own bodily form. Effectively, these maidens are independent, partial, alter-ego personifications of Rādhā's personality. It is no wonder that she, like the other Gopīs, is rejected by Krishna due to pride, considering these cowherd maidens are extensions of herself. The tradition conveys, however, the superlative status of Rādhā's divinity by expressing that she is, in effect, the whole who is greater than the sum total of all the parts, the Gopīs, combined.

Additionally, according to the Caitanya theology, the Gopīs are personified embodiments of the range of Rādhā's various emotions. Since she is envisioned as the special Gopī at the center of the Rāsa *maṇḍala,* the Rāsa Līlā is essentially an expression of Rādhā-Krishna *līlā.* Rādhā encircles Krishna with numerous manifestations of her very own emotions in the forms of the cowherd maidens, and Krishna manifests as multiple duplicates in order to attend intimately to each and every manifestation of Rādhā.

Although an explicit description of Rādhā's place in the Rāsa dance is absent from the text, and the uncultivated eye does not see her at the center of the Rāsa-*maṇḍala* with Krishna, she is surely there, as so many artistic renderings reveal. The theological and scriptural portraits of the intimate dimensions of Krishna's divinity are not in conflict; rather, to the esoteric eye they support and enrich each other. Not only is Krishna in the middle of the circle of the Rāsa dance, but, according to the teachers of the Caitanya school, he is there with "the queen of Vrindāvana, Rādhā," because she is the superlative Gopī and the "cause" of the Rāsa dance itself.

The Rāsa Līlā drama, therefore, turns out to be a portrait of the divine couple, Rādhā and Krishna, as well as a portrait of each of the Gopīs with her beloved Krishna. Rādhā's role, esoterically perceived as central in this most worshiped portion of the *Bhāgavata,* has now become widely accepted and recognized by all Hindus. In modern-day pilgrimage dramas and artistic renderings, Rādhā appears most often at the center of the Rāsa dance, along with her beloved Krishna.

3

Messages of the Text

DEVOTIONAL YOGA TRANSCENDS DEATH

The relationship of the devoted soul to the world and such a soul's passage from this world through death is a subtle but prominent theme in the Rāsa Līlā story line. The Gopīs' departure from their homes symbolizes a type of death, that is, a shift from one body to another, and from one world to another. This shift is observable in the narrator's description of the Gopīs' three types of bodies, which could be described as physical, nonphysical, and illusory, although the exact relationship between these bodies is unclear.

The first is a body "composed of material elements," a body influenced by the "underlying forces of nature," that is abandoned upon hearing Krishna's flute (RL 1.11). This body fulfills the responsibilities of an ideal Indian woman as dictated by dharma, by maintaining faithfulness to the family, performing household work, milking cows, and feeding the children and husband (RL 1.5–7). The abrupt abandonment, or death, of the physical body occurs in the first scene of the drama, when the Gopīs suddenly drop all types of vital household activities upon hearing the flute music of their beloved Lord.

The second type of body—understood by inference since it is not explicitly described—is presumably a body not composed of material elements and not influenced by the forces of nature; a kind of "resurrected" body suitable for relating to God, facilitating the passionate love of the cowherd maidens. The Gopīs give up their dharmic bodies as they abandon their duties, by escaping either outwardly to the forest or inwardly into meditation. My contention here is that in either case, the Gopīs require a new body that is not bound by dharmic restrictions. The author of the *Bhāgavata,* however, addresses this new body only in relation to the maidens who are unable to be with Krishna, in the following verse:

Certainly, he is the supreme Soul,
 though they knew him
 intimately as their lover.
They relinquished their bodies
 composed of material elements,
 and any worldly bondage
 was instantly destroyed.
(RL 1.11)

Thus, the Gopīs who cannot depart from their families instead depart by means of yogic meditation, embracing Krishna from within. In either case, the physical body is abandoned, and they find themselves in a new body that is perfect for engaging in loving affairs with their beloved. The maidens lose themselves in their Lord in utter self-forgetfulness, whether they move inwardly, embracing Krishna deeply within the heart, or outwardly, embracing him in the forest of Vraja. The Gopīs interact with Krishna throughout the drama in this devotional body, which can be understood either as a transformation of the original body or a different body into which the soul has been transported (although, in the latter scenario, there is no explicit mention of a body that remains behind).

We do not hear of the third type, the illusory body, until the final scene of the drama. Arranged by Yogamāyā, this body is designed to create an appearance of the maidens in their homes as if they had never left. The illusory or substitute body is maintained while, simultaneously, the Gopīs are engaged in *līlā* with Krishna, in their nonphysical, devotional bodies. We are told that the cowherd husbands continue to feel the presence of their wives in their homes and are peaceful, apparently unaware of the dual role that their wives are playing:

The husband cowherds of Vraja
 felt no jealousy whatsoever
 toward Krishna.
Deluded by his power of Māyā,
 each husband thought his wife
 had remained all the while by his side.
(RL 5.38)

To further complicate matters, the cowherd maidens, at the end of the night of the Rāsa dance, return to their homes: "During the sacred hour before dawn, . . . the Gopīs returned to their homes, though reluctantly, for they so loved the Beloved Lord" (RL 5.39). It is certainly enigmatic that the devotional body returns home, where the illusory body has remained all along. This apparent discrepancy is further discussed below. For now, let us take a look at the pervasive role of yoga throughout the text.

Those cowherd maidens who are not able to abandon their everyday lives by externally leaving are, nevertheless, successful in giving up their lives, through the internal yogic means of deep devotional contemplation:

> Some Gopīs,
> unable to leave,
> had gone inside their homes.
> With eyes closed,
> fully absorbed in love,
> they meditated upon Krishna.
>
> The intense burning
> of unbearable separation
> from their dearest beloved
> disrupted all inauspiciousness;
> Due to the joy
> of embracing Acyuta
> attained through meditation,
> even their worldly happiness was lost.
> (RL 1.9–10)

The Gopīs referred to here are forced to turn inward due to their family circumstances, and it may appear as if this is their misfortune. However, Krishna himself coyly prescribes meditation (*dhyāna*) even to the maidens who have successfully united with him in the forest, in lieu of leaving their homes at such a questionable hour (RL 1.27).

The Vaishnava commentators from the Caitanya school make virtually no comment on the application of yoga in the devotion of the Gopīs. Perhaps an explanation for this is that the relationship of yoga to bhakti had been already established in the *Bhagavad Gītā,* and therefore within the minds of the traditional teachers. The *Yoga Sūtra* of Patañjali, the famous classical and comprehensive exposition on the practice and philosophy of yoga, also recognizes devotion to the deity within its prescribed practice; thus, the inclusion of yoga within bhakti and throughout the *Bhāgavata* text should not be surprising. In fact, the narrator of the Rāsa Līlā confirms that service to the feet of the supreme deity is achieved by the power of yoga: "They whose bondage to karma has been shaken off by the power of yoga are fully satisfied by humble service to the dust of the lotus feet of the Lord" (RL 5.35ab).

The meditation of the Gopīs who could not escape to the forest constitutes the penultimate step, called *dhyāna,* of the "eight-limbed" (*aṣṭāṅga*) system of yoga.[1] Meditation (*dhyāna*) is defined as "the single continuous movement [of the mind] toward an object," and in this case the object of the Gopīs' meditation is their beloved Lord, in whose beauty they revel unceasingly. It is through their meditation that they are able to overcome the pain of separation from Krishna (RL 1.10). The detained maidens then go on to further achieve the perfection of yoga as *samādhi,* the final step of the eightfold process of yoga, that is, meditation in its purest and deepest form.[2] Such meditation allows them to be "fully absorbed in love" as they are able to experience the "joy of embracing Acyuta" (RL 1.9–10). Although the *Yoga Sūtra* and *Bhāgavata* both promote loving meditation on a personal and worshipful deity, the *Bhāgavata*'s focus is especially on the beautiful and adorable attributes of God, the intimate deity, which effectively transforms *dhyāna* and *samādhi* into more spontaneous and erotically intense experiences within *bhakti.*[3]

Yoga is also used by the Gopīs as a threat directed toward Krishna in their songs of longing. The cowherd maidens boldly ask Krishna to "extinguish the fire burning within our hearts." They then threaten him with these words: "For if you don't, we shall place our bodies in the fire born of separation from you. Then, O friend, by means of meditation, we shall go to the abode of your feet" (RL 1.35). It is significant that some Gopīs choose to connect with Krishna by meditating on his beautiful form, even while in his presence:

1. The eight limbs of yoga are as follows: (1) *yama:* principles of self-restraint; (2) *niyama:* established observances; (3) *āsana:* physical postures; (4) *prāṇāyāma:* control over the breathing; (5) *pratyāhāra:* withdrawal of the senses from sense objects; (6) *dhāraṇa:* concentration; (7) *dhyāna:* meditation; and (8) *samādhi:* pure and total absorption (YS 2.29).

2. "The perfection of pure meditation is accomplished by devotional surrender to God" (*samādhi-siddhi īśvara-praṇidhānāt,* YS 2.45). See also other texts that emphasize the "self-surrender to God" (*īśvara-praṇidhāna*): YS 1.23, 2.1, and 2.32.

3. See YS 1.24, which equates *īśvara* ("the supreme Lord") with *puruṣa* ("the supreme Person"). Krishna, in the *Bhagavad Gītā,* declares that a yogi ultimately becomes a *bhakta* or devotee (BG 6.47). The cowherd maidens, however, have already perfected the process of yoga in their meditation on Krishna, and they resort to yoga as an expression of their intense love for him. Such practice does not merely legitimize the devotion of the Gopīs; the cowherd maidens utilize yoga as a technique for intimacy.

One of them took him
into her heart through
the aperture of her eyes;
then closing her eyes,
she embraced him within.
She became elated with
bodily ripplings of joy,
as the body of a yogi
is overcome with bliss.
(RL 4.8)

This verse makes it clear that yoga, in the devotion of the Gopīs, is used as a tool for love. All the cowherd maidens are effectively *yoginīs* of love, whose minds and hearts are ever fixed on their beloved Lord. Krishna is called, in several places throughout the drama, the "Lord of all masters of yoga," *yogeśvareśvara,* and the Gopīs are certainly such masters of yoga.

Whether the Gopīs attain Krishna's audience through appearing before him or through internal yogic meditation, the tradition understands this "new" body of each of the maidens to be a spiritual, perfected body (*siddha-deha*), a body that the devoted soul ultimately develops during the course of pursuing the process of bhakti.[4] It is in such a spiritual body that complete absorption in the service of the Lord becomes possible:

Within the mind of one whose
own body is spiritually perfect,
One contemplates day and night
the service of Krishna in Vraja.
(CC 2.22.157)

The development of a spiritual body does not, however, preclude the possibility of maintaining a physical body. In other words, it is plausible to remain in this world while living in a spiritual body. This is illustrated by the cowherd maidens who, at the end of the drama, re-

4. The process of bhakti has two general phases. The first is *vaidhī-bhakti,* "devotional love in the various forms of discipline"; and the second is *rāgānugā-bhakti,* "devotional love following the *rāga-bhaktas,* or pure spontaneous associates of the Lord," in which a spiritual body is said to develop. For a thorough treatment of *rāgānuga-bhakti,* see David L. Haberman, *Acting as a Way of Salvation: A Study of Rāgānugā Bhakti Sādhana* (New York: Oxford University Press, 1988).

turn to their homes. The tradition suggests that the life of a practitioner becomes this coalescence of the devotional body with the illusory physical body—performing in the world according to dharma, and simultaneously living in the devotional world of the heart.

Indeed, for the Caitanya school, meditation on the Rāsa Līlā enables the absorbed devotee to develop a spiritual form so that one is able to be even more fully immersed in devotion:

> For one who hears or one who recites [the Rāsa Līlā]—
> the benefit for such a person is
> Full absorption in love,
> serving [the Lord] day and night.
>
> What can be said of the benefit for such a person?
> It is simply impossible to convey.
> One is eternally perfect,
> and one acquires a perfect body.
>
> (CC 3.5.49–50)

Having acquired such a perfected spiritual body, the devotee is only concerned about devotional service, no matter where it may take place, in this world or the next. The desire to please the deity lifts the devotee from the world, even while living in it. The *Bhakti Sūtra* tells us that "the essential nature of devotional love is immortality" (NBS 3–4). In comparison, the biblical Song of Solomon informs us that "love is as strong as death."[5] In bhakti, however, it is clear that love is stronger than death, as it carries the soul beyond death, even while the soul is in the embodied state prior to death.

The Caitanya vision of death presents an understanding distinctly opposing that of the greater Hindu complex. The difference between the two could be described as death according to karma versus death according to *kṛpā;* or, death as the cumulative result of one's own actions and what one has earned (the traditional concept of karma), in contrast to death as a result of attracting God's grace (the Caitanya school's concept of *kṛpā*). The bhakti tradition puts forward a process that ultimately transcends any of the pan-Hindu requirements. This is possible because the very practice of bhakti is both intrinsically the means to liberation and itself constitutes liberation. Death, then, becomes a shift in location and does not consist merely of release from

5. Song of Solomon 8.4.

the world, as the devotee is already liberated from this world through his or her loving service to God (*sevā*).

Death is not merely an isolated incident at the end of one's life for which the devotee is preparing, nor is death any concern at all once the soul is absorbed in loving service to the deity. Like the Gopīs in their illusory bodies, the devoted soul is active in this world, and similar to the Gopīs in their devotional bodies, the devotee is all the while deeply fixing the mind and heart on God. The inner life of such a soul, then, allows one to be engaged in worldly affairs and, simultaneously, to be detached from such affairs, due to one's absorption in devotional love.

Both the cause and result of being so absorbed are the same—the singular attention of the devoted soul being fully directed to the supreme. The reward for such complete absorption is the absorption itself. The following sutra text is reminiscent of the Gopīs' devotion:

> Having attained devotional love,
> one sees only the Beloved,
> one hears only the Beloved,
> one thinks only of the Beloved.
> (NBS 55)

According to the *Bhagavad Gītā*, after obtaining such an elevated state of devotion, the soul is guaranteed to join the supreme upon departure from this world (BG 8.5). Thus it is the way of life that determines the outcome of death for the devotee, who, unlike the practitioner within the pan-Hindu context, does not consider the cause, time, and place of death, or other such externals. For the devoted soul, death is conquered within this life through deep absorption in the beloved object.

ETHICAL BOUNDARIES AND BOUNDLESS LOVE

We have already seen how the boundless love of the Gopīs causes them to cross bodily boundaries and manifest other types of bodies. Such boundless love also crosses social and ethical boundaries for both Krishna and the Gopīs. It is Krishna's identity as the divine lover of the cowherd maidens that raises the question of ethics. The Caitanya school considers the play of the amorous and erotic Krishna with Rādhā and her cowherd girlfriends as the ultimate display of pure love between the deity and devotee. At the same time, the divine cowherd is understood as the originator of all religious and ethical principles (*dharma*). Some scholars, even among specialists in the Caitanya tradition, have been confounded as to how God, the source of dharma, can also be the amorous deity whose affairs with the Gopīs can appear to be unethical.[6] Indeed, even the king to whom the story is narrated inquires from the narrator, Śuka, regarding this ethical question:

> How could he—the teacher,
> executor, and protector
> of the limits of dharma—
> O knower of Brahman,
> act in contrary ways
> by touching others' wives?
> (RL 5.28)

The answer to the king's question lies not so much in the narrator's direct response as in the divine identities of the hero and heroines and the dialogue that ensues between them.

Śuka, in short, states that great and powerful persons, not to mention the Lord, are exempt from the ethical norms of this world. A much more compelling argument that undergirds the complete story, however, may be that Krishna is the most intimate spouse or dearest friend of all living beings because, as the supreme Lord, he is the soul within all souls. In fact, there is at least one expression of this intimate presence of God in each act of the drama. The narrator recognizes Krishna as "the supreme Person who is present internally and externally for all living beings, as heavenly air pervades all beings, within and without" (RL 2.4). He also states that Krishna is "the true companion of all souls" (RL 4.13), and is the one who "dwells within the Gopīs and within their husbands" (RL 5.36). The Gopīs themselves describe their beloved as "the Witness residing in the hearts of all

6. Perhaps the most thoroughgoing scholarship on the Caitanya school has been presented by S. K. De, in his *Early History of the Vaiṣṇava Faith and Movement in Bengal* (Calcutta: Firma K. L. Mukhopadhyay, 1961). In this rich presentation of the historical, literary, and theological tradition, the one confounding factor for De was the question of ethics in relation to the tradition's erotic mysticism of Krishna. See the chapter "Ritualism and Devotional Practices," especially section three of this chapter, entitled "Ethics of Bengal Vaisnavism" (pp. 542–555). Also, see his criticism of Krishnadas Kaviraja's *Govinda Līlāmṛta* as an erotic text that ignores the ethical and presents what he describes as an "excessive load of sexual passion" (pp. 610–611).

embodied beings" (RL 3.4) and, in conversation with Krishna, acknowledge that he is "the dearest beloved of all living beings, the most intimate relation" (RL 1.32). A natural conclusion, then, is that Krishna, who resides eternally within the heart, is the true spouse of everyone. The cowherd husbands of the Gopīs, on the other hand, are temporary relations in this life, and therefore illusory. From this it could be argued that since Krishna is the intimate and eternal spouse of the maidens, the cowherd husbands are married to another's wife!

Throughout the *Bhāgavata Purāṇa,* we find that God, being omnipotent, is capable of embracing and transcending dharma at the same time. This ethical paradox is observable in the Rāsa Līlā in the apparently duplicitous, teasing words of Krishna to the Gopīs. Such words cleverly demonstrate how Krishna supports dharma in the everyday world and, simultaneously, passionate devotion in the transcendent world. Likewise, the greater *Bhāgavata* text maintains that normative social roles and identities leading one to the service of God should be preserved, and it also promotes a breaking away, an antithetical approach to social convention that is particularly notable with regard to the cowherd maidens of Vraja.

In the Rāsa Līlā, there is no better expression of the supreme Lord both maintaining and transcending dharma than in the third scene of act 1, when Krishna greets the Gopīs just after they have left their homes. Commentators delight in the double entendre of Krishna's words in several verses here, allowing him to both uphold and overlook dharma.[7] In the following verse, for example, Krishna attempts to "frighten" the Gopīs into doing the "right thing," while ostensibly offering protective words:

> Night has a frightening appearance;
> inhabiting this place are
> fearsome creatures!
> Please return to Vraja—
> women should not remain here,
> O ones with beautiful waists.
> (RL 1.19)

But commentators point out that the ways in which the Sanskrit words are combined in the above verse, as well as the varying ways

7. In order to understand further how, in Sanskrit, it is possible for a verse to possess opposite meanings, see "Notes and Comments" for these verses.

that negatives can be applied to particular words, can produce opposite meanings, which allow Krishna to suggest to the Gopīs that they *should* remain with him in the forest:

> Night is without a frightening appearance (*aghora-rūpa*);
> inhabiting this place are
> creatures that are not fearsome (*aghora-sattva*).
> Please do not return to Vraja (*pratiyata vrajam na*)—
> women should remain here (*iha stheyam*),
> O ones with beautiful waists.

A few verses later, Krishna seems concerned about the proper dharmic behavior for the cowherd maidens, which clearly would be to return to their families. He explicitly encourages them to be faithful to their dharmic duties:

> Please go to the village without delay!
> O chaste ladies, attend your husbands.
> Your calves and children are crying for you—
> you must go feed and nurse them.
> (RL 1.22)

This verse can also be interpreted, however, as Krishna attempting to persuade the Gopīs that there is no need for them to conform to dharmic obligations and, instead, to stay with him:

> Please do not go back right away
> to attend your husbands, O chaste ladies.
> Your calves and children are crying for others;
> you need not feed and nurse them.

Two verses later, Krishna further emphasizes to the Gopīs the importance of following dharma, by making a declaration of what their "highest dharmic" obligation (*parodharma*) is:

> For every woman the highest dharma (*parodharma*)
> is to serve her husband without falsity,
> Be agreeable toward his family members,
> and nourish the children.
> (RL 1.24)

Here again, there is a double entendre. Commentators point out that Krishna is also saying to the cowherd maidens:

> For the dharma of all other women (*parodharma*)
> is to serve false husbands . . .

In this instance, the word *parodharma,* instead of meaning "the highest dharma," is taken as "the dharma of other women," who Krishna claims are serving only "false husbands."[8] By implication, he is proclaiming himself to be the only true husband of the Gopīs. Thus, their highest duty or *parodharma,* which was initially understood in relation to their cowherd husbands, is now to be seen in relation to Krishna, their "true husband." In fact, the word *parodharma* refers to the highest dharma of loving devotion to God, or bhakti:

> The highest dharma (*parodharma*) for all humans is
> certainly devotion (*bhakti*) unto the transcendent Lord;
> It is selfless and unremitting, and it is that
> by which the self is most deeply satisfied.
>
> (BhP 1.2.6)

Here, the true meaning of *parodharma* is clearly defined by the *Bhāgavata* text itself, supporting the idea that the highest dharma is ultimately devotional love for the supreme Lord.

Following Krishna's playful words, the Gopīs, in response to his apparently duplicitous words, cleverly retort using his reversible logic to serve their own desires:

> O dear one, as you
> who knows dharma
> have stated,
> The proper duty for women
> is to be loyal to husbands,
> children and close friends.

8. The prefix *paro-* used with *dharma* in the first instance utilizes the sense of degree, that is, "the higher," or in the superlative sense, "the highest" (the latter sense of which is used throughout this study as meaning specifically bhakti, or devotion). In the second instance commentators also cleverly interpret the prefix in its sense of relation, that is, "other," "strange," or "different."

Let this dharma of ours be for you,
O Lord, since you are
the true object of such teachings.
Truly you are the dearest
beloved of all living beings,
the most intimate relation,
for you are the supreme Soul.
(RL 1.32)

It appears from this verse that for the maidens the idea of relinquishing normative social conventions is impossible to resist, since for them Krishna is the most beloved of all beings; therefore, an exclusive relationship with him would be fulfilling the highest dharma.

The passionate devotion of the cowherd maidens is clear. They are irresistibly drawn to their Lord, and certainly leaving their husbands along with all worldly dharmic duties is an expression of their passion and utter self-sacrifice for him. The humility of the Gopīs is also clear. They wish to follow their "true" dharma and submit themselves to Krishna, who is their "real" husband, thus relinquishing their "false" husbands. In so doing, however, their honorable social status could be destroyed by apparent dharmic transgressions. Traditional commentators interpret the cowherd maidens' apparent abandonment of family and social obligations as dharmic transcendence, and therefore find it to be not only acceptable but even highly desirable; whereas the *Bhāgavata* text is less willing to see the Gopīs' transgression as a transcendent movement crossing beyond dharmic boundaries. Instead, the *Bhāgavata* attempts to recover dharma and compensate for the subversive behavior of the maidens through Yogamāyā's arrangement of illusory bodies, which preserves their dharmic position in the home and yet allows for their ostensibly transgressive participation in God's *līlā*.

As we have seen, Krishna cleverly pacifies the husbands of the Gopīs while virtually borrowing their wives (RL 5.38), indicating that the Lord regards the upholding of dharmic obligations to be crucial, even if it is toward "false husbands" (RL 1.24). It is interesting that in the *Harivaṁśa* and *Vishnu Purāṇa* versions of the story, the cowherd maidens are *not* given duplicate forms by which their husbands at home would be pacified. The *Bhāgavata* distinguishes itself ethically by ensuring that the cowherd husbands remain satisfied, even while their wives are with Krishna for the night. This synthesis of dharma with *parodharma* preserves the ethical boundaries of dharma while giving full expression to the boundless love of the cowherd maidens.

The key to understanding the Caitanya school's approach to the *parodharma* of bhakti is found in the way it views the subordinate role of women, specifically the women of Vraja, within the ancient Indian social order known as *varṇāśrama.*[9] The position of women was somewhat removed from the laws of dharma, since their social identity was always in relation to a male's, whether it be a father, brother, or husband. That a woman did not possess a status of her own proved to be conducive to the life of devotion. Furthermore, her feminine nature was taken to be that of inherent humility and meekness in service to both the worldly male and the supreme "male," thereby satisfying dharmic obligations as well as transcending them.

The subservient, loving role of women is employed by the school as the model for illuminating and exemplifying the highest and most intense form of bhakti, demonstrated in the devotion of the Gopīs. Caitanya, who is Krishna himself, understood by his followers to be the embodiment of the love shared between Rādhā and Krishna, descended in order to experience the nature of the Gopīs' devotion, specifically that of Rādhā.[10] The description of such pure devotion, found in the *Bhakti Sūtra* of Nārada, presents the model of the Gopīs, who embody the humility of an eternal servant (*nitya-dāsa*) and the

9. The *varṇāśrama* consists of both *varṇa* and *āśrama.* This system has to do with four hierarchically arranged social-vocational strata of society, or *varṇas*, which, in ancient India, consisted of the educational class (*brāhmaṇa*) as the highest, the governmental class (*kṣatriya*), the business or agricultural class (*vaiśya*), and the working class (*śudra*). The four stages, or *āśramas*, of the life cycle began with the student stage (*brahmacārya*), then moved into the marital stage (*gṛhastha*), then the retired stage (*vanaprastha*), and finally the renounced stage (*sannyāsa*). The divisions of *varṇa* are often mistaken for the "caste system," which has to do with finer subdivisions or distinctions within each of the *varṇas*, known as *jāti* or "class," also translated as "caste," historically a much later development than the overall *varṇāśrama* system.

10. The divine identity of Caitanya is complex, and an elaborate theological discussion of this identity can be found in CC 1.4. Krishna not only appears as Caitanya to experience the superior love and intense feelings of the Gopīs or Rādhā, he himself is said to be the embodiment of the love between Rādhā and Krishna. The root cause of Krishna's appearance as Caitanya arises from his identity described in the significant phrase *rasika-śekhara,* the Lord as "the supreme connoisseur of divine relationships" (CC 1.4.103; also in CC 1.4.16, 1.7.7, 2.14–155, and 2.15.140). As the supreme Lord, Krishna must remain supreme in all ways, including his experience of love. However, when the Gopīs experience a love for him so much greater than his for them, he must take the form of Caitanya in order to attain the experience of his greatest devotees, the cowherd maidens. Krishnadāsa Kavirāja claims that Caitanya is the full *avatāra* of Krishna himself, who descends for two essential reasons: first, to experience the relationship of pure selfless love of God, *prema-rasa,* and second, to establish the religious path of spontaneous attraction to God, *rāga-marga* (CC 1.4.15).

passion of an eternal lover (*nitya-kānta*).[11] Caitanya, as the paradigmatic devotee, sets the stage for the school's ethics of devotion by desiring to become the humble servant of the servant of the servant of the lotus feet of the Lord of the Gopīs.

For the Vaishnava, then, the combination of humility and passion in devotion is an essential balance, exhibited by the Gopīs. The intimate deity is emphasized over the cosmic or almighty deity and yet, for the devotee, they are always experienced in dialectical tension with one another. Neither is excluded; rather, the one is implicitly or explicitly experienced while the other is in the background. The intimate deity inspires a passionate devotion, and the cosmic or powerful deity, a devotion of humility. The devotee "knows" the greatness of God, but due to being absorbed in devotional passion, appears to "forget" this dimension. With *parodharma* in the foreground, however, the devoted soul continues to apprehend, in the background, the ethical dimension of dharma that flows from the divinity.

Veneration and awe for the greatness of the deity create an atmosphere of deep reverence and humble admiration among followers; whereas intimacy with the divine elevates the devotee into a transethical sphere of love and amorous play with the Lord, as well as affectionate fellowship with other devotees. This intimacy is nowhere else demonstrated more dramatically than in the Rāsa dance itself, in which the Gopīs join hands in fellowship, and simultaneously, as individuals, interact exclusively and amorously with their beloved.

Although the Rāsa dance is the culmination of the drama, the Gopīs experience and express their most intense feelings for Krishna in his absence, specifically in the middle act, "The Song of the Gopīs." The greatest form of intimacy with the deity is understood by this school as *viraha-bhakti*, "devotional love in the experience of the absence of God." The *Bhakti Sūtra* describes *viraha*, out of eleven different types of loving attachment to God, as the highest process: "Devotion in separation from the Beloved is the highest devotion of all."[12] The Caitanya school not only accepts this statement but indeed models its devotion specifically on "the attainment of service in separation," known as *vipralambha-sevā*.[13] It is especially this type of loving service that balances humility and passion in devotion.

11. *Bhakti Sūtra,* text 66: "devotional love manifests as the self constantly devoted to God as an eternal servant and eternal lover. One should cultivate pure love, *premā,* for God, and pure love alone."

12. *Bhakti Sūtra,* text 82.

13. The literal meaning of *vipralambha-sevā* is "performing service (*sevā*) while having

In contrast, the intimacy of union with God, as we have seen in the fifth act, can lead to "forgetfulness" of the knowledge of God's greatness, causing humility to remain in the background of passion. Whereas when the Gopīs either anticipate or actually experience separation from Krishna, they are more conscious of his almighty attributes which, in turn, stimulates humility. At times though, even in Krishna's presence, the Gopīs, fearing separation, are humbled by his supreme status: "O unattainable one, do not reject us—accept us as your devotees just as you, the Lord, the original Person, accept those who desire liberation" (RL 1.31). Here the maidens, while present before their beloved, fear his rejection; in anticipation of Krishna's imminent absence, both their humility in service and passion in devotion are heightened (RL 1.38). Humility, then, intensifies passion, and conversely, passion augments humility.

Thus, the cowherd maidens exhibit the essential dynamic within bhakti: the experience of an ever-intensifying dialectical tension between the absence and presence of God exhibited in various phases of separation and union. It is precisely because of this dialectical balance that any concern about an excessive emotionalism on the part of practitioners is unfounded. Passion and humility synergistically combine in the hearts of the devoted followers of the Caitanya tradition, forming an axiological core of an ethics of devotion that is also embedded in the Rāsa Līlā text. These ethical dimensions have yet to be discovered and further illuminated by scholars both inside and outside the tradition.

THE VISION OF DEVOTIONAL LOVE

Toward the beginning of this study it was suggested that the Gopīs' love for Krishna could appear to be passionate and selfish in ways that mirror worldly relationships of lust and, perhaps surprisingly, that this is intentional on the part of the author. The Rāsa Līlā displays divine love while distinguishing it from worldly love, since the special nature of *līlā* is both playful and didactic. Although *līlā* is for the pleasure of Krishna and his devotees, and everything that occurs in *līlā* contributes to the delight and celebration of supreme love and beauty, there are aspects that also instruct those who have yet to enter into its esoteric domain.

---

attained (*lambha*) distance (*vipra*)." In the Caitanya tradition, distance or separation in divine love creates a most positive experience of union, paradoxically, and not the negative experience associated with the way lovers of this world agonize when apart.

The pure love of the Gopīs in *līlā* is therefore displayed in the drama, and the reader is simultaneously instructed about the impure love found in this world, love that is tainted by selfishness and pride.

The major lesson that the Rāsa Līlā offers, then, is on the nature of love. Krishna instructs the cowherd maidens about various types of pure and impure love, and we learn that he regards the Gopīs' love for him as perfect and unconditional (RL 4.20–22). Krishna's dalliance with the one special Gopī is meant to contrast love of God with the degraded love of this world that is exhibited in adulterous affairs (RL 2.34), and he teaches, through his sudden disappearance from the maidens, that God disappears from those whose love is mixed with pride (RL 1.47–48). In order to appreciate more fully the passionate love of the Gopīs and the difference between worldly and divine passion, we need to become aware of the nuances of words used throughout the drama to express love.

In Sanskrit, there are numerous words for "love," and the author of the *Bhāgavata* engages many of them in the Rāsa Līlā. The most frequently used words are those verbs and nouns derived from four verbal roots that essentially mean "to love": *prī-*, *bhaj-*, *kam-*, and *ram-*.[14] Words derived from the first two, *prī-* and *bhaj-*, carry the sense of a pure love, affection, or adoration—a selfless love untainted by desire or self-concern—resembling the Greek word *agapé*. Some meanings of words derived from the verb root *prī-* are to "love," "please," and "delight."[15] Senses of words coming from the verb root *bhaj-* are to "adore," "worship," and "reciprocate."[16] These words are associated

14. Other words meaning "love" also appear in the passage: *bhāvanā*, "love" (RL 1.9), "imitation" (RL 2.16), and "absorbed" (RL 2.44); *manmatha*, "amorous passion," which can also be a name for the god of love (RL 4.2); *anaṅga*, "love" (RL 1.4), another name for the god of love, literally, "the limbless one"; *aṅga*, "O dear one," literally, "O limb" (RL 1.32 and 1.40); *anuvṛtti*, "following," "acting suitably to," "having regard or respect," "the act of continuance," and "(true) love" (RL 1.32, 4.20, and 4.21); *sauhṛda*, "devotional affection" (RL 1.15), "endearment" or "endearing" (RL 4.17 and 4.18); and *vallabha*, "beloved" (RL 5.15).

15. Translations and forms of this root found in the episode are the following: *prīta*, "pleased" (RL 2.28 and 5.2); *prīti*, "affection" (RL 2.8 and 4.3); *premā*, "love" (RL 2.5, 3.10, 3.17, 4.6, 5.21, and 5.24); *preṣṭha*, "beloved" (RL 1.10, 1.30, and 4.3) and the superlative form, "most dear" (RL 1.32) or "darling beloved" (RL 2.39); *priya* (masc.) and *priyā* (fem.), "beloved" (this word for "lover," "beloved," or "dear," is the most frequently used among words of affection and love, appearing 26 times throughout the episode: RL 1.2 [twice], 1.13, 1.18, 1.28, 1.30, 1.33, 1.36, 1.43, 2.3 [twice], 2.7, 2.11, 2.12, 2.31-1, 2.32, 2.36, 2.38, 2.40, 3.10, 3.19, 4.21 [twice], 5.6, 5.9, and 5.39); *vipriya*, "unpleasant" (RL 1.28); *preyas* (the comparative of *priya*, "dearer," "a dear friend," or "lover"), "beloved" (RL 2.31-1 and 2.32); and the verbal forms *prīyatā*, "pleased" (RL 5.10) and *prīyante*, "being dear" (RL 1.23).

16. Forms and translations appearing in the Rāsa Līlā text are the following: *bhakti*, "devotion" (RL 5.40); *bhakta* (masc.) and *bhaktā* (fem.), "devotee" (RL 1.31) or "devoted one"

with a nonerotic, giving, and affectionate love that could be applied to a variety of love relations.

On the other hand, words derived from the second two verbal roots, *kam-* and *ram-*, carry the sense of passionate love, including sexual connotations. Meanings of words derived from the verb root *ram-* are to "delight," "please," and "enjoy sensually."[17] Some senses of words derived from the verb root *kam-* are to "desire," "long for," and "be enamored of"; and the noun *kāma*, prominent in the *Bhāgavata* text, means "pleasure," "lust," and "passion."[18] These words describe erotic love, love of passionate desire, and generally refer to the love within amorous relationships, much like the Greek word *eros.*[19]

From the meanings of words derived from these four verbal roots, we can understand that both pure and erotic senses of love are woven together throughout the Rāsa Līlā. The question remains, how does the boundless love of the Gopīs, who are overflowing with romantic desire and amorous affection, express the purity of love that the author of the drama claims they possess, and that many Vaishnava traditions honor and even celebrate? What is the relation of the erotic and passionate to the pure and selfless? In the last verse of the Rāsa Līlā episode, it is stated that *kāma* will be cleansed from the heart of a faithful soul (RL 5.40), yet the emotions and actions of the Gopīs in their love toward Krishna arise from *kāma* (RL 1.38). The Caitanya school has treated this apparent contradiction extensively.

The tradition's interpretation of the terms *kāma* ("passionate love") and *premā* ("pure love") is crucial for understanding the concept of selfless devotion. Krishnadāsa, in his work *Caitanya Caritāmṛta,*

(RL 5.37); and various verbal forms, *bhajatā*, "love" (RL 4.21); *bhajasva*, "please accept" (RL 1.31); *bhajanti*, "love" (RL 4.16 [twice], 17, 18, 19, 21); *abhajataḥ*, "love" (RL 4.16, 18, 19, 20); and *bhajate*, "accept" (RL 1.31), "honor" (RL 2.36), and "worship" (RL 5.37).

17. Forms and translations appearing in the Rāsa Līlā text are the following: the infinitive *rantum*, "to enjoy love" (RL 1.1); *rati*, "attraction" (RL 1.33), "love" (RL 1.46), "amorous" (RL 5.9 and 5.21), and "enjoyment" (RL 5.24); *ramaṇa*, "enjoyment" (RL 1.39), "darling one" (RL 2.39), and "charming lover" (RL 3.13); *ramayām*, "enjoying" (RL 1.46); *rata*, "enjoys" (RL 2.34); *reme*, "enjoying" (RL 5.9, 5.21, 5.17, 5.20, and 5.24); *surata*, "erotic love" (RL 3.2) and "amorous joy" (RL 3.13); and *saurata*, "sexual desire" (RL 5.26).

18. The idea of *kāma* is one of the "four aims of life," *puruṣārthas*, along with *dharma*, *artha*, and *mokṣa*. The word *kāma* can mean "desire or carnal gratification," "lust," "the god of love," or "the name of Baladeva, Pradyumna, and the Supreme Being" (VA).

19. The meanings of the verb *kam-* can be to "desire," "long for," and so on. Translations and forms of this root appearing in this passage are *kāma*, "desire" (RL 1.15, 1.38, 2.36, 3.5, and 3.13) and "lustfulness" (RL 5.40); *kānta* (masc.) and *kāntā* (fem.), "beloved" (RL 1.4, 2.31.b, 2.33, 3.5, and 3.11), "lover" (RL 5.15), and "desired one" (RL 1.12 and 2.11); *kāmin* (masc.) and *kāminyāḥ* (fem.), "the amorous one" (RL 2.31–2), "one desirous of love" (RL 2.33), and "lustful one" (RL 2.34).

applies these most widely used terms in order to distinguish between "worldly love" and "divine love." Perhaps the most concise explanation of the difference between the two is found in the fourth chapter of the Ādi Līlā:

> The desire to please one's own senses,
> in my opinion, is to be called *kāma.*
> The desire to please the senses of Krishna
> takes the name *premā.*
>
> (CC 1.4.165)

The distinctions between *kāma* and *premā* are even more sharply defined when *kāma* is compared to "blind darkness," and *premā* is compared to the "pure light of the sun" (CC 1.4.171).[20]

Generally speaking, the word *kāma* refers to love in the sense of worldly pleasure, and *premā* to love in the sense of spiritual pleasure. Krishnadāsa describes the Gopīs as the paradigmatic exemplars of *premā,* emphasizing the intention behind their love rather than the form in which the love appears:

> They [the Gopīs] give up everything
> for the sake of Krishna.
> The motive of their pure
> and passionate love
> is the happiness of Krishna.
>
> (CC 1.4.175)

This passage clearly indicates that the Gopīs' love is not tainted by any selfish concern. Krishnadāsa is careful to point out that the singular

20. The Caitanya school has a more limited or strict sense of the word *premā* than that demonstrated in the *Bhāgavata.* For the school, *premā* indicates only "spiritual" love. The love in *premā* occurs only between human and divine beings or between one divine personage and another, and therefore cannot be applied to the love between one human and another. In the *Bhāgavata,* however, the numerous applications of the word would suggest a much broader meaning.

The *Bhāgavata* applies this word *premā* in the sense of pure love to the conjugal relationships of this world (see BhP 3.23.5, 4.28.43, 6.19.17, 7.11.27, 9.18.20, 10.58.8, and 10.81.26). Paternal *premā* is found (see BhP 1.9.11, 4.9.43 and 48), and fraternal *premā* is also demonstrated (see BhP 4.20.18). A more carnal type of *premā* can be found (see BhP 4.25.25), which is unusual. A human's love for the earth can be expressed as *premā* (see BhP 4.18.28), and for an animal (BhP 5.8.21 and 10.13.35). However, *premā* is most commonly found in expressions of the soul's love for the deity (see BhP 1.8.45, 1.10.16, 9.10.38, 10.14.49, 10.15.20, 10.17.16, 10.38.36, 10.46.27, 10.55.39, 10.73.35, 10.84.66, and 18.85.38).

"motive" of the Gopīs is "the happiness of Krishna" (*kṛṣṇa-sukha-hetu*), even while they experience and express their amorous and passionate devotion to him. He finds a radical difference between the soul with selfish motives and the soul with no motive other than the intense desire to please God, and repeatedly contrasts the theocentric motivation of the Gopīs with the egocentric motivation characteristic of worldly love (CC 2.8.217). He states that the love of the Gopīs is naturally pure, not tainted by the impurities of *kāma*:

> The natural love of the Gopīs
> is without any trace of *kāma*;
> It is without fault,
> and it resembles the beauty
> and purity of molten gold.
> (CC 1.4.209)

The Gopīs "have achieved the perfection of loving service," for they have only Krishna as their desired object of love (CC 1.4.212).

The word *kāma* has for its most essential meaning simply "desire." Used in the contradevotional sense, the word has a selfish or self-serving objective, and thus Krishnadāsa calls it *prākṛta-kāma,* "worldly desire," which can be further understood as "lustfulness." The distinction between desire that is truly loving and the desire of lustfulness is again contrasted by Krishnadāsa:

> Therefore the happiness [of the Gopīs]
> nourishes the happiness of Krishna,
> Because there is no fault of lustfulness (*kāma-doṣe*)
> in the pure love of the Gopīs (*gopī-preme*).
> (CC 1.4.195)

The word *kāma* is not restricted, however, to a negative connotation. In fact, as it is applied to the Gopīs in the Rāsa Līlā, *kāma* can mean, paradoxically, "desire" that is "utterly unselfish" or "unself-serving," that is, "selfless." Thus, *kāma* indicates a force within humans that is either the path to worldly bondage and suffering or the path to liberation. It is plainly stated that the Gopīs "discarded all desires for his sake" (RL 1.30). Yet it is also explicitly stated, throughout the *Bhāgavata,* that the Gopīs attain liberation on account of their desire or *kāma* for Krishna (BhP 7.1.30, 31): "Those women [the Gopīs] who desired me (*mat-kāmā*) knew me as their amorous lover and paramour, although they did not know my true nature" (BhP 11.12.13ab).

It is interesting to observe the first instance of the word *kāma* within the Rāsa Līlā, found in the theological discourse of the narrator to his listener:

> Desire (*kāma*), anger, fear, and
> certainly loving attachment,
> intimacy, and affection
> Should always be directed toward Hari;
> by so doing, persons become
> fully absorbed in God.
>
> (RL 1.15)

Here, the positive engagement of *kāma* sharply contrasts with the negative application of the word generally found in the *Bhagavad Gītā,* where *kāma* designates an unfavorable state of being in which the soul is controlled by the three worldly forces, or *tri-guṇas.* In the seventh chapter of the *Gītā,* however, an exception is found in which Krishna declares, "I am *kāma*" (BG 7.12). This singular positive use of the word in the *Gītā* anticipates its more favorable usage in the Rāsa Līlā. Although the negative sense of *kāma* is also prevalent in the *Bhāgavata* text, the theme of directing all desire to God is clearly more prominent, thereby engaging *kāma* in a positive way. This is in contrast with the theme of transcending desire, which engages the unfavorable sense of the term that runs throughout the *Gītā.*

Favorable usages of *kāma* in relation to both Krishna and the Gopīs occur frequently in the Rāsa Līlā. It is said that Krishna fulfills all desires, *kāma-dam,* in the following line of a verse: "O beloved, please place on our heads your hand, beautiful as a lotus, that fulfills all wishes" (RL 3.5). And the cowherd maidens, who are "burning" with desire for their beloved Krishna, have all desires satisfied through serving him: "O jewel among men, please grant unto us whose hearts are burning with intense desire, inspired by your beautiful glances and smiles, the chance to serve you" (RL 1.38). Furthermore, not only do the Gopīs attain liberation by means of *kāma* but the various ways in which *kāma* manifests in their liberated state also becomes, for Vaishnavas, the model of passionate devotional love.

The word *kāma,* then, can mean "desire" in the neutral sense of being innately a part of the human character—desire that can be directed either to worldly pleasures or to the pleasure of the divine. When *kāma* is directed toward satisfying the self, it serves as a means of bondage to worldly existence; whereas when directed toward pleasing the divine, it serves as a means of liberation—and it can become the very expression of devotion even after one has attained the liberated state.

According to the Caitanya school, the word *kāma* can be understood as "divine passion" in those *līlās* of Krishna in which the Gopīs display an intensity of *premā*. The love of the Gopīs can appear in the form and image of *kāma* or worldly love, and thus the word can be used to describe certain aspects of *premā*, which, as we have seen, has the sole intention of Krishna's happiness:

> The love (*premā*) of the Gopīs is natural,
> it is not worldly love (*prākṛta kāma*).
> Because it [appears to be] the same
> as the activities of worldly love (*kāma-krīḍā*),
> I will refer to such activities by the term *kāma*.
> (CC 2.8.215)

Whatever emotionally charged expressions of love the Gopīs exhibit must be recognized, according to Krishnadāsa, as existing only for Krishna's pleasure. Indeed, if there is any happiness or pleasure on the part of the maidens, it manifests only to serve the happiness of their beloved. Krishnadāsa provides the principle for understanding what can appear to be excessive emotionalism on the part of the Gopīs:

> So whatever affection we observe
> in the Gopīs' own forms,
> Know for certain that it must be
> for Krishna only.
> (CC 1.4.181)

This verse describes Krishnadāsa's hermeneutic for appreciating the heightened emotionalism of the cowherd maidens to be utterly theocentric, and therefore pure and selfless. In such exemplary devotional love, the soul loses itself in the beloved object.

SYMBOLISM IN THE RĀSA LĪLĀ

The early twentieth-century theologian and comparativist Rudolf Otto states that the scholar of religion must find a religious tradition's "deepest and most characteristic element, as its peculiar and central idea—or better, as its peculiar gift, the last and highest good which it has to give to humanity."[21] The Rāsa Līlā, which carries the special message of supreme love, easily could be considered one of Vaishnavism's greatest gifts to the world. The Caitanya school speaks of the dynamic aspects of such devotional love in great detail. Although it is not within the scope of this study to review the sophisticated and elaborate theological analyses of Rūpa and Jīva Gosvāmins concerning devotion in its various stages, I would like to demonstrate briefly how the Rāsa Līlā story reveals eight distinct phases of supreme love.

In the development of the love of the cowherd maidens for Krishna these eight aspects can be observed, appearing in the acts of the drama as shown in table 2. The awakening stage of supreme love is symbolized by the Gopīs hearing the sound of Krishna's flute, and the stage of anticipation is represented when they run from their homes into the forest. The meeting phase is experienced during the time they achieve the presence of Krishna. The conflict stage manifests in the Gopīs' pride and in Krishna's disappearance; the phase of separation, in their search for Krishna in the forest; and the stage of loss, in their songs of longing and torment. The reunion phase occurs when Krishna rejoins the cowherd maidens, and finally, the phase of rejoicing in the triumph of love takes place when Krishna and the Gopīs perform the wondrous circle dance of the Rāsa.

Each of the eight phases constitutes a positive dimension of supreme love, no matter how devastating the phase may appear to be. I propose that these eight stages, in part or in whole, within the given sequence or even a different one, can be identified in the expressions of supreme love found in other mystical traditions as well, such as the Song of Solomon or even in the story of Jesus. While each phase is a

TABLE 2. EIGHT PHASES OF SUPREME LOVE WITHIN THE RĀSA LĪLĀ

Act 1	Act 2	Act 3	Act 4	Act 5
(1) Awakening (2) Anticipation (3) Meeting (4) Conflict	(5) Separation	(6) Loss	(7) Reunion	(8) Rejoicing in the triumph of love

21. Rudolf Otto, *India's Religion of Grace and Christianity Compared and Contrasted*, translated by Frank Hugh Foster (New York: Macmillan, 1930), p. 12.

constituent of supreme love, certain phases may be emphasized in a particular tradition; one aspect may be elevated above the others as its primary focus for contemplation and worship. For example, the phase of "loss" symbolized in the Cross, representing the crucifixion of Christ, has become the ultimate focal point of worship for Christians. This symbol, however, does not preclude the highly celebrated phase of rejoicing in the triumph of love, found in the resurrection of Christ.

Similarly, as we have seen, Vaishnavas honor the phase of "loss" demonstrated in *vipralambha-sevā* (literally meaning "the attainment of distance from the beloved in loving service") above all other phases, in the model of the grieving cowherd maidens in the second and third acts, after the disappearance of their beloved. The Caitanya school's emphasis on loss is especially demonstrated by the repetition of the climactic verse of the middle act (RL 3.19), which is found four times in the *Caitanya Caritāmṛta*—the only verse of the drama repeated so often in Krishnadāsa's work.[22] Clearly, the phase of rejoicing in love is also elevated, as symbolized by the wondrous circle of the divine Rāsa dance. Moreover, this final stage of triumphant love is represented in the worshiped images of Rādhā and Krishna, the focal point of liturgical practices for the Caitanya school, along with other Vaishnava sects.

The circle of the Rāsa, which represents the ultimate phase of supreme love, is known as the Rāsa Maṇḍala. The word *maṇḍala* means "circle" or "round," and comes from the verb root *maṇḍ*, which means "to adorn" or "to decorate." Various *maṇḍala* configurations and designs were incorporated in ancient sacrificial rites during the Vedic period because they were thought to be powerfully emblematic of the cosmos. Such configurations also functioned on a more internal level as an aid in various forms of yogic and tantric meditation, stimulating subtle energies within the body.[23] The *maṇḍala* of the Rāsa dance, however, is not made up of static or graphic geometric configurations. Rather, it is dynamic and ecstatic, its circle consisting of special souls dancing with the divinity, meditation upon which cultivates the innermost emotions of the heart.

22. These repetitions are evenly distributed throughout the work: CC 1.4.173, 2.8.219, 2.18.65, and 3.7.40. Out of the sixteen different verses of the RL quoted by Krishnadāsa, only one other is quoted even three times (RL 4.22).

23. See Mircea Eliade's relevant discussion on "Maṇḍala" in his work *Yoga: Immortality and Freedom*, translated from the French by Willard R. Trask (Princeton: Princeton University Press, [1958] 1969), pp. 219–227.

The Rāsa Līlā drama is famous for its *maṇḍala* of maidens, and we find the words describing the formation of this *maṇḍala* at the start of the climactic scene of the drama: "The festival of the Rāsa dance commenced with a circular formation of Gopīs" (RL 5.3) (see the frontispiece of this book). The scene depicting the Rāsa Maṇḍala, "the wondrous circle of the Rāsa dance," is to this day the most celebrated among all scenes from the story, and is widely presented in various art forms, dramatic performances, and poetic works.

According to Carl G. Jung, the *maṇḍala* is "an archetypal image whose occurrence is attested throughout the ages."[24] The *maṇḍala* is a God-image for Jung, and "signifies the *wholeness of the self.*"[25] Additionally, it serves as a threshold into the spiritual—thus Jung characterizes the *maṇḍala* as a "window on eternity."[26] The *maṇḍala* in the Jungian psychical context parallels the *maṇḍala* in the Vaishnava sacred literary context. Psychologically, the *maṇḍala* represents the fulfillment of the self as well as a window into the deeper recesses of the spiritual self. Similarly, the Rāsa Maṇḍala is the climactic event of the Rāsa Līlā, which in turn is the ultimate fulfillment of all scripture, and the *maṇḍala* also functions canonically as a window into the more esoteric *līlās* of Rādhā and Krishna.

The Rāsa Maṇḍala functions canonically in two primary ways: first, it is enthroned by other exoteric traditional works; and second, the *maṇḍala* itself enthrones even more esoteric works. It is enthroned by the encircling canonical literature as the ultimate revelation of the intimate deity. Imagine all the scriptural texts accepted by the Caitanya school being placed within the concentric *maṇḍala*-like arrangement of petals forming the whorl of a lotus flower—the outer leaves forming the foundational texts, and the inner circling petals, as they move closer to the center, enthroning the highest revelational text, the *Bhāgavata,* found in the very center of the flower. In the middle of this center pod are the Vraja *līlās* of the tenth book, at the heart of which is the Rāsa Līlā, the essence of which is the Rāsa Maṇḍala. This, then, is the exoteric arrangement of the Vaishnava canon (see figure 12).

The Rāsa Maṇḍala, which is the very center of the lotus and ultimate focal point of all exoteric scriptural texts, also serves to enthrone other more subjective, personal visions in literary works about the

24. C. G. Jung, *Memories, Dreams, Reflections,* recorded and edited by Aniela Jaffé, translated from the German by Richard and Clara Winston (New York: Vintage Books, [1961] 1965), pp. 334–335.

25. Ibid., p. 335. Italics are in original.

26. Ibid., p. 197.

intimate deity. The *maṇḍala* becomes the outer petals of another lotus, enthroning esoteric visions of Vraja *līlās*, especially those focusing on intimate *līlās* of the supreme Goddess, Rādhā, and her consort, Krishna. In many ways, the living tradition embodies these visions and develops them in a variety of cultural and literary productions. Utilizing the Rāsa Maṇḍala as the threshold into such esoteric expressions, pilgrimage dramas from Vraja introduce every dramatic performance of Krishna's *līlās* with a reenactment of the Rāsa Maṇḍala. These regularly performed plays are named after the Rāsa Līlā, and are known as *rās līlās.*[27]

In his study of such dramas, Norvin Hein states that the reenactment of the Rāsa dance is their "most sacred component" and "recurrent feature."[28] Such performances invoke this most exalted *līlā* in order to usher in a performance of any one of the numerous divine acts of Krishna.[29] When the Rāsa Līlā story itself is performed as a drama, it is known by the name *mahārās*, or "the great Rāsa dance."[30] Even the stage or the physical platform arena on which the dramas are enacted is often circular, and is called the *rāsmaṇḍal,* a name, adopted from the story, which describes the circle of dancers in the Rāsa dance.[31]

The pilgrimage performances of Vraja, then, initially invoke images of the Rāsa Līlā, yet go beyond the *Bhāgavata* by means of dramatic content into more esoteric realms. Hein explains that the literary source of the many dozens of dramatic themes enacted in these productions is indeed the *Bhāgavata,* though the dramas are

27. The spelling *rās līlā* is Hindi for Rāsa Līlā from the Sanskrit.

28. Norvin Hein, *The Miracle Plays of Mathurā* (New Haven: Yale University Press, 1972), p. 129. Hein states that "The analysis of a rāslīlā performance must begin with notice of its two radically different parts, the rās and the līlā. The rās portion, so named because its principal feature is the set of dances called the rās, is a ritual reenactment of the most sacred of all Kṛishṇaite stories, the incident of Kṛishṇa's dance with the gopīs. . . . Thus we have in the rāslīlā a coupling of an enactment of the moonlight dance of Kṛishṇa with a dramatization of some other deed of his" (pp. 142–143). Hein presents ten various segments within the Rāsa dance as "(A) The open circle (B) The closed circle (C) The mimicking of Kṛishṇa (D) The three hops (E) Kṛishṇa's solo dance on his knees (F) The adjusting of Rādhā's ornaments (G) The promenade (H) The whirling of partners (I) The dalliance of Rādhā and Kṛishṇa (J) The clapping circle," pp. 145–147.

29. Hein states that "the number of distinct *līlās* which are played by the troupes of Braj probably approaches 150" (ibid., p. 154).

30. For a transcription of a *mahārās* performance, see chapter 4, "The Great Circle Dance," in *At Play with Krishna: Pilgrimage Dramas from Brindavan,* by John Stratton Hawley in association with Shrivatsa Goswami (Princeton: Princeton University Press, 1981), pp. 155–226.

31. Hein, *Miracle Plays of Mathurā,* p. 137.

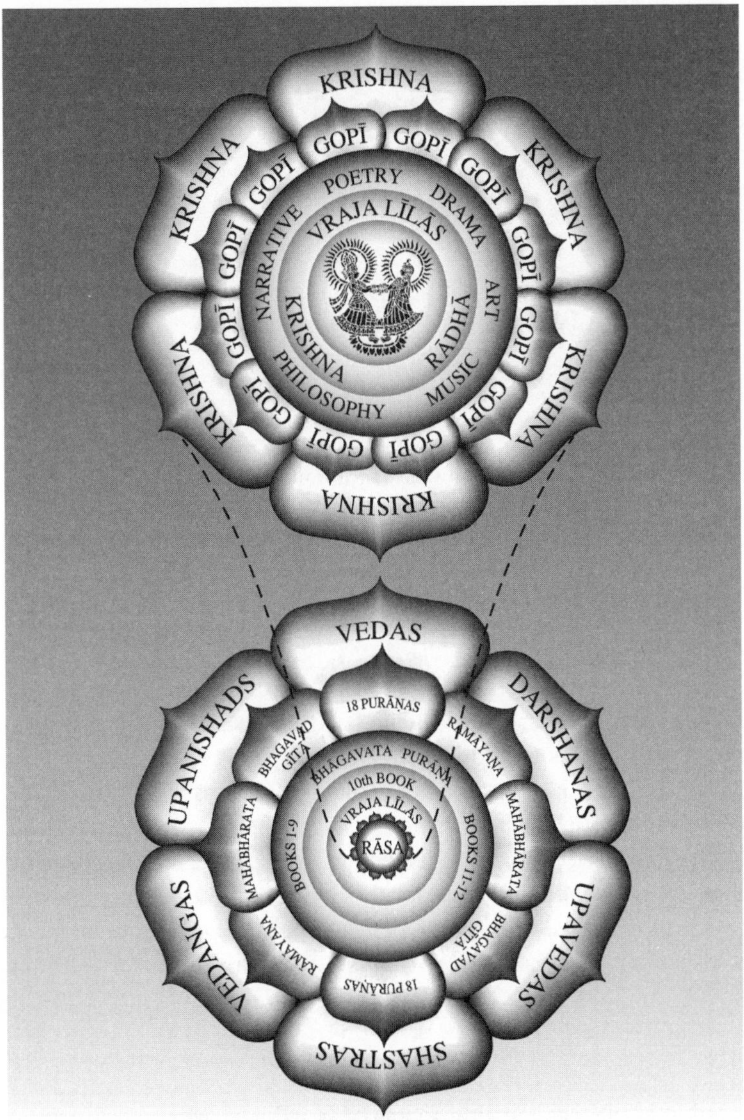

Figure 12. Rāsa Līlā at the heart of all exoteric literature (lower *maṇḍala*) and Rāsa Līlā as the window into esoteric visions (upper *maṇḍala*). Graphic art by Gregory Golem.

Figure 13. Young boys play the parts of the cowherd maidens dancing in the circular Rāsa dance around Krishna in a Vraja drama troupe performance. Photograph courtesy of Robyn Beeche, Sri Caitanya Prem Samsthan, Vrindāvana.

often based on the poetry and song of bhakti poets, who have derived their inspiration from the *Bhāgavata*.[32] In addition, there is a large body of literature that retells, embellishes, or reminisces about the specific story or particular themes of the Rāsa Līlā.[33] Like Indian music that begins with a basic melodic formula known as *rāga*, in which the musician expands upon and develops his piece from a single formulaic melody line, so, on the stage, a performance introduced by the Rāsa dance "borrows" its theme from the greater *Bhāgavata* or the Rāsa story itself and develops the theme in its retelling.

As the *maṇḍala* of the Rāsa dance enthrones pilgrimage dramas, it also poses as a calendrical *maṇḍala* that introduces the autumn

32. Ibid., p. 157.

33. To name just a few, the work entitled *Aścarya Rāsa Pravandha* ("The Story of the Marvelous Rāsa Dance"), by Prabodhānanda Sarasvatī, who lived around the time of Caitanya or perhaps just after him in the sixteenth century, is a work that retells the various scenes of the Rāsa Līlā with great poetic detail. Rāmānanda Rāya, a contemporary of Caitanya, writes a drama that is his own re-vision of the Rāsa Līlā drama, known as the *Jagannātha Vallabha Nāṭaka*. And in his retelling of key Vraja *līlās* in *Ānanda Vṛndāvana Campu*, Kavikarṇapūra of the sixteenth century devotes much attention to his own retelling of the Rāsa Līlā toward the end of the work. Krishnadāsa Kavirāja Gosvāmin does the same in his *Govinda Līlāmṛta*, supplying in some cases exquisitely detailed embellishments on the Rāsa story, even a technical discussion on the types of music being sung during the Rāsa dance. There are many others, too numerous to list here. A modern retelling of the tenth book of the *Bhāgavata*, including the Rāsa Līlā chapters with interwoven commentary, is *Kṛṣṇa: The Supreme Personality of Godhead*, by A. C. Bhaktivedanta Swami.

month known as Kārttik, the most sacred month of the Vaishnava lunar calendar. This month is ushered in on a special holy day that commemorates the Rāsa dance, a day when the full moon rises as it does in the Rāsa Līlā story. Another example of the *maṇḍala* acting in the life of the practitioner is found in the recitation of the divine names in the form of the *mahāmantra*, "the greatest (*mahā*) prayer-formula (*mantra*) for deliverance." This mantra is virtually a sonic reenactment of the Rāsa Maṇḍala, consisting of a series of alternating names of God in the vocative case, both calling out for and praising the presence of the divine. When the mantra is recited repeatedly in meditation or song, it worshipfully enthrones the Soul of the soul within the heart of the devotee, forming a sonic *maṇḍala*.

The circuitous arrangement of the words of this *mahāmantra* consists of an alternating pattern between an equal number of feminine (as *hare*) and masculine (as *kṛṣṇa*—the transliterated form of the name Krishna—and as *rāma*) names of the divine. The sacred thirty-two-syllable *mantra* appears as follows: *hare kṛṣṇa / hare kṛṣṇa / kṛṣṇa kṛṣṇa / hare hare / hare rāma / hare rāma / rāma rāma / hare hare.* The patterned movement of eight pairs of feminine and masculine names of the divine can be observed in the mantra. Within four of the pairs (the first, second, fifth, and sixth) the feminine and masculine names appear alternately. In the other four pairs (the third, fourth, seventh, and eighth) two masculine names appear together in one pair, followed by two feminine names in the next pair. Thus the dancelike movement can be observed both within and between pairs. Additionally, the mantra begins and ends with feminine names, enclosing the masculine names, just as the Gopīs engulf Krishna when they encircle him during the commencement of the Rāsa dance. When practitioners recite the mantra over and over, the divine names form a circular pattern imitative of the exchange between the feminine and masculine partners in the Rāsa dance. It can be seen, then, that the presence of the Rāsa Maṇḍala is archetypal in Vaishnava practices.

The Rāsa Maṇḍala is a symbol of supreme love for those traditions that honor the *Bhāgavata*'s Rāsā Līlā as their highest revelation. The question arises—can this symbol speak to those beyond the boundaries of its tradition to communicate a universal message? All symbols derive their power and depth of meaning from the tradition out of which they come. But there is a certain point at which a symbol bursts through the boundaries of its own tradition and culture, and begins to speak to the greater human community. As a symbol once enclosed within its limited realm moves beyond itself, its ultimate intrinsic value takes on an extrinsic purpose.

The Rāsa dance is perhaps one such symbol. The cowherd maidens linking arms in the dance represent the linking of human hearts and the solidarity of the human community of devoted souls. All souls, collectively, are invited to dance together with God, while simultaneously each individual soul is able to dance with God personally and exclusively. The Rāsa dance symbolizes the humility and passion of the devoted soul—the humility of love expressed through linking with other human beings, and the passion of love through souls linking with the supreme. This linking is the meaning of yoga, of which, as we have seen, the Gopīs are masters.

The divine circle of the Rāsa dance could be seen as symbolizing a genuine religious pluralism in which human beings of different faiths can love God, or the divine, in joyous harmony, and individually, as each soul receives God's singular and superlative attention. Diana L. Eck sees the Rāsa Līlā as presenting a symbol of supreme love when she states that the theological message of the story is essentially "God's infinite capacity to love."[34] Her statement is supported by her observation that "there was plenty of Krishna to go around, an abundance of Krishna's presence."[35] Thus, it is only after devoted souls come together to surround the divinity in a great circle, their arms linked in affectionate fellowship, that the deity agrees to connect personally with each soul—implying that God is indebted toward those who bond with other souls for the purpose of honoring, serving, and loving him.

Ontologically speaking, it is impossible for a finite being to possess the infinite. It is plausible, however, according to Vaishnava teachings, not only for a soul to possess God but also for God to be conquered by a soul with a pure devotional heart. The idea of the soul's love conquering God is presented by the *Bhāgavata:* although the Lord is unconquerable by anyone in all the three worlds, he is conquered by those who are devoted to him (BhP 10.14.3). Moreover, it is significant that Krishna's bluish complexion appears to change to green, "like a magnificent emerald," as he consorts with the Gopīs in the Rāsa dance (RL 5.7). The Gopīs' love is so powerful that Krishna's color changes, signifying that he is conquered by their love.

34. Diana L. Eck, *Encountering God: A Spiritual Journey from Bozeman to Banaras* (Boston: Beacon, 1993), p. 47.

35. Ibid., p. 46.

Jīva Gosvāmin, in his theological work, presents many verses from the Rāsa Līlā, especially from the second scene of the fifth act, that further demonstrate how the love of devoted souls can control God.[36] Viśvanātha Cakravartin also sees the Rāsa Līlā as expressing this power of the soul's love by stating in his commentary: "the Rāsa Līlā is the loving smile of the intimate devotee of the Lord, the most victorious, praised for the ability to bring Krishna under control" (SD 5.40). What is more, traditional commentators speak about how divine possessiveness is desirable and considered a special form of grace. Possessiveness out of love for the beloved object, completely devoid of worldly pride, jealousy, and self-interest, arises from devotional passion and pure love. But possessiveness tainted with pride and self-concern can lead to destructiveness and take one away from God's love.[37]

In the Rāsa dance, this possessing of God represents one of the greatest miracles of divine love. Eck, however, explains that: "the moment the milkmaids became possessive, each thinking that Krishna was dancing with her alone, Krishna disappeared." This statement appears to represent a misreading of the text, and perhaps misses an essential message of the Rāsa dance—when the Gopīs experience Krishna's exclusive attention, this is presented by the author of the text as a wonderful achievement. Eck seems to confuse this positive exclusivity or possessiveness of divine love occurring in the beginning of the fifth act with the apparent egocentrism of the Gopīs found at the end of the first act:

> Thus those who received honor
>   from the Beloved Lord,
>   Krishna, the great Soul,
> Thought themselves the best
>   among all women in the world—
>   they then became filled with pride.
>
> (RL 1.47)

36. In PrS 130, Jīva quotes RL 1.1 and 42, as well as RL 5.17, 21, 22, and 24 as examples of how Krishna is controlled by his devotee. See PrS 295–299 for further discussion on how the different types of intimate devotees control the Lord. Jīva states that the ability to control God by love is also available in other *rasas,* not just the *rasa* of passionate love. See PrS 127–129.

37. For more discussion on the idea of divine "possessiveness" and related ideas, see "Notes and Comments" for verses RL 2.28, 2.38, 2.41, 4.6, 4.22, 5.24, and 5.40.

From this verse, it could be understood that at the precise moment one insists on having a relationship with the divinity while excluding other souls, one loses God's favor. Krishna vanishes from the Gopīs only when they feel themselves to be the best women in the world, although, as he explains to the maidens, they were never out of his sight (RL 4.21). The lesson here is that our vision of God is lost when we become self-interested, though as we are told, we are never lost to God's vision. It is not possessiveness or jealousy that consumes the Gopīs; rather, it is pride, the setting of themselves apart from others and a corresponding lack of humility.[38]

Furthermore, in the *Bhāgavata* text, Krishna does not leave the Gopīs during the Rāsa dance, as Eck implies. Indeed, it is the Gopīs who return to their homes and take Krishna's leave at the end of this timeless and magical night:

> During the sacred hour before dawn,
> at the end of the night of Brahmā,
> and with the consent of Vāsudeva,
> The Gopīs returned to their homes,
> though reluctantly
> for they so loved the Beloved Lord
> and they were so loved by him.
> (RL 5.39)

Thus, the dance lasts an entire "night of Brahmā" which, in cosmic terms, is equivalent to at least 432,000,000 human years!

AMONG ALL SCRIPTURAL TEXTS of India, originating with the Vedas, the Rāsa Līlā episode becomes the most important revelation of supreme love. As a story, the Rāsa Līlā has a beginning and an end. As a sacred love story, however, it is the timeless dance in which God and the soul lose themselves forever in the rhythms, melodies, and movements of divine love. The drama of the Rāsa is a celebration of souls joining together to glorify God's unlimited power to love, and further, of God's capacity to love each soul intimately.

38. Eck makes the following compelling statement: "The point is one that speaks to us all: The moment we human beings grasp God with jealousy and possessiveness, we lose hold of God. One might add that the religious point here is quite the opposite of God's jealousy, of which we hear so much in the Old Testament; it is God's infinite capacity to love and the problem of *human* jealousy" (*Encountering God*, p. 47).

We have seen in the Rāsa drama that the hero and heroines are not ordinary—indeed, they are explicitly and eloquently described as extraordinary. The language and tenor of the text also reveal this love story to be otherworldly, yet it speaks personally to us in this world. The traditions that honor the story make the claim that all love is but a spark of the archetypal fire of the Rāsa's divine love, and it is by hearing or reciting the Rāsa story that we too will go beyond the spark to be consumed by this fire of Love. In the West, the famous words of the Latin poet Virgil resonate even today: "Love conquers all things; we too should surrender unto Love."[39] Viśvanātha Cakravartin, in his final comment on the Rāsa story, seems to answer Virgil's calling when he proclaims, "Indeed, we have thus become conquered by pure love."[40]

Among sacred love stories of the world, the Rāsa Līlā is prominent. Other such stories are necessarily allegorical in order to be valued as sacred. In this regard, the Rāsa Līlā appears exceptional. It has been demonstrated how the dramatic story presents rich poetry and deep symbolism, but it is also much more than this. Its text is understood as the ultimate revelation of divine love that becomes the window into esoteric visions of the very center of the godhead—the love between Rādhā and Krishna. This love of the divine couple becomes a song, as well as a dance, and the reader is invited to join the celebration, along with the chorus of celestial singers. In fact, Caitanya himself inquires, "Among all songs, which song is the very essence of the soul?" Rāmānanda replies, "That which is about the loving encounters of Rādhā and Krishna—this is the inmost heart of all songs" (CC 2.8.250). Thus, the Rāsa story can truly be called the song of songs of India.

Divine love, as we have seen, is a type of eternal dance in which souls continually move toward and apart from God within the various phases of love—love that is ever-increasing in intensity, at every moment. The culmination of these phases is the dance itself, the festive exultation of supreme love that is ever beckoning all souls to join in the triumph of divine love. The hearts of those who are already a part of the dance, for whom passionate and exclusive intimacy with God is already attained, melt with compassion for those who have not yet arrived, and yearn for all to delight in the dance of divine love.

39. *Omnia vincit amor, et nos cedamus amori* (Eclogues X.1.69).
40. *premnā jitā evābhūmeti,* SD 5.40.

Figure 14. A young boy in elaborate costume playing the part of Krishna for a Vraja drama troupe. Photograph courtesy of Nityatripta Devi Dasi.

Part III

NOTES AND COMMENTS

Introduction

The notes and comments are intended to furnish the specialist as well as the general reader with additional literary and philosophical information on the Rāsa Līlā text by focusing on the meanings and analyses of particular verses. This section of the book assumes that the reader will have already been exposed to earlier discussions on verses and ideas in the introductory and textual illuminations portions of this work, and therefore these previous discussions will generally not be repeated here. I will also present the various interpretations on the text by key teachers of the Caitanya school. Some of the dramatic and poetic features found within each act of the Rāsa Līlā are provided in an introductory note that precedes the comments on individual verses of each act.

The general format of the notes is to list, under each verse commented upon, some broader observations and more specific notes concerning meanings, definitions, and alternate translations of certain words or phrases found within the verses. The notes also provide preferred senses of words according to traditional commentators from within the Caitanya sect. Additionally, the esoteric vision of these teachers on particular verses is presented, and there are interesting concepts for which I will provide some extended comments and analyses for further clarification.

The sheer quantity of traditional commentarial writing from the Caitanya school of Vaishnavaism related to this specific text is too vast to present here. The direct commentaries of the school on the *Bhāgavata Purāṇa* are too numerous, not to mention the indirect commentaries, works written about or related to the *Bhāgavata*'s Rāsa Līlā. Although I have relied on many commentaries to guide my translation and illumination of the Rāsa Līlā text, I present here only selected comments from the most important direct and indirect traditional commentaries as their words can further illuminate the meanings of the text.

There are several works from which I have drawn for writing and assembling these notes and comments. I first draw from the *Bhāgavata*'s original commentary predating Caitanya, known as the *Bhāvārthabodhinī*, by Śrīdhara Svāmi (fourteenth century), since later commentators of the Caitanya school rely upon and react to his work, which they regard as authoritative. Śrīdhara is generally accepted as the venerable and original commentator of the *Bhāgavata*, and Caitanya himself, as depicted in his biography, insists that Śrīdhara's work be consulted first when commenting upon the *Bhāgavata* text (CC 3.7.113–116 and 133). I have consulted the works of Rūpa Gosvāmin (fifteenth century), especially *Bhaktirasāmṛtasindhu* and *Ujjvalanīlamaṇī*, but engage these less often in the notes and comments than other texts. Particularly noteworthy is the work of Jīva Gosvāmin (sixteenth century). I have relied heavily on his *Bhakti* and *Prīti Sandarbhas*, and at times some of his other *Sandarbha* texts, as well as his direct commentary on the *Bhāgavata*, *Krama Sandarbha*. Additionally, the great biography of Caitanya and perhaps the most important theological treatise of the Caitanya school, the *Caitanya Caritāmṛta* by Krishnadāsa Kavirāja Gosvāmin (sixteenth century), has been greatly utilized here. The other commentarial work on which I have depended extensively is the *Sārārtha Darśinī* of Viśvanātha Cakravartin (seventeenth century). At times, rather than acknowledge the particular text from which information is derived, I will simply use the name of the commentarial author of the work. This applies only to the direct commentarial texts of Śrīdhara (BB), Jīva (KrS), and Viśvanātha (SD). Other primary works have been consulted from which I have drawn information found in these notes and comments, and many of these are listed in the bibliography.

Act One

The drama commences with an act that presents the "opening scene" (*mukha-sandhi*) comprising the first eleven verses, presented in the narrative voice. The narrator immediately and boldly introduces Krishna, the hero or leading figure (*nāyaka*), in the first verse. Here, the narrator suggests the purpose of the drama (*arthopakṣepaka*) when Krishna "turns his mind toward love's delights." The Gopīs, his leading counterparts (*nāyikās*), are gradually introduced from the first verse on, almost imperceptibly. The cowherd maidens are subtly presented by way of metaphor in the initial verse, then in the third verse, as "fair maidens with beautiful eyes" who become mesmerized by the sound of Krishna's flute, and again in the fourth verse, as those who run off to be with their beloved Lord. The momentum of the scene intensifies as these ladies abandon their dharmic duties, even their physical bodies, and hastily leave for the forest. By the scene's end, the Gopīs fully blossom in the presence of Krishna.

This opening scene also hints at some of the elements of a "prologue" (*prastāvanā*) that develop more fully in the second scene. Natural beauty is celebrated in the first three verses in a kind of poetic invocation (*nāndī*) that commonly occurs in prologues. Thus, the descriptions of jasmine and night-blooming lotus flowers glowing in the dark forest, the rising of the full autumn moon, and the horizon splashed with reddish-colored moon rays all invoke auspiciousness. This rich poetic imagery and metaphor become a form of praise (*prarocanā*) for the time and place of the drama, as well as the drama's theme of love. When descriptions of the season and natural setting are used to exemplify actions or characteristics of the hero and heroines, another quality of dramatic prologue emerges (*pravartaka*), as vividly demonstrated in the second verse:

Then the moon,
  king among stars, arose,
spreading soothing reddish rays
  over the face of the eastern horizon;
Dispelling the sorrow
  from those who looked on,
As a lover caresses his beloved's blushed face,
  consoling her after long separation.

Both the opening scene and prologue-like beginning are imbued with an erotic tone (*śṛṅgāra-rasa*) that is to pervade the whole drama—a heavenly erotic tone, not to be mistaken for worldly romance. A challenging question from the primary listener of the narration, the king, ushers in the second scene, interrupting the narration launched in the first scene with a brief, clever dialogue (*āmukha*), another feature common to dramatic prologue. This theological discourse further enlightens the reader as to the transcendent character of the hero and heroines of the story, thus establishing their divine status and the special nature of this love affair.

As Krishna greets the Gopīs who have arrived in the forest, a dialogue ensues between them in a "progressive scene" (*pratimukha-sandhi*) that furthers the theme of the opening scene. In this third scene (RL 17–41), Krishna first speaks to the cowherd maidens in a stream of ten terse verses. Greeting them with politeness and aloofness, he inquires from them as to their purpose in coming to the forest so late at night. In flowery language (*puṣpa*) that is filled with poetic double entendre (*śleṣa-alaṅkāra*), Krishna cleverly presents reasons why the Gopīs should promptly retreat to their homes, while urging them, at the same time, to remain with him in the forest. The maidens respond to Krishna's requests emotionally, in eleven longer, embellished verses of the *vasantatilakā* meter, pleading with him to allow them to stay. They express torment (*tāpana*) at the idea of returning home after they have sacrificed so much. With rational argument (*upanyāsa*), they point out that Krishna is the source of all laws of dharma, and insist that it would not be an ethical transgression for them to remain there with him.

The fourth and final scene of this first act is a narration of only seven verses (RL 42–48). The dialogue has ended and Krishna enacts playful activities with the Gopīs that cease when he abruptly disappears from them, because they have become prideful of the attention he has given them. Characteristic of this type of "developmental scene" (*garbha-sandhi*) is attainment and nonattainment of a particular goal; in this case, the maidens had attained Krishna's attention, but then lost it due to becoming "intoxicated with their good fortune."

Verse 1.1

It is customary for traditional writers and commentators from the devotional-theistic school of Caitanya to begin their writing with words of praise for God, for significant teachers, and for the subject matter of their work. By so doing, writers offer their ideas with confidence, because they feel that their praise is reciprocated by blessings from these divine sources of guidance, which they need in order to present words that are truly enlightening, endearing, and lasting. Commentaries open with devotional words of acknowledgment, not only as an entrance into the topic at hand but also, and especially, as a form of verbal worship, since the words function as such when reactivated by the reader. The five chapters of the Rāsa Līlā are hardly the beginning words of the *Bhāgavata;* indeed, the story appears in the 230th chapter of this very long text consisting of 335 chapters—a little over two-thirds of the way into the work. Yet commentators are compelled to offer words of praise for this unique five-chapter story, demonstrating how the Rāsa Līlā has ultimate significance as a special, independent story within the greater *Bhāgavata.*

Following this tradition, Viśvanātha Cakravartin, in his opening remarks to the Rāsa Līlā, offers words of honor and worship. First, he offers respects to his immediate spiritual teacher, then to a teacher preceding his own, next to Caitanya, the founder of the school, and finally to Krishna himself, regarded as the ultimate spiritual teacher. His respects are also offered to the sage Śuka, the narrator of the *Bhāgavata.* Viśvanātha offers himself and his life to the almighty deity, "the darling of the cowherd maidens," for whom he hopes to be able to perform service. He states that the five chapters of the Rāsa Līlā of Hari can be compared to the five vital life-airs of the body.[1] Finally, he states that this story is the prize jewel among the treasury of all *līlās,* and praises the Rāsa dance itself. Later, he repeats praise for this *līlā* by stating that it is "the crown-jewel of all divine acts," *sarva-līlā-cūḍa-maṇi.*

1. These life-airs function in various ways throughout the body: *prāṇa* (ascending breath from the navel, for inhalation and exhalation); *apāna* (breath associated with the lower half of trunk); *vyāna* (diffuse breath circulating in all the limbs); *udāna* (the "up-breath" in *cakra* centers, associated with speech and with higher states of consciousness); and *samāna* (breath in the abdominal region, associated with the digestive process).

Teachers of the Caitanya school describe the divine acts of the supreme deity as being of three types. When these acts demonstrate God's power and might, and are cosmic or ontological in nature, they belong to the category of *aiśvarya-līlā*. When the acts are centered upon the deity's compassion for souls and his protection of them from demonic forces, they are called *kāruṇya-līlā*. And when the divine acts are tender and intimate, even amorous or passionate, they are in the category of *mādhurya-līlā* (PrS 158). Jīva Gosvāmin states that Krishna's *mādhurya* nature can be observed in the first verse. He goes on to say that this verse demonstrates the power of love in its beginning stages, known as *pūrva-rāga*. The power of love facilitated by Yogamāyā is meant to allow Krishna to fulfill the unlimited spiritual desires of the numerous cowherd maidens (PrS 296–297).

Śrīdhara summarizes the story line of the act, and presents his dramatic explanation that Kandarpa, the worldly god of love, had become too proud upon conquering elevated beings such as Brahmā, the god of creation. He goes on to say that Krishna "destroys the pride" (*darpahā*) of Kandarpa (or *kandarpadarpahā*, "destroying the power of the force of lust"), and then praises Krishna as he appears in the Rāsa Līlā: "All praise is given to the Lord of the Goddess Śrī, decorated by the wondrous circle of cowherd maidens in the Rāsa dance" (*jayati śrīpatir gopī-rāsa-maṇḍala-maṇḍanaḥ*). Śrīdhara acknowledges that it may be questioned how the story can be presenting a victory over the god of love, even though the Rāsa Līlā itself includes Krishna's rendezvous with others' wives. In contrast, he claims that there are many passages in the story that confirm Krishna's divinely independent and aloof status (RL 1.1, 1.42, and 5.26). The paradox of Krishna's apparently erotic interests juxtaposed with statements expressing complete detachment therefore points to a special kind of love, a theme that is pursued throughout the story. Śrīdhara insists, then, that this story announces Krishna's complete victory over Kandarpa, and the *līlā* also serves as a declaration of conquest over Cupid. He writes that the purpose of these five chapters is to demonstrate renunciation, although such purpose is perhaps disguised by the amorous love story (BB).

The romantic tone of the story is established in this first verse. Theorists of classical Sanskrit dramaturgy colorfully describe the very first indication of the plot as a "seed" (*bīja*), planted at the beginning (*ārambha*) of the drama. The function of this seed parallels that of the well-known invocative seed (*bīja-mantra*) of the sacred syllable "om" (or "aum") known as *oṁkāra*, found as the first utterance in many sacred hymns and texts, which invokes auspiciousness and blessings; thus, it is understood as preparing the atmosphere with an elevated level of sanctity. As "om" is said to symbolically represent the whole of the universe in its seed sound, so this verse presents the *bīja* of the Rāsa Līlā, from which the essential theme and principal elements of the drama sprout into the drama as a whole.

An indication of the central theme is present in "love's delights." The *kārya,* or ultimate object of the plot is the celebration of love between the hero and heroines of the story as they come together at the end of the story to consummate (*phalāgama*) their love, expressed in the Rāsa dance. In this verse, the *prayatna,* or the means by which the Beloved Lord can achieve his goal, is presented: he takes full refuge in the power, Yogamāyā, who arranges for the consummation of love.

The illustrious son of Vyāsa, *bādarāyani.* The narrator of the Rāsa Līlā episode, the sage Śuka, is introduced and identified by the name *bādarāyani,* which means "the son of Badarāyana," or Vyāsa, the "compiler of the Vedas." Other Sanskrit editions of this episode use simply *śrī-śuka,* which is how he is presented throughout the rest of the Rāsa Līlā story and most of the *Bhāgavata* text.

The Beloved Lord, *bhagavān.* The Sanskrit word *bhagavān,* referring to Krishna, who is identified by this proper name in RL 1.3, is understood by the Caitanya school as the intimate and personal "supreme Lord." The significance of the meaning of this term is discussed in "Krishna: Lord of Love and Beauty," in the "Aspects of the Story" portion of "Textual Illuminations."

The Beloved Lord's experience of allurement (*vilobhana*), desire (*upakṣepa*), and resolve (*yukti*) are declared by the following three sequential actions in the verse: first, he sees the beauty of the autumn nights subtly reminiscent of his beloveds, the heroines (lines 1–4); second, he turns his attention to love (lines 5–6); and third, he takes refuge in the illusive power of Yogamāyā (lines 7–8).

Those nights, *tā rātrīḥ.* The word *rātriḥ* is the feminine plural. Although this image ostensibly presents the natural elements of "autumn nights" and "blooming jasmine," it also subtly paints a picture of the heroines of the story. The word *rātrī* is the name for the goddess who is a personification of night, a divine mother in the celestial order known as *ṛta,* presented in the *Ṛg Veda* in the following passages:

"I call on Night who gives rest to all moving life" (RV 1.35.1); "Night, sent away for Savitar's uprising, hath yielded up a birth-place for the Morning" (RV 1.113.1); a hymn completely dedicated to her (RV 10.127); and "Night and Morning" (RV 1.142.7 and 1.188.6). In the present verse, the goddess Night is profusely decorated with blooming jasmine flowers known for their exotic scent. The image of the many nights decorated with jasmine flowers is a parallel image to the collective cowherd maidens, who are also decorated with jasmine flowers (see RL 5.11). The implication is that these beautiful autumn nights, perfumed by night-blooming jasmine flowers, remind Krishna of the beautiful goddesslike damsels of Vraja.

Turned his mind toward love's delights, *rantuṁ manaś-cakre.* This phrase, the predicate of this verse, consists of the finite verb "turned," *cakre,* the object of the finite verb "mind," *manas,* and the infinitive "to enjoy love," *rantum.*[2] This particular form of the finite verb *cakre* is significant. It is formed from the verb root *kṛ* in the *ātmanepada* voice, providing the sense that Krishna "made up his mind" or "decided for himself." The verb *rantum* is an infinitive of purpose that completes the finite verb in the literal phrase, "he decided to delight in love." Furthermore, the infinitive takes on the *ātmanepada* voice of the accompanying finite verb, providing, according to commentators, a significant theological sense: the Beloved Lord decides to delight in love for a divine purpose, internal in nature.[3]

Viśvanātha observes that these words indicate that this *līlā* of Krishna is not an external or superficial episode. The verb *cakre* is intentionally used, the middle voice (*ātmanepada*) of the verb, indicating that the enjoyment of this *līlā* is for his own divine satisfaction. He points out that Krishna's internal purpose of enjoyment is demonstrated by the purity of the Gopīs' love for him, and in turn, by his own pure interest, since he is self-satisfied even while enjoying love with them. Viśvanātha further provides support for the profundity of Krishna's acceptance of the Gopīs by quoting two verses, one from the

2. The following words are other possible translations for the Sanskrit verbal infinitive *rantum:* to "delight," "make happy," "enjoy carnally," "be glad," "be pleased," "be delighted," "be fond," "rejoice," "enjoy oneself," "play or sport," "amuse," "dally," and so on. The middle voice (*ātmanepada*) of the verb is used, indicating to the commentator that "love's delights" in this *līlā* is for God's own divine self-satisfaction, and it is part of God's very being "to delight in love in his innermost supreme self."

3. J. S. Speijer, in his work *Sanskrit Syntax* (Delhi: Motilal Banarsidass, [1886] 1973), section 387, explains that the infinitive takes on the voice of the accompanying finite verb.

Viṣṇu Purāṇa and the other from the *Harivaṁśa,* in which Krishna is described as "honoring (*mānayan*)" the cowherd maidens.

Furthermore, commentators insist that this divine *līlā* is in no way a frivolous affair. They argue that because God is full and complete in all ways, there is no need for the deity to enjoy frivolously, nor are his actions merely a false or cheap imitation of human activity, in which humans seek out others for selfish interest (SD). If the verb "delighting in love" had been put into the active *parasmaipada* voice, it would have indicated that Krishna's enjoyment was focused externally on the maidens, evidence of some lacking or selfish need on his part. The very fact that the enjoyment of love, for Krishna, is internal and selfless, bespeaks the purity of the Gopīs' love for him (SD).

It is interesting that this phrase has prominence in the first verses of the two other synoptic stories, the *Harivaṁśa* and *Viṣṇu Purāṇa.* Among the many similar features these verses share, the phrase *manaś cakre ratiṁ prati,* "turned his mind toward love's delights," is virtually identical to the RL version:

> When Krishna saw the youthfulness
> of the fresh moon during one night,
> He, during those autumn nights,
> turned his mind toward love's delights.[4]
> (HV 63.15)

> When Krishna saw the clear sky
> by the light of the autumn moon,
> Then the night-blooming lotus flowers
> in the pond, perfuming the air everywhere,
> And seeing the forest groves
> garlanded with buzzing bees,
> He, together with the Gopīs,
> turned his mind toward love's delights.[5]
> (VP 13.14–15)

4. *kṛṣṇas tu yauvanaṁ dṛṣṭvā | niśi candramaso navam |*
śāradīnāṁ niśānāṁ ca | manaś cakre ratiṁ prati || 15 ||
5. *kṛṣṇas tu vimalaṁ vyoma | śarac-candrasya candrikām |*
tathā kumudinīṁ phullām | āmodita-dig-antaram || 14 ||
vana-rājīṁ tathā kūjad- | bhṛṅga-mālā-manoramām |
vilokya saha gopībhir | manaś cakre ratiṁ prati || 15 ||

Fully taking refuge in Yogamāyā's illusive powers, *yogamāyām upāśrita.* The word *upāśrita* means "taking refuge with," "relying upon," or "abiding in." According to Jīva, the prefix *upa-*, of the word *upāśritaḥ,* indicates the sense of *samīpe,* or "being near," "easy to attain," "approaching," "being in the presence of," and so on (MW). Śrīdhara points out that the prefix *upa-* indicates an adverbally qualifying meaning that provides the word with the sense of *ādhikyena,* "submitting fully" or "submitting to the authority or supremacy," of Yogamāyā.[6]

That the Beloved Lord "fully takes refuge in Yogamāyā" is a unique event in the relationship between Krishna and Yogamāyā, that is, one that has never been described as having taken place, before or after this statement, anywhere in the *Bhāgavata* text. The word *upāśritaḥ,* "fulling taking refuge in," is significant in its application as a past participle within this verse, because it is the key word for understanding this unique event at the start of the Rāsa Līlā and the relationship that the subject, the Beloved Lord, has with Yogamāyā. Once again, an extraordinary event is communicated here: God is truly omnipotent, precisely because his power allows him to submit to the power of love and simultaneously to remain all-powerful. God is powerful enough to disempower himself, that is, to allow another power (relatively speaking outside of himself, yet ultimately coming from himself) to overtake his divine self for the sake of love.

This verse, in the original Sanskrit, consists of fourteen words (seven words per half-verse line), and the ordering of its words subtly prepares the reader for what is to come. An interesting rhythm of alternating groups of masculine and feminine words is established:

6. This participle modifies the subject, and has several lexical meanings that are worth listing here: "resorting to," "lying or resting upon," "leaning against," "clinging to," "having recourse to," "relying upon," "taking refuge with," "taking one's self to," "approached," "arrived at," and "abiding in" (MW). The prefix *upa-* can indicate another meaning for this word that provides the adverbial sense of *ādhikyena,* meaning, resorting "fully," or resorting with "supremacy" or "authority," to Yogamāyā (BB). Others (KrS) have suggested that the prefix *upa-* in the word *upāśritaḥ* indicates the sense of *samīpe,* that is, "being near," "easy to attain," "approaching," or "being in the presence of" (MW). Bhagavān's relationship to Yogamāyā expressed by the word *upāśritaḥ* is indeed one of nearness (that is, indicated by the prefix "*upa-*" meaning "toward," "near to," "by the side of," and "with"), and can have many senses, "but generally involving the idea of subordination or inferiority" (VA).

1 2 3 4 5 6 7
bhagavān api tā rātrīḥ śāradotphulla-mallikāḥ |

8 9 10 11 12 13 14
vīkṣya rantuṁ manaś-cakre yoga-māyām upāśritaḥ || 1 ||

Sanskrit is a highly inflected language, in which the syntactical ordering of words does not depend upon their actual sequence within the line or sentence. Rather, the relations between words are indicated and controlled by the changeable endings appended to noun stems, indicating gender and syntax. The groupings of words according to gender are the following:

	Word Count
Masculine 1–2	2
Feminine 3–7	5
Masculine 8–11	4
Feminine 12–13	2
Masculine 14	1

Half of the total number of words in the verse consists of words in or connected to the masculine gender, and the other half of words in the feminine gender. The word count within the masculine and feminine groupings is significantly greater in the groupings within the middle of the verse, contributing a dramatic swell to its expression. In my translation, I have tried to simulate this balance of masculine and feminine by placing the masculine words in lines 1, and 5 through 7, and the feminine in lines 2 through 4, and 8:

Even the Beloved Lord,	1	Masculine
seeing those nights	2	Feminine
in autumn filled with	3	Feminine
blooming jasmine flowers,	4	Feminine
Turned his mind	5	Masculine
toward love's delights,	6	Masculine
fully taking refuge in	7	Masculine
Yogamāyā's illusive powers.	8	Feminine

The balanced alternation between masculine-feminine words and imagery is immediately reflective of what is to come, the "dancing" or dialectical movements between the masculine and feminine voices of the hero and heroines of the drama.

Verse 1.2

This verse, in the original, moves with rich poetic rhythms and metaphor. The narrator launches into the action of the episode, by the dramatic jump from the *anuṣṭubh* meter of the first verse to the longer-flowing *jagatī* meter (four twelve-syllable quarter-verse lines) in this and the following two introductory verses.

The moon rises in the sky, spreading its "soothing reddish rays" over the horizon, in the same way that a husband or lover dispels the sorrow of separation for his beloved, "caressing" her blushed face upon his arrival.[7] Commentators suggest that the reddish face of the beloved is created by the spreading of soothing saffron *kuṅkuma* powder by the husband who has been absent for a long time (BB and SD). Note that the face of the Goddess Ramā in the following verse is "reddish as fresh saffron *kuṅkuma*," suggesting the Indian custom of soothing the beloved woman's face with this powder.

This poetic figure has further metaphorical significance. The compound word *uḍurājaḥ* literally means "king (*rājaḥ*) of stars (*uḍu*)," an epithet that refers to the moon. The image of the moon surrounded by stars in this verse anticipates the use of this image as a metaphor for Krishna surrounded by the Gopīs: "He was glowing like the full moon surrounded by stars" (RL 1.43). Later, the moon and stars become an audience for Krishna and the maidens in the Rāsa dance: "even the moon with its constellations became amazed" (RL 5.19). A mirroring of the moon-stars metaphor can be found in another verse: "he [Krishna] appeared radiant, like the supreme Person with his splendorous powers" (RL 4.10). Mirroring images utilizing bees (RL 2.7, 5.23, etc.) and elephants (RL 2.1, 5.25, etc.), as well as others, are found throughout the passage.

The moon is a great symbol of illumination and nourishment in Indian culture. Krishna, whose most prominent *līlā* takes place at night, is compared to the moon, the most prominent luminary of the night. In the *Bhagavad Gītā,* Krishna declares himself to be Soma, the

7. The phrase "spreading soothing . . . rays" in this verse translates *karair,* meaning literally "spreading with soothing hands." Commentators suggest that "hands" means metaphor-

deity of the moon, which nourishes all plant life with its essence, or *rasa* (BG 15.3). Indeed, the moon's rays are pleasing, and the moon itself conveys the source of aesthetic delight metaphorically. In the Rāsa Līlā passage, this lunar metaphor is invoked to suggest the aesthetic *rasa* (see RL 5.26).

Verse 1.3

Certain elements in the first three verses convey the sublime beauty by which Krishna's heart is so moved that he begins to produce mesmerizing music on the flute, alluring the cowherd maidens. These elements, forming a seductive paradisial scene, include the night-blooming lotus and jasmine flowers, and the moon beaming with the brilliance of the Goddess, its rich reddish rays coloring the forest during the autumn nights.

The passage mentions that the antecedent subject, the Beloved Lord, begins to make sweet music, and it is understood that such music is produced by him on the flute (see RL 1.40, 2.18, and 3.14). The powerful effect of such music is a recurring theme in the RL: Krishna's flute music is known to ignite the fire burning within the hearts of the Gopīs (RL 1.35), and the sweet melodious music causes them to abandon their noble character (RL 1.40). From the story, it is apparent that the flute music of this intimate deity is a kind of divine love call.

The special quality or power of Krishna's music is indicated by the words "melting the hearts of fair maidens with beautiful eyes" (*vāma-dṛṣāṁ manoharam*), enhancing the experience of *ādi-rasa,* or "ultimate relationship with God in divine intimacy" (KrS). The beautiful-eyed maidens are the young cowherd women of Vraja, first introduced explicitly here, and in the following several verses the effect of Krishna's flute music on them is delightfully presented. But it is not until the ninth verse that they are introduced to the reader as the "Gopīs," the most frequent name for the heroines found throughout the drama and the *Bhāgavata* text.

Viśvanātha suggests that upon witnessing the rising of the moon, a "transformation of Love" (*kandarpa-vikāraḥ*) takes place. The word *kandarpa* is a name for the god of Love, or "Cupid," or it simply means "love." The meanings of the word *vikāraḥ* are "change of form or nature" or "transformation," or it can mean "emotion," "agitation," or "passion"

---

ically "with the rays," *raśmi* ("ray of light" or "splendor" [MW]) (KrS). The synonym *kiraṇa* (a "ray" or "beam of light" [MW]) is also suggested (SD).

(MW). These senses support the Caitanya school's understanding of Krishna, who is the divinely impassioned supreme God of Love.

Lotus flowers, *kumut.* Śrīdhara states that this word refers to a special kind of lotus flower that blossoms at night. Viśvanātha, offering two possible ways to understand the meaning of the word *kumut,* states that the word can refer to special lotus flowers that open at night in the presence of the moon, or can indicate that the moon's presence gives pleasure, *mud,* to the earth, *ku.*

Ancient India has had a fascination with the lotus, revealed by the number of synonymns in the Sanskrit language that are provided to refer to this flower. It often symbolizes the divine, the erotic, beauty, and so on. Words for the flower are usually epithets describing its color, the time of day for blossoming, its place of origin, or other qualities. Here is a sample list: *padma* (the lotus that closes toward evening); *kuvalaya* (a variety of water lily that opens at night); *paṅkaja* (a lotus that closes in the evening; literally, "one who is born from the mud"); *ambhoja* ("the water-born" day lotus); *nalina* (a lotus or water lily); *mahotpala* (a large water lily); *abja* ("water-born"; lotus); *ambuja* ("one which is born from the water"; lotus); *sarasija* ("that which is born in lakes or ponds"; lotus); *sarasiruha,* ("that which is growing in a lake or pond"; lotus); *kamala* (a more general term for lotus, possibly with the specific color of rose); *utpala* (literally, "to burst open," referring to the blue lotus); *kumuda* (literally, "exciting with joy"; lotus, referring to the white water lily); *puṣkara* (a blue lotus); *puṇḍarīka* (a white lotus expressive of beauty); and *aravinda* (possibly, "one who gains obedience or devotion"; lotus); and so on.

Ramā. A name for the Goddess Lakṣmī, the divine consort of Lord Nārāyaṇa. The Goddess, in her form as Ramā, is mentioned in this verse because the radiance of the full moon is compared to her radiance, since she is especially known for her luster that is described as more illuminating than lightning when it strikes against a mountain of marble (BhP 8.8.8–9). Her other pure qualities include all-auspiciousness, good fortune, and unsurpassable beauty. She is completely devoted to bringing pleasure to the supreme Lord. Her grand image is invoked in this verse to express the power of the moon's splendorous presence that autumn evening. It is a common feature of this poetic drama to invoke images from the majestic, powerful, and cosmic dimensions of the divinity as Vishnu or Nārāyaṇa (*aiśvarya*), in order to express the power of the intimacy or sweetness of the deity Krishna (*mādhurya*). Thus the image of the Great Goddess is invoked here to enhance the sweetness of the village girls, the cowherd maidens.

Kuṅkuma. The word *kuṅkuma* indicates a brilliant or deep reddish powder, often translated as "saffron" (MW and VA). It is produced from the plant and flower pollen of the botanical *Crocus sativus* (MW). The role of *kuṅkuma* in the RL is an interesting one: this substance is found either on the bodies or the clothing of the Gopīs, or on Krishna's garland after having embraced a woman on whose breast the *kuṅkuma* is spread. The maidens fear Krishna's rejection from the forest and begin to cry, "washing away the *kuṅkuma* on their breasts" (RL 1.29). When Krishna returns after a period of separation from them, the narrator explains that "Using their delicate shawls, colored by reddish *kuṅkuma* from their breasts, they arranged a seat for the true companion of all souls" (RL 4.13). When the *kuṁkuma* is on Krishna's garland, it is a sign that he has embraced a lover, either apart from the group of cowherd maidens (RL 2.11), or together with them during the Rāsa dance: "His garland, crushed by their limbs joined together with his, was colored with the reddish *kuṅkuma* that covered their breasts" (RL 5.23).

Verse 1.4

This verse expresses the powerful effect of Krishna's divine love call on the young women of Vraja. In fact, traditional teachers refer to the verse as an example of emotionally intensive forms of divine love known as "madness," or *unmāda* (PrS 345), as well as "anxiousness," "eagerness," or "impatience," known as *autsukya* (PrS 357). The minds of the cowherd maidens are no longer their own, as indicated by the verse: "the young women of Vraja whose minds were captured by Krishna" (*vraja-striyaḥ kṛṣṇa-gṛhīta-mānasāḥ*). They have, in effect, "lost" their minds to Krishna and have become self-forgetful, even completely unaware of each other, as they hastily depart to be with their beloved.

This state of forgetfulness or mindlessness is described at times by using the image of God as a divine thief. The narrator of the Rāsa Līlā states about the Gopīs that "their hearts had been stolen by Govinda," *govindāpahṛtātmānaḥ* (RL 1.8), and they themselves claim that "while in our homes, our minds were easily stolen by you," *cittaṁ sukhena bhavatāpahṛtaṁ gṛheṣu* (RL 1.34). The idea of "self-forgetfulness" is also seen in various other places within the *Bhāgavata* text, as in the following:

In sleeping, sitting, and walking,
conversing, playing, and bathing,
and in all other activities,
The Vṛṣṇis, whose minds
were absorbed in Krishna,
were not even aware
of themselves being present.
(BhP 10.90.46)

This state of self-unawareness, due to exclusive focus on the beloved object and complete abandonment of the world, symbolizes the one-pointed devotion that is ideal for bhakti and is a recurring trait in the behavior of the devoted soul. Elsewhere in the RL, it states that the Gopīs forget their homes and even themselves (RL 2.43), and indeed, it is Krishna who is responsible for causing forgetfulness of all such attachments (RL 3.14).

The innermost part of the godhead is the pinnacle of ultimate beauty, and once situated in this divine realm, the intimate devotee experiences a type of supranormal aesthetic delight causing total self-forgetfulness:

Krishna is all attractive, all pleasing,
the greatest source of all *rasa;*
By his own divine power,
he causes forgetfulness of all else.
(CC 2.24.38)

Thus, self-forgetfulness is incidental to the soul's total and irresistible attraction to God, and moreover, it is caused by his divine power. The present verse demonstrates this power in the form of Krishna's flute music that causes the cowherd maidens to abandon suddenly everything they are doing to run off to be with their beloved Lord.

An essential message of this text is that an incidental result of true love is total forgetfulness or concern for the self and the world. The underlying statement is that true renunciation can only be the result of pure love, and renunciation is artificial if it is not a derivative of such devotional love. This approach to the conception of renunciation constitutes a major departure of bhakti traditions from pan-Indian traditions that strive for renunciation either for its own sake or for the sake of achieving liberation. In bhakti, the self seeks nothing for the self and everything for the beloved object, and only this can constitute true renunciation.

Passion, *anaṅga.* The translation "passion" is a connotative sense of the word *anaṅga,* whose literal meaning is "without limbs," "bodiless," and "incorporeal" (MW). Passion, on the one hand, is formless, the feeling between two persons. Yet the word can also refer to the personification of love, known by the name Kāmadeva, the equivalent of Cupid, who is paradoxically the "bodiless" or "formless" one (VA). In the verses that follow, the Gopīs pay no attention to their bodily forms or anything connected with them. Furthermore, their love for Krishna is so strong that, as we shall see, they abandon their own physical bodies out of intense passionate love for the supreme beloved (see RL 1.11).

The Lord's activities are of two types: "connections by means of loving feelings," *bhāva-sambandhinī;* and "actions filled with joy from his own being," *svābhāvika-vinodamaya.* This verse is demonstrative of the first type (PrS 304). The verse also demonstrates the stage of separation, *purva-rāga,* leading to its fulfillment in *sambhoga* (PrS 383).

Verse 1.5

This and several following verses express how the Gopīs' various household activities and duties, even the preparations for their personal bodily appearance, are abruptly dropped, leaving these tasks only partially completed, at the moment they hear the divine love call of Krishna's flute music. The author has returned to the common and more terse *anuṣṭubh*-metered epic verse for this and several verses to follow, providing greater movement and tension in the storyline. This dramatic behavior of the cowherd maidens symbolizes the transformation of the self that takes place in bhakti, or devotional love: the soul is transferred from an intrinsically self-centered orientation to a completely theocentric orientation. Incidental to the theocentric orientation is self-forgetfulness and a form of natural renunciation, as spoken of above. Thus, commentators speak of the Gopīs as abandoning all their activities based on worldly "my-ness" (*mamatā*) and "I-ness" (*ahaṁtā*) (SD), and cite this verse as an example of "great haste" in pure love, *avega,* due to the uncontrollable urges of the devotional heart (PrS 344).

Verse 1.6

The word for "milk" (*payaḥ*) in this verse is a point of contention for traditional commentators. Jīva insists that *payaḥ* means "cow's milk" rather than "mother's milk." This means, according to Jīva, that the Gopīs are unmarried women and therefore are not nursing their own children from their breasts; rather they are assisting the children of other married women, such as their sisters or sisters-in-law. This understanding of the word reflects Jīva's idea that the cowherd maidens are truly the "wives" of Krishna (*svakīya*) and not the so-called "adulterous" lovers of Krishna (*parakīya*). He claims that the maidens are not actually mothers, nor are they wives of others; rather, they are women who are legitimately eligible to be the wives of Krishna.

Krishnadāsa, however, clearly favors the idea that *parakīya bhāva* is the highest love for God. He explains that *madhura-rasa,* amorous love for God, includes two types: *svakīyā bhāva* and *parakīyā bhāva* (CC 1.4.46), and then states that in *parakīyā-bhāva* the greater intensity of love exists, found only in the *līlās* of Vraja (CC 1.4.47). The text supports or makes room for either or both conceptions.

Verse 1.7

Śrīdhara states that the second pair of *padas* indicates that the Gopīs, whose minds are intensely attached to Krishna, perform activities that are solely intended for his satisfaction, even if executed imperfectly, as in their chaotic and disorderly dressing before rushing to meet him. Viśvanātha explains that some of the maidens are in such a frenzy to meet Krishna that they fail to identify properly parts of their own bodies, and thus dress themselves improperly.

Jīva cites this verse as an example of *vibhrama* (PrS 328). A form of *anubhāva* is *vibhrama,* which is described by Jīva, quoting Rūpa (UNM), as the misplacement of various ornamental and decorative objects on the body due to love.

Verse 1.8

Śrīdhara explains that those whose minds are attracted to Krishna cannot be affected by any distractions, including dear family members. Viśvanātha comments that the cowherd maidens forget everything but Krishna, due to their pure love, which is facilitated by Yogamāyā. Viśvanātha explains that the Gopīs, whose husbands and other relatives attempt to stop them from leaving, are given imaginary forms by Yogamāyā, which allow them to appear to remain with their families and continue with their household duties, as if they had never left (RL 5.38).

Govinda is another proper name for Krishna. A variety of proper names, as well as epithetical names, are used by both narrator and the Gopīs to refer to Krishna. This name is found in seven instances throughout the story (RL 1.8, 1.28, 2.7, 2.28, 2.29, 2.30, and 5.2).

Their hearts had been stolen by Govinda, *govindāpahṛtātmāno.* The word *ātmā* in its plural form is translated as "hearts," although it can mean "souls," "minds," "selves," and so on.

Entranced, *mohitaḥ.* This word would typically be translated as "bewildered," as in other places within the RL. Bewilderment (from the Sanskrit root *muh-*) is a state found throughout the drama (RL 1.8, 1.17, 1.40, 2.35, 2.40, 3.8, 3.16, 3.17, and 5.38). Jīva suggests that the restlessness, or *cāpalya,* of the Gopīs can appear to be conflicting with their state of bewilderment. There is no conflict between these two, however, since the combination contributes to the intensity of their love for Krishna (PrS 201).

Verse 1.9

In this verse, the reader is informed that those Gopīs who are unable to escape successfully from their homes, in order to be in the presence of Krishna externally, resort to being in his presence internally through yogic meditation. The interesting relationship between yoga and devotional love or bhakti is raised in the present verse as well as others throughout the RL. For example, we find that the cowherd maidens meditate on Krishna in his absence and in his presence. While separated from their Beloved, they find auspicious things upon which to base their meditations, such as his smiles, loving glances, and playfulness (RL 3.10), as well as his lotus feet (RL 3.13). Later, when Krishna returns to them and they gaze insatiably upon his beautiful face, they are compared to saintly persons who meditate insatiably upon his holy feet (RL 4.7).

It is clear that the Gopīs prefer the physical presence of Krishna over that of his presence within meditation, yet the latter is a method to which they always resort if his absence is unavoidable. From the perspective of the *Bhagavad Gītā,* it is clear that the maidens have reached the ultimate stage of yoga:

> Indeed, among all practitioners of yoga,
> the one whose inner self is centered upon me,
> Who possesses faith and worships me,
> such a person is considered the most devoted to me.
> (BG 6.47)

One might ask, are the cowherd maidens practicing yoga in their devotion to Krishna? According to the *Yoga Sūtra* of Patañjali, "Yoga is the practice which controls the movement of thoughts," *yogaḥ cittavṛtti nirodhaḥ* (YS 1.2), and this is described in the above verse. Moreover, "Meditation (*dhyāna*) is the single continuous movement [of the mind] toward an object," *tatra pratyayaikatānatā dhyānam* (YS 3.2), and for the Gopīs, the singular object of all thought is certainly Krishna. Furthermore, "meditation (*dhyāna*) is according to what is pleasing" *yathābhimata-dhyānāt vā* (YS 1.39), and it is clear that the supremely pleasing object for the maidens is Krishna.

Although the Gopīs resort to a yogic form of meditation at various times, their general state of consciousness is one of complete and total absorption of love, or *samādhi,* the highest step of the "eight-limbed" (*aṣṭāṅga*) yoga system. As the *Yoga Sūtra* itself states, "The perfection of pure meditation is accomplished by devotion to the supreme Lord," *samādhi-siddhi īśvara-praṇidhānāt* (YS 2.45). From this statement, we can assume that the maidens are already accomplished in *dhyāna-yoga,* and primarily use meditation during periods of separation from Krishna. Even while in his presence, however, they sometimes meditate on him, as described in RL 4.8. The Gopīs, then, at times "climb down" the yoga ladder to the *dhyāna* rung (when the "eight limbs" are viewed hierarchically), which serves to enhance their state of absorption in *samādhi.*

The cowherd maidens are not ordinary human beings, according to Viśvanātha, referring to Rūpa Gosvāmin and Kavi Karṇapūra's commentaries on this verse. They are viewed as eternally perfected beings, *nitya-siddhas,* co-eternal with the supreme Lord, or as beings perfected by practice, *sādhana-siddhas,* who ultimately attain a co-eternal position with the supreme Lord. Rūpa Gosvāmin is acknowledged as having categorized the different types and subtypes of Gopīs in his work *Ujjvala-nīlamaṇi.* Kavi Karṇapūra understands that some of the maidens were originally great sages who were not yet fully freed from the contamination of this world, and therefore it was arranged by Yogamāyā for them to be born into the families of Gopīs and Gopas (cowherd men), in order to develop the highest stage of pure love for Krishna by associating with other eternally liberated Gopīs. The maidens, by the power of Yogamāyā, are never tainted by mundane sexual contact with worldly husbands, since they possess pure spiritual bodies (SD).

Jīva presents the following verse to show how they are able to achieve Krishna without being directly in his presence:

> Those of you who could not sport with me
> during that night in the forest
> remained in Vraja.
> O fortunate ones, those who were unable
> to attend the Rāsa dance achieved me
> by contemplating my prowess.
> (BhP 10.47.37)

Jīva states that the Gopīs who cannot attend the Rāsa dance are able to experience Krishna's presence through his *aprakaṭa-prakāśa,* and therefore achieve him internally (KS 164, 170).

This verse is an example of *mṛti,* "death" or "dying," or the departure from the body (PrS 349).

Verse 1.10

In this verse, the Gopīs who are unable to leave their homes instead connect with their beloved through meditation, and embrace him from within. In fact, Krishna himself speaks to the maidens who successfully escape from their homes and achieve his physical presence about the various alternative methods for experiencing his presence, one of which is meditation (*dhyāna* RL 1.27).

Acyuta is another name for Krishna, meaning "the infallible one." Special attention is given to this name in "Krishna: Lord of Love and Beauty," in Textual Illuminations.

Meditation, *dhyāna.* This verse, and the previous one, demonstrate that the Gopīs are naturally accomplished in yoga, as they were formerly great sages in a previous life, according to traditional teachers. For the cowherd maidens, the practices of yoga are simply a means for achieving their passionate and devotional connection with Krishna and not merely a step toward *samādhi,* as they are already totally absorbed in him.

Verse 1.11

Jīva states that the phrase *jāra-buddhyā* means that the Gopīs think of themselves as Krishna's paramours, but in reality have nothing to do with adulterous love as found in this world. Because of the intensity of their pure love for Krishna, they could easily appear as his paramours, transgressing ethical boundaries, though their love is in no way susceptible to breaking rules of morality. In addition, the material bodies that are left behind by the maidens are specially constructed by Yogamāyā, since they depart in their nonmaterial forms to be with Krishna (KS 145).

This verse and the previous two verses are cited as examples of death, or a departure from the body, due to the intensity of pure love for Krishna (PrS 349). The Gopīs, as a result of *dhyāna* and *samādhi,* transcend their bodies or attain a state of bodilessness. The *Yoga Sūtra* speaks of the experience of "bodilessness" in the following sutra text: "For those who are situated in material nature, the experience of bodilessness may arise (when engaged in the practice of yoga)" (YS 1.19). Aspects of the Rāsa Līlā story symbolize the transfigurative power of bhakti, for the relationship of the *bhakta* to the world and to death is a subtle but prominent theme in the story line. This theme is discussed at length in "Devotional Yoga Transcends Death," in "Textual Illuminations."

Viśvanātha explains that the narrator of the Rāsa Līlā, the sage Śuka, gives both exoteric and esoteric messages simultaneously in this verse, so that the internal meaning can be exposed to confidential devotees without being revealed to outsiders. The external meaning of this verse is the subject matter of the liberation of the cowherd maidens. The internal meaning is the subject of the spiritual emotions within divine intimacy that the Gopīs attain, and how the experience of this intimacy can appear contrary to worldly expectations, as it expresses the intensity and selflessness of pure love for God.

Verse 1.12

Greatest lover, *paraṁ kāntam.* Śrīdhara's translation of the words *paraṁ kānta* is "the only desirable (lover)." He states that the word *paraṁ* means "only," and the word *kāntam,* "desirable." Alternatively, the phrase could be translated as "they knew him as their only desirable object," or as "the supreme lover."

Brahman. The word possesses the broad meanings of "the absolute reality," "supreme spirit," or perhaps simply "God." More specifically, *brahman* can be one of three manifestations of the supreme, as the manifestation of "the supreme impersonal spirit." The other two manifestations are the "supreme soul," *paramātman,* and "the supreme Lord," *bhagavān.* These distinctions are the three primary identities of God as defined by the Vaishnava theologians, derived from the *Bhāgavata* text itself.

Jīva cites verse 10 above, along with this verse, to emphasize that the Gopīs are not interested in the liberation associated with *śānta-rasa,* and that these verses do not actually constitute a mixture of *śānta* and *mādhurya rasas* (PrS 178). Jīva insists that these verses simply express how the maidens overcome various obstacles in their goal to be with Krishna, and this does not constitute a "mixture of *rasas,*" or, *rasābhāsa.*

Verse 1.13

King of Cedi is Śiśupāla. In the assembly of many great personalities and elders about to witness the performance of the *rājasūya* sacrifice, Śiśupāla, after hearing much praise for Krishna who was seated there, got up and directed various intolerable insults toward Krishna. Some members of the assembly rushed to kill the king, but Krishna stopped them. Instead, he beheaded Śiśupāla himself with his own *cakra* (supernatural discus), awarding Śiśupāla the opportunity to merge with his divine body and thereby granting him one of the several kinds of liberation. This story is found in BhP 10.74.30–46.

Verse 1.15

Intimacy, *aikyaṁ.* Śrīdhara states that the word *aikyam* means "relationship." The word *aikyam* means, literally, "oneness," and I have translated it as "intimacy" to be consistent with the series of emotional experiences presented in this verse.

Affection, *sauhṛdam.* The word can also mean "friendship." Śrīdhara provides the meaning of bhakti for the word.

Note that the first pada of this verse lists three negative emotions, "desire," "anger," and "fear." The second *pada* lists three positive emotions—loving attachment, intimacy, and affection—that could be interpreted in any of three ways. Each quality can be seen as belonging to a progressively higher realm of existence, that is, the *sneha* of this world, the *aikya* (taken in the sense of "oneness") of transcendence, and the *sauhṛda* of Krishna's highest heaven. Also, all three of these emotions can be viewed as different emotions found in persons of this world; or alternatively, the three can be understood as essential emotions within the *rasa*s between Krishna and his associates of the divine world.

The phrase *tan-mayatām* refers to "full absorption in God," which liberates souls. All the emotions presented above, whether positive or negative, allow souls to become fully absorbed in God. Jīva states, however, that persons with positive emotions directed toward God ultimately achieve much more than those who possess negative ones (KS 145). See BhP 3.2.10 for a related verse.

Verse 1.16

This verse answers the question as to why Krishna descends to this world. In this connection, Jīva quotes a phrase from BhP 10.90.48, stating that Krishna's presence extinguishes evil among all moving and nonmoving beings (KS 115).

The present verse is cited by Haridāsa Thākura, when speaking to Caitanya. Haridāsa praises his mission to liberate all the living beings of this world and therefore quotes this verse, especially because of the phrase, "By him this entire world is liberated" (CC 2.3.84).

Verse 1.17

This verse introduces the dialogue between Krishna and the Gopīs, which comprises verses 17 through 41, or what I have designated as scene 3 of act one.

With playful words, *vācaḥ peśair.* According to Śrīdhara, the words *vācaḥ peśair* mean *vāg-vilāsaih,* or "with playful words." Commentators discuss the various implied contrary meanings and senses, both of Krishna's clever words with double meanings in verses 18 through 27 and of the Gopīs' words containing hidden senses in verses 31 through 41. The different interpretations by Jīva and Viśvanātha of each of these conversational verses of Krishna and the cowherd maidens will be reviewed below.

Verse 1.18

Quoting Rūpa's UNM, Jīva points out that conversation in *anubhāva-prakāraṇa* is called *samlāpa.* Krishna has two purposes in his *samlāpa* with the Gopīs: to attract the Gopīs, who are mesmerized by his flute and other qualities, and to test their love with jesting and rejecting language. In return, the maidens have two purposes in their *samlāpa* with Krishna: to reject Krishna's words of rejection, and to express in their words of rejection their longing to be with him. Both Krishna and the Gopīs are equally eloquent and clever in this *samlāpa* or dialogue, and this equality is affirmed by Krishna in this verse. Such dialogue therefore increases their *rasa.* Jīva comments on verses RL 1.18 through 1.41 as examples of *samlāpa* (PrS 332).

Verse 1.19

Krishna speaks "playful words" to the Gopīs, as the narrator of the Rāsa Līlā informs us two verses earlier (1.17), introducing Krishna's duplicitous words. This verse is the first among several in which Krishna's words possess double entendre. Commentators point out that these playful words express his divinely paradoxical interests and motives: his recommendation to the Gopīs that they fulfill their essential worldly obligations and duties (*dharma*) as women, and at the same time renounce such responsibilities and take up the highest calling (*parodharma*), which is to be with him, the Beloved Lord, the worshipable deity in the hearts of all beings. The original Sanskrit language and grammar of this verse allows for such contradictory expressions. Since the English language does not accommodate this type and degree of double entendre, I present in the translation the more apparent meanings of verses that express Krishna's advice to act according to social expectations, and then provide in footnotes the more subtle alternative translations that are simultaneously communicated. A discussion of these double-entendre verses is presented in "Ethical Boundaries and Boundless Love," in "Textual Illuminations."

After Krishna greets the Gopīs in the previous verse, as if unaware of their motive for coming to the forest, he speaks words of warning to them. On the face of it, Krishna attempts to alarm them into doing the right thing, while ostensibly offering protective words. He states that the night is frightening, as are the animals in the forest, and urges the cowherd maidens to return to the village since, clearly, the forest is not a safe place. The verse concludes, however, with Krishna addressing the Gopīs teasingly as "ones with beautiful waists," hinting at his double motive, thus preparing the reader for the playfulness of double-word meanings in following verses. While attempting to frighten the maidens with the dangers of the night, Krishna also encourages them to stay with him in the forest where there is no cause for fear.

This double message is not communicated connotatively, but through the actual grammar and syntax of the verse. For example, the four words in the first quarter line of RL 1.19 are *rajany eṣā ghora-rūpā.* In the original characters of the Sanskrit language, these transliterated words appear merged as *rajanyeṣāghorarūpā,* according to the rules of euphonic combination in which the endings of words are combined or merged in sonorous fashion with the beginnings of following words, known as *sandhi.* Thus, when the demonstrative pronoun *eṣā* ("this") is merged with the word following it, an adjective, it appears as *eṣāghora.* However, the text presents an ambiguity here. The exact spelling of the word following *eṣā* is unclear: it can be either the positive form of *ghora* ("frightening"), or the negative (with the prefix *a-*) *aghora* ("non-frightening"), because both positive and negative forms of this adjective appear the same when either of these words is combined with the preceding word *eṣā.* The same ambiguity conveniently occurs in this verse the second time the word *ghora/aghora* is used, combined with its preceding word *rūpā,* as *rūpāghora-sattva* ("frightening beings" or "non-frightening beings").

Unlike English, whose syntax depends upon word order or placement within the sentence, Sanskrit, being an inflected language, does not require word order; syntactical force and meaning are indicated through the endings of nouns and verbs. Therefore, when the negative particle *na,* meaning "no" or "not" is found in a verse, it can be applied singularly or in multiple ways. In this verse, if the negative is applied in a singular fashion, then the only negative would be "women should *not* stay here," and this application of the negative serves Krishna's motive to encourage *dharma.* But if the negative is not applied here, and instead applied to other elements in the verse in a multiple fashion, these various negatives then serve Krishna's motive to encourage the positive notion that the Gopīs should remain with him in the forest.

Psychological subtleties of meaning derived from the double entendre of this verse have inspired further interpretations (SD). Krishna, in this verse, could be saying that the Gopīs should not be afraid of staying with him in the forest because the animals themselves are not frightened by the night, and therefore why should they be frightened? Or, Viśvanātha suggests, it may be Krishna's intent that the Gopīs should not be fearful of staying with him, even if there are frightening animals residing there, precisely because such terrifying animals will keep their worried family members away from the forest, thus protecting the maidens from being discovered with Krishna.

Verse 1.20
This verse also displays a possible double meaning, according to Viśvanātha. Thus Krishna's words are teasing and playful, though in the guise of being concerned and understanding.

Verse 1.22
Again, Krishna is playful in his words. Viśvanātha recognizes the double meaning of this verse. Jīva suggests that this verse could be making even more emphatic statements such as: "Do not attend your husbands," "your calves and children are not crying," and therefore "you need not feed and nurse them." The various double meanings of these verses allow Krishna to be morally proper and mischievous at the same time.

Verse 1.23
Jīva anticipates a moral objection to Krishna's words in this verse: "How can Krishna encourage the Gopīs to break the vow of faithful service to husbands in marriage?" Jīva states that the next verse answers this objection (PrS 332).

Verse 1.24

The highest dharma, *paro dharmo.* Viśvanātha points out the two possible but very different meanings of the words *paro dharmaḥ,* which can be understood as "the duty of another," that is, someone else's duty," or as "the highest duty." Viśvanātha suggests that this ambiguity of meaning allows Krishna to imply either that the Gopīs should go back and serve their husbands or that they should stay, since the duty of serving husbands is for other women and not for them. A thorough discussion on these two possible understandings is presented in "Ethical Boundaries and Boundless Love," in "Textual Illuminations."

Without falsity, *amāyayā.* The word *amāyayā* can be translated literally as "without *māyā,*" "without illusion," or "without duplicity." In translating this statement, I have attempted to preserve the ambiguity of the object of the prepositional phrase, "without falsity, or Māyā," since the commentators stress one or the other object to which "without Māyā" can refer. This word is interpreted as meaning both that the Gopīs' service to their husbands should be sincere, that is, without duplicity or interest in other men, and that their service should be to a husband who is without falsity or worldly qualities. In the latter sense, Krishna implies that he is the only qualified husband for the cowherd maidens, yet at the same time appears to encourage them to behave morally and return to their worldly husbands.

Viśvanātha considers that Krishna is making a very clever statement here. He states that the implication in Krishna's instruction to the Gopīs is that they should serve their husbands "without unfaithfulness," without being interested in other men. Jīva, on the other hand, understands the object of the prepositional phrase, "without *māyā*," as the word *bhartuḥ* or "husbands," indicating that Krishna is instructing the Gopīs to serve a husband who is without falsity or who is not of the realm of this world. Stated in positive terms, they should be serving Krishna, who is not subject to falsity, or the temporary world of Māyā.

Jīva interprets this final statement as Krishna saying to the cowherd maidens that they should continue serving him as they have from their childhood. He points out that the implied message in Krishna's words is that the Gopīs have never been married, and that their so-called husbands are actually false. Therefore, there is nothing wrong in abandoning false husbands (PrS 332).

Krishnadāsa Kavirāja explains that, at times, the devotee of Krishna may not follow his supreme order due to feelings of *premā*, or love. Greater intimacy with God is the higher principle, and other rules of dharma can be broken for the sake of achieving this divine intimacy. Here, Krishna is explaining to the Gopīs what their duties are according to dharma; however, they refuse to obey these rules for the sake of being with him. In this regard, Krishnadāsa states that Caitanya gave Nityānanda the order to remain in Bengal. Instead, Nityānanda went to see Caitanya due to his great love for him (CC 2.10.5). Krishnadāsa goes on to say that sometimes the devotee who is absorbed in *anurāga*, or "passionate love for God," breaks an order or does not care for a rule or injunction, in order to achieve greater intimacy (*saṅga*) with God (CC 2.10.6). Then he states the following:

> In the Rāsa Līlā story, for example, the Gopīs
> were given the order to return to their homes.
> His [Krishna's] order was broken and instead
> they remained in intimate association with him.
> (CC 2.10.7)

Thus in bhakti, greater achievements in divine intimacy are to be favored over that of obedience to regular rules and injunctions, even if such instructions come from God himself.

Verse 1.25

Krishna's words in this verse could be interpreted as saying that the husbands of the Gopīs are fallen because they are envious of him. Since their husbands are fallen, the maidens have no obligation to serve them, and therefore should abandon them in order to be with Krishna (PrS 332).

Verse 1.26

Adultery, *aupapatyam*. Jīva gives an opposing double meaning for this word as "one who remains near a husband." This meaning would change the sense of the verse to imply that staying near a husband should be condemned, since it does not allow such a woman to attain heaven (*asvargyam*) (PrS 332).

Everywhere, *sarvatra*. Viśvanātha suggests that the word *sarvatra* could be taken to modify, alternatively and ambiguously, the word *aupapatyam*, meaning that adultery, which is found everywhere, is nevertheless condemned. The second two *padas* could be translated as follows:

> Women from good families know
> adultery is found everywhere
> and should be condemned.

Krishna would be implying here that it is adulterous for all women to relate to worldly husbands, since it is he who is the only true and eternal husband.

Verse 1.27

This verse resembles many of the prescriptive formulations for bhakti practice found in the *Bhagavad Gītā*. The first two *padas* of the present verse remind one specifically of the following verse:

> Be absorbed in thinking of me, be devoted to me,
> sacrifice everything for me and bow down to me.
> You will certainly come to me, having engaged
> your very self completely in devotion to me.
> (BG 9.34)

Jīva implies that the present verse could be taken to mean that there are many processes through which to relate to Krishna; however, the result of these processes is not the same as being directly with Krishna or in close physical proximity. Thus, the implied meaning of Krishna's words is that the cowherd maidens should stay with him in the forest at night (PrS 332).

Verse 1.28

Govinda. Viśvanātha suggests that the name Govinda is used here because it conveys the sense of someone "who utilizes (*vindate*) playful speech (*gāḥ*)." Jīva feels that the Gopīs do not understand the hidden message within Krishna's playful and clever words because, as the narrator Śuka describes, they become saddened by his words (PrS 332).

Verse 1.29

Viśvanātha describes the tears of the Gopīs as not trickling, rather as "streaming," or flowing bountifully enough to carry the various types of cosmetics worn on their eyes and breasts before being soaked up by their garments.

Jīva presents this verse as an example of *dhyāna,* or meditation (PrS 355).

Kajjala. A blackish substance, sometimes considered a collyrium, applied to the eyelashes or eyelids as decorative makeup.

Verse 1.31

Jīva points out that this, as well as other verses, includes words of irony and punning, demonstrating the compatible combining of *rasas.* Here, Krishna is addressed intimately by the Gopīs, identified by them as the expositor of dharma and the all-pervading divinity in the hearts of all beings, the dearest friend of all and the supreme Self (PrS 199). Jīva is concerned that the maidens' words not be taken as a conflict of *rasa.* It is characteristic that the Gopīs use words of humility, words that one would expect from someone in the *śānta rasa,* as well as words of passion, naturally found in *śṛṅgāra rasa* (PrS 182).

Cruelly, *nṛ-śaṁsam.* Viśvanātha also suggests other meanings, such as "injurious" and "murderous."

Original Person translates the phrase *ādi-puruṣaḥ.*

Verse 1.32

Proper duty, *sva-dharma.* Jīva states that the word can be construed as *su adharma,* meaning "great lack of dharma" or "very much without dharma." This would give a different meaning to the verse:

O dear one, it may be true
as you, who knows dharma, have stated,
That it is very much against dharma for women
to be loyal to husbands, children, and close friends.

If taken in this way, the words "you who knows dharma" are spoken facetiously by the Gopīs (KrS). Jīva also points out that the word *upadeśapāda,* translated here as the "object of these teachings," can be used to indicate a "teacher." This would also give a different sense of the third *pada* in the verse:

Let this dharma of ours be for you, O Lord,
since you are the teacher [of this dharma].

The supreme Soul, *ātmā.* Śrīdhara states that the word *ātmā* refers to the *īśa,* or the supreme Lord. Viśvanātha also identifies the supreme Lord as the "supreme soul." The Gopīs acknowledged Krishna's form of majesty as the supreme soul within all beings, due to their anticipatory feelings of separation. If they felt secure in their position of union with Krishna, then any awareness of his supreme excellences would not be present.

Verse 1.33

Jīva suggests some double meanings in this verse, conveying contrary senses: "Why not appreciate our husbands and children who don't cause us much trouble?" and "O supreme Lord, who causes us much trouble, be merciful unto us—please destroy our longing for you who does not appreciate us!"

The spiritually advanced, *kuśalāḥ.* Śrīdhara suggests that the word *kuśalāḥ* means "those who are authorities in the scriptures." Viśvanātha declares that such persons who are *kuśalāḥ* are full of faith, or very attached to and affectionate toward Krishna. Here I have translated the word *kuśalāḥ* simply as "the spiritually advanced."

Verse 1.34

Jīva suggests that this verse indicates *bhāva,* or "feeling" without any outer ecstatic signs, the first of twenty types of *alaṅkāra-anubhāva* (PrS 318). While the cowherd maidens are in their homes, they show no outer signs of being absorbed in love for Krishna. Jīva points out an implied meaning in the statement of the Gopīs: "If you had not come along, we would have remained happily engaged in work in our homes" (PrS 332).

Verse 1.35

The Gopīs themselves threaten Krishna that they will achieve the abode of his feet by means of meditation if he refuses to extinguish the fire burning within their hearts. In other words, they declare, "if you refuse to come to us, then we'll go to you by means of meditation. We always have access to you by this means."

This verse is cited by Caitanya when speaking to Sanātana Gosvamin. Caitanya discusses how the attainment of Krishna is not possible by voluntarily giving up one's body, or suicide; it is only through bhakti that one can attain Krishna (CC 2.4.55–58, 60). He further elaborates that sometimes a devotee, due to intense feelings of separation, may desire to leave the physical body (CC 2.4.62). This statement of Caitanya introduces the quotation of the present verse (CC 2.4.64) as an expression of this idea—in particular, the last two *pada*s in which the Gopīs threaten Krishna that they will place their bodies "in the fire . . . [and] by means of meditation we will go to the abode of your feet."

Verse 1.38

This verse is cited by Jīva as an example of *dainya,* or the experience of despair and helplessness (PrS 338).

Verse 1.39

Your face encircled, *āvṛta-mukham.* Śrīdhara understands the word *āvṛta-mukham* as "surrounding your face," rather than "covering" the face. I have used the translation "encircled" as a synonym for Śrīdhara's idea.

When discussing the ways in which the beauty and bodily features of Krishna attract the minds of the Gopīs, Caitanya quotes this verse (CC 2.24.50). Furthermore, after coming out of unconsciousness from a devotional trance (CC 3.15.57–59), Caitanya longs for the sight of Krishna who holds the flute to his mouth (CC 3.15.60–62). He begins to recite a verse spoken by Rādhā (CC 3.15.63) and describes Krishna further in his own words (CC 3.15.64–69), after which he recites this verse of the Rāsa Līlā (CC 3.15.70).

Verse 1.40

Ripplings of bodily bliss, *pulakāny.* For an exegetical analysis of the word *pulaka* and other related words, and a discussion on the difficulty of translating this word and similar words, refer to the section entitled "Devotional Yoga Transcends Death" in "Textual Illuminations."

Jīva presents this verse among others to describe how the Lord makes it possible for his devotees to be drawn to him through love. Jīva also quotes the verse to demonstrate the exquisite beauty of Krishna (KS 178) and to illustrate how the Gopīs find themselves immersed in pure love for him (PrS 83). Elsewhere Jīva states that Krishna's flute music is a cause of *rasa,* giving the present verse as an example (PrS 111). Furthermore, the verse is understood as an example of *ālāpa,* "very affectionate speech" (PrS 330).

In Krishnadāsa's work, Caitanya recites this verse to show the power of Krishna's flute music and how Krishna attracts the minds of all young girls (CC 2.24.56). In one incident, Caitanya requests his intimate associate Svarūpa Dāmodara to recite something about Krishna, his flute music, and the Gopīs (CC 2.17.28–29). Svarūpa chooses to recite this verse to satisfy him (CC 2.17.31). Caitanya becomes absorbed in an ecstatic state and begins elaborating upon this verse in the eighteen verses that follow (CC 3.17.32–49), beginning with the verse below:

> *śuni' prabhu gopībhāve āviṣṭa hailā*
> *bhāgavatera ślokera artha karite lāgilā*
>
> Hearing this, the Master became absorbed
> in the emotions of the Gopīs.
> He began to explain the meaning
> of this verse from the *Bhāgavata.*
> (CC 3.17.32)

Verse 1.42

Jīva cites this verse as another of several verses in the RL expressing how Krishna comes under the influence or control of his devotees' love for him (PrS 296-297).

The supreme Lord among masters of yoga, *yogeśvareśvaraḥ.* Jīva highlights the epithetical name for Krishna, *yogeśvareśvaraḥ,* indicating that he is the supreme controller who arranges for all supramundane activities by his inconceivable powers.

Despondent words, *viklavitaṁ.* Jīva states that the word *viklavitaṁ,* meaning literally "words of distress," refers to "words of helplessness."

Arranged for the pleasure, *arīramat.* Jīva suggests that just as the most prominent of children arranges the agenda for their playing, so the word *arīramat* means that Krishna "arranged for the enjoyment" of the Gopīs.

Verse 1.43

Jīva cites this verse to demonstrate the supreme love of the Gopīs for Krishna. Here, he also desires to establish the spiritual forms of the cowherd maidens and Krishna (PrS 280), and similarly cites verses RL 4.10 (PrS 282) and RL 5.7 (PrS 281).

Actions, *ceṣṭitam.* Viśvanātha states in his commentary to this verse that the word *ceṣṭitam* refers to God's *līlā.*

Verse 1.47

The great Soul, *mahātmanaḥ.* Jīva states that *mahātmanaḥ* means "great soul," in the sense of Krishna as the most excellent of all lovers, worldly or divine. Viśvanātha confirms this meaning given by Jīva, and adds that it also means that the manifestation of Krishna is the original form of the Lord.

Verse 1.48

Jīva cites this verse to answer the question of how it is possible for the dear devotees of the Lord to be rivals of one another. However, even such contrary behavior on the part of a devotee is exhibited for the purpose of contributing to love of God (PrS 287).

Bestowing upon them his grace, *prasādāya.* Jīva states that the word can be taken in several ways. The sense of "grace" or "mercy" can be understood, because Krishna puts the cowherd maidens in a position of longing for him. It can also be understood to mean "for the purpose of satisfying" the Gopīs' passion, ultimately in the Rāsa dance. It can also mean "for delighting" the maidens in the Rāsa (PrS 288).

To quell, *praśamāya.* The word *praśamāya,* a causative form of the verb *śam,* which I have translated as "to calm," has other senses that could apply, such as "to appease," "to extinguish," "to conquer," or "to subdue."

Pride, *mānam.* Jīva suggests that the Gopīs' pride is their "great fortune," *saubhaga-madam* within *praṇaya-māna,* or the "pride of loving intimacy." This verse is cited by Jīva as identifying *praṇaya-māna,* and the idea is further developed in PrS 84 and 386.

This verse is recited by Caitanya (CC 2.15.81) who, as he continues to describe Krishna, becomes forlorn in his feelings of separation from him. Caitanya then requests Svarūpa Dāmodara to recite poetry that will absorb his consciousness in Krishna. This devoted follower chooses the following refrain found in verses from the *Gīta Govinda,* which he recites repeatedly for Caitanya (CC 2.15.84–91):

> *rāse harim iha vihita-vilāsam |*
> *smarati mano mama kṛta-parihāsam ||*
>
> In the Rāsa dance, here Hari was playing lovingly.
> My mind remembers how he was laughing teasingly.
> (GG 2.2–9)

The repetition of this refrain sends Caitanya into an ecstatic state of mind and wild dancing.

Act Two

The second act opens with a "pausing scene" (*vimarṣa-sandhi*) in which the heroines act out their torment of being separated from Krishna. The Gopīs imitate Krishna's actions and movements, and inquire of his whereabouts from inhabitants of the forest (RL 1–23). Although the second scene (RL 24–44) is a further development of the pausing scene, a clear shift is indicated by the introduction of a "subplot" (*patākā*). The Gopīs track footprints and discover that Krishna has left the group of cowherdesses with a special Gopī. They find this maiden, also deserted by Krishna, in the forest. Together, they continue the search for Krishna, while constantly speaking about him until darkness falls upon them.

Verse 2.1

This verse is cited as an example of *eka-līlā-gata* (found in one *līlā*) within *pūrva-rāga* (the separation of lovers who were previously intimately associated, but have been separated due to their being in different places) (PrS 390). Jīva cites this verse and the following two as examples of *līlā,* or "acting out of Krishna's divine play," an aspect of the experience of *anubhāva-prakaraṇa.* The *līlā-anubhāva,* or imitation of Krishna's activities, is seen throughout the first half of this act. In this *anubhāva,* the Gopīs are completely identified with Krishna (PrS 324–325). Jīva also cites this verse as an example of "the state of being separated from the beloved by a shorter distance," *kiñcid-dūra-gamana-maya,* within "the state of separation from the beloved," a type of *pravāsa* found in *vipralambha* (PrS 390).

Verse 2.2

Viśvanātha explains that when the Gopīs act out Krishna's *līlās*, it has the effect of an intense and powerful meditation characterized as *sañcāri-bhāva,* specifically known as *unmāda,* or a type of "madness" in which one loses self-awareness and identifies oneself completely with Krishna. Thus "their minds were absorbed in him." The phrase *tad-ātmika,* "being fully absorbed in him," indicates, according to Viśvanātha, the stage of *unmāda.* Once the Gopīs attain this state of madness, their minds, intelligence, indeed their very souls are of him, Krishna (SD). The phrase *tad-ātmika* is found again in the next verse.

The word *vibhrama* is translated in this verse simply as "passionate" or "passion" (in the first and second quarter verses, respectively), which hardly conveys the complex psychological state that Viśvanātha explains is indicated here. He defines it as a certain intense frenzy, which prevents the mind from functioning while experiencing amorous feelings. The word *ākṣipta* means in this context, according to Śrīdhara, *ākṛṣṭa* (literally "drawn to") or "utterly captivated." The word means "cast," "thrown down," "caught," "seized," "overcome," "charmed," or "transported." Viśvanātha states that *ākṣipta* describes the state of the Gopīs' minds, which become unsubstantial, and thus appear to the maidens to be leaving their bodies.

Verse 2.3

The behavior of the Gopīs is not a "state of self-worship," *ahaṅgrahopāsanā*; rather, it exhibits the state of *tad-ātmika.* The phrase *tad-ātmika* is used again here, a repetition from the previous verse. Thus, their state is one in which the various movements of the beloved overtake their minds and senses, *cittendriya-mayī,* and their very selves assume a likeness to Krishna (SD).

Became similar, *pratirūḍha.* Śrīdhara states that this word means *āviṣṭa,* or "filled." Jīva states that the word means *sadṛśī-bhūta,* or "became similar."

Verse 2.4

The madness of the cowherd maidens is seen in their behavior of talking to the plants and vines of the forest, and imitating the behavior of Krishna because of identifying with him. According to Jīva, this madness is an appreciation, based on pure love, of God's presence everywhere, allowing one to see God manifest in everything. The behavior of the Gopīs in this verse is identified as "bewilderment of the heart," *unmāda* (PrS 345).

God appears to the maidens within their own hearts, and he appears to them in the forms of the trees, vines, and flowers of the Vrindāvana forest. In support of his exegesis, Jīva quotes a later text stating that, "just as the vines and trees of the forest were revealing an abundance of flowers, they [the Gopīs] were revealing Vishnu in their own hearts" (*vana-latās tarava ātmani viṣṇuṁ vyañjayantya iva puṣpa-latāḍhyāḥ,* BhP 10.35.9). Viśvanātha states that although Krishna is alone with the presiding goddess of Vrindāvana, he is aware of the questions that the Gopīs ask in their state of love intoxication and madness of separation, since he is all-pervading (KrS 2.4).

Caitanya quotes this verse (CC 2.25.130) during his talk with Prakaśānanda, when he is describing how one should inquire about the supreme Person. Thus the example of the Gopīs inquiring from every plant in the forest demonstrates this mood of inquiry (CC 2.25.122–123), and how a devotee looks everywhere and sees only Krishna (CC 2.25.127).

Supreme Person, *puruṣaṁ.* The Sanskrit word *puruṣa* means "person" in its simple denotative definition. The term also carries the Vedic sense of "the primaeval man as the soul and original source of the universe" (MW), and can be an epithet for Vishnu, "the all-pervading One." It is clear from the modifying terms in the sentence that *puruṣa* identifies Krishna.

All living beings, *bhūteṣu.* The word *bhūteṣu,* according to Jīva, refers here specifically to "living" (*prāṇiṣu*) beings.

Verse 2.6

Rāma is the shortened version of the name Balarāma, a form of Krishna who assumes the role of his older brother. The bodily forms of Krishna and Balarāma are identical, with the exception of color (CC 1.1.68)—Krishna being described as dark or bluish, and Balarāma as white. Despite the divine identities, the two boys tend calves and cows and fight off demons that threaten the residents of Vraja. Balarāma is solely responsible for killing such demons as Pralambhāsura (BhP 10.18), the Dvivida Gorilla demon (BhP 10.67), and for slaying Rukmi, the bad-hearted brother of Krishna's principal queen in Dvāraka (BhP 10.61). In order to console the Gopīs during their long separation from Krishna when he goes off to Mathurā, Balarāma remains with them in Vraja. They enjoy each other's company nightly in a forest grove along the shores of the Yamunā River (BhP 10.65.17– 18). Śrīdhara states that the Gopīs who are not able to participate in Krishna's Rāsa Līlā, due to their young age, instead enjoy these amorous dealings with Balarāma. Jīva also quotes a phrase that confirms this statement (BhP 10.15.8). Jīva states that the Gopīs with whom Balarāma sports during certain festivals are not the same Gopīs with whom Krishna sports. Viśvanātha agrees with this statement (BhP 10.65.18).

Verse 2.7

The Gopīs are talking to the *tulasī* plants because they know that the delicate blossoms of *tulasī* are always included among the other flowers in Krishna's garlands. Their understanding is made more explicit in Verse 12 of this act.

When Caitanya finds a flower garden and wanders through it, he thinks he is in the Vrindāvana forest. Becoming absorbed in love (*premāveśe*), he begins to search for Krishna. While in his ecstasy and loving madness, he emulates the behavior of the Gopīs in their madness of separation and thus begins to quote their words, as they search for Krishna in the forest (CC 2.15.30–31). Caitanya then quotes the present verse (RL 2.7) in CC 2.15.33, and other verses from the present scene, expressing his state of mind.

Verse 2.8

The Gopīs know how attracted Krishna is to jasmine flowers, evidenced by their talking to varieties of jasmine in the Vraja forest, when they search for him in their madness: "O Mālati [jasmine]," Mallikā, Jāti, and Yūthikā!"

As with the previous verse, Caitanya quotes this verse and the next to describe his state of mind, which is similar to that of the Gopīs in this act (CC 2.15.34).

Verse 2.9

Arka plant. A very insignificant vine, which expresses how desperate the Gopīs are to find Krishna, and the lack of response they are getting from the more prominent plants and trees in the forest (KrS).

We are losing our minds, *rahitātmanāṁaḥ.* Another sense of the word *rahita* in this context is "deserted." Understood in this latter sense, the Gopīs have deserted themselves, or their souls, *ātmanām.*

Krishnadāsa explains the reason why the trees and plants that are questioned by the cowherd maidens do not respond—they may be male, and as Krishna's friends, will not reveal his whereabouts. Krishnadāsa further describes how the Gopīs then inquire from the female plants. Upon still receiving no response, they think that these plants must be maidservants of Krishna, and out of fear, cannot speak (CC 2.15.32–42).

Verse 2.10

Jīva makes a distinction between *prema,* or intimate and pure love for God, and *aiśvarya-jñāna,* or love mixed with knowledge of God's greatness and power. This verse illustrates both types of love: the first two *padas* express the intimacy of *mādhurya-bhāva,* and the second two express love combined with *aiśvarya-jñāna* (KrS). Jīva suggests that both the third and fourth *padas* regarding the *aiśvarya* forms of Krishna are actually rhetorical questions. In other words, the ecstatic bristling hair-like grasses of the earth rise not because of Urukrama or Varāha, but are certainly due to the touch of Krishna's feet (PrS 310-312).

The Gopīs appear to be projecting their own emotions onto the earth when they interpret the earth's erect grasses to be signs of ecstasy, due to having been in the presence of Krishna. The hairs of the earth that the maidens observe are the grasses and sprouts growing from its surface, which stand on end because Krishna walks the earth (SD).

Urukrama is a name for Krishna meaning "the wide-striding one." Another name for Urukrama is Vāmana, the dwarf incarnation of Krishna. Posing as the son of a brāhmaṇa, Vāmana appeared before King Bali, asking in charity for only three paces of land. Bali granted the Lord his wish against the advice of his demonic spiritual master. Vāmana then proceeded to expand his body, assuming the immense form of Lord Vishnu, and covered the entire world's surface, the sky, and all directions with his first step. With his second step, he covered the complete upper planetary system. Bali, who understood that Lord Vishnu had no space left for his final footstep, then offered his head as a suitable place for the Lord's third step. The story of Urukrama can be found in BhP 8.17–23.

Varāha is a name for Krishna's incarnation as the divine boar. Due to a disturbance created by certain demons, the earth's floating condition had been disrupted, and it had subsequently fallen into the Garbhodaka Ocean. Varāha, the Lord in the form of a gigantic boar, saved the earth by lifting it out of the water with his huge tusks, which he then used for piercing the demon Hiranyākṣa. Some commentators emphasize that the Lord's significant snout was also used for carrying the planet earth. This incident is described in BhP 3.13.

Verse 2.11
Jīva states that the words "his beloved" refer to Krishna's dearest Goddess consort, Rādhā (PrS 108). The Gopī speaking the words in this verse is a *sakhī,* or "friend." This is clear when the speaker calls out to the deer as *sakhī,* "O friend," and the cowherd maidens treat the deer as they treat each other—as friends. Elsewhere, Jīva states that this verse and the next are examples of Gopīs who enjoy loving interactions with Krishna directly (PrS 369).

Jīva presents four types of Gopī personalities in relation to Rādhā: *sakhī,* those who act as a "friend"; *suhṛt,* those who are "good hearted" or "kindly"; *taṭasthā,* those who are "neutral" or "marginal" in character; and *prātipakṣikī,* those who are "adversarial" or "rival" in nature (PrS 286). These special characteristic behaviors of the maidens are elaborated upon by Jīva throughout his *Prīti Sandarbha* (PrS 429). Jīva identifies the particular types of Gopīs in various verses throughout the second act (PrS 286–240).

Pleasure, *nivṛtim.* The synonymn, according to Viśvanātha, for the word *nirvṛtim* is *ānandam,* meaning "bliss," "joy," or as translated here, "pleasure."

Lord of this group, *kula-pati.* According to Viśvanātha, this phrase means the "enjoyer of the Gopīs." The word *pati* can mean "husband" or "lord," and in a compound, "head" or "chief"; and *kula* means "herd," "troop," "flock," and so on. Viśvanātha explains that the maidens are trying to tell the deer that Krishna should be the *kula-patiḥ,* instead of being alone with one Gopī.

This verse is recited by Caitanya (CC 2.15.44). Krishnadāsa explains that the deer, upon hearing the Gopīs speak, do not respond to their desperate inquiry simply because they are not able to hear the maidens, also due to their feeling intense separation from Krishna (CC 2.15.48).

Verse 2.12
Rāma is the shortened name for Krishna's brother, Balarāma (*bala* and *rāma,* "one who enjoys great strength"). The name Rāma is also a name for the *avatāra* of Krishna as Rāmacandra, found in the epic *Rāmāyana* written by Vālmīki, but this personality is not referred to here.

The Gopīs perceive the trees and plants, whose branches are heavy with fruits and flowers during the harvest season, to be bowing before Krishna, having just seen him pass by. The reason the trees do not answer the maidens is that they have apparently become unconscious, due to the unhappiness they experience in separation from Krishna (CC 2.15.52–54). Krishnadāsa interprets this verse (CC 2.15.49–50), which Caitanya recites (CC 2.15.51).

Verse 2.13
Here the Gopīs wish to inquire from the vines, which are embracing their husbands' arms, the branches of the trees. As both Viśvanātha and Śrīdhara suggest, the cowherd maidens are sure that the vines have had contact with Krishna, since they could not be experiencing ecstatic eruptions (*utpulakāni*) due simply to contact with their husband-tree (BB and SD). The words of this verse are spoken by a Gopī who is neutral, or *taṭasthā* (PrS 286).

Rising ripplings of bliss, *utpulakāny.* See the section entitled "Devotional Yoga Transcends Death" in "Textual Illuminations" for an explanation of this translation of the word *pulaka.*

Verse 2.15
Pūtanā is a demonness who transformed herself into a beautiful woman and entered Vraja with the intent of killing baby Krishna by nursing him from her poisoned breast. As the baby squeezed her breast, however, he sucked out the poison and the life of Pūtanā as well. This episode is in BhP 10.6.1–44.

Pretended to be a cart, *śakaṭāyatīm.* Krishna as a baby had been placed briefly underneath a handcart. With a simple kick of his delicate soft leg, the handcart was overturned and broken into many pieces, and the metal utensils on it went flying here and there. Some commentators explain that a demon named Śakatāsura had taken the form of the handcart in order to kill the child; instead, however, baby Krishna killed the demon. This episode is presented in BhP 10.7.6–12.

Verse 2.16
A demon carrying away another. In this verse, Krishna's episode with the demon Tṛṇāvarta is imitated by the Gopīs. In the form of a great whirlwind or tornado, this demon carried the infant Krishna into the

sky, far away from his mother. Krishna then made himself heavier than a mountain and choked the demon to death, returning to Vraja unharmed. This story is presented in BhP 10.7.18–32.

With the tinkling of ankle bells. Special attention is given to the ankle bells of Krishna in BhP 10.8.22 when he is an infant, and in BhP 10.11.39 when he is older.

Verse 2.17

The calf demon is known by the name Vatsa, and disguised himself as a calf with the intention of killing Krishna. Catching the demon's hind legs and twirling his body around, Krishna threw him into a tree which then fell to the ground along with the dead demon. This episode is described in BhP 10.11.41–45.

The crane. The demon in the guise of a giant crane is named Baka. Krishna, who was devoured by this demon, made himself like fire, burning the throat of the demon, who immediately vomited. Once released from Baka, Krishna, who was not harmed, was attacked by the giant bird. In the presence of his cowherd friends, the Lord then bifurcated the demon's beak, causing his death. This incident is mentioned in BhP 10.11.46–54.

Verse 2.18

Jīva cites this verse as another example of *līlā-anubhāva.* He points out that as the Gopīs are overcome with love in separation from Krishna, they act out his marvelous activities to relieve themselves of the intense agony. He describes how the cowherd maidens lose themselves in their imitations of Krishna in the way actors lose themselves in their roles within a drama. In doing so, their love for Krishna increases.

Although the commentators do not indicate it, the acting out of cows wandering off seems to invoke a particular *līlā.* This verse appears to refer to the trick that Brahma played on Krishna when he wanted to demonstrate his own power and better perceive the power of Krishna. The story goes as follows: while Krishna was engaged in searching for some wandering calves, Brahma kidnapped the remaining cowherd boys and calves. Understanding that this was Brahma's trick, Krishna multiplied himself so as to assume the identity of each of the stolen calves and children, thereby keeping their family members in Vraja completely satisfied. When Brahma witnessed this phenomenon, he became bewildered and amazed by Krishna's supreme potency, and offered him respectful prayers. This story is found in BhP 10.13 and 14.

Verse 2.19

When the Gopīs act out Krishna's *līlās,* it has the effect of an extremely intense and powerful meditation characterized as *sañcāri-bhāva,* specifically known as *unmāda,* or a type of "madness" in which one loses self-awareness and identifies oneself completely with Krishna (SD).

Verse 2.20

Upper garment, *ambaram.* According to Śrīdhara, the word *ambaram* means "upper garment." The Gopī in this verse is imitating Krishna in the episode of lifting the hill known as Govardhana by lifting her upper garment, as Krishna lifted Govardhana. The god Indra became upset when Krishna convinced the residents of Vraja to discontinue their sacrifice for him, and instead to offer a sacrifice for the pleasure of the brāhmaṇas, the cows, and Govardhana. Indra then sent torrential rains and wind as a form of pusnishment. Lifting Govardhana with just one finger, Krishna had the Vraja residents enter underneath, and used the hill for seven days as an umbrella of protection for his devotees. This episode is presented in BhP10.24 and 25.

Verse 2. 21

O wicked snake, *duṣṭāhe.* The snake in this incident is known as Kāliya, a venomous serpent that was contaminating the Yamunā River with its poison. Krishna jumped into Kāliya's lake, where he was wrapped in the coils of the serpent. When Krishna understood that the residents of Vraja were in acute anxiety over his condition, he expanded himself, breaking out of the serpent's grip, and then began to dance upon the hoods of Kāliya, easily conquering him. This episode is presented in BhP.10.16 and 17.

Verse 2.22

Raging forest fire, *dāvāgniṁ . . . ulbaṇam.* This Gopī is referring to the incident in which the cows wandered into the dense forest, searching for green grass. After the cowherd boys found their cherished cows, they were faced with a sudden forest fire of great magnitude, and cried out for help from Krishna and Balarāma. Krishna then swallowed the fierce fire, saving his friends with his yogic power. This story is found in BhP10.19.

Verse 2.23

This episode acted out by the cowherd maidens is cited as another example of *līlā-anubhāva* by Jīva. Moreover, he points out that the *līlās* acted out by the Gopīs are not any of those found within the *śṛṅgāra rasa.* Rather, they are *līlās* from other *rasas* and with various demons. Even so, the love for Krishna in *śṛṅgāra rasa* remains constant for the maidens throughout their dramatic acting (PrS 177, 324–325).

The one who has broken the butter pots. A Gopī imitates Krishna, pretending to be fearful of his mother, in the last line of this verse. In this story, Krishna, as a young boy, mischievously broke the butter pots of his foster mother, Yaśodā, and then stole the butter. Yaśodā attempted to tie him up with a rope in order to prevent him from further misbehaving. Mystically, however, each time she tried, using longer and longer ropes, the rope was always too short to bind the child Krishna. Finally, the divine cowherd allowed her to tie him up out of love, and is therefore known by the name of Dāmodara, "one who is bound (*dāma-*) at the waist (*-udara*)." This *līlā* is presented in BhP10.9.

Verse 2.24

Viśvanātha states that the Gopīs forget their own selves and identify only with their beloved when their madness, caused by their feelings of separation from Krishna, reaches its highest point (SD).

Verse 2.25

Viśvanātha explains that this verse refers to the six divine marks found on Krishna's right foot: the disc, flag, lotus flower, thunderbolt, elephant goad, and barleycorn. Other marks are discussed by Sanātana Gosvāmin in his *Vaiṣṇava-Toṣanī,* such as certain lines, an umbrella, a group of four *svāstikās* in the four cardinal directions, and so on. Viśvanātha goes on to explain that marks are also found on the left foot, such as the conch shell, the broken bow of Cupid, and others, with a total of nineteen images on both feet combined. Due to these decorations on the soles of his feet, his footprints are easily recognized by the Gopīs.

Verse 2.27

Rūpa Gosvāmin is acknowledged as having categorized the different types and subtypes of Gopīs in his work *Ujjvala-nīlamaṇi.* Jīva also distinguishes between Gopīs in relation to Rādhā, for she is the jewel among all the cowherd maidens. These various relations to Rādhā can be observed in the varying reactions of the maidens upon coming across the footprints of Krishna and the special Gopī (RL 2.27–33). Jīva quotes these passages on the Gopīs' detective work in the final section of the PrS, in which he states that the *Bhāgavata* describes Śrī Rādhā, who is the foremost of all fortunate ladies (PrS 429). The section describing Rādhā includes the RL 2.27–34.

Verse 2.28

The Beloved Lord, the supreme Lord (*īśvaraḥ*) **Hari**, and **Govinda**. Viśvanātha presents the significance of the various names of God employed. Hari means one who "removes the distress of the devotees." The word Bhagavān, as the Beloved Lord, can be identified with Lord Nārāyaṇa, or it can mean "beautiful one, agitated by amorous desire." Beauty is understood to be one among many excellences, as acknowledged by Jīva and Krishnadāsa. *Īśvara,* normally understood as "the supreme controller," also means "the one who is capable of trickery" and "the one who fulfills the desires of his devotees." The literal translation of Govinda can be "one who has taken (*vindati*) another's senses (*gāḥ*) in order to enjoy them for himself," or "he who causes one's senses to enjoy (*vindayati*)."

Worshiped . . . perfectly, *anayārādhitaḥ.* The significance of this verse for the early teachers of the Caitanya school is great, because this is the first verse in which the identity of Rādhā, Krishna's dearest Gopī consort, is revealed. The words in this verse, according to Jīva, are spoken by a maiden who is kindly, *suhṛt* (PrS 286). Jīva confirms later that this verse is spoken by Rādhā's kindly or good-hearted associates (PrS 429). This verse is seen as expressing the great glory of Rādhā (PrS 367). It is here that the name of the supreme Goddess consort of Krishna is said to be presented within the verbal form *anayārādhitaḥ,* the one who "perfectly worshiped" (PrS 108). It is explained that the name Rādhā is hidden in the word *ārādhitaḥ* (KS 178), and that this verse acknowledges that the cowherd maidens know that Rādhā has Krishna under her control (PrS 109). Jīva states that each of the Gopīs exhibits a different level of intensity of passion, among which Rādhā's is the most intense because she has the greatest ability to bring Krishna under her control (PrS 279).

Rādhā's name is withheld by the narrator, Śuka, until this verse. He reveals her personal name through the letters of the verbal adjective *ārādhita,* meaning the "resplendent" or "worshiped" one (SD), in which the first four consecutive letters of Rādhā's five-lettered name are embedded (*ā–rādh–ita*). This is the verse in which Rādhā is announced, and it is explained that her specially marked footprints, which also possess nineteen marks (as enumerated by Rūpa Gosvāmin in UNM), are recognized by the other cowherd maidens. Even though she is the dear friend of many of these maidens, they pretend not to recognize her footprints for the sake of the larger company of many types of Gopīs present. Those who are able to recognize her footprints inwardly and joyfully acknowledge her great fortune to be with Krishna exclusively, despite their outward expressions of discovery and bewilderment.

This verse is quoted twice in the CC. First, when Krishnadāsa gives an elaborate theological description of the supreme Goddess, Rādhā, the verse is introduced (CC 1.4.88). Later in the work, Rāmānanda describes Rādhā to Caitanya and quotes, among other texts, this verse (CC 2.8.100), before he goes on to describe her role in relation to the other cowherd maidens and Krishna within the Rāsa Līlā story. This verse is highly significant for the early teachers of the Caitanya school because it is the only verse in which the identity of Rādhā is implicitly revealed through the Gopīs' description of her.

Verse 2.29

The words of this verse are spoken by Gopīs who are neither adversarial nor friendly, but neutral in character, or *taṭasthā* (PrS 286 and 429).

Verse 2.30

This verse is spoken by a Gopī who is considered a rival or adversary, a *prātipakṣikī,* to the other maidens (PrS 287). The verse exemplifies the quality of *asūyā,* meaning "envy" (PrS 360).

Verse 2.34

Jīva points out that there is nothing wrong with the pride of the Gopīs, as expressed by this verse. He presents a discussion describing how Krishna desires to show the lowly condition of worldly love. Although the love of the special Gopī identified as Rādhā may appear to be that of worldly love, it is actually wondrous and glorious spiritual love for God (PrS 288). Thus, commentators discuss how Rādhā's behavior is both revealed and concealed. The author of the *Bhāgavata* appears to be saying that Krishna's enjoyment also teaches dharma by "showing the degraded condition of lustful men and lowly women."

Bad-hearted women, *durātmatām.* For further elaboration on this phrase, see comments on verse 2.41 below.

Verse 2.35
This verse demonstrates how special this particular Gopī is among all the numerous cowherd maidens. Jīva identifies her as Rādhā (PrS 288). This example of exclusive attention, apart from the other Gopīs, is attainable only after the highest limit of *premā* is demonstrated, wherein intimacy increases in intensity. In this case, the special maiden, Rādhā, controls Krishna (KrS).

Verse 2.36
This verse and the next two are presented by Caitanya in his instructions to Rūpa Gosvāmin (CC 2.19.207–209), and are cited as examples of *praṇaya-māna* (PrS 386); see "Notes and Comments" on RL 1.48 for the first instance of this. When Caitanya explains the intricacies of the five *rasas,* these verses are quoted by him to demonstrate the nature of *kevala śuddha-prema,* or "unqualified pure love" (CC 2.19.203).

Verse 2.37
She became proud, *dṛptā.* The Gopī's "pride" is expressed in this passage by the word *dṛptā.* There are two levels of pride, or *māna,* which are further expressions of the pure love of the cowherd maidens: the first is *sthāyi-mayī,* prideful ecstasy that is only experienced when the beloved is present; and the second is *sthāyi-mayī bhāva,* which occurs when others are also present. The mood exhibited by this special maiden is called *kevala-sthāyi-mayī bhāva,* which is a sustained state of her love for Krishna, *anurāga* (KrS).

Verse 2.38
Krishna's departure is actually a kind of trick that is performed to stretch the limits of *premā,* or pure love, through the extreme humiliation and bewilderment of separation. This example of separation is appropriate only after the highest limit of *premā* is demonstrated in the form of direct enjoyment (of *sambhoga*). In this case, intimacy in-

creases in intensity as the special Gopī, Rādhā, controls Krishna (KrS). It is possible for Krishna, due to the divine potency of *līlā*, to be unaware of what is going on in the mind of the Gopī. This example demonstrates that the tradition accepts the power of love as the supreme power, even over Krishna, although he is the very source of that power (SD).

This verse is cited as an example of *eka-līlā-gata* (found in one *līlā*) within *pūrva-rāga*, the separation of lovers who were previously intimately associated, but have been separated due to their being in different places (PrS 390).

Verse 2.39

The meaning of this verse for the tradition is that Rādhā is the highest among all the queens of Dvāraka and Mathurā, as well as among all the Gopīs of Vraja (CC 1.6.71).

This verse illustrates *audārya* as a characteristic of *alaṁkāra-anubhāva*. The sign of *audārya* is consistently humble behavior (PrS 322). The verse is also an example of *pralāpa* within the state of *pravāsa* (being far away from one's beloved), the fourth type of *vipralambha* (separation from one's beloved) (PrS 391). This verse is a specific example of *kiñcid-dūra-gamana-maya* (the state of being separated from the beloved by a shorter distance) within the state of *pravāsa* (PrS 390).

Caitanya's words resonate with these words of longing and prayer coming from the special Gopī, as in the following passage:

> Where is the one whose figure is curved in three places?
> Where is the sweet song of his flute?
> Where is the bank of the river Yamunā?
> Where is the play of the Rāsa dance?
> Where is the dancing, singing, and laughter?
> Where is my Lord, Madan Mohan?
>
> (CC 2.2.56)

Verse 2.40

When the cowherd maidens are separated from Krishna, all of them, in spite of their differences in character type, feel a kinship with each other. According to Jīva, the words of this verse express that kinship. The purpose of Krishna's separation from the Gopīs, who are the greatest lovers of God, is to increase their love for him (PrS 288).

Verse 2.41

Self-indulgence, *daurātmyād.* The meaning of the word *daurātmyāt* is "bad-heartedness" or "wickedness," according to both Jīva and Viśvanātha, and is meant to express how this Gopī is thinking of her own prideful words and humiliation. The word actually indicates that the Gopī is feeling "herself (*ātmā*) so far away (*dūra*)" from Krishna, or feeling that "the soul (*ātmā*, or Krishna) is so far away (*dūra*)" from her (KrS and SD 2.41). Thus pride, according to the commentators, is actually a positive element in the Gopīs' unconditional love for Krishna. Viśvanātha explains that from this verse (RL 2.41) it is clear that the cowherd maidens abandon all their activities based on the negative worldly quality of "my-ness" (*mamatā*) and "I-ness" (*ahaṁtā*) (SD 1.5). Jīva speaks of a worldly *mamatā*, or "my-ness" (PrS 180). Yet he also speaks of "my-ness" or "possessiveness," using the same word *mamatā*, as a sign of love of God, even a sign of higher levels of loving God. He states that *mamatā* is the distinguishing characteristic that separates higher *rasas* from *śānta rasa.* He also discusses *ananya-mamatā*, that is, the Lord is experienced as "their only possession." Furthermore, he speaks of degrees of possessiveness (PrS 160, 168), and gives the example of RL 4.6 as pride in divine love (PrS 156).

Verse 2.43

They were fully absorbed in him, *tad-ātmikāḥ.* Śrīdhara states that the phrase *tad-ātmikāḥ* means that he was their very self, or that they were completely absorbed in thoughts of him.

Act Three

The third act consists of only one scene containing nineteen verses of monologue, or prayerful soliloquy. This is another pausing scene, like that found in the beginning of act two, but at a heightened level of expression. The calamity of Krishna's disappearance and inability on the part of the cowherd maidens to find him lead them to prayerful song in this third act.

These combined verses form a climactic plateau in which the Gopīs' agony of separation reaches a sustained pitch of intensity, expressed in eighteen verses in the *triṣṭubh* meter, and culminating in the nineteenth and final verse in the *śakvarī* meter. This act is effectively placed at the very center of the drama, framed by the other four acts. Although the climactic event of the story is found in the first scene of the fifth act, the greatest expression of emotion is present within the verses of this third act.

The emotional pitch sustained throughout the scene is achieved in several ways. First, there is no descriptive narrative or didactic discourse—only verses spoken directly by the Gopīs. Second, among the five acts this is the only one in which verses of the shortest and most common purāṇic meter of *anuṣṭubh* are completely absent. The *triṣṭubh* meter is introduced here, and is utilized only twice thereafter, once in the fourth act (RL 4.20) and once in the fifth (RL 5.17). In the latter two instances, the *upajāti* form of the *triṣṭubh* meter is used, whereas in this act the *rājahaṁsī* form is engaged. It is as if the author saved this particular flowing songlike meter for this one-scene act.[1] Third, this scene presents the greatest consecutive number of longer-metered verses of any scene or act.

1. Contributing further to the songlike quality of the Rājahaṁsī verse is the repetition of the first syllable consonant of each quarter verse line within the seventh syllable of the same line. For example, in the first verse of this act, the "j" consonant is found within the first quarter verse in the first and seventh syllables; the "ś" sound within the second quarter verse is found in the first and seventh syllables, and so on. Most verses have only a few lines with this consonantal repetition (vv. 2, 5, 6, 7, 8, 10, 13, 14, 15, 16, and 17); one verse has no such repetition (v. 12); and some verses have each quarter verse with repetitions (vv. 1, 3, 4, and 18).

The central act has been characterized as containing verses of song, and thus has been popularly named "The Song of the Gopīs," or Gopī Gīta. The scene takes place on the banks of the Yamunā River, where the Gopīs praise Krishna and yearn for his company through song. The singing of the cowherd maidens is explicitly described in the final two verses of the preceding act and in the act that follows. Thus, the narrator states that the maidens "praise Krishna's qualities in song" (RL 2.43), and sit together as they "sing about Krishna" (RL 2.44); then the fourth act begins by acknowledging that they "sang out for him" (RL 4.1).

The verses in act 3 have also been cited as expressions of "lamentation" known as *pralāpa* (PrS 392). *Pralāpa* is one of the nine characteristics found within a certain type of *vipralambha,* or "separation" in devotional love, known as *pravāsa.*[2] This specific type of separation involves the parting of lovers who were previously intimately associated but have been separated by being in different places. Many of the qualities found within both *pravāsa* and *pralāpa,* such as "anxiety," "trembling," "torment," "madness," "bewilderment," and "dying," can be observed here.

Every verse in this act glorifies Krishna, at least implicitly. Such praise is for his qualities of intimacy (*mādhurya*) or his qualities of greatness (*aiśvarya*). Praise of these attributes of intimacy yields expressions of passion, whereas glorification of his omnipotence and divine power yields expressions of humility. In both cases, there is often a weaving together of reflective and emotive qualities. For example, in the first verse of the act, the cowherd maidens state that Vraja is wonderful since it is the place of Krishna's birth; but in the same breath, they express both the desperation of looking for Krishna and their absolute dependence on him. In another verse expressing their passion for him, the Gopīs reflect upon the beauty of Krishna's eyes in the first half of the verse, and in the second half, explode with emotion:

With your eyes,
  you steal the beauty
  of the center
Of an exquisite fully bloomed
  lotus flower, rising out
  of a serene autumn pond,

2. See note to RL 2.39 (PrS 391).

O Lord of love,
  and it is killing us—
  your voluntary maidservants!
O bestower of benedictions,
  in this world,
  is this not murder?
(RL 3.2)

Therefore, act 3, though uneventful with regard to action within the plot, is as eventful emotionally as the rest of the drama in its story line. It is no wonder that the verses in this act, with their intense emotional content, have received special attention from the Caitanya school because of their expression of *viraha bhakti,* devotional love in separation from God. These verses are said to possess the "fragrance of the honey" of pure love, attracting Krishna who is compared to a "bee" (SD 3.1).

Jīva devotes at least one section of his Prīti Sandarbha to quoting the verses of this act in full, tracing their emotional expressions and essential meanings (PrS 391–392). Indeed, more verses are quoted in the CC from this act and the previous one, both of which focus on the absence of Krishna, than from any of the other three acts. The final verse of this act is quoted four times throughout the CC, more than any other single verse in the complete drama. Verses here are not randomly placed together, as they might appear upon a first reading; rather, they are effectively arranged as they orchestrate expressions of increasing emotional intensity—love, longing, humility, and passion, all of which are experienced by the Gopīs in Krishna's absence.

Verse 3.1

This verse opens with lines of praise for Vraja, a land so special that it attracts the eternal service of the Goddess Śrī. The deity is described as both with and without birth. Here, the Gopīs speak of Vraja as the land of Krishna's birth. In the first act, however, the narrator explains that Krishna "is without birth" (RL 1.16). The first half of the verse consists of reflective words of the cowherd maidens, and the second half, strongly emotive words—the prominent expression throughout the act. They express passionate selfless dedication to Krishna in the final verse, in the phrase, "our lives are only for you," and explain that their "very life-breath" is found in him; other words express their fervent search for him.

The essential message of the Gopīs in the verses of this act is "please allow us to see you," or "please appear to us" (BB). The message of this particular verse is that Krishna should appear before the cowherd maidens out of fear, otherwise, of being accused of murdering so many women (SD). This verse is an example of *pūrva-rāga,* the beginning phase of loving Krishna experienced by the Gopīs (PrS 290).

The Gopīs spoke, *gopya ūcuḥ.* The verb "spoke" is the plural of the perfect past tense, introducing all the verses in this act (BB). Each of the verses is a singular voice of one of the Gopīs speaking on behalf of the group, as confirmed by commentators. Although the first person plural is utilized throughout, in some verses the Gopī speaking is clearly representing the group, especially when using the third person to refer to the others. An example of this is v. 8.

Glorious is Vraja, *jayati . . . vraja.* The first word of this act, *jayati,* is a simple present tense verb meaning literally to "conquer" or "excel," and thus the Gopīs state, "Vraja conquers or excels [all other lands in all ways]." The word *jayati* is commonly used as an opening word in hymns of praise.

Surpassing all, *adhikam.* This word emphasizes the superlative status of the realm of Vraja, which "conquers" all other places, including the heavenly spiritual realm of Vaikuṇṭha, and therefore is considered superexcellent. Vraja is considered to be the best of all places (SD).

The Goddess Indirā is a name for Lakṣmī, also known as Śrī, the consort of Nārāyaṇa throughout the RL. In the highest sphere of Vraja, Lakṣmī is serving; whereas in Vaikuṇṭha, with the cosmic form of Vishnu, she is being served. Thus, the extraordinary status and superlative nature of Vraja is expressed by the Great Goddess's residence here (SD). Śrī is referred to by the Gopīs three more times in this act; see vv. 5, 7, and 17.

Please allow your maidservants to see you, *dṛśyatām.* Grammatically, this imperative verb can mean quite the opposite, as in "please look at us," or "please come to see us." Alternative readings of this imperative verb have been suggested: "you should be seen by us," or "these Gopīs should be seen by you—you should search for them" (BB). Both meanings in this ambiguity apply, but the former is more consistent with the maidens' words, expressing their search for Krishna.

Sustained, *dhṛta.* The word has been taken to mean "offered," as in the alternative reading of the phrase, "to you we have offered our very lives" (SD). If we use the alternative translations of both *dṛśyatām* and *dhṛta,* a possible alternative reading of the second half of the verse could be as follows:

O beloved, please allow
your maidservants to see you!
We have offered our very life-breath to you;
we search everywhere for you.
(RL 3.1cd)

Verse 3.2

O Lord of love, *surata-nātha.* The word *surata* has a sexual or erotic overtone. This epithet for Krishna can be understood as the synonym *sambhoga-pate,* "O Lord of intimate enjoyment" (BB).

Verse 3.3

The Gopīs are wondering, in this verse, how Krishna can protect them so many times from death and in a variety of dangerous incidents, yet can now neglect them (BB). Their thoughts could be as follows: "As you have rescued everyone from these various demons in the past, you must certainly rescue us now" (PrS 392). The cowherd maidens desire to be saved from the "demon" of separation from him and, as in all other circumstances, he is the only one who can do it.

It is interesting that the last two stories described in this verse, presenting the bull demon and Vyomāsura, sequentially follow the Rāsa Līlā, and therefore appear chronologically later in the *Bhāgavata* than does the Rāsa event. Some commentators account for this by understanding that the Gopīs' devotional love for Krishna allows them to develop knowledge of Krishna's future. Others state that the maidens are aware of Krishna's astrological charts provided by such sages as Garga and Bhāguri, which predict these events as well as others (SD).

From poisonous waters is generally understood as referring to the serpent Kāliya, on whose many heads Krishna danced when he conquered the demon. The story of Krishna and the Kāliya serpent is found in BhP 10.16–17. This *līlā* was acted out by the Gopīs in the earlier part of the previous act; see RL 2.21 and the comments on 2.21 above.

A fearsome demon can refer to any number of demons, including Kāliya, who was unambiguously indicated in the preceding phrase, "from poisonous waters," but is generally taken as the huge snake demon by the name of Agha. The story of Agha is found in BhP 10.12.

From torrential rains, wind storms, and fiery thunderbolts, refers to the *līlā* of Krishna lifting Govardhana hill and the humbling of the god Indra. See the comments on 2.20 for more detailed explanation. Some commentators state that the phrase "wind storms" is an indication of the *līlā* of Krishna killing the Tṛnāvarta, or whirlwind demon; see the comments on 2.16.

The bull is a demon known as Ariṣṭāsura. The demon, terrorizing the cowherd village of Vraja as he caused the earth to tremble with his hooves and bellowing, was provoked by Krishna's words. The gigantic bull furiously charged Krishna, who seized Ariṣṭāsura by the horns, kicked him to the ground and thrashed him, then struck him with the demon's torn-off horn until he died. This story is related in BhP10.36.1–16.

The son of Maya is Vyomāsura. The episode of Krishna slaying Vyomāsura is found in BhP 10.37.28–33.

Verse 3.4

The cowherd maidens in this verse are using indignant words to express their feelings that it is very inappropriate for Krishna, who has descended to protect the whole world, to neglect his devotees (BB). The following statements are examples, often using the first-person voice, of the types of thoughts and feelings that commentators imagine the Gopīs to possess: If Krishna has come to protect the whole world, then why shouldn't he protect the maidens who are also part of this world? How is it that Krishna can happily sit within the hearts of all souls, while witnessing the unhappiness of so many? Krishna was not born to the soft-hearted Gopī, his foster mother Yaśodā. Rather, he arose from the family of the Sātvata Dynasty, hiding his divine identity by transgressing his own religious and moral laws, such as those prohibiting the stealing of other men's wives (SD).

This verse is cited as an example of the Gopīs' awareness that the *aiśvarya* of Krishna can be combined with their vision of his sweetness in *mādhurya* (PrS 178). The concern for the Caitanya tradition is whether or not there is an improper mixture of *rasas*, in this case that of the *śānta rasa* with the *śṛṅgāra rasa*. Jīva insists that there is no fault in this apparent mixture of *śānta* and *śṛṅgāra rasa*s since there is actually no mixture at all, the implication being that the *aiśvarya* perceptions of the Gopīs are merely supplementing the *mādhurya*. Some commentators insist that the *aiśvarya* perceptions of the cowherd maidens only occur during their periods of fearing separation or actual separation from Krishna, and not when they are fully united with him (SD).

The first half of this verse declares that Krishna is not the son of a Gopī (his foster mother Yaśodā), and in reality is the indwelling supreme Soul of all souls. The manifestation of Krishna as the supreme Soul remains aloof from the joy and suffering of souls. The implication is that it is because of this manifestation that he remains aloof from the Gopīs' suffering. In the second half of the verse, the maidens observe that the creator of the universe requested Krishna to descend to protect this world, and he managed to appear. So, why should he not honor their request to appear before them (PrS 392)?

The Witness residing in the hearts, *antarātma-dṛk*. The word *dṛk,* or "witness," indicates that Krishna is the indwelling controller of all beings, *antar-yāmī* (SD). The idea of an indwelling Lord is found throughout the story; see RL 1.32, 2.4, 4.14, and 5.36.

When Vikhanas prayed to you for protection of the universe. When the earth planet was burdened by powerful demons who were ruling as kings, Mother Earth in the form of a cow approached Brahmā for assistance. Brahmā then traveled, along with other powerful gods and Mother Earth, to the shore of the ocean of milk where Lord Vishnu was lying on an island. There, the gods collectively worshiped him by reciting Vedic mantras. Brahmā, while in trance, understood Lord Vishnu's intention to manifest on earth in order to relieve the earth's burden. As Krishna states in the *Bhagavad Gītā:*

> When and wherever there are
> discrepancies of dharma, O Bhārata,
> And an arising of no dharma,
> at that time I descend.
>
> For the deliverance of the good
> and the destruction of those who are evil,
> For the purpose of establishing dharma,
> I manifest myself age after age.
>
> (BG 4.7–8)

The gods and their wives were to accompany Krishna by appearing in the Yadu Dynasty. Krishna would manifest as the son of Vasudeva, along with his potency known as Yogamāyā and his elder brother, Baladeva. This incident is described in BhP 10.1.17–26.

Verse 3.5

This verse with the following three verses comprise four prayers containing specific requests of the Gopīs (BB). In this verse, the cowherd maidens request Krishna to place his divine hand on their heads. In the next, they request him to accept them as his maidservants and allow them to see his beautiful face. In the following verse, they request Krishna to place his feet on their breasts, removing the desires lying within their hearts. And in the last of the four, they request their "hero" to restore them to life with a kiss.

As those who wish to become free from the cycle of endless suffering, *saṁsāra,* approach Krishna's feet, similarly, the Gopīs also wish to become free of their suffering in his absence. They question, if you liberate others from suffering, then why don't you liberate us from our suffering simply by appearing before us (PrS 392)?

O leader of the Vṛṣṇis. An epithet of Krishna indicating his descent to this world as one belonging to the family of Nanda and among the people of Vraja, all of whom are born in the special dynasty of the Yadus (PrS 392).

Fulfills all wishes, *kāma-daṁ.* Another meaning for this compound is "destroys lust" (SD).

Verse 3.6

This verse is quoted by Krishnadāsa (CC 1.6.67) to demonstrate how the Gopīs, the greatest of lovers of God, still take pride (*-abhimāna*) in considering themselves the servants (*dāsī-*) of Krishna (CC 1.6.65–66). In one phrase they beg, "Show us your beautiful face," and in another, "always accept us as your maidservants." The point made here is similarly made in the following phrase in a *sūtra* text: "the self is absorbed in worshiping the Beloved as an eternal servant and as an eternal lover" (NBS 66).

Verse 3.7

The selfless love of the cowherd maidens is explicitly described in this verse (SD). Although it appears to display demanding and perhaps selfish motives on their part, commentators insist that it expresses their unconditional love. The Gopīs demonstrate the highest level of pure love for God because every action of body and mind, indeed, every thought is for the sole purpose of pleasing Krishna. The seemingly selfish words spoken by them are only for the sake of serving the supreme, and they have no interest in avoiding unhappiness or gaining happiness for themselves (SD).

Verse 3.8

Prior to this verse, the Gopīs have praised the sweetness of Krishna's eyes, feet, and hands, and now they praise his words, voice, and lips. The sweetness of Krishna's words has enchanted the maidens, and only the intoxicating medicine of his lips will revive them from their delirium. Yet they find it difficult to attain his intoxicating lips, because their elders and family members try to keep them in their homes (PrS 392). The implication here is, "We are here now, but where are you?"

Verse 3.9

Bestowing the greatest riches, *bhūri-dā.* The word *bhūri-dā* means a person who "gives the greatest riches." Such a person is the cause of a kind of death to other persons belonging to this world of duality. These gentle souls commit genocide by giving the greatest riches to persons of this world—riches that destroy the source of misery and suffering, arising from the contamination of material existence (SD).

Krishnadāsa describes how the king of Orissa, Pratāparudra, would please Caitanya by reciting the verses of the Rāsa Līlā to him (CC 2.14.8). When the king recited this particular verse to Caitanya (CC 2.14.13), he found himself elated, and requested the king to recite it over and over again (CC 2.14.12). Thus, the king won the favor of Caitanya with the recitation of this verse.

Verse 3.10

Intimate playful ways, *viharaṇaṁ.* The synonymn *samprayogaḥ,* "loving intimacy" or "loving connection," is suggested here (SD). The word *samprayogaḥ* has the following meanings: "joining together," "attaching," "conjunction," "union," "matrimonial," or "sexual union" (MW).

Agitate, *kṣobhayanti.* The synonymn *vyākulayanti* is offered for this word (SD).

Verse 3.12
From cows is implied in the Sanskrit and suggested by Śrīdhara.

Loving memory, *smaram.* The word *smaram,* which means literally "memory," "recollection," "loving recollection," and so on, can also mean "the god of love," or more connotatively, "passionate thoughts."

Verse 3.13
Krishna's feet relieve suffering, as well as grant satisfaction and delight. Indeed, they are worshipable. As noted earlier, the Gopīs worship his feet uniquely by placing them on their breasts. Mere meditation on Krishna's feet, while liberating for others, is not adequate for the cowherd maidens. In fact, meditating on their beloved Lord's feet in his absence causes more pain and grants virtually no relief, due to their intense love for him (KS 169).

One born from the lotus flower, *padmaja.* This phrase refers to the god of creation, Brahmā, who appeared from the lotus flower sprouting from the navel of Vishnu.

Verse 3.14
Pure love of God results in peacefulness. However, the intense love that the Gopīs have for Krishna creates an unpeaceful state of mind. This verse spoken by the maidens, expressing the longing they have for Krishna's lips, is cited as an example of this unpeaceful state (PrS 51).

This verse is recited by Caitanya (CC 2.16.117). Caitanya had just eaten foodstuffs that had been first offered to and enjoyed by the deity, known as *prasāda.* After he marveled at the taste of this food that had been touched by the mouth of Krishna, Caitanya spoke about the "nectar of Krishna's mouth" (CC 2.16.107–116). Then he quoted the Gopīs' statement, "O hero, bestow upon us this nectar of your lips."

Verse 3.15
The most intense form of spiritual emotion, known as *mahābhāva,* is expressed in this verse (KrS). Ordinary humans delight in gazing upon Krishna, but the Gopīs become angry at the creator for interrupting their gaze by allowing their eyelids to blink [PrS 92].

Krishnadāsa presents the following verses that precede his quotation of the present verse:

All minds are attracted
upon hearing and seeing [Krishna].
Krishna makes efforts
to taste his own attractiveness.

One who constantly drinks
the nectar of this sweetness
Never satisfies one's thirst;
rather, such thirst increases endlessly.
(CC 1.4.148–149)

Krishnadāsa continues by saying that such a person who is never satisfied begins to criticize the creator god, Brahmā, who provides souls with only two eyes, and even they interrupt one's vision by blinking (CC 1.4.150–151). He then quotes this verse (CC 1.4.152).

Another instance of this verse occurs when Caitanya, speaking to Sanātana Goswami about cosmology and the omnipotent forms of Krishna (*aiśvarya*), is reminded of Krishna's beautiful intimate form (*mādhurya*). Caitanya recites this verse (CC 2.21.124) to Sanātana when speaking of the beauty of "Krishna's sweet form" that is attractive to the lives of all (CC 2.21.102).

Verse 3.16

This verse is given as an example of *amarṣa,* impatience, indignation, or passion (PrS 359).

This verse is presented by Caitanya in his instructions to Rūpa Gosvāmin (CC 2.19.210). When Caitanya explains the intricacies of the five *rasas,* this verse is quoted by him to demonstrate the nature of *kevala śuddha-prema,* or "unqualified pure love" (CC 2.19.203). Caitanya cites this verse in another instance (CC 2.7.42), where he introduces it with the following words:

The pure love (*śuddha-prema*) of the Gopīs
is without knowledge of God's omnipotence.
When there is reprimanding,
this is a sign of such pure love.

Verse 3.19

This verse is clearly the climactic expression of the Gopīs' longing for Krishna. It is the last verse, in the whole of the Rāsa Līlā story, to express their feelings of separation that have been building up since

Krishna suddenly disappeared at the end of act 1 (RL 1.48). Following a stream of eighteen verses in the songlike *triṣṭubh rājahaṁsī* meter (11-syllable count per quarter verse), expressing a variety of intense feelings of bereavement, this verse, presented in the flowing *śakvarī vasantatilakā* (14-syllable count per quarter verse), brings the Gopīs' expression to a dramatic pitch, ending with the phrase of unrequited love, "Our very lives are only for you."

Very lives, *āyuṣām.* The word *āyus* means "life," "vital power," "vigor," "health," "duration of life," "long life" (MW). Thus the word indicates the whole or full duration of one's life.

Our very lives are only for you, *bhavad-āyuṣāṁ naḥ.* A simple literal translation of this final phrase could be, "You are our very life." The third act of the Rāsa Līlā, expressing agonizing feelings of separation from Krishna, concludes with these words of pure dedication. The Gopīs have given everything, offered everything—and there is nothing left. They could be stating in this last line that they have given their lives completely to Krishna because they feel they are dying, or as if they are just about to lose their lives. Other translations are possible for this phrase, attempting to express how the maidens have given up everything for Krishna, even the vitality of life (*āyus*) itself: "We have offered our very lives unto you" implies that the Gopīs have used up their "duration of life," and that they are about to expire due to intolerable separation from Krishna (SD). In effect, the devotional love and dedication of the cowherd maidens for Krishna is even to the point of death.

This last verse demonstrates "pure love of God," or *śuddha-prīti,* and is to be distinguished from "worldly love," or *kāma.* Worldly love and passion essentially involve the desire to please oneself. If there is a desire to please the beloved within such love, it is only secondary. On the other hand, if love and passion are directed toward God exclusively as the beloved object, then it is possible for such feelings to exist selflessly and purely for his sake (PrS 84).

This verse is presented as an example of *sākṣād-upabhogātmaka* (the "direct enjoyment of love" with Krishna) in *sthāyi-bhāva* ("enduring feelings of love" for God) in *śṛṅgāra* ("amorous love") (PrS 365). The two causes of *sthāyi-bhāva* are Krishna's nature, and the nature of the female lover (PrS 363–364). This verse exemplifies the second cause of *sthāyi-bhāva,* that is, the Gopīs. Here, the maidens desire direct enjoyment of love with Krishna in his *līlā*. The different types of this love among the maidens are demonstrated in six verses of the following act (RL 4.4–9) (PrS 366).

As already noted, it is significant that this verse from the RL is quoted a total of four times throughout the CC, more than any other verse from the RL and, I suspect, more than any other verse from any of the numerous texts from which Krishnadāsa draws for his great work. This verse is used to demonstrate the purity of the Gopīs' love for Krishna. Their "love" (*anurāga*) is "pure" (*svaccha*) and "clean" (*dhauta*), and has "no trace of worldly lust" (*nāhi kāma-gandha*). The maidens' love is "only for Krishna's happiness" (*kṛṣṇa-sukha lāgi mātra*) (CC 1.4.170–173). See also CC 2.8.219, 2.18.65, and 3.7.40.

Act Four

The fourth act consists of two developmental scenes, the first a narrative (RL 1–14) and the second a dialogue (RL 15–22). In the first scene, Krishna suddenly reappears and the Gopīs react in various emotional ways. In the second scene, the cowherd maidens inquire about the various ways that souls reciprocate love. Krishna responds in three didactic verses in the commonly found epic meter *anuṣṭubh*, by explaining conditional love, unconditional love, and aloofness toward love. The final three verses, also spoken by Krishna, exhibit longer quatrains and varying meters, each verse incrementally longer than the previous one, indicating an increasing intensity of emotion on Krishna's part. Here he expresses the reason for his absence, then his gratefulness and indebtedness to the maidens for their love.

Verse 4.1
Wondrous ways, *citradhā.* This is the meaning according to Śrīdhara (BB). For Viśvanātha, it implies that the Gopīs are singing in the most elaborate musical arrangements, crying out for Krishna with their sweet voices (SD).

Verse 4.2
Śauri is the name used here because it indicates Krishna's appearance in the dynasty of Śūra, conveying the heroic character of Krishna as he suddenly appears before the Gopīs. Here, his character as a member of royalty conveys aloofness to those women who possess more intimate love for him (SD).

The supreme God of love stood directly before them, alluring even the love-god, *sākṣān manmatha-manmathaḥ.* As the natural surroundings of Vraja during the autumn evenings arouse passion in Krishna, so he can awaken the god of love in the Gopīs. Śuka states that Krishna appeared directly as the god of love filled with amorous passion. Śrīdhara explains that the phrase used here, *sākṣān manmatha-manmathaḥ,* means "the passion arising from the mind of amorous passion personified," a passion that stuns even personified love himself. Similarly, Viśvanātha understands this phrase to mean "directly the bewilderer of the mind of the god of love." The sense is that even the god of love is overtaken by love itself, and this is the case with both Krishna and the cowherd maidens within their affectionate exchanges. Viśvanātha states further that the spiritual love exchanged between them is not that of the Cupid who bewilders this world; rather, their love has only to do with the Cupid who belongs to the internal nature of God.

The word *manmatha* means connotatively either an emotional state of love, that is, "amorous passion," or it refers to a personification of this emotional state of love, that is, "the god of love" who "stirs up persons' minds." Śrīdhara states that this *pada* refers to Krishna who disturbs the mind of even passion personified, who himself disturbs the whole world (BB). Jīva points out that Krishna as the *sākṣān manmatha* is one of the manifested forms of Krishna, the God of the gods of love (KS), and the one who agitates Cupid (PrS 275). Viśvanātha confirms the former commentators' remarks and elaborates further. Krishna, who is the original God of Love, stuns the mind, or strikes the heart, of even the Cupid who disturbs the minds and hearts of humans in this world. Thus, he is the supreme spiritual Cupid who exists only within the internal realm of God, and has nothing to do with the Cupids of this world. Finally, Viśvanātha points out that Krishna appears to the Gopīs as the supreme God of Love in order to cause them to forget the agony of separation from him.

The word *sākṣāt* means most literally "with the eyes," having various connotative meanings such as "evidently," "manifestly," "clearly," "in person," "in bodily form," "immediately," and "directly" (MW). The word *manmatha* is an intensive of the verbal root *math* (which adds the prefixed reduplicated-syllable *man-*). Or the word is a compound consisting of the word *manas* ("mind") added to the verb *matha*, meaning "disturbing of the mind" (MW).[1]

THIS VERSE IS AN EXAMPLE of *sambhoga*, the other side of *vipralambha* in the amorous love of *śṛṅgāra-rasa*, as the enjoyment of the presence of the beloved. The first stage of *sambhoga* is exemplified by RL 4.9, and the second stage by RL 4.13 (PrS 393). Jīva states that

1. Meanings of the verbal root *math* are worth reviewing here to give the rich and powerful senses of the word *manmatha*. Vedic meanings of the verb *math* are "to stir" or "to whirl around." Epic senses of the verb contribute to its meaning here. With the word *agni* ("fire"), it means "to produce fire by rapidly whirling round or rotating a dry stick in another dry stick prepared to receive it" (MW); in the *Harivaṁśa*, it means "to use friction

this verse presents the *ālambana,* or "foundation" for emotion in *rasa,* and the *viśaya,* or Krishna as the "object" of emotion (PrS 275). For further explanation of these two components within the scheme of *vibhāvas* (or "excitants"), see S. K. De, *Early History of the Vaiṣṇava Faith and Movement,* pp. 183–184.

This verse is quoted several times throughout the *Caitanya Caritāmṛta.* First, Krishnadāsa describes the leading deity of Vrindāvana (*vṛndāvana-purandara*) as the one who is the Rāsa-*vilāsī,* "the playful dancer of the Rāsa," known as Madan Gopāla, and particularly who is a manifestation of the form of the God among all gods of love, *manmatha-manmatha-rūpa.* This verse is quoted to establish these attributes of Krishna (CC 1.5.214). Second, when Rāmānanda introduces to Caitanya the *kānta-prema,* that is, "the passionate love of God" in *mādhurya-rasa,* as the highest of all *rasas,* he quotes this verse (CC 2.8.81). Then, within the same chapter, this verse is quoted fully again (CC 2.8.140) by Rāmānanda in the following:

> The hearts of all men and women,
> all moving and non-moving beings,
> Are completely attracted directly by the one
> who captivates the god of love [Krishna].
> (CC 2.8.139)

Verse 4.3

This verse illustrates *vilāsa-anubhāva,* the expressions and graceful motions of the face, eyes, and other bodily features while walking, sitting, or standing, caused by contact with the beloved (PrS 326).

Verse 4.4

This verse and the following five verses, through RL 4.9, are examples of variety in the types of love the Gopīs have for Krishna. Jīva presents each of these verses to demonstrate this variety among the cowherd maidens. This verse expresses a mutual loving adoration and respect (PrS 366–367). See related ideas in the comments on verse 3.19.

---

upon any part of the body with the object of producing offspring from it" (MW); and in the *Bhāgavata,* "to churn" or "to produce by churning [milk into butter]" (MW). Other similar senses are found, such as "to stir up," "shake," "agitate," "trouble," "disturb," "afflict," and "destroy" (MW).

Jīva suggests that the words in verse 4 describe two Gopīs who are very intimate friends of Rādhā. The first half of the verse refers to the maiden named Lalitā, also known as Anurādhā; the maiden named Śyāmalā is spoken of in the second half of the verse. Jīva uses the name Śyāmalā to identify this Gopī as one of the eight principal Gopīs. He does not identify her as Rādhā, as Viśvanātha does in his comment to RL 5.12.

Verse 4.5

The principal rival of Rādhā is known by the name of Candrāvalī. The mood of those Gopīs who follow her, such as Padmā and Śaibya, is expressed in this verse (PrS 367).

Verse 4.6

This verse expresses a form of love known as *māna,* or "pride" (PrS 87). It is also cited as an example of *vibhoka,* a form of *anubhāva.* The phenomenon of *vibhoka* occurs when the heroine pretends to be angry and unappreciative of something given by the hero (PrS 328). This verse is said to be describing the possessive feelings and mood of Rādhā (PrS 367).

An indication of the varieties of amorous love for Krishna can be found in the Gopīs' statements upon seeing him in the beginning of the fourth act, after his sudden disappearance at the end of the first act (PrS 367). Jīva identifies specific Gopīs by name, according to their varied emotional reactions to Krishna's arrival. For example, he identifies the special Gopī, Rādhā, in this sixth verse, who expresses a type of possessive love that is considered exalted (PrS 367). It is a more passionate and intensive love than that found in RL 4.4. He also discusses *ananya-mamatā,* that is, the Lord is experienced as "their only possession." Furthermore, he speaks of degrees of possessiveness (PrS 160 and 168), and gives the example of this verse as pride in divine love (PrS 156).

Verse 4.7

This verse and the following are said to describe the character of Rādhā and her friends such as Anurādhā, also named Lalitā, and Viśākhā (PrS 367). According to Jīva, these dearest friends express a mood of love similar to that of Rādhā, described in this verse and the next.

Verse 4.8

Took him into her heart, *hṛdi kṛtvā.* Śrīdhara suggests the similar phrase, "leading into her heart." Viśvanātha suggests that this Gopī is attempting to keep her "fickle lover" Krishna from escaping, by closing her eyes after she "led Krishna into her heart" through her eyes.

Ripplings functions conveniently, in a poetic way, to convey the two ways in which this phenomenon is manifest in the cowherd maidens—either from within the body to the outside (displayed on the skin as eruptions), or from the outside to the inside. When the Gopīs meditate on Krishna, it is the former, as illustrated in this verse; whereas when they are physically touched by Krishna, it is the latter, as illustrated by RL 5.12. See the comments on 1.40 for an in-depth discussion on the phenomenon of "bodily ripplings of bliss."

Yogi is one who practices the physical and mental internal discipline of yoga. The word *yogi* is taken by Jīva as neuter in gender, which results in a slightly different translation of the second half of this verse:

> She became elated with
> bodily ripplings of joy,
> as yogic union with him
> is flooded with bliss.

The word *yogi* is taken here as a state of relation between Krishna and the Gopīs. Jīva is concerned that the verse not be taken as possessing the improper "mixture of *rasas*," known as *rasābhāsa* (PrS 178).

VIŚVANĀTHA STATES THAT out of innumerable Gopīs, there are eight principal ones. Of all the cowherd maidens, Rādhā is the dearest to Vishnu (*yathā rādhā priyā viṣṇos*), and the most beloved of Vishnu (Viśvanātha gets this idea from the *Padma Purāṇa*: *sarva-gopīṣu saivaikā viṣṇor atyanta-vallabhā*).

Verse 4.9

This and preceding verses of this act describe the first stage of being relieved from painful separation from Krishna. The second stage of relief begins in RL 4.13 below; and the final and complete stage of relief is the first verse of the next act (PrS 393).

The maiden described in this verse is identified as Bhadrā, another rival Gopī, who is associated with these words (PrS 367).

Verse 4.10

Like the supreme Person with his splendorous powers, *puruṣaḥ śaktibhir yathā.* Śrīdhara defines *puruṣaḥ* as the supreme soul in all of creation, or the cosmic Lord lying at the foundation of the material creation, along with his various energies (BB). Jīva and Viśvanātha both recognize that this phrase refers to Bhagavān, the supreme Lord along with his *śaktis,* or internal spiritual energies. Jīva cites the verse to describe the relationship of the Gopīs to Krishna in the form of his spiritual powers (PrS 282).

The Caitanya school sees the cowherd maidens as persons who possess spiritual bodies, as *śaktis* of Krishna, and not physical material bodies. Its theology begins with the idea that God (*īśvara-tattva*) is the possessor of all energy or power (*śaktimat*), and all existences consist of his manifestations and energies (*śaktis*). This theological construction is also found in the Rāsa Līlā when the narrator describes Krishna, surrounded by the Gopīs, as he "appeared radiant, like the supreme Person (*puruṣa*) with his splendorous powers (*śaktis*)."

Verse 4.11

The almighty one, *vibhuḥ.* An epithetical name for Krishna is used in this verse. The word *vibhuḥ* has many rich meanings: "being everywhere," "far-extending," "all-pervading," "omnipresent," and so on; "mighty," "powerful," "excellent," "great," and so on; "a lord," "ruler," "sovereign," and so on (MW).

Verse 4.13

This verse describes the second stage of the Gopīs' relief from their separation from Krishna (PrS 393).

Revealed scriptures refers to the *śrūtis,* the revelational scriptures of the Vedas.

Verse 4.14

Krishna, who is referred to as *yogeśvara,* "the Lord of yoga," is understood by Viśvanātha to duplicate himself while sitting with the Gopīs. Viśvanātha suggests that Krishna is sitting on many different seats prepared by the maidens, and this multiple appearance of Krishna, on so many seats made by different groups of Gopīs, is made possible by the power of Yogamāyā.

The concept of Yogamāyā, or simply Māyā, can also be implied by the word yoga within compound phrases, which serve as epithets for Krishna, such as *yogeśvara,* "master of yoga" (for example, RL 4.14 and 5.3) and other similar phrases throughout the passage.

Verse 4.15

This verse is an example of *avahitthā* or the suppression of feelings. Jīva explains that although the cowherd maidens honor Krishna upon his return, they attempt to conceal their anger about the situation (PrS 353). The verse is cited as an example of "veneration and pride," *ādaraṇīya-māna,* describing how the Gopīs become slightly angered with Krishna for having disappeared (PrS 384).

The one who ignited the passion of their love, *anaṅga-dīpanaṁ.* This phrase means either that Krishna is the one in whom "amorous passion arises," or that he is the one who "kindles amorous passion" within the Gopīs.

Verse 4.16

Viśvanātha names the three types of persons about whom the Gopīs are inquiring, based on verses in which Krishna is about to speak (RL 4.17–19). Persons who love could be summarized as those who love conditionally, those who love unconditionally, and those who are indifferent to love. Viśvanātha suggests that those persons who love because others love them have conditional love, *sopādhi-prīti.* In this type of love, persons reciprocate only if they find a worthy object, indicating that their affection is conditional. Those who love others whether or not they return such love have unconditional love, *nirupādhi-prīti.* Such persons love regardless of the nature of the object, have no ulterior motive or expectation of result, and do not desire love for themselves. Others, because their desires are fulfilled, are indifferent, *svakāma-sampādaka.* Under this category, which includes all who are indifferent to loving conditionally or unconditionally, are those who are hateful and envious, and who neither love anyone nor are loved by anyone (SD).

From this verse to the end of the act, verbs derived from the root *bhaj* are used extensively. This is the same root from which the important noun *bhakti,* meaning "devotion," "worship," or "love" is derived. I have translated the verbal form in this and following verses simply as "love," since it is clear from this verse that it is the concern of the Gopīs to understand what kind of love Krishna can have for them, in light of his painful departure from them. In fact, Jīva points out in his one-line comment to this verse, that "there the Gopīs were desirous of establishing the hardness [rather than the love] of *bhagavān*—this is the significance of the word *bhajataḥ*" (*tatra bhagavataḥ kāṭhinyam āpādayitu-kāmāḥ pṛcchanti—bhajata iti*). The word "love" is intended to convey a level of meaning and affective state that words derivative of *bhaj* carry. See "Devotional Love of the Gopīs" in "Textual Illuminations" for a discussion on the words for "love" in Sanskrit, used throughout the Rāsa Līlā.

Verse 4.17

Viśvanātha discusses the difference between selfish love and true love, *sauhṛdam,* which he treats as a synonym for the word *prema.* Selfish love involves being wholly intent on one's own interest, *svārtha-parāḥ.* Such persons who are full of desires, *kāmina,* have as their goal a love filled with conditions or selfish motives, *sopādhi-prītimantaḥ.* He states that "in such persons there are no endearing qualities or purity of love," *tatra teṣu sauhṛdaṁ prema nāsti.* Jīva discusses the phrase *svātmārtham,* "one's own sake," and relates this idea to the ulterior motives of a person. Such a person who possesses this selfishness, according to Jīva, only worships him or herself. Jīva cites this and the following verse as a presentation on "pure love," or *śuddha-prīti* (PrS 70).

Verse 4.18

In relation to the statement "those who love others who may not love in return are either parents or persons of compassion," Jīva quotes (PrS 94) a line from the *Bhāgavata, pitror abhyadkhikā prītir ātmajeṣv ātmano 'pi hi,* meaning "parents, indeed, love their children even more than their own lives" (BhP 10.45.21).

Viśvanātha explains that Krishna is presenting two types of unconditional love: that of compassionate persons, *kārunāḥ,* and that of nurturing parents, *pitarau,* rather than including *pitarau* as an example of *kārunāḥ.* The compassionate person is described as the "pure devotee," *śuddha-bhakta,* and the name of Prahlāda is given as an example of such pure devotion

The story of Prahlāda is in the seventh book of the *Bhāgavata Purāṇa.* Prahlāda was the son of Hiranyakāśipu, a powerful demon who attempted in many ways to end the life of his son because of the latter's devotion to God. Due to Prahlāda's compassionate nature, however, he never felt anger or revenge toward his father. He only desired for his father to be liberated from conditioned existence within the cycle of birth and death, *saṁsāra.* The commentator explains that both compassionate and parental persons are selfless in that they have no concern for any personal benefit. He explains that in happiness or misery, they do not give up their love for others. Of these two types of unconditional love, compassionate love is the "best," *śreṣṭhaḥ.* But persons who possess either type of unconditional love are "faultless," *nirapavāda,* in their dharma because they are free from any expectation of result, and because their love is both "endearing," *sauhṛdam,* and "pure," *premā.*

Verse 4.19

Viśvanātha mentions that there are four types of persons discussed in this verse: those who are "self-satisfied," *ātmārāmāḥ,* who have no external vision or who are completely focused on the self; those who are "fulfilled in their desires," *āpta-kāmāḥ,* who have external vision but do not desire any "sensual enjoyment," *bhoga,* from another person because they are already fulfilled; those who are "ungrateful persons," *akṛta-jñāḥ,* because they do not recognize the help that persons give them even though they desire sense enjoyment from others; and finally, those who are "hateful persons," *guru-druhaḥ,* who are not only ungrateful but are resentful toward persons worthy of respect, described as persons who are "without motive," *nirhetuka.* Such ungrateful persons betray good faith and may be hateful to humble superiors who offer them protection. Viśvanātha explains that there are many subcategories of this last type.

Verse 4.20

Viśvanātha quotes Krishna's promise from the *Bhagavad Gītā* (4.11): "As persons submit themselves unto me, in the same way I return my love to them," *ye yathā māṁ prapadyante tāṁs tathaiva bhajāmy aham.* He quotes this half verse, demonstrating that Krishna always reciprocates with his devotee. According to Krishna, the Gopīs may not understand how or in what ways he reciprocates with them, as the verses of this act express, beginning with verse 16.

The Lord sometimes intentionally places his devotees in a stressful condition in order to increase their devotion, and this is seen in the present verse, in which both the devotee's humility and passion increase (PrS 121). This condition of absence yielding greater presence is a theme in the *Bhāgavata:*

> As the minds of women are fully absorbed
> in their beloved when he is far away,
> So when he is present before their eyes
> he is not as much in their thoughts.
> (BhP 10.47.66)

Verse RL 4.20 is cited by Jīva in a few instances. First, he refers to the verse to illustrate a love that is even more than *śuddha-prīti,* or pure love, which is presented in verses 17 and 18 above (PrS 71). The love spoken of in this verse illustrates a further intensification of pure love. In another instance, he presents this verse in order to show how the Lord separates himself from his dear devotees to increase their love (PrS 288). He also cites this verse to demonstrate that *śṛṅgāra* cannot reach its fullness without the "attainment of distance," or *vipralambha* (PrS 370).

To strengthen their love, *anuvṛtti vṛttaye.* Since Viśvanātha gives words derivative of *bhaj* as synonyms for *anuvṛtti,* I translate the word as "love."[2]

Verse 4.21

Viśvanātha explains that Krishna admits to the injustice of leaving the cowherd maidens, even though he does so out of love for them. He points out that the words *priyam* and *priyāḥ* are thus provided (by Krishna) as reasons for the Gopīs not to blame him, *atra priyamiti priyā iti ca hetuḥ.* Finally, he states that lovers (*priyāḥ*) certainly do not wish to bring to mind the fault of the beloved (*priyasya*), *priyasya doṣaḥ priyāḥ khalu na manasyānayastītyarthaḥ.* He comments that the maidens have, on the one hand, an unrequited selfless love for Krishna due to their love for him in his absence, and on the other hand, a

2. The meanings of the words in the phrase *anuvṛtti-vṛttaye* are worth reviewing here. The word *vṛttaye* in the dative case can mean, as Viśvanātha indicates, "for sustaining" or "for strengthening"; or it can mean "for being in a particular state," "for remaining," "abiding," or "being" (VA). The word *anuvṛtti* can mean "continuation," "remembrance," "previous course of conduct," "continuance in," "gratifying," or "pleasing" (VA). For the word *vṛttaye* Viśvanātha also supplies the synonym *jīvikāyai,* meaning "for the sustenance" or "for strengthening."

love that is reciprocated by Krishna in his appearance before them, *darśana.* This verse and the following are cited as examples of how Krishna attempts to assuage the slightly angered pride of the Gopīs (PrS 385).

O dearest ones, I am your beloved! *tat priyaṁ priyāḥ.* This phrase appears at the end of this penultimate verse expressing Krishna's loving dedication to the cowherd maidens. This statement parallels the last phrase of the final verse of the Gopīs' songs of bereavement from the previous act, in which they express their loving dedication to Krishna and say, "Our very lives are only for you" (RL 3.19).

In his discussion on the purity (*śuddha*) of love and attachment (*anurāga*), Krishnadāsa quotes this verse in which Krishna acknowledges the Gopīs' sacrifice (*parityāga*) for him (CC 1.4.176). This verse anticipates this act's final climactic and much-quoted verse of Krishna's expression of gratefulness to the maidens, which Krishnadāsa quotes in full just a few verses later (CC 1.4.180).

Verse 4.22

As the last verse of the previous act becomes a climax of the expression of the Gopīs' devotion in separation, this last verse of the present act could easily be seen as a climax of Krishna's expression of love and indebtedness to the maidens. The commentators quote this verse often to show how even the Lord comes under the control of his devotees, and how he becomes indebted to such devoted souls. Krishna's response to the Gopīs' question in verse 16 of this act, about the nature of love, appears in the final six verses of the act, beginning with three verses in the typical epic *śloka* or *anuṣṭubh* meter (8-syllable quarter verse). As the emotional content of Krishna's words intensifies, the longer *triṣṭubh* metered verses (11-syllable quarter verses) are found in the following two verses, and the climactic verse of the act appears in the 12-syllable quarter *jagatī* meter.

Jīva points out that this verse demonstrates how the Lord can be controlled by the love of his devotee. Krishna's word *niravadya* ("purity" or "pure love") indicates that he recognizes the purity of the Gopīs' love for him; the words *sva-sādhu-kṛtyam* ("reciprocate your own purity") indicate the greatest love for him; and *na paraye* ("I am unable") indicates the Gopīs' ability to control Krishna. From this verse, it is concluded that the cowherd maidens are emblematic of all pure lovers of God found within the five *rasas*, and specifically that the Lord in *śṛṅgāra rasa* is controlled by the devotee's love (PrS 84, 130).

In his comments to verse 20 above and to the present verse, Viśvanātha quotes Krishna's promise from the *Bhagavad Gītā* (4.11ab), as Krishnadāsa also does. The first half of this verse (*ye yathā māṁ prapadyante tāṁs tathaiva bhajāmy aham*) demonstrates that Krishna always reciprocates with his devotee. According to Krishna, the Gopīs may not understand how or in what ways he reciprocates with them, as expressed in the verses of this act, beginning with verse 16. When quoting the *Bhagavad Gītā* verse in his comments on the present verse, Viśvanātha states that even though Krishna promises to reciprocate their love, the love of the maidens is so powerful that he is unable to do so. He therefore states that their own saintly behavior will have to be their reward.

Finally, he claims that lovers (*priyāḥ*) certainly do not wish to bring to mind the fault of the beloved (*priyasya*) (*priyasya doṣaḥ priyāḥ khalu na manasyānayastītyarthaḥ*) (SD). The concluding verse of the fourth act is seen by the early teachers as an expression of Krishna's appreciation of the power of the Gopīs' love for him. To some, it is evidence of the power that the most intimate devotee has to control the supreme controller, that of love. Viśvanātha ends his commentary to this act by stating, "Indeed, we have thus become conquered by love," *premnā jitā evābhūmeti.*

Your own purity, *sva-sādhu.* The word *sādhu,* according to lexical sources, has many meanings that express the quality of the love of the Gopīs for Krishna. The meanings "faithful," "perfect," "saintly," "effective," "good," "virtuous," "honest," "proper," "chaste," "kind," and so on, are all appropriate in describing the "purity" of love of the Gopīs. The use of the word "purity" in the translation of this verse is intended to reflect Viśvanātha's discussion on the *nirupādhi* of "unconditional love," of which the Gopīs are the recognized exemplars.

Your own purity, *sādhunā.* Śrīdhara understands the meaning of *sādhunā* as *sādhu-kṛtyena,* "by the reward of the purity [of your love]." In other words, it is only through the pure behavior of the Gopīs that they receive any reward, and not through compensation from Krishna.

Krishnadāsa states that Krishna makes a promise of reciprocity with his devotees according to the ways they worship him. To confirm this, he quotes the following verse from *Bhagavad Gītā:*

As they submit themselves to me,
  I, accordingly, reciprocate lovingly with them.
In every way, humans follow my path,
  O son of Pṛthā.

(BG 4.11)

However, Krishnadāsa insists that Krishna himself breaks this promise by his inability to reciprocate the superlative way in which the cowherd maidens have honored him:

This promise was broken
  due to the worship of the Gopīs.
The authority for this is in the words
  coming from the beautiful mouth of Krishna.

(CC 1.4.179)

Later, Rāmānanda, who similarly quotes BG 4.11 (CC 2.8.91), comments on the final verse of this act in the following statement:

This form of pure love, *premā,*
  cannot be reciprocated.
Therefore, [Krishna] becomes a debtor—
  thus it is stated in the *Bhāgavata.*

(CC 2.8.92)

According to Rāmānanda, Krishna is understood to be indebted to the devotee who loves him in the manner of the Gopīs. Rāmānanda then quotes the present verse in CC 2.8.93.

The verse RL 4.22 is quoted in the CC for the final time when Caitanya is speaking with Vallabha Bhaṭṭa about how the worship of the cowherd maidens is the best of all (*sarvottama-bhajana,* CC 2.7.44). Caitanya quotes Krishna as saying, "I am indebted to you" (*āmi tomāra ṛṇī*).

Krishnadāsa states that Krishna with the Gopīs, that is, *bhagavat* with his *śaktis,* is confounded by the level of enjoyment that his *śaktis* experience from being loved by him. Indeed, their enjoyment is the highest, yet ever-increasing. Since it is Krishna who loves his devotees supremely, being the ultimate beloved object, his devotees, though unmotivated, receive an unsought and unsurpassable bliss that even he longs to experience. For the discussion on the Gopīs' unending and ever increasing bliss excelling even that of Krishna's, see CC 1.4.185–221.

Act Five

The final act of the Rāsa Līlā consists of four scenes. The first (RL5.1–20) is called the "culmination scene" (*nirvahaṇa-sandhi*). The "seed" (*bīja*) of the drama, that is, Krishna turning his mind toward "love's delights" (RL 1.1), fructifies fully in this scene in which the formation and commencement of the Rāsa dance takes place (RL 5.1–7). The narrative description of Krishna and the Gopīs dancing in the Rāsa occurs in verses 8 through 20.

The eighth verse, the longest metered verse in the complete text, is the first to describe exactly how Krishna and the cowherd maidens dance together, and here the Rāsa dance is fully initiated. The name of the meter type used in verse 8 is revealing: *mandākrāntā,* which literally translates as "approaching slowly," as in the beginning of a dance. Every type of verse meter that is employed throughout the dramatic poem is engaged in this scene, most appropriately, in a back-and-forth pattern (see table 3).

The quarter-verse syllabic pattern in verse 8 exhibits seven distinct shifts between short and long syllables (see "Poetic Meters in the Sanskrit Text"); and within this scene of twenty verses there are seven shifts between different meter types. In short, the dance narrative is supported by dancelike movements within the climactic verse, as well as between verses within the climactic scene.

The second scene (RL 5.21–26) is a narrative of the affectionate activities that follow the dancing and singing, and is itself another culminating scene. It is erotic in tone and imagery, yet delightfully playful and romantic. Here, the story's climax of intimate union abounds in metaphor, yet explicitly states that this is not a sexual encounter (RL 5.26), again asserting the otherworldly nature of its drama. The first and fourth quarters of verse 26 are a recapitulation and allusion to the beginning of the work (*pūrva-vākya*), lending the drama a sense of finality:

> Thus he allowed himself to be
> subdued by those nights
> made so brilliant
> by the rays of the moon;
>
> . . .
>
> Inspired by the narrations
> and poetry of autumn,
> all those moonlit nights
> found their refuge in *rasa.*

It is clear that, through these words concluding the second scene, the "achievement of the story's goal" (*ānanda*) has now been attained.

Next, an epilogue-like penultimate scene begins with verse 27, in which the king inquires from the sage narrator, as he did in the second scene of the drama. Again, a didactic discourse ensues; now, however, it addresses the ethical concern of Krishna dancing with other men's wives (RL 5.27–35). The king, in three verses, questions whether or not Krishna's behavior with the Gopīs can be considered dharmic. The sage responds in five verses of *anuṣṭubh* meter, then dramatically in the last verse uses the lengthy *vasantatilakā* meter, ending the discourse with a rhetorical question.

The final scene introduces a quiet transition from the dialogue between the sage and the king to an explanation of the special nature of Krishna's divine manifestations and *līlā.* The subtle shift to this fourth and last scene of the final act is indicated by a gradual return to the narration of the story, though the narrator continues to be somewhat didactic. For example, the first part of verse 36 informs us that while the drama is taking place, Krishna, as the Witness, "dwells within the Gopīs and within their husbands," which contributes to both the narrative and didactic voices of the scene; whereas in the second part of

TABLE 3. METER TYPES IN SCENE ONE OF ACT FIVE

Verses	Meter Type	Syllable Length (per quarter verse)
Verses 1–7	*anuṣṭubh*	(8)
Verse 8	*mandākrāntā*	(17)
Verses 9–15	*anuṣṭubh*	(8)
Verse 16	*vasantatilakā*	(14)
Verse 17	*upajāti*	(11)
Verse 18	*viṣamacatuṣpadī*	(12)
Verses 19–20	*anuṣṭubh*	(8)

the verse and in the following verse, the narrator teaches that Krishna comes to this world to perform his divine *līlā* as an act of grace. Verse 38 then returns to a blend of narrative and didactic explanation when Śuka explains that the husband cowherds of the Gopīs are unaffected by their wives' sudden departure, which is arranged by the divine feminine power of the Goddess. The penultimate verse of exclusive narration states that the Gopīs return home after their activities with Krishna that autumn night. The final verse of the story is "benedictory" (*praśanti*), and states that hearing or reciting this *līlā* of the cowherd maidens with Vishnu will cure the disease of the heart and grant the highest devotion to God.

Verse 5.1

The enchanting words, *su-peśalāḥ.* The meaning of this phrase is suggested by Viśvanātha.

Simply by touching his limbs, *tad-aṅgopacitāśīṣaḥ.* Viśvanātha points out that this phrase could be understood to be modifying Krishna, the one whose desires are fulfilled by touching the limbs of the cowherd maidens. The phrase in the verse, however, modifies the Gopīs as the ones whose desires are being fulfilled. The ambiguity of the object of modification for this adjectival phrase demonstrates the mutuality of devotion between Krishna and the maidens.

When anger, or praṇaya-māna, has completely disappeared, then *sambhoga,* or union in *śṛṅgāra-rasa,* begins to develop, as indicated in this verse (PrS 386).

Verse 5.2

Rāsa. Rāsa is the name of a specific dance form performed by village people in ancient India. A deeper significance, however, is found in the word. Viśvanātha points out that Rāsa refers to the sum of all *rasa*s or intimate experiences with the supreme. Jīva states that Rāsa is an aspect of *sambhoga,* or union in *śṛṅgāra-rasa* (PrS 425-427).

We have very little information regarding the exact type of dance that the ancient Rāsa was. See *Viraha Bhakti* by Friedhelm Hardy for information on this subject.

Verse 5.3

Circular formation, *maṇḍala-maṇḍitaḥ.* The word *maṇḍala* means "circle," "circular," "round," "wheel," "orb," "ring," or "the path or orbit of a heavenly body" (especially of the sun or moon); the word can even mean "a multitude," "group," or "whole body." These different meanings of *maṇḍala* can be applied to different aspects of the Rāsa Līlā. The verbal active voice (*parasmaipada*) of *maṇḍ* means "to deck" and "adorn"; the verbal reflexive voice (*ātmanepada*) means "to distribute" or "clothe," "to glorify" or "extol," and "to rejoice" or "exhilarate" (MW).

The supreme Lord of yoga, *yogeśvara.* This translation is intended to reflect the understanding of the commentators. Jīva, along with Śrīdhara, states that the word yoga refers to Krishna's *acintya-śakti,* or "incomprehensible power." Viśvanātha expounds upon this meaning by stating that the compound indicates that God is the source of all artistic ability. He refers to the definitions of yoga in the Amarakośa, such as "a process of attaching," "meditation," "a process of bringing together," or an "arrangement," and associates this phrase with Yogamāyā, who "arranges the impossible." The ambiguity of whether or not Krishna is present before every Gopī in the dance, or whether he is present between each pair of maidens is resolved, because Yogamāyā arranges for each Gopī to experience an individual manifestation of Krishna.

Krishna is called *yogeśvareśvara* in the first act (RL 1.42), and in this verse of the last act. The epithet of Krishna as *yogeśvareśvara,* "the Lord of all masters of yoga," found in this verse, is also related to Yogamāyā by the concept of *acintya-śakti.*

This verse presents the first description of the arrangement of the Gopīs with Krishna in the Rāsa dance. Viśvanātha states that the Rāsa dance, which is eternally blissful for the eyes and minds of devotees, is presented by Krishna himself as the most excellent of all his *śaktis* and *līlās*. Even such divine personages as Lakṣmī are unable to attain the Rāsa dance.

It appears that the Rāsa dance begins with the formation of a "circle of Gopīs" (*gopī-maṇḍala*) whose arms, as the previous verse states, are "linked with one another." Krishna, from the middle of the circle of Gopīs, multiplies himself as many times as there are pairs of maidens, sharing one side of himself, through his duplicate forms, with each Gopī. The words "entering between all pairs of them" *tāsāṁ madhye dvayor dvayoḥ,* seem to make this point. Even so, as this verse states, each of the maidens "thought she alone was at his side." Śrīdhara asks, how did each of the cowherd maidens think that she was receiving Krishna's attention exclusively? Krishna is able to accomplish this because he is *yogeśvara,* "the supreme Lord of yoga," as identified in this verse.

Later in this act, it appears that the number of Krishna's own duplications equals the number of Gopīs present, so that there is a direct one-to-one Krishna-to-Gopī correspondence, eliminating the sharing of Krishna by two maidens (RL 5.20). Viśvanātha states that the present verse can be taken to mean either that there is one Krishna for every two Gopīs or one Krishna for each Gopī, because how one counts a "pair of Gopīs" can effectively yield either result. More specifically, if every maiden is counted as pairing off with each of the maidens on either side of her, then there are as many Krishnas as there are Gopīs, that is, each Gopī is seen as participating in two different pairs. If, on the other hand, as Śrīdhara takes it, it is assumed that each cowherd maiden participates in only one pair of maidens, then there is one Krishna for every two maidens.

Viśvanātha quotes a verse from Bilvamaṅgala's *Krishna Karnāmṛtam* that reveals the ambiguity of the number of Krishnas to Gopīs:

aṅganām aṅganām antare mādhavo
mādhavaṁ mādhavaṁ cā 'ntareṇā 'ṅganā |
ittham ākalpite maṇḍale madhya-gaḥ
saṁjagau veṇunā devakī-nandanaḥ ||

Between every pair of lovely maidens was a Mādhava;
and between every pair of Mādhavas was a lovely maiden.
At the center of those thus assembled in the *maṇḍala,*
the son of Devakī sang and made music with his flute.
(KK II 35)

From this colorful stanza, we can deduce the several possible ways this verse can be interpreted. If each Gopī is counted as participating in only one pair of maidens, then the formation would appear as the first line of Bilvamaṅgala's stanza suggests:

Gopī-Krishna-Gopī / Gopī-Krishna-Gopī / Gopī-Krishna-Gopī / etc.

Similarly, if each Krishna or Mādhava is counted as participating in only one pair of Mādhavas, then the formation would appear as the second line suggests:

Krishna-Gopī-Krishna / Krishna-Gopī-Krishna /
Krishna-Gopī-Krishna / etc.

But if either the Gopīs or the Krishnas participate in two pairs at once, considering both the first and second lines of the stanza, the formation would essentially become a one-to-one correspondence between all the maidens and Krishnas:

Gopī-Krishna-Gopī-Krishna-Gopī-Krishna-Gopī-Krishna, etc.

Viśvanātha insists that there is no contradiction in this ambiguity, since the power of Yogamāyā arranges for each cowherd maiden to experience only one form of Krishna, no matter how we may attempt to comprehend the *maṇḍala* pattern. Precision on the number of maidens to the number of Krishnas is not sought by the text, nor by the tradition that follows it. The mind cannot fathom the many possible ways that the Gopī-Krishna combinations could be envisioned, and consequently one finds great variety in the artistic depictions of the Rāsa Maṇḍala.

Bilvimaṅgala delights in the ambiguity of the different possibilities of Krishnas to Gopīs, and adds that Krishna both sings and makes music with his flute from the middle of the arena. In the *Bhāgavata* story itself, however, there is no mention of Krishna playing the flute during the Rāsa dance. In the very beginning of the episode (RL 1.3), Krishna makes music on his flute only briefly in order to draw the Gopīs into the forest. After this initial sounding of the flute, there is no mention of Krishna again playing the flute throughout the rest of the drama. The power and beauty of Krishna's flute music is described, however, by the cowherd maidens, when they beg him to allow them to remain with him toward the end of the first act, and while they sing songs of separation, reminiscing about his flute music in the third act.

Krishnadāsa explains that when "the one body of the Lord becomes many forms" and when there "is no difference in appearance," these forms being the "same in essence," such duplicated forms of the Lord are understood as *prakāśa* forms (CC 1.1.69–70). This is seen in the examples of Krishna's marriage to the many queens or the duplicate Krishnas attending the numerous Gopīs in the Rāsa dance, Krishnadāsa quotes BhP 10.69.2 concerning the queens (CC 1.1.71), and then quotes verses from the fifth act of the Rāsa Līlā, beginning with the present verse. He explains the special duplication form of Krishna that extends to the each of the Gopīs:

'svayaṁ-rūpa' 'svayaṁ-prakāśa'—dui rūpe sphūrti
svayaṁ-rūpe—eka 'kṛṣṇa' vraje gopa-mūrti

Svayaṁ-rūpa and Svayaṁ-prakāśa—
["God's original form" and
"God's original manifestation," respectively]
these are the two manifestations of God's own form—
In the Svayaṁ-rūpa,
the form of a cowherd boy in Vraja
is the one [original] 'Krishna.'

'prābhava-vaibhava'-rūpe dvividha prakāśe
eka-vapu bahu rūpa yaiche haila rāse

In the Svayaṁ-prakāśa
there exists in God's form
a division of two manifestations:
prābhava and *vaibhava.*
The one form
[of God in his *prābhava* manifestation]
becomes a form of many,
as was the case in the Rāsa Līlā.

(CC 2.20.166–167)

Verse 5.4

It is clear from this verse that the Rāsa dance of Krishna and the Gopīs is hardly an isolated event, away from all other persons. Not only do the heavenly denizens observe the Rāsa dance but they also participate in it with their musical accompaniment, as will be explained in the following verse.

Verse 5.5

Gandharvas are the heavenly beings who produce exquisite instrumental and vocal music.

Verse 5.6

The musical accompaniment for the Rāsa dance, then, consists of the sounds coming from the jewelry on the moving limbs of the Gopīs, and from the musical instruments and voices of hundreds of heavenly Gandharvas situated above the dance, in the sky.

Verse 5.7

A magnificent emerald, *mahā-marakato.* Commentators explain that the prefixed word *mahā-* metaphorically expresses Krishna's ability to replicate himself so that he can stand next to each Gopī simultaneously. Thus, I have translated *mahā-*, meaning literally "great," as "magnificent," in order to convey the sense of Krishna's ability to "magnify" himself.

The author describes Krishna here using a simile: he is like a brilliant glowing emerald-colored gem at the center of the circle, or *maṇḍala,* of Gopīs, who are compared to golden ornaments. Curiously, the glowing gem that represents Krishna is green rather than the deep blue color that is typically associated with this deity. The very name "Krishna" means "black," "dark," or "dark blue" (VA). Indeed, a prominent and distinguishing characteristic of the deity Krishna is his blackish or bluish bodily hue, often compared to the rich array of deep blues and blackish grays of a new monsoon rain cloud, or to the deep blue of a sapphire gem. In fact, it is unusual that Krishna's complexion is described anywhere as appearing to be green. Yet suddenly in this verse, just preceding the verse in which the Rāsa Līlā story reaches its climax, we are told that he is the green color of a "magnificent emerald" (*mahā-marakato*).[1]

The word used here for emerald is *marakataḥ,* meaning, literally, "emerald" (MW). Despite this, some commentaries (BB), as if correcting the text, insist that the word *marakataḥ* actually means *nīlamaṇi* ("deep blue gem"), referring to a sapphire, in keeping with Krishna's traditional image. An attempt to resolve this problem can be found in a later prominent commentary (SD). Viśvanātha explains, as the verse indicates, that although Krishna is the son of Devakī and a member of the *kṣatriya* class, and even though he is Bhagavān himself, the one completely satisfied and supremely full in all six excellences, still, his bodily hue becomes amazingly transformed when dancing with the village girls in the circle dance of the Rāsa *maṇḍala.*[2]

1. There are five places in the *Bhāgavata* text in which Krishna's complexion is described as emerald-like, two prior to the instance in the RL and two following: in BhP 8.6.3 *marakata-śyāma* and BhP 8.16.35 *marakata-śyāma-vapuṣe,* he is depicted as having a "dark complexion like an emerald"; in BhP 10.38.33 *mārakata-śaila,* he is described as being similar to an "emerald mountain"; and in 12.9.22 *mahā-markata-śyāmam,* as "dark like a great emerald," in the form of an infant engulfed by a large green leaf of a banyan tree. Krishna is described as "the one who is dark blue and a great emerald." Krishna, in his divine cosmic function, appears as an infant lying on his back in the middle of a large green leaf.

2. Interestingly, Jīva expresses the opinion that Devakī in this verse actually refers to Yaśodā. In one of his *Sandarbhas,* Jīva cites this verse as demonstrating the spiritual forms of

His beautiful sapphire-like complexion appears to change into an exquisite emerald color when intimately mingling with the golden-complexioned Gopīs. Thus when the primary color of blue is mixed with gold or yellow, the result is the secondary color green, expressing the great intimacy between the numerous Krishnas and cowherd maidens.

It is significant that it is Krishna's complexion that appears to change color, and not that of the maidens. Jīva presents this verse, along with others, as a demonstration of the exquisite beauty of Krishna. Note that his supreme beauty in this verse is yet even further enhanced by the proximate beauty of the Gopīs (KS 178). Again, a major theological message of this devotional tradition is that the pure love of the devotee has power over the omnipotent supreme Lord, who can be transformed by the intense devotional love of his worshipers. The influence of the Gopīs' love on Krishna is expressed in the following statement: "Although the superlative beauty of Krishna is the greatest sweetness, still his divine sweetness increases when interacting with the goddesses of Vraja, the Gopīs" (CC 2.8.94). Moreover, Krishna is described as a "magnificent" (*mahā*) emerald, an indication of the way in which this divine jewel brilliantly radiates through his own duplicated forms for each maiden in the *maṇḍala* of the Rāsa dance.

The poet Bilvamaṅgala continues this tradition of describing Krishna's complexion as the color of an emerald: "Oh that I may see the boy who has the deep green complexion of an emerald" (Wilson trans., KK 1.64), and "His top-knot has a peacock plume and his body the beauty of an emerald pillar" (Wilson trans., KK 1.57). He further honors the emerald color of the divine cowherd:

> I do homage to the large emerald,
> the central stone in the necklace of milkmaids
> and the only ornament in the whole world
> which adorns the jar-like breasts of Lakṣmī.
> (Wilson trans., KK 1.90)

the Gopīs and Krishna (PrS 281), and similarly cites the verses RL 1.43 (PrS 280) and RL 4.10 (PrS 282).

Bilvamaṅgala also describes Krishna as deep blue in color (KK1.73), sapphire blue (KK2.10), or as a lovely sapphire (KK2.97).

Rāmānanda speaks to Caitanya about how the beauty of Krishna is unexcelled when he mingles with the Gopīs, his greatest devotees:

yadyapi kṛṣṇa-saundarya—mādhuryera dhurya
vraja-devīra saṅge tāṅra bāḍaye mādhurya

Even though the supreme beauty of Krishna
is the highest sweetness,
His sweetness increases when commingling
with the goddesses of Vraja.

CC 2.8.94

These words introduce the present verse of the RL to the *Caitanya Caritāmṛta* text (CC 2.8.95).

Verse 5.8

It can easily be argued that this verse forms the climactic point of the whole story of the Rāsa Līlā. It is this verse toward which all previous verses build, and it is this verse from which all subsequent verses wind down. A couple of simple but compelling observations can be made to support this idea. First, the story line culminates at this point, toward the end of the episode, in which Krishna and the Gopīs finally unite in their joyous dance of divine love and passion, the Rāsa. Second, the verse displays the longest verse meter of the complete episode. Whereas the longer meters found in the rest of the drama are of the *śakvarī* type, consisting of 14-syllable quarter lines, this verse is the very dramatic *mandākrāntā* form of *atyaṣṭi* variety, comprising 17-syllable quarter lines. Therefore, from a strictly literary perspective, this verse can be seen as the climax of the story.

In the direct and indirect commentaries consulted here, no special attention is given to the verse at hand. There is much greater attention given to the various subclimax points throughout the story that build toward this moment. These points are more relevant to the tradition's concept of the process of bhakti, which emphasizes separation from the Beloved in devotional love over union with God.

This verse and the following two verses are cited by Jīva to exhibit the exquisite musical performance occurring during the actual Rāsa dance (PrS 283). Krishna's flute music is seen as the ultimate source of the music in this world. According to both Jīva and Viśvanātha, the singing of the cowherd maidens during the Rāsa dance, inaugurated by Krishna's flute music, is the origin of the sixteen thousand musical *rāgas* (KS and SD).

The spiritual wives of Krishna, *kṛṣṇa-vadhvo.* Viśvanātha states that the word *vadhū* can mean "wife," "sister-in-law," or "woman." Although he argues that the Gopīs are not the wives of Krishna, they are just like wives because they embrace only him, are sheltered by him alone, and are enjoyed only by him. Perhaps it would be fair to say that Viśvanātha here resolves the *parakīya* versus *svakīya* debate. The cowherd maidens are technically, that is, socially, not married to Krishna, but because of their intimate and eternal relation to him, they can be considered his wives. When explaining the position of the Gopīs as the highest among all the Lakṣmīs or goddesses of prosperity and beauty, Jīva quotes this verse as an expression of their supreme status (KS 186).

With waists bending, *bhajyan madhyaiḥ.* Viśvanātha describes the waists of the Gopīs as being bent, due to the swinging movements of their dancing.

Like lustrous flashes of radiant lightning engulfed by a ring of dark clouds, *taḍita iva tā megha-cakre virejuḥ.* Here the Gopīs are compared to "flashes of radiant lightning" and Krishna to a "ring of dark clouds." This metaphor for Krishna and the Gopīs is one among several, including a magnificent emerald set in golden ornaments, the full moon among many stars, and so on.

Verse 5.9

As the Gopīs overflow with love, their love spills over into the universe with song. Thus music originates as a celebration of that love. Again, both Jīva and Viśvanātha explain that this singing of the maidens during the Rāsa dance is the origin of music. Furthermore, this verse is cited by Jīva as an example of *saṅgānam,* singing and musical ensemble, which is a division of *sambhoga,* or union in *śṛṅgāra-rasa* (PrS 424).

The whole universe, *idam.* The word *idam* is a simple demonstrative pronoun that Śrīdhara states implies the object "universe." Jīva agrees with this (PrS 283).

Verse 5.10

Jīva suggests that even the gods Brahmā, Śiva, and Indra cannot understand how Krishna and the Gopīs are able to achieve the highest level of expertise in musical artistry and ensemble. He explains that the word *svarāḥ* indicates the seven-note scale beginning on the sixth note, and *jāyataḥ* indicates the *rāga* coming from this particular scale. The word *amisrataḥ* means that the melodies sung by Krishna and the cowherd maidens are not mixed, and the tonality of their voices is pure. The words *pūjitā tena* indicate that Krishna is worshiped by the sweet voices of the Gopīs, and the word *dhruvam* means that the melody is sung in the *dhruvam* rhythm (PrS 284).[3]

Verse 5.11

Carrying a baton, *gadā-bhṛtaḥ*. Jīva states that *gadā* refers to a kind of club or baton, used for herding cows or by a leader of dancers. The particular Gopī spoken of in this verse is identified by Jīva Gosvāmin as "the daughter of Vṛṣabhānu," or Rādhā. Jīva speaks of Rādhā as the "chief of all the Gopīs," because of her intimate actions with Krishna that place her, in a certain way, in a superior position to Krishna.

This verse illustrates *mādhurya* as one among many types of *alaṁkāra-anubhāva*. The characteristic feature of *mādhurya* is loveliness and gracefulness of all one's actions (PrS 320–321).

Verse 5.12

Elated with bodily ripplings of bliss, *hṛṣṭa-romā*. The phrase means literally "having the hair of the body bristling or thrilling" (MW), and is translated here to be consistent with the translations of the similar word *pulaka*, found in earlier passages. See the comments on verse 1.40 for a discussion on the translation of these terms.

According to Viśvanātha, the same behavior exhibited in the previous verse is found again in this verse, and therefore the Gopī spoken of here is also Rādhā, whom he refers to as Śyāmalā. Jīva uses the name Śyāmalā, as we have seen above in his comments on RL 4.4, to identify one of the eight principal Gopīs, and does not identify her as Rādhā, as Viśvanātha does in his comments to this verse.

This verse, Jīva suggests, provides an example of *sāttvika-anubhāva*, or the type of manifest feeling arising out of one's nature (*sāttvika*).

3. Guy Beck helped me to understand the two musical styles referred to in this verse: one highly structured as *dhruvam*, and the other a spontaneous and improvisational coloratura.

Here the blissful nature of the Gopī is presented (PrS 316–317). The verse also illustrates *prāgalbhya* as one of many characteristics of *alaṁkāra-anubhāva.* This feature consists of uninhibited action toward the beloved within an amorous relationship (PrS 322).

Verse 5.13

Viśvanātha continues to identify the Gopīs. This verse exhibits the actions of the rival Gopī, Śaibyā, identified by Jīva in RL 4.5.

Verse 5.14

The cowherd maiden spoken of in this verse is identified as Candrāvalī (SD). There are several rival Gopīs recognized in this final verse of the series of verses identifying specific maidens. One characteristic feature of Candrāvalī's behavior, that of grabbing Krishna's hand, is exhibited, according to Viśvanātha, in this verse. He also states that another Gopī by the name of Padmā, along with Candrāvalī, brings Krishna's hand to her breast in order to stop the burning sensation. Viśvanātha suggests that the behavior of the Gopī Bhadrā, although not strongly indicated, is described here as well.

Verse 5.17

This verse, according to Jīva, demonstrates how Krishna comes under the control of the love of his devotees (PrS 298–299).

Plays with his own reflection, *sva-pratibimba-vibhramaḥ.* Viśvanātha explains that when Krishna plays with the Gopīs it is similar to his playing, *vibhramaḥ,* with his own reflection, *pratibimba.* This is because the cowherd maidens are all part of his *hlādinī-śakti,* or "pleasure power," since they are an essential part of Krishna's internal being and nature, *svarūpa-bhūta* (SD).

Verse 5.18

This verse is an example of *udbhāsvara-anubhāva.* There are four types of *anubhāvas,* or the outer physical or emotional characteristics formed by or arising from deep inner feelings. One type is observed in one's radiant beauty, *udbhāsvara.* Thus, the outer disheveled appearance of the Gopīs is due to their overflowing joy, making them appear especially beautiful (PrS 316-317). This condition of the cowherd maidens is also characterized as *mada,* rapture or excitement, that is, becoming so intoxicated with love that one loses normal sensibility (PrS 340).

Verse 5.20
Jīva refers to this verse to express how Krishna is pleased by the love of his devotees (PrS 84). Jīva confirms that this verse emphasizes how Krishna duplicates or multiplies himself as many times as there are Gopīs.

Having multiplied himself, *kṛtvā tāvantam ātmānaṁ*. I have translated the word *ātmānam* as the third-person reflexive pronoun "himself," referring to Krishna, as Jīva suggests. Jīva cites this verse in his extensive discussion on Krishna's ability to duplicate his form, and to operate on many levels through which he manifests his divine presence (KS 155).

As many forms as there were cowherd women, *yāvatīr gopa-yoṣitaḥ*. Krishna expands or duplicates himself as many times as there are cowherd maidens. It is this verse that justifies the depictions of the Rāsa-*maṇḍala* as a circle of Gopīs, with every Gopī enjoying an exclusive duplication of Krishna.

This divine play, *līlā*. The word *līlayā* ("by the *līlā*") indicates that a force separate from Krishna, that is, *līlā-śakti,* makes this event possible (PrS 152).

Verse 5.21
A type of *alaṁkāra-anubhāva* is *śobhā,* characteristics derived from the glow of love, or from having enjoyed passionate love. This verse and the following two verses, according to Jīva, illustrate *śobhā* (PrS 320–321). This verse is also cited as an example of *śrama* or fatigue (PrS 339).

The compassionate one lovingly wiped their faces, *vadanāni saḥ prāmṛjat karuṇaḥ premṇā*. In this verse, Krishna is very moved by the love of the Gopīs. Jīva states that the words *premnaḥ karuṇaḥ* mean "with tears in his eyes." Jīva quotes a verse from the *Viṣṇu Purāṇa* (5.13.54) that is parallel to this verse (PrS 126).

Verse 5.23
Breaking down any boundaries, *bhinna-setuḥ*. Viśvanātha points out that these words carry the sense of breaking the boundaries of worldly morality.

KRISHNADĀSA DESCRIBES how Caitanya recites all of the verses of the Rāsa Līlā (CC 2.18.24). When Caitanya recites this very verse (CC 2.18.25), in which a description of the *jala-keli* or "water play" begins, he becomes inspired to run toward the sea and, mistaking it for the Yamunā, jumps in, almost drowning himself (CC 2.18.26–32).

Verse 5.24

This simile of frolicking male and female elephants is indicative of the erotic tenor of the text, expressed in the pleasure and actions of the deity as a lover. This verse is cited by Jīva as an example of how the devotee controls the Lord (PrS 299). The *jala-krīḍa,* or water play, is an aspect of *sambhoga,* or union in *śṛṅgāra-rasa,* amorous love of God (PrS 425–427).

Verse 5.25

When Krishna plays with the Gopīs in the forest, this is called *vṛndāvana-vihāra,* or forest play. This play is a dimension of union or *sambhoga* in *śṛṅgāra-rasa* (PrS 425–427).

Verse 5.26

This verse invokes images from the very first verse of the Rāsa Līlā episode. Technically, this is the last verse of the narrative (just before the narrator's theological discourse). Here, Krishna is moved "by those nights," described in the words of the first verse as "seeing those nights in autumn filled with blooming jasmine flowers" (RL 1.1). In the present verse, those "moonlit nights found their refuge in *rasa,*" and in the first verse, Krishna "turned his mind toward love's delights." Krishna is "subdued" in the present verse, mirroring "fully taking refuge in Yogamāyā's illusive powers" (RL 1.1). These "beautiful nights" are, in the present verse, "made so brilliant by the rays of the moon," and similarly, in the third verse of the first act, Krishna sees "the forest colored by the moon's gentle rays" (RL 1.3).

Jīva states the Lord's purpose does not arise from worldly passion but rather from pure love. Jīva mentions that *līlā* serves two purposes: one, for the Lord to offer his love to his devotees, and two, for the Lord to teach renunciation to persons of this world. What in *līlā* can appear to be worldly passion is truly an expression of pure love, and there is no fault in the Lord's divine acts (PrS 143). This verse is cited as the concluding verse of the Rāsa dance (PrS 429).

Viśvanātha states that these special autumn nights are the "very source of all poetic narrations of *rasa,* or the intimate experiences with God." He goes on to say that these poetic narrations are unlimited, and that poets in the past and future will never be able to reach the end of them.

Subdued, *siṣeva.* I have translated the verb *siṣeva* as the word "subdued" in light of Viśvanātha's comments on this verse. These beautiful autumn nights, *niśāḥ,* which inspire intimacy between the Gopīs and Krishna, are arranged by the power of Yogamāyā. As stated in the very first verse of the Rāsa Līlā, Krishna "fully took refuge in" Yogamāyā's power, in order to enjoy intimacy with his dear ones. Viśvanātha states that these intimate sports have nothing to do with this illusory world; rather, they are *satya-kāmaḥ,* "essentially real."

Rasa. For a discussion on the meaning of *rasa,* see "Textual Illuminations," "Devotional Love as 'Rasa.'" The moon is often associated with *rasa,* as in the present verse, and in the first several verses of the Rāsa story.[4]

This verse is cited by Svarūpa Dāmodara Gosvāmin to Caitanya, in his discussion on pride in the Gopīs' love for Krishna (CC 2.14.140–153). He states the following about Krishna:

> Dāmodara said, "Krishna is the foremost
> enjoyer of loving *rasa* (*rasika-śekhara*),
> The one who enjoys tasting *rasa,*
> and his body is fully endowed with *rasa.*"
> (CC 2.14.155)

Several verses later, Svarūpa quotes the present verse (CC 2.14.158) to demonstrate that both Krishna and the Gopīs are absorbed and subdued by the poetic beauty of nature, which itself inspires *rasa.*

Verse 5.27–28

These two verses and the following one demonstrate how the author of the *Bhāgavata* text anticipates that it may be difficult for persons to understand how God could apparently behave immorally while he

4. In the *Bhagavad Gītā,* Krishna identifies the moon, or Soma, with himself, because the moon supplies nourishment to all plant life through its power or *rasa* (BG 15.13).

himself is the originator of all morality. Here, doubts are raised as to the morality of this *līlā,* and both Jīva and Viśvanātha explain that Parīkṣit raises this doubt on behalf of the other listeners in the audience, anticipating their confusion.

Verse 5.29

Whose desires are supremely fulfilled, *āpta-kāmo.* Jīva states that the implication of the king's question in this verse is that the Lord, who is already "fulfilled in all desires," would therefore not have any purpose in committing such immoral actions. Viśvanātha points out that the Lord does not perform the Rāsa Līlā to fulfill his own desires. And since Krishna is the Lord of the Yadus, who are themselves very religious, Viśvanātha rhetorically asks how Krishna could be otherwise.

O strict sage, *su-vrata.* The king addresses Śuka in this verse as *su-vrata* (literally, "one who is very strict in following one's *vratas* or vows") implying that Krishna may not be so strict and consistent. Those in the assembly are puzzled, since they see the narrator's appreciation for this *līlā* and at the same time, his strictness in renunciation. Viśvanātha explains that even though Krishna is self-satisfied and fulfilled in all desires, it is natural for him to enjoy with the Gopīs, who belong to the internal nature of his pure loving energy (*premānanda-svarūpa*).

Verse 5.31

Rudra is a name for Śiva, the god of cosmic dissolution. In this story, Śiva drinks the *kālakūṭa* poison that has been generated from the churning of the ocean. Together, various divinities including Vishnu himself, as well as the demons, pulled a great snake named Vāsuki back and forth across the Mandara mountain, which was being used as a churning rod in order to obtain an intoxicating nectar from the ocean. This churning motion, however, produced a large quantity of poison along with the nectar. The divinities and Vishnu approached the powerful Śiva, offering prayers and pleading for relief from the fiery poison, which was rapidly spreading. Śiva, who offers protection to all dependents struggling for existence, compassionately agreed to drink the poison, for the happiness of all. The poison marked Śiva's neck with a bluish line, considered beautiful and ornamental (BhP 8.7).

Viśvanātha points out that if anyone else were to drink poison, such a person would perish. Rudra, on the other hand, is invulnerable to the poison. Indeed, he becomes strikingly beautiful upon drinking it; specifically, his neck turns a bluish hue, one of the special marks of Śiva.

Verse 5.34

From the piety or impiety of creatures, *kuśalākuśalānvayaḥ.* Jīva suggests that the words *kuśalākuśala* are equivalent to *puṇya-pāpābhyām,* or "both the piety and impiety," and *anvaya* is equivalent to *samparka,* or "connection."

Verse 5.35

By the power of yoga, *yoga-prabhāva.* Viśvanātha indicates that the use of the word yoga in this verse means specifically *bhakti-yoga,* or "the method of attaining perfection by loving devotion."

Dust, *parāga.* The word *parāga* can also mean "flower pollen," implying the positive quality of this dust. Moreover, in India, even the dust from the feet of a great personage, not to mention of a god or the supreme God, is considered to have inestimable value, expressing simultaneously the humility of the worshiper and the greatness of the worshiped.

Verse 5.36

The tradition has presented conflicting understandings on this question regarding whom the Gopīs are married to. Some say that they are married to cowherd men, causing their love for Krishna to be illicit, or *parakīya,* the love for a paramour. Others say that the cowherd maidens are in reality married to Krishna, and therefore their love is licit conjugal love, or *svakīya,* "love for one's own spouse." Although this study cannot present the details of this debate, some of the important commentators address this question in the following discussion.

Śrīdhara insists that the Gopīs cannot be considered the wives of other men, as the Lord never consorts with the wives of others. Viśvanātha asks a rhetorical question: How can there be any fault in the one who is the supreme soul and internal witness (*antaḥ adhyakṣaḥ*), who dwells secretly within all living beings, to embrace any of these beings externally in a secret place?

Jīva cites this verse to demonstrate that Krishna is not adulterous and therefore is not behaving immorally in his relationships with the Gopīs (PrS 103). As discussed in the notes on RL 1.6, the Gopīs are indeed unmarried women and therefore are only assisting other married women in nursing *their* children. This understanding reflects Jīva's idea that the Gopīs are Krishna's "own wives," *svakīya-rasa,* and not the so-called "adulterous" lovers of Krishna, *parakīya-rasa.* On the one hand, the cowherd maidens do not act as wives of Krishna, because they love him passionately as a woman loves a paramour; on the other hand, Jīva states that the Gopīs should not be considered adulteresses because their only true husband is Krishna. Jīva acknowledges that the behavior of Krishna with the Gopīs can appear to be the selfish love of illicit lovers, and even quotes the Gopīs when they say "lovers abandon women after having enjoyed love with them" (Bhramara Gīta, BhP 10.47.8). From a worldly perspective, it appears that the Gopīs are already married to other husbands. From the spiritual perspective, these so-called husbands only exist as a manifestation of God's internal energy for the purpose of his *līlā* (PrS 279).

Jīva argues that this verse demonstrates that the true husband of the Gopīs is Krishna, since he is *para-brahman,* the "supreme Brahman," *sarvāṁśitva,* the "one from whom all portions of existence emanate," *sarva-pātṛtva,* the "protector of all," and therefore is *patitva,* the "essential or ultimate husband." The words *gopīnāṁ tat-patīnāṁ ca,* translated here as "within the Gopīs and within their husbands," are interpreted by Jīva as "among all the Gopīs as their husbands" (KS 177).

Jīva understands the following verse as presenting the three essential identifications of Krishna in a hierarchical arrangement:

> Full of passionate love for me
> as a husband, as a lover,
> And not for my supreme nature,
> these women knew me.
> Hundreds and thousands
> of these women achieved me,
> The supreme Brahman,
> by intimate contact with me.
> (BhP 11.12.13)

Jīva observes that the BhP identifies Krishna as being three different types of beloveds for the Gopīs, each one having successively greater weight over the previous identification: Krishna as paramour (*jāra,* which can also mean "lover"); Krishna as husband (*ramaṇa,* which can mean either "lover" or "husband"—Jīva takes great pains to show that the word's application in other BhP verses is clearly the latter sense rather than the former); and Krishna as the supreme Brahman (*brahma paramam*). Although the word order in Jīva's list is different from that of the verse itself, Jīva justifies his reordering of the words *ramaṇa* and *jāra* by a hermeneutic rule, which states that word order is not as powerful as the order of ideas in the greater context of the written work. Thus, Krishna as a husband is a more powerful identity than Krishna as a lover. Indeed, after referencing verses BhP 10.47.34–37, Jīva claims that the conception of Krishna as the paramour of the Gopīs is a very dangerous interpretation and one that is not consonant with the understandings of other scriptural sources (KS 177).

Jīva insists that the notion that the Gopīs are married to others and not to Krishna is a view that comes from the residents of Vraja themselves. In the pain of their separation from Krishna when he departs from Vraja, the residents imagine the Gopīs as having other husbands, and mistakenly perceive the Gopīs as Krishna's paramours. Jīva states that the authorities on *rasa* come to the conclusion that Krishna does not transgress dharma or the rules of ethical behavior (KS 177).

There are two types of unethical amorous relations: *pārakīya* ("adulterous relations") and *pārasparśa* ("improper contact with another"). Jīva argues that Krishna could not be engaged in either of these unethical interactions with the maidens, as this would be countering the requirements of *rasa.* He states, invoking Śuka's explanation in verses RL 5.30–37, that although Krishna may appear to perform actions of an ordinary person, he is powerful beyond the human realm and thus not subject to requirements of this world (KS 177).

Jīva states that this verse describes both Krishna's divine acts in *prakaṭa* and *aprakaṭa* forms realized in the *svārasikī* experience of the Gopīs. Krishna's appearance is revealed to the *svārasikī* in his *prakaṭa* form when he enjoys his *līlā*s in Vraja with the Gopīs, their husbands, and everyone else; and in his *aprakaṭa* form as the internal Witness within the hearts of the Gopīs, their husbands, and everyone (KS 172).

Krishnadāsa clearly favors the idea that *parakīya bhāva* is the highest love for God. He explains that *madhura-rasa,* amorous love for God, includes two types: *svakīya bhāva* and *parakīya bhāva* (CC 1.4.46), and then states that the *parakīya-bhāva* knows the greater intensity of love, found only in Vraja (CC 1.4.47).

Verse 5.37

Human-like form, *mānuṣaṁ deham.* According to Viśvanātha, God comes in a form that resembles that of humans, a "human-like form," while at the same time directly appearing in his internal identity.

Śrīdhara explains that one purpose of God's appearance within the Rāsa Līlā is to transform the minds of those who are absorbed in worldly sexuality instead of devotion to God. Viśvanātha adds that

God reveals this particular Rāsa Līlā as a special act of grace, as it has, compared to other *līlās*, the greatest inconceivable power, like magical jewels, mantras, or powerful medicinal herbs. Moreover, the principal reason for God's appearance in a human-like form is to allow his devotees to relate with him directly or intimately.

According to Jīva, the Lord exhibits relationships with his devotees that may reveal pride, passion, and so on. Indeed, the Lord himself displays four characteristics in the *śṛṅgāra-rasa,* or the relationship of amorous love, which can be described as follows: *dakṣiṇa,* "sincere" or "pleasing"; *anukūla,* "faithful," "kind," or "obliging"; *śaṭha,* "false," "deceitful," or "cheating"; and *dhṛṣṭa,* "bold," "daring," or "audacious." These are the various characteristics of Krishna that the Gopīs may experience in his presence due to *līlā śakti,* "the power of the revelational drama" (PrS 288).

This verse is cited in the important fourth chapter of the Ādi Līlā of the *Caitanya Caritāmṛta* (CC 1.4.34). Krishnadāsa, in his presentation of the reasons for Krishna's descent as Caitanya, explains how the Lord is often known to this world by his omnipotent forms, and not by his intimate forms that interact with personages within the higher *rasa*s, namely, *sakhya, vātsalya,* and *mādhurya.* The Gopīs are specially mentioned in this regard.

Verse 5.38

Deluded by his power of Māyā, *mohitās tasya māyayā.* Again, Yogamāyā is observable in the simple word Māyā. Viśvanātha indicates that the word Māyā, in the instrumental case, means specifically Yogamāyā. Thus it is by means of Yogamāyā that the husbands and family members of the Gopīs experience the full presence of those Gopīs who abandon them and depart for the forest to meet Krishna. Jīva explains that the Gopīs at home are simply illusory forms and only appear to be standing by the sides of their husbands, while the actual Gopīs depart for the forest. When they return to their homes, the actual maidens replace their illusory forms. All this is made possible by Yogamāyā.

Jīva cites this verse to show that the Gopīs have no contact with any other husbands, and therefore cannot be considered as behaving in immoral ways. The verse establishes for him that these husbands only exist through Krishna's "spiritual power," *cit-śakti,* and have no existence or purpose apart from it (PrS 279).

Here Jīva acquiesces to the idea that even if the Gopīs are married and in fact do run off to dance with Krishna, such an act normally considered inauspicious becomes auspicious. After all, the true forms of the Gopīs are the ones that are married to Krishna, the spiritual forms attained when they depart to join him in the forest, and not their illusory forms that remain with their so-called husbands. Jīva states that Yogamāyā protects the rules (*maryāda*) of dharma and allows the Gopīs' pure love for Krishna to be acted upon without anxiety. The relationships of the Gopīs to these so-called husbands are illusory, since the Gopīs' illusory forms are but a shadow transformation of themselves that remain with the cowherd men, and not the true Gopīs. Jīva explains that the Gopīs, by the power of Yogamāyā, are never tainted by mundane sexual contact with worldly husbands, since they possess pure spiritual bodies. The very fact that the husband cowherd men, as this verse states, feel no jealousy whatsoever is further proof that the Gopīs are not truly their wives. Furthermore, since the Gopīs are apparently not under the control of their husbands, it cannot be said that they have husbands. Rather, they are controlled or allured by Krishna's flute music and his beauty—therefore Krishna is their only true husband. Moreover, if the Gopīs are truly the wives of the cowherd men, then they would not desire to run off, nor would they be able to run off as they do (KS 177).

Whenever the husbands of the Gopīs are referred to by Krishna, it is to be understood as Krishna's jesting, for the purpose of amusement. By so doing, there is no "conflict within the rules governing *rasa*" (known as *rasābhāsa*). By accepting the direct meanings of words regarding the Gopīs as having husbands, then the problematic distortion of *rasa* occurs. According to Jīva, this distortion would interrupt the purity of aesthetic delight that the RL passage itself claims to possess, expressed in RL 5.26. Thus, the indirect meaning of the word "husband" is to be taken here, since it is Krishna who is the true husband. The *rasa* of the RL passage becomes seriously defective if the Gopīs are understood as having abandoned their own children to run off to be with Krishna. Since nowhere in the RL is it stated that these children whom the Gopīs abandon are their own, according to Jīva, they are certainly not theirs (KS 177).

Verse 5.39

At the end of the night of Brahmā, *brahma-rātra upāvṛtte.* Śrīdhara states that the words *brahma-rātre* are to be understood as *brāhma-muhūrta* (a certain auspicious period of time about an hour before sunrise, marking the beginning of a new day), and *upāvṛtte* as "arriving." According to these understandings, the translation for this part of the verse might be, "on that night, when the *brāhma-muhūrta* hour had arrived." In contrast to Śrīdhara's understanding, but not necessarily in contradiction to it, Viśvanātha suggests that *brahma-rātre* refers to "a night of the creator, Brahmā," which consists of a duration of one thousand *yugas.* The idea is that the duration of one night for God is significantly longer than one night for mortals of this world. Because both meanings of the phrase in the Sanskrit resonate strongly here, I have included in my translation of this verse phrases that accommodate both.

Vāsudeva is another name for Krishna that means "the son of Vasudeva."

Verse 5.40

Highest devotion, *bhaktiṁ parāṁ.* This phrase appears only once in the entire *Bhāgavata Purāṇa.* There is no phrase similar to it that promises the highest devotion to God, even among the numerous benedictory verses found at the ends of various stories, thus setting this particular story apart from all others in the *Bhāgavata.*

This phrase also appears in two verses spoken by Krishna toward the end of the *Bhagavad Gītā:*

> One whose being is absorbed in *brahman,*
> whose self is full of serenity,
> who does not lament or hanker,
> Who is equal to all beings,
> such a person gains
> the highest devotion (*bhaktiṁ parām*) to me.
> (BG 18.54)

> One who explains this supreme secret
> to my devotees (*bhaktas*)
> Having performed the highest devotion (*bhaktiṁ parām*),
> shall come to me without doubt.
> (BG 18.68)

Lust, the disease of the heart, *kāmaṁ hṛd-rogam.* The narrator of the Rāsa Līlā states that the effect of hearing this episode of the *Bhāgavata* is to rid one of lust, the disease of the heart.

Peaceful and wise, *dhīraḥ*. The Sanskrit word possesses many meanings, which relate either to "gravity" or "wisdom," that is, a state of saintly behavior or learnedness. Thus I have provided two words in the translation that convey these two senses. Synonyms such as "saintly," "sober," "equipoised," "solemn," "sedate," "prudent," "composed," "calm," "gentle," "soft," and "collected," relate to the former; and "realized," "learned," "intelligent," "sensible," and "clever" relate to the latter. One who is *dhīraḥ* is a "learned" or "wise" person, *paṇḍitaḥ,* as Viśvanātha suggests.

Śrīdhara, confirming the statement made in this final verse of the *līlā,* declares that one becomes a wise soul (*dhīra*) when one hears and recites the Rāsa Līlā, which destroys *kāma,* or lustfulness, the disease of the heart. Furthermore, he states that the *līlā* serves as a declaration of God's conquest over Cupid, who apparently became proud of his conquest over Brahmā and other gods. Now, in the Rāsa Līlā, Krishna takes away the pride of even Cupid (RL 5.36).

Jīva states that spiritual love is permanently established by hearing the *līlās* of Krishna, displacing worldly love and lust, and quotes this last verse of the RL to confirm this (PrS 84). Viśvanātha begins his commentary to the verse by again declaring that this work is the "crown-jewel of all *līlās,*" *sarva-līlā-cūḍā-maṇi* (see the comments on verse 1.1). Furthermore, he states that the Rāsa Līlā is supremely glorious, and is therefore known as the loving smile of God for the devotee—for in the Rāsa dance, God himself is controlled by love.

This final verse of the Rāsa Līlā is quoted in full (CC 2.5.48) by Caitanya during his discussion on the elevated spiritual status of Rāmānanda Rāya (CC 2.5.37–51). Prior to the quotation and presentation of the meaning of this verse, Caitanya offers his exegetical rewording of the verse as follows:

> The play of the Rāsa and other *līlās* of Krishna
>   in the intimate association of
>   the young women of Vraja,
> Which, if a person describes
>   or hears with great faith,
> Will destroy at that time the disease
>   of lust in one's heart,
> And the agitation of
>   the three worldly qualities will cease
>   as one becomes greatly realized (*mahā-dhīra*).
>
> (CC 2.5.45–46)

Following the quotation of this last RL verse, Caitanya gives the following exegesis emphasizing the power of simply hearing or reciting the Rāsa Līlā:

> Those who hear and those who recite,
>   this is the effect on such persons.
> Such a person becomes deeply absorbed in emotion
>   and serves in this way both day and night.
>
> What shall I say about its effect?
>   It is not possible to describe
> Such a person who is eternally perfect,
>   who has become perfect though still having a body.
> (CC 2.5.49–50)

In the verse that follows the above passage, Caitanya insists that Rāmānanda is on the spontaneous path of passionate devotion, *rāgānuga-mārga,* and possesses a *siddha-deha,* a spiritual body:

> I know that the devotion of [Rāmānanda] Rāya is
>   on the path of the followers of passionate devotion—
> Therefore he possesses a spiritual body (*siddha-deha*)
>   and his mind is not affected by worldly nature.
> (CC 2.5.51)

Figure 15. Devout pilgrim reading the *Bhāgavata* before the sacred *tulasī* plant in Rādhā Kund, Vraja. Photograph by the author.

Part IV

THE SANSKRIT TEXT

Introduction

The original Sanskrit text and its English transliteration are provided in this section of the book. To date, a critical edition of the *Bhāgavata Purāṇa* has not been produced. I have consulted several Sanskrit texts, however, and have found that the alternate wordings of the Rāsa Līlā are few and negligible. Such variant readings as exist do not change the dramatic content and theological concepts of the Rāsa Līlā. In the service of scholarship, however, I have provided these variations of particular verses in footnotes to the original text that I use for my English translation. The non-italicized words in footnotes to verses indicate the variant readings of such verses.

The transliterated text as it appears here has been formatted for the nonspecialist reader to gain a visual sense of the versification of the original Sanskrit. The eight-syllable quarter lined metered verses, or *anuṣṭubh,* appear as couplets of Sanskrit text, the quarter lines indicated by an inserted comma in each line. The other five types of longer metered verse forms appear as quatrains, easily distinguishable from the more common two-lined *anuṣṭubh* verses by the four lines of elaborate and embellished metered verses. (See "Poetic Meters in Sanskrit Text" for an analysis of verse meters used in the Rāsa Līlā text.) The English translation also imitates this visual distinction between the couplet appearance of *anuṣṭubh* verses and the quatrain formation of longer verses. This is accomplished in the translated *anuṣṭubh* verses by presenting two "leading lines," or nonindented lines of text, under each of which one or several indented lines appear; likewise, for the more complex metered verses in translation, I have presented four leading lines, each followed by one or more indented lines.

In some editions of the text there are differences in verse divisions and numbering, particularly in the second and fifth chapters of the episode. This lack of consistency does not pose a challenge, however, since it was the habit of medieval commentators to identify verses by the first several words of the first line, without reference to any sequential numeration. Any confusion in attempting to identify my translation with other original texts containing differing verse divisions is avoided by presenting each verse of the original Sanskrit text, coupled with its English transliteration.

Act One

Bhāgavata Purāṇa Book 10 Chapter 29

श्रीबादरायणिरुवाच
भगवानपि ता रात्रीः शारदोत्फुल्लमल्लिकाः ।
वीक्ष्य रन्तुं मनश्चक्रे योगमायामुपाश्रितः ॥ १ ॥

śrī-bādarāyaṇir uvāca
bhagavān api tā rātrīḥ, śāradotphulla-mallikāḥ |
vīkṣya rantuṁ manaś-cakre, yoga-māyām upāśritaḥ || 1 ||[1]

तदोडुराजः ककुभः करैर्मुखं
प्राच्या विलिम्पन्नरुणेन शन्तमैः ।
स चर्षणीनामुदगाच्छुचो मृजन्
प्रियः प्रियाया इव दीर्घदर्शनः ॥ २ ॥

tadoḍurājaḥ kakubhaḥ karair mukhaṁ
prācyā vilimpann aruṇena śantamaiḥ |
sa carṣaṇīnām udagāc chuco mṛjan
priyaḥ priyāyā iva dīrgha-darśanaḥ || 2 ||

दृष्ट्वा कुमुद्वन्तमखण्डमण्डलं
रमाननाभं नवकुंकुमारुणम् ।
वनं च तत्कोमलगोभी रञ्जितं
जगौ कलं वामदृशां मनोहरम् ॥ ३ ॥

dṛṣṭvā kumudvantam akhaṇḍa-maṇḍalaṁ
ramānanābhaṁ nava-kuṅkumāruṇam |
vanaṁ ca tat-komala-gobhī rañjitaṁ
jagau kalaṁ vāma-dṛśāṁ manoharam || 3 ||

1. *śri* śuka *uvāca*

निशम्य गीतं तदनङ्गवर्धनं
 व्रजस्त्रियः कृष्णगृहीतमानसाः ।
आजग्मुरन्योन्यमलक्षितोद्यमाः
 स यत्र कान्तो जवलोलकुण्डलाः ॥४॥

niśamya gītaṁ tad anaṅga-vardhanaṁ
 vraja-striyaḥ kṛṣṇa-gṛhīta-mānasāḥ|
ājagmur anyonyam alakṣitodyamāḥ
 sa yatra kānto java-lola-kuṇḍalāḥ || 4 ||

दुहन्त्योऽभिययुः काश्चिद्दोहं हित्वा समुत्सुकाः ।
पयोऽधिश्रित्य संयावमनुद्वास्यापरा ययुः ॥५॥

duhantyo 'bhiyayuḥ kāścid, doham hitvā samutsukāḥ |
payo 'dhiśritya saṁyāvam, anudvāsyāparā yayuḥ || 5 ||

परिवेषयन्त्यस्तद्धित्वा पाययन्त्यः शिशून् पयः ।
शुश्रूषन्त्यः पतीन् काश्चिदश्नन्त्योऽपास्य भोजनम् ॥६॥

pariveṣayantyas tad dhitvā, pāyayantyaḥ śiśūn payaḥ |
śuśrūṣantyaḥ patīn kāścid, aśnantyo 'pāsya bhojanam || 6 ||

लिम्पन्त्यः प्रमृजन्त्योऽन्या अञ्जन्त्यः काश्च लोचने ।
व्यत्यस्तवस्त्राभरणाः काश्चित्कृष्णान्तिकं ययुः ॥७॥

limpantyaḥ pramṛjantyo 'nyā, añjantyaḥ kāśca locane |
vyatyasta-vastrābharaṇāḥ, kāścit kṛṣṇāntikaṁ yayuḥ || 7 ||

ता वार्यमाणाः पतिभिः पितृभिर्भ्रातृबन्धुभिः ।
गोविन्दापहृतात्मानो न न्यवर्तन्त मोहिताः ॥८॥

tā vāryamāṇāḥ patibhiḥ, pitṛbhir bhrātṛ-bandhubhiḥ |
govindāpahṛtātmāno, na nyavartanta mohitāḥ || 8 ||

अन्तर्गृहगताः काश्चिद् गोप्योऽलब्धविनिर्गमाः ।
कृष्णं तद्भावनायुक्ता दध्युर्मीलितलोचनाः ॥९॥

antar-gṛha-gatāḥ kāścid, gopyo 'labdha-vinirgamāḥ |
kṛṣṇaṁ tad-bhāvanā-yuktā, dadhyur mīlita-locanāḥ || 9 ||

दुःसहप्रेष्ठविरहतीव्रतापधुताशुभाः ।
ध्यानप्राप्ताच्युताश्लेषनिर्वृत्या क्षीणमङ्गलाः ॥१०॥

duḥsaha-preṣṭha-viraha-, tīvra-tāpa-dhutāśubhāḥ |
dhyāna-prāptācyutāśleṣa-, nirvṛtyā kṣīṇa-maṅgalāḥ || 10 ||

तमेव परमात्मानं जारबुद्ध्यापि सङ्गताः ।
जहुर्गुणमयं देहं सद्यः प्रक्षीणबन्धनाः ॥११॥

tam eva paramātmānaṁ, jāra-buddhyāpi saṅgatāḥ |
jahur guṇa-mayaṁ dehaṁ, sadyaḥ prakṣīṇa-bandhanāḥ || 11 ||

श्रीपरीक्षिदुवाच
कृष्णं विदुः परं कान्तं न तु ब्रह्मतया मुने ।
गुणप्रवाहोपरमस्तासां गुणधियां कथम ॥१२॥

śrī-parīkṣid uvāca
kṛṣṇaṁ viduḥ paraṁ kāntaṁ, na tu brahmatayā mune |
guṇa-pravāhoparamas, tāsāṁ guṇa-dhiyāṁ katham || 12 ||

श्रीशुक उवाच
उक्तं पुरस्तादेतत्ते चैद्यः सिद्धिं यथा गतः ।
द्विषन्नपि हृषीकेशं किमुताधोक्षजप्रियाः ॥१३॥

śrī-śuka uvāca
uktaṁ purastād etat te, caidyaḥ siddhiṁ yathā gataḥ |
dviṣann api hṛṣīkeśaṁ, kim utādhokṣaja-priyāḥ || 13 ||

नृणां निःश्रेयसार्थाय व्यक्तिर्भगवतो नृप ।
अव्ययस्याप्रमेयस्य निर्गुणस्य गुणात्मनः ॥१४॥

nṛṇāṁ niḥśreyasārthāya, vyaktir bhagavato nṛpa |
avyayasyāprameyasya, nirguṇasya guṇātmanaḥ || 14 ||

कामं क्रोधं भयं स्नेहमैक्यं सौहृदमेव च ।
नित्यं हरौ विदधतो यान्ति तन्मयतां हि ते ॥१५॥

kāmaṁ krodhaṁ bhayaṁ sneham, aikyaṁ sauhṛdam eva ca |
nityaṁ harau vidadhato, yānti tan-mayatāṁ hi te || 15 ||

न चैवं विस्मयः कार्यो भवता भगवत्यजे ।
योगेश्वरेश्वरे कृष्णे यत एतद्विमुच्यते ॥१६॥

na caivaṁ vismayaḥ kāryo, bhavatā bhagavaty aje |
yogeśvareśvare kṛṣṇe, yata etad vimucyate || 16 ||

ता दृष्ट्वान्तिकमायाता भगवान् व्रजयोषितः ।
अवदद्वदतां श्रेष्ठो वाचः पेशैर्विमोहयन् ॥१७॥

tā dṛṣṭvāntikam āyātā, bhagavān vraja-yoṣitaḥ |
avadad vadatāṁ śreṣṭho, vācaḥ peśair vimohayan || 17 ||

श्रीभगवानुवाच
स्वागतं वो महाभागाः प्रियं किं करवाणि वः ।
व्रजस्यानामयं कच्चिद् ब्रूतागमनकारणम् ॥१८॥

śrī-bhagavān uvāca
svāgataṁ vo mahā-bhāgāḥ, priyaṁ kiṁ karavāṇi vaḥ |
vrajasyānāmayaṁ kaccid, brūtāgamana-kāraṇam || 18 ||

रजन्येषा घोररूपा घोरसत्त्वनिषेविता ।
प्रतियात व्रजं नेह स्थेयं स्त्रीभिः सुमध्यमाः ॥१९॥

rajany eṣā ghora-rūpā, ghora-sattva-niṣevitā |
pratiyāta vrajaṁ neha, stheyaṁ strībhiḥ su-madhyamāḥ || 19 ||

मातरः पितरः पुत्रा भ्रातरः पतयश्च वः ।
विचिन्वन्ति ह्यपश्यन्तो मा कृद्ध्वं बन्धुसाध्वसम् ॥२०॥

mātaraḥ pitaraḥ putrā, bhrātaraḥ patayaś ca vaḥ |
vicinvanti hy apaśyanto, mā kṛdhvaṁ bandhu-sādhvasam || 20 ||

दृष्टं वनं कुसुमितं राकेशकररञ्जितम् ।
यमुनानिललीलैजत्तरुपल्लवशोभितम् ॥२१॥

dṛṣṭaṁ vanaṁ kusumitaṁ, rākeśa-kara-rañjitam |
yamunānila-līlaijat, taru-pallava-śobhitam || 21 ||[2]

2. 21a *dṛṣṭaṁ vanaṁ* kumuditaṁ

तद्यात मा चिरं गोष्ठं शुश्रूषध्वं पतीन् सतीः ।
क्रन्दन्ति वत्सा बालाश्च तान् पाययत दुह्यत ॥२२॥

tad yāta mā ciraṁ goṣṭhaṁ, śuśrūṣadhvaṁ patīn satīḥ |
krandanti vatsā bālāś ca, tān pāyayata duhyata || 22 ||[3]

अथ वा मदभिस्नेहाद् भवत्यो यन्त्रिताशयाः ।
आगता ह्युपपन्नं वः प्रीयन्ते मयि जन्तवः ॥२३॥

atha vā mad-abhisnehād, bhavatyo yantritāśayāḥ |
āgatā hy upapannaṁ vaḥ, prīyante mayi jantavaḥ || 23 ||

भर्तुः शुश्रूषणं स्त्रीणां परो धर्मो ह्यमायया ।
तद्बन्धूनां च कल्याणः प्रजानां चानुपोषणम् ॥२४॥

bhartuḥ śuśrūṣaṇaṁ strīṇāṁ, paro dharmo hy amāyayā |
tad-bandhūnāṁ ca kalyāṇaḥ, prajānāṁ cānupoṣaṇam || 24 ||

दुःशीलो दुर्भगो वृद्धो जडो रोग्यधनोऽपि वा ।
पतिः स्त्रीभिर्न हातव्यो लोकेप्सुभिरपातकी ॥२५॥

duḥśīlo durbhago vṛddho, jaḍo rogy adhano 'pi vā |
patiḥ strībhir na hātavyo, lokepsubhir apātakī || 25 ||

अस्वर्ग्यमयशस्यं च फल्गु कृच्छ्रं भयावहम् ।
जुगुप्सितं च सर्वत्र ह्यौपपत्यं कुलस्त्रियः ॥२६॥

asvargyam ayaśasyaṁ ca, phalgu kṛcchraṁ bhayāvaham |
jugupsitaṁ ca sarvatra, hy aupapatyaṁ kula-striyaḥ || 26 ||

श्रवणाद्दर्शनाद्ध्यानान्मयि भावोऽनुकीर्तनात् ।
न तथा सन्निकर्षेण प्रतियात ततो गृहान् ॥२७॥

śravaṇād darśanād dhyānān, mayi bhāvo 'nukīrtanāt |
na tathā sannikarṣeṇa, pratiyāta tato gṛhān || 27 ||

3. 22a *tad yāta mā ciraṁ* ghoṣaṁ

श्रीशुक उवाच
इति विप्रियमाकर्ण्य गोप्यो गोविन्दभाषितम् ।
विषण्णा भग्नसङ्कल्पाश्चिन्तामापुर्दुरत्ययाम् ॥२८॥

śrī-śuka uvāca
iti vipriyam ākarṇya, gopyo govinda-bhāṣitam |
viṣaṇṇā bhagna-saṅkalpāś, cintām āpur duratyayām || 28 ||

कृत्वा मुखान्यव शुचः श्वसनेन शुष्यद्
बिम्बाधराणि चरणेन भुवः लिखन्त्यः ।
अस्त्रैरुपात्तमसिभिः कुचकुंकुमानि
तस्थुर्मृजन्त्य उरुदुःखभराः स्म तुष्णीम् ॥२९॥

kṛtvā mukhāny ava śucaḥ śvasanena śuṣyad
bimbādharāṇi caraṇena bhuvaḥ likhantyaḥ |
asrair upātta-masibhiḥ kuca-kuṅkumāni
tasthur mṛjantya uru-duḥkha-bharāḥ sma tūṣṇīm || 29 ||

प्रेष्ठं प्रियेतरमिव प्रतिभाषमाणं
कृष्णं तदर्थविनिवर्तितसर्वकामाः ।
नेत्रे विमृज्य रुदितोपहते स्म किञ्चित्
संरम्भगद्गदगिरोऽब्रुवतानुरक्ताः ॥३०॥

preṣṭhaṁ priyetaram iva pratibhāṣamāṇaṁ
kṛṣṇaṁ tad-artha-vinivartita-sarva-kāmāḥ |
netre vimṛjya ruditopahate sma kiñcit
saṁrambha-gadgada-giro 'bruvatānuraktāḥ || 30 ||

श्रीगोप्य ऊचुः
मैवं विभोऽर्हति भवान् गदितुं नृशंसं
सन्त्यज्य सर्वविषयांस्तव पादमूलम् ।
भक्ता भजस्व दुरवग्रह मा त्यजास्मान्
देवो यथादिपुरुषो भजते मुमुक्षून् ॥ ३१ ॥

śrī-gopya ūcuḥ
maivaṁ vibho 'rhati bhavān gadituṁ nṛ-śaṁsaṁ
santyajya sarva-viṣayāṁs tava pāda-mūlam |
bhaktā bhajasva duravagraha mā tyajāsmān
devo yathādi-puruṣo bhajate mumukṣūn || 31 || [4]

यत्पत्यपत्यसुहृदामनुवृत्तिरङ्ग
स्त्रीणां स्वधर्म इति धर्मविदा त्वयोक्तम् ।
अस्त्वेवमेतदुपदेशपदे त्वयीशे
प्रेष्ठो भवांस्तनुभृतां किल बन्धुरात्मा ॥ ३२ ॥

yat paty-apatya-suhṛdām anuvṛttir aṅga
strīṇāṁ sva-dharma iti dharma-vidā tvayoktam |
astv evam etad upadeśa-pade tvayīśe
preṣṭho bhavāṁs tanu-bhṛtāṁ kila bandhur ātmā || 32 ||

कुर्वन्ति हि त्वयि रतिं कुशलाः स्व आत्मन्
नित्यप्रिये पतिसुतादिभिरार्तिदैः किम् ।
तन्नः प्रसीद परमेश्वर मा स्म छिन्द्या
आशां धृतां त्वयि चिरादरविन्दनेत्र ॥ ३३ ॥

kurvanti hi trayi ratiṁ kuśalāḥ sva ātman
nitya-priye pati-sutādibhir ārti-daiḥ kim |
tan naḥ prasīda parameśvara mā sma chindyā
āśāṁ dhṛtāṁ tvayi cirād aravinda-netra || 33 ||[5]

4. 31d *devo yathādi-puruṣo* bhajato *mumukṣūn*
5. 33c *tan naḥ prasīda* varadeśvara *mā sma chindyā*

चित्तं सुखेन भवतापहृतं गृहेषु
यन्निर्विशत्युत करावपि गृह्यकृत्ये ।
पादौ पदं न चलतस्तव पादमूलाद्
यामः कथं व्रजमथो करवाम किं वा ॥ ३४ ॥

cittaṁ sukhena bhavatāpahṛtaṁ gṛheṣu
yan nirviśaty uta karāv api gṛhya-kṛtye |
pādau padaṁ na calatas tava pāda-mūlād
yāmaḥ kathaṁ vrajam atho karavāma kiṁ vā || 34 ||[6]

सिञ्चाङ्ग नस्त्वदधरामृतपूरकेण
हासावलोककलगीतजहृच्छयाग्निम् ।
नो चेद्वयं विरहजाग्न्युपयुक्तदेहा
ध्यानेन याम पदयोः पदवीं सखे ते ॥ ३५ ॥

siñcāṅga nas tvad-adharāmṛta-pūrakeṇa
hāsāvaloka-kala-gīta-ja-hṛc-chayāgnim |
no ced vayaṁ virahajāgny-upayukta-dehā
dhyānena yāma padayoḥ padavīṁ sakhe te || 35 ||

यर्ह्यम्बुजाक्ष तव पादतलं रमाया
दत्तक्षणं क्वचिदरण्यजनप्रियस्य ।
अस्प्राक्ष्म तत्प्रभृति नान्यसमक्षमञ्जः
स्थातुंस्त्वयाभिरमिता बत पारयामः ॥ ३६ ॥

yarhy ambujākṣa tava pāda-talaṁ ramāyā
datta-kṣaṇaṁ kvacid araṇya-jana-priyasya |
asprākṣma tat-prabhṛti nānya-samakṣam añjaḥ
sthātuṁs tvayābhiramitā bata pārayāmaḥ || 36 ||

6. 34d *yāmaḥ kathaṁ vrajam* maho *karavāma kiṁ vā*

श्रीर्यत्पदाम्बुजरजश्चकमे तुलस्या
  लब्ध्वापि वक्षसि पदं किल भृत्यजुष्टम् ।
यस्याः स्ववीक्षण उतान्यसुरप्रयासस्
  तद्वद्वयं च तव पादरजः प्रपन्नाः ॥ ३७ ॥

śrīr yat padāmbuja-rajaś cakame tulasyā
  labdhvāpi vakṣasi padaṁ kila bhṛtya-juṣṭam |
yasyāḥ sva-vīkṣaṇa utānya-sura-prayāsas
  tadvad vayaṁ ca tava pāda-rajaḥ prapannāḥ || 37 ||

तन्नः प्रसीद वृजिनार्दन तेऽङ्घ्रिमूलं
  प्राप्ता विसृज्य वसतीस्त्वदुपासनाशाः ।
त्वत्सुन्दरस्मितनिरीक्षणतीव्रकाम-
  तप्तात्मनां पुरुषभूषण देहि दास्यम् ॥ ३८ ॥

tan naḥ prasīda vṛjinārdana te 'ṅghri-mūlaṁ
  prāptā visṛjya vasatīs tvad-upāsanāśāḥ |
tvat-sundara-smita-nirīkṣaṇa-tīvra-kāma-
  taptātmanāṁ puruṣa-bhūṣaṇa dehi dāsyam || 38 ||

वीक्ष्यालकावृतमुखं तव कुण्डलश्री-
  गण्डस्थलाधरसुधं हसितावलोकम् ।
दत्ताभयं च भुजदण्डयुगं विलोक्य
  वक्षः श्रियैकरमणं च भवाम दास्यः ॥ ३९ ॥

vīkṣyālakāvṛta-mukhaṁ tava kuṇḍala-śrī-
  gaṇḍa-sthalādhara-sudhaṁ hasitāvalokam |
dattābhayaṁ ca bhuja-daṇḍa-yugaṁ vilokya
  vakṣaḥ śriyaika-ramaṇaṁ ca bhavāma dāsyaḥ || 39 ||

का स्त्र्यङ्ग ते कलपदायतवेणुगीत-
सम्मोहितार्यचरितान्न चलेत्त्रिलोक्याम् ।
त्रैलोक्यसौभगमिदं च निरीक्ष्य रूपं
यद् गोद्विजद्रुममृगाः पुलकान्यबिभ्रन् ॥४०॥

kā stry aṅga te kala-padāyata-veṇu-gīta-
sammohitārya-caritān na calet tri-lokyām |
trailokya-saubhagam idaṁ ca nirīkṣya rūpaṁ
yad go-dvija-druma-mṛgāḥ pulakāny abibhran || 40 || [7]

व्यक्तं भवान् व्रजभयार्तिहरोऽभिजातो
देवो यथादिपुरुषः सुरलोकगोप्ता ।
तन्नो निधेहि करपङ्कजमार्तबन्धो
तप्तस्तनेषु च शिरःसु च किङ्करीणाम् ॥४१॥

vyaktaṁ bhavān vraja-bhayārti-haro 'bhijāto
devo yathādi-puruṣaḥ sura-loka-goptā |
tan no nidhehi kara-paṅkajam ārta-bandho
tapta-staneṣu ca śiraḥsu ca kiṅkarīṇām || 41 || [8]

श्रीशुक उवाच
इति विक्लवितं तासां श्रुत्वा योगेश्वरेश्वरः ।
प्रहस्य सदयं गोपीरात्मारामोऽप्यरीरमत् ॥४२॥

śrī-śuka uvāca
iti viklavitaṁ tāsāṁ, śrutvā yogeśvareśvaraḥ |
prahasya sa-dayaṁ gopīr, ātmārāmo 'py arīramat || 42 ||

7. 40a *kā stry aṅga te kala-padāyata-*mūrcchitena OR
*kā stry aṅga te kala-*padāmṛta-*venu-gīta-*
8. 41a *vyaktaṁ bhavān vraja-*janārti-*haro 'bhijāto*

ताभिः समेताभिरुदारचेष्टितः
  प्रियेक्षणोत्फुल्लमुखीभिरच्युतः ।
उदारहासद्विजकुन्ददीधतिर्
  व्यरोचतैणाङ्क इवोडुभिर्वृतः ॥४३॥

tābhiḥ sametābhir udāra-ceṣṭitaḥ
priyekṣaṇotphulla-mukhībhir acyutaḥ |
udāra-hāsa-dvija-kunda-dīdhatir
vyarocataiṇāṅka ivoḍubhir vṛtaḥ || 43 ||

उपगीयमान उद्गायन् वनिताशतयूथपः ।
मालां बिभ्रद्वैजयन्तीं व्यचरन्मण्डयन् वनम् ॥४४॥

upagīyamāna udgāyan, vanitā-śata-yūthapaḥ |
mālāṁ bibhrad vaijayantīṁ, vyacaran maṇḍayan vanam || 44 || [9]

नद्याः पुलिनमाविश्य गोपीभिर्हिमवालुकम् ।
जुष्टं तत्तरलानन्दिकुमुदामोदवायुना ॥४५॥

nadyāḥ pulinam āviśya, gopībhir hima-vālukam |
juṣṭaṁ tat-taralānandi-, kumudāmoda-vāyunā || 45 ||[10]

बाहुप्रसारपरिरम्भकरालकोरु-
  नीवीस्तनालभननर्मनखाग्रपातैः ।
क्ष्वेल्यावलोकहसितैर्व्रजसुन्दरीणाम्
  उत्तम्भयन् रतिपतिं रमयां चकार ॥४६॥

bāhu-prasāra-parirambha-karālakoru-
nīvī-stanālabhana-narma-nakhāgra-pātaiḥ |
kṣvelyāvaloka-hasitair vraja-sundarīṇām
uttambhayan rati-patiṁ ramayāṁ cakāra || 46 ||

एवं भगवतः कृष्णाल्लब्धमाना महात्मनः ।
आत्मानं मेनिरे स्त्रीणां मानिन्यो ह्यधिकं भुवि ॥४७॥

evaṁ bhagavataḥ kṛṣṇāl, labdha-mānā mahātmanaḥ |
ātmānaṁ menire strīṇāṁ, māninyo hy adhikaṁ bhuvi || 47 ||

9. 44d vyacarat savanād danam
10. 45c reme *tat-taralānandi-*

तासां तत्सौभगमदं वीक्ष्य मानं च केशवः ।
प्रशमाय प्रसादाय तत्रैवान्तरधीयत ॥४८॥

tāsāṁ tat-saubhaga-madaṁ, vīkṣya mānaṁ ca keśavaḥ |
praśamāya prasādāya, tatraivāntaradhīyata || 48 ||

Act Two

Bhāgavata Purāṇa Book 10 Chapter 30

श्रीशुक उवाच
अन्तर्हिते भगवति सहसैव व्रजाङ्गनाः ।
अतप्यंस्तमचक्षाणाः करिण्य इव यूथपम् ॥१॥

śrī-śuka uvāca
antarhite bhagavati, sahasaiva vrajāṅganāḥ |
atapyaṁs tam acakṣāṇāḥ, kariṇya iva yūthapam || 1 ||

गत्यानुरागस्मितविभ्रमेक्षितैर्
मनोरमालापविहारविभ्रमैः ।
आक्षिप्तचित्ताः प्रमदा रमापतेस्
तास्ता विचेष्टा जगृहुस्तदात्मिकाः ॥२॥

gatyānurāga-smita-vibhramekṣitair
mano-ramālāpa-vihāra-vibhramaiḥ |
ākṣipta-cittāḥ pramadā ramā-pates
tās tā viceṣṭā jagṛhus tad-ātmikāḥ || 2 ||

गतिस्मितप्रेक्षणभाषणादिषु
प्रियाः प्रियस्य प्रतिरूढमूर्तयः ।
असावहं त्वित्यबलास्तदात्मिका
न्यवेदिषुः कृष्णविहारविभ्रमाः ॥३॥

gati-smita-prekṣaṇa-bhāṣaṇādiṣu
priyāḥ priyasya pratirūḍha-mūrtayaḥ |
asāv ahaṁ tv ity abalās tad-ātmikā
nyavediṣuḥ kṛṣṇa-vihāra-vibhramāḥ || 3 ||

गायन्त्य उच्चैरमुमेव संहता
  विचिक्युरुन्मत्तकवद् वनाद् वनम् ।
पप्रच्छुराकाशवदन्तरं बहिर्
  भूतेषु सन्तं पुरुषं वनस्पतीन् ॥४॥

gāyantya uccair amum eva saṁhatā
  vicikyur unmattaka-vad vanād vanam |
papracchur ākāśa-vad antaraṁ bahir
  bhūteṣu santaṁ puruṣaṁ vanaspatīn || 4 ||

दृष्टो वः कच्चिदश्वत्थ प्लक्ष न्यग्रोध नो मनः ।
नन्दसूनुर्गतो हृत्वा प्रेमहासावलोकनैः ॥५॥

dṛṣṭo vaḥ kaccid aśvattha, plakṣa nyagrodha no manaḥ |
nanda-sūnur gato hṛtvā, prema-hāsāvalokanaiḥ || 5 ||

कच्चित्कुरबकाशोकनागपुन्नागचम्पकाः ।
रामानुजो मानिनीनामितो दर्पहरस्मितः ॥६॥

kaccit kurabakāśoka-, nāga-punnāga-campakāḥ |
rāmānujo māninīnām, ito darpa-hara smitaḥ || 6 ||

कच्चित्तुलसि कल्याणि गोविन्दचरणप्रिये ।
सह त्वालिकुलैर्बिभ्रद् दृष्टस्तेऽतिप्रियोऽच्युतः ॥७॥

kaccit tulasi kalyāṇi, govinda-caraṇa-priye |
saha tvāli-kulair bibhrad, dṛṣṭas te 'ti-priyo 'cyutaḥ || 7 ||

मालत्यदर्शि वः कच्चिन्मल्लिके जातियूथिके ।
प्रीतिं वो जनयन् यातः करस्पर्शेन माधवः ॥८॥

mālaty adarśi vaḥ kaccin, mallike jāti-yūthike |
prītiṁ vo janayan yātaḥ, kara-sparśena mādhavaḥ || 8 ||

चूतप्रियालपनसासनकोविदार-
जम्ब्वर्कबिल्वबकुलाम्रकदम्बनीपाः ।
येऽन्ये परार्थभवका यमुनोपकूलाः
शंसन्तु कृष्णपदवीं रहितात्मनां नः ॥९॥

cūta-priyāla-panasāsana-kovidāra-
jambv-arka-bilva-bakulāmra-kadamba-nīpāḥ |
ye 'nye parārtha-bhavakā yamunopakūlāḥ
śaṁsantu kṛṣṇa-padavīṁ rahitātmanāṁ naḥ || 9 ||[1]

किं ते कृतं क्षिति तपो बत केशवाङ्घ्रि-
स्पर्शोत्सवोत्पुलकिताङ्गरुहैर्विभासि ।
अप्यङ्घ्रिसम्भव उरुक्रमविक्रमाद् वा
आहो वराहवपुषः परिरम्भणेन ॥१०॥

kiṁ te kṛtaṁ kṣiti tapo bata keśavāṅghri-
sparśotsavotpulakitāṅga-ruhair vibhāsi |
apy aṅghri-sambhava urukrama-vikramād vā
āho varāha-vapuṣaḥ parirambhaṇena || 10 ||

अप्येणपत्न्युपगतः प्रिययेह गात्रैस्
तन्वन् दृशां सखि सुनिर्वृतिमच्युतो वः ।
कान्ताङ्गसङ्गकुचकुंकुमरञ्जितायाः
कुन्दस्रजः कुलपतेरिह वाति गन्धः ॥११॥

apy eṇa-patny upagataḥ priyayeha gātrais
tanvan dṛśāṁ sakhi su-nirvṛtim acyuto vaḥ |
kāntāṅga-saṅga-kuca-kuṅkuma-rañjitāyāḥ
kunda-srajaḥ kula-pater iha vāti gandhaḥ || 11 ||

1. 9b jambīra-*bilva-bakulāmra-kadamba-nīpāḥ*

बाहुं प्रियांस उपधाय गृहीतपद्मो
  रामानुजस्तुलसिकालिकुलैर्मदान्धैः ।
अन्वीयमान इह वस्तरवः प्रणामं
  किं वाभिनन्दति चरन् प्रणयावलोकैः ॥१२॥

bāhuṁ priyāṁsa upadhāya gṛhīta-padmo
  rāmānujas tulasikāli-kulair madāndhaiḥ |
anvīyamāna iha vas taravaḥ praṇāmaṁ
  kiṁ vābhinandati caran praṇayāvalokaiḥ || 12 ||

पृच्छतेमा लता बाहूनप्याश्लिष्टा वनस्पतेः ।
नूनं तत्करजस्पृष्टा बिभ्रत्युत्पुलकान्यहो ॥१३॥

pṛcchatemā latā bāhūn, apy āśliṣṭā vanaspateḥ |
nūnaṁ tat-karaja-spṛṣṭā, bibhraty utpulakāny aho || 13 ||

इत्युन्मत्तवचो गोप्यः कृष्णान्वेषणकातराः ।
लीला भगवतस्तास्ता ह्यनुचक्रुस्तदात्मिकाः ॥१४॥

ity unmatta-vaco gopyaḥ, kṛṣṇānveṣaṇa-kātarāḥ |
līlā bhagavatas tās tā, hy anucakrus tad-ātmikāḥ || 14 ||

कस्याचित्पूतनायन्त्याः कृष्णायन्त्यपिबत्स्तनम् ।
तोकयित्वा रुदत्यन्या पदाहन् शकटायतीम् ॥१५॥

kasyācit pūtanāyantyāḥ, kṛṣṇāyanty apibat stanam |
tokayitvā rudaty anyā, padāhan śakaṭāyatīm || 15 ||[2]

दैत्यायित्वा जहारान्यामेको कृष्णार्भभावनाम् ।
रिङ्गायामास काप्यङ्घ्री कर्षन्ती घोषनिःस्वनैः ॥१६॥

daityāyitvā jahārānyām, eko kṛṣṇārbha-bhāvanām |
riṅgayām āsa kāpy aṅghrī, karṣantī ghoṣa-niḥsvanaiḥ || 16 ||

2. 15c tokāyitvā *rudaty anyā*

कृष्णरामायिते द्वे तु गोपायन्त्यश्च काश्चन ।
वत्सायतीं हन्ति चान्या तत्रैका तु बकायतीम् ॥१७॥
kṛṣṇa-rāmāyite dve tu, gopāyantyaś ca kāścana |
vatsāyatīṁ hanti cānyā, tatraikā tu bakāyatīm || 17 || [3]

आहूय दूरगा यद्वत्कृष्णस्तमनुवर्ततीम् ।
वेणुं क्वणन्तीं क्रीडन्तीमन्याः शंसन्ति साध्विति ॥१८॥
āhūya dūra-gā yadvat, kṛṣṇas tam anuvartatīm |
veṇuṁ kvaṇantīṁ krīḍantīm, anyāḥ śaṁsanti sādhv iti || 18 ||

कस्याञ्चित्स्वभुजं न्यस्य चलन्त्याहापरा ननु ।
कृष्णोऽहं पश्यत गतिं ललितामिति तन्मनाः ॥१९॥
kasyāñcit sva-bhujaṁ nyasya, calanty āhāparā nanu |
kṛṣṇo 'haṁ paśyata gatiṁ, lalitām iti tan-manāḥ || 19 ||

मा भैष्ट वातवर्षाभ्यां तत्त्राणं विहितं मया ।
इत्युक्त्वैकेन हस्तेन यतन्त्युन्निदधेऽम्बरम् ॥२०॥
mā bhaiṣṭa vāta-varṣābhyāṁ, tat-trāṇaṁ vihitaṁ mayā |
ity uktvaikena hastena, yatanty unnidadhe 'mbaram || 20 ||

आरुह्यैका पदाक्रम्य शिरस्याहापरां नृप ।
दुष्टाहे गच्छ जातोऽहं खलानां ननु दण्डकृत् ॥२१॥
āruhyaikā padākramya, śirasy āhāparāṁ nṛpa |
duṣṭāhe gaccha jāto 'haṁ, khalānāṁ nanu daṇḍa-kṛt || 21 ||

तत्रैकोवाच हे गोपा दावाग्निं पश्यतोल्बणम् ।
चक्षूंष्याश्वपिदध्वं वो विधास्ये क्षेममञ्जसा ॥२२॥
tatraikovāca he gopā, dāvāgniṁ paśyatolbaṇam |
cakṣūṁṣy āśv apidadhvaṁ vo, vidhāsye kṣemam añjasā || 22 ||

3. 17 vatsāyitān gṛhītvānyān bhrāmayitvā nyapāathat |
kṛṣṇāyitān jaghānānyāntatrekāṁ tu bakāyitām ||
17b gopāvatsāyitāḥ parāḥ

बद्धान्यया स्रजा काचित्तन्वी तत्र उलूखले ।
बध्नामि भाण्डभेत्तारं हैयङ्गवमुषं त्विति ।
भीता सुदृक् पिधायास्यं भेजे भीतिविडम्बनम् ॥२३॥

baddhānyayā srajā kācit, tanvī tatra ulūkhale |
badhnāmi bhāṇḍa bhettāraṁ, haiyaṅgava-muṣaṁ tv iti |
bhītā su-dṛk pidhāyāsyaṁ, bheje bhīti-viḍambanam || 23 ||[4]

एवं कृष्णं पृच्छमाना वृन्दावनलतास्तरून्
व्यचक्षत वनोद्देशे पदानि परमात्मनः ॥२४॥

evaṁ kṛṣṇaṁ pṛcchamānā, vṛndāvana-latās tarūn |
vyacakṣata vanoddeśe, padāni paramātmanaḥ || 24 ||

पदानि व्यक्तमेतानि नन्दसूनोर्महात्मनः ।
लक्ष्यन्ते हि ध्वजाम्भोजवज्राङ्कुशयवादिभिः ॥२५॥

padāni vyaktam etāni, nanda-sūnor mahātmanaḥ |
lakṣyante hi dhvajāmbhoja-, vajrāṅkuśa-yavādibhiḥ || 25 ||[5]

तैस्तैः पदैस्तत्पदवीमन्विच्छन्त्योऽग्रतोऽबलाः ।
वध्वाः पदैः सुपृक्तानि विलोक्यार्ताः समब्रुवन् ॥२६॥

tais taiḥ padais tat-padavīm, anvicchantyo 'grato 'balāḥ |
vadhvāḥ padaiḥ su-pṛktāni, vilokyārtāḥ samabruvan || 26 ||

कस्याः पदानि चैतानि याताया नन्दसूनुना ।
अंसन्यस्तप्रकोष्ठायाः करेणोः करिणा यथा ॥२७॥

kasyāḥ padāni caitāni, yātāyā nanda-sūnunā |
aṁsa-nyasta-prakoṣṭhāyāḥ, kareṇoḥ kariṇā yathā || 27 ||

अनयाराधितो नूनं भगवान् हरिरीश्वरः ।
यन् नो विहाय गोविन्दः प्रीतो यामनयद् रहः ॥२८॥

anayārādhito nūnaṁ, bhagavān harir īśvaraḥ |
yan no vihāya govindaḥ, prīto yām anayad rahaḥ || 28 ||

4. 23ab *baghnantyanyaāṁ srajaikāha tvāmayolūkhale hare* |
Some editions of BhP do not include the third line (23ef).
5. 25cd *lakṣyante hi* yadambhojdhvajavajrāṅkuśādibhiḥ |

धन्या अहो अमी आल्यो गोविन्दाङ्घ्र्यब्जरेणवः ।
यान् ब्रह्मेशौ रमा देवी दधुर्मूर्ध्न्यघनुत्तये ॥२९॥

dhanyā aho amī ālyo, govindāṅghry-abja-reṇavaḥ |
yān brahmeśau ramā devī, dadhur mūrdhny agha-nuttaye || 29 ||

तस्या अमूनि नः क्षोभं कुर्वन्त्युच्चैः पदानि यत् ।
यैकापहृत्य गोपीनां रहो भुङ्क्तेऽच्युताधरम् ॥३०॥

tasyā amūni naḥ kṣobhaṁ, kurvanty uccaiḥ padāni yat |
yaikāpahṛtya gopīnāṁ, raho bhuṅkte 'cyutādharam || 30 ||

न लक्ष्यन्ते पदान्यत्र तस्या नूनं तृणाङ्कुरैः ।
खिद्यत्सुजाताङ्घ्रितलामुन्निन्ये प्रेयसीं प्रियः ॥३१-१॥

na lakṣyante padāny atra, tasyā nūnaṁ tṛṇāṅkuraiḥ |
khidyat-sujātāṅghri-talām, unninye preyasīṁ priyaḥ || 31–1 ||

इमान्यधिकमग्नानि पदानि वहतो वधूम् ।
गोप्यः पश्यत कृष्णस्य भाराक्रान्तस्य कामिनः ।
अत्रावरोपिता कान्ता पुष्पहेतोर्महात्मना ॥३१-२॥

imāny adhika-magnāni, padāni vahato vadhūm |
gopyaḥ paśyata kṛṣṇasya, bhārākrāntasya kāminaḥ |
atrāvaropitā kāntā, puṣpa-hetor mahātmanā || 31–2 ||[6]

अत्र प्रसूनावचयः प्रियार्थे प्रेयसा कृतः ।
प्रपदाक्रमण एते पश्यतासकले पदे ॥३२॥

atra prasūnāvacayaḥ, priyārthe preyasā kṛtaḥ |
prapadākramaṇa ete, paśyatāsakale pade || 32 ||

केशप्रसाधनं त्वत्र कामिन्याः कामिना कृतम् ।
तानि चूडयता कान्तामुपविष्टमिह ध्रुवम् ॥३३॥

keśa-prasādhanaṁ tv atra, kāminyāḥ kāminā kṛtam |
tāni cūḍayatā kāntām, upaviṣṭam iha dhruvam || 33 ||

6. 31–2 This verse is not found in some editions of the BhP.
The third line (31–2ef) of this verse is not included in some editions that present the first two lines of this verse (31–2a-d).
31–2d *bhārākrāntasya* gāminaḥ

रेमे तया चात्मरत आत्मारामोऽप्यखण्डितः ।
कामिनां दर्शयन् दैन्यं स्त्रीणां चैव दुरात्मताम् ॥३४॥

reme tayā cātma-rata, ātmārāmo 'py akhaṇḍitaḥ |
kāminām̐ darśayan dainyam̐, strīṇām̐ caiva durātmatām || 34 ||

इत्येवं दर्शयन्त्यस्ताश्चेरुर्गोप्यो विचेतसः ।
यां गोपीमनयत्कृष्णो विहायान्याः स्त्रियो वने ॥३५॥

ity evam̐ darśayantyas tāś, cerur gopyo vicetasaḥ |
yām̐ gopīm anayat kṛṣṇo, vihāyānyāḥ striyo vane || 35 ||

सा च मेने तदात्मानं वरिष्ठं सर्वयोषिताम् ।
हित्वा गोपीः कामयाना मामसौ भजते प्रियः ॥३६॥

sā ca mene tadātmānam̐, variṣṭham̐ sarva-yoṣitām |
hitvā gopīḥ kāma-yānā, mām asau bhajate priyaḥ || 36 ||

ततो गत्वा वनोद्देशं दृप्ता केशवमब्रवीत् ।
न पारयेऽहं चलितुं नय मां यत्र ते मनः ॥३७॥

tato gatvā vanoddeśam̐, dṛptā keśavam abravīt |
na pāraye 'ham̐ calitum̐, naya mām̐ yatra te manaḥ || 37 ||

एवमुक्तः प्रियामाह स्कन्ध आरुह्यतामिति ।
ततश्चान्तर्दधे कृष्णः सा वधूरन्वतप्यत ॥३८॥

evam uktaḥ priyām āha, skandha āruhyatām iti |
tataś cāntardadhe kṛṣṇaḥ, sā vadhūr anvatapyata || 38 ||

हा नाथ रमण प्रेष्ठ क्वासि क्वासि महाभुज ।
दास्यास्ते कृपणाया मे सखे दर्शय सन्निधिम् ॥३९॥

hā nātha ramaṇa preṣṭha, kvāsi kvāsi mahā-bhuja |
dāsyās te kṛpaṇāyā me, sakhe darśaya sannidhim || 39 ||

श्रीशुक उवाच
अन्विच्छन्त्यो भगवतो मार्गं गोप्योऽविदूरितः ।
ददृशुः प्रियविश्लेषान्मोहितां दुःखितां सखीम् ॥४०॥

śrī-śuka-uvāca
anvicchantyo bhagavato, mārgaṁ gopyo 'vidūritaḥ |
dadṛśuḥ priya-viśleṣān, mohitāṁ duḥkhitāṁ sakhīm || 40 ||

तया कथितमाकर्ण्य मानप्राप्तिं च माधवात् ।
अवमानं च दौरात्म्याद् विस्मयं परमं ययुः ॥४१॥

tayā kathitam ākarṇya, māna-prāptiṁ ca mādhavāt |
avamānaṁ ca daurātmyād, vismayaṁ paramaṁ yayuḥ || 41 ||

ततोऽविशन् वनं चन्द्रज्योत्स्ना यावद् विभाव्यते ।
तमः प्रविष्टमालक्ष्य ततो निववृतुः स्त्रियः ॥४२॥

tato 'viśan vanaṁ candra-, jyotsnā yāvad vibhāvyate |
tamaḥ praviṣṭam ālakṣya, tato nivavṛtuḥ striyaḥ || 42 ||

तन्मनस्कास्तदालापास्तद्विचेष्टास्तदात्मिकाः ।
तद्गुणानेव गायन्त्यो नात्मागाराणि सस्मरुः ॥४३॥

tan-manaskās tad-ālāpās, tad-viceṣṭās tad-ātmikāḥ |
tad-guṇān eva gāyantyo, nātmāgārāṇi sasmaruḥ || 43 ||

पुनः पुलिनमागत्य कालिन्द्याः कृष्णभावनाः ।
समवेता जगुः कृष्णं तदागमनकाङ्क्षिताः ॥४४॥

punaḥ pulinam āgatya, kālindyāḥ kṛṣṇa-bhāvanāḥ |
samavetā jaguḥ kṛṣṇaṁ, tad-āgamana-kāṅkṣitāḥ || 44 ||

Act Three

Bhāgavata Purāṇa Book 10 Chapter 31

गोप्य ऊचुः
जयति तेऽधिकं जन्मना व्रजः
श्रयत इन्दिरा शश्वदत्र हि ।
दयित दृश्यतां दिक्षु तावकास्
त्वयि धृतासवस्त्वां विचिन्वते ॥१॥

gopya ūcuḥ
jayati te 'dhikaṁ janmanā vrajaḥ
śrayata indirā śaśvad atra hi |
dayita dṛśyatāṁ dikṣu tāvakās
tvayi dhṛtāsavas tvāṁ vicinvate || 1 ||

शरदुदाशये साधुजातसत्-
सरसिजोदरश्रीमुषा दृशा ।
सुरतनाथ तेऽशुल्कदासिका
वरद निघ्नतो नेह किं वधः ॥२॥

śarad-udāśaye sādhu-jāta-sat-
sarasijodara-śrī-muṣā dṛśā |
surata-nātha te'śulka-dāsikā
vara-da nighnato neha kiṁ vadhaḥ || 2 ||

विषजलाप्ययाद् व्यालराक्षसाद्
वर्षमारुताद्वैद्युतानलात् ।
वृषमयात्मजाद्विश्वतो भयाद्
ऋषभ ते वयं रक्षिता मुहुः ॥३॥

viṣa-jalāpyayād vyāla-rākṣasād
varṣa-mārutād vaidyutānalāt |
vṛṣa-mayātmajād viśvato bhayād
ṛṣabha te vayaṁ rakṣitā muhuḥ || 3 ||[17]

1. 3a *viṣa*-jalāśayā *vyāla-rākṣusād*

न खलु गोपिकानन्दनो भवान्
अखिलदेहिनामन्तरात्मदृक् ।
विखनसार्थितो विश्वगुप्तये
सख उदेयिवान् सात्वतां कुले ॥४॥

na khalu gopikā-nandano bhavān
akhila-dehinām antarātma-dṛk |
vikhanasārthito viśva-guptaye
sakha udeyivān sātvatāṁ kule || 4 ||

विरचिताभयं वृष्णिधूर्य ते
चरनमीयुषां संसृतेर्भयात् ।
करसरोरुहं कान्त कामदं
शिरसि धेहि नः श्रीकरग्रहम् ॥५॥

viracitābhayaṁ vṛṣṇi-dhūrya te
caraṇam īyuṣāṁ saṁsṛter bhayāt |
kara-saroruhaṁ kānta kāma-daṁ
śirasi dhehi naḥ śrī-kara-graham || 5 ||

व्रजजनार्तिहन् वीर योषितां
निजजनस्मयध्वंसनस्मित ।
भज सखे भवत्किङ्करीः स्म नो
जलरुहाननं चारु दर्शय ॥६॥

vraja-janārti-han vīra yoṣitāṁ
nija-jana-smaya-dhvaṁsana-smita |
bhaja sakhe bhavat-kiṅkarīḥ sma no
jalaruhānanaṁ cāru darśaya || 6 ||

प्रणतदेहिनां पापकर्षणं
तृणचरानुगं श्रीनिकेतनम् ।
फणिफणार्पितं ते पदाम्बुजं
कृणु कुचेषु नः कृन्धि हृच्छयम् ॥७॥

praṇata-dehināṁ pāpa-karṣaṇaṁ
tṛṇa-carānugaṁ śrī-niketanam |
phaṇi-phaṇārpitaṁ te padāmbujaṁ
kṛṇu kuceṣu naḥ kṛndhi hṛc-chayam || 7 ||

मधुरया गिरा वल्गुवाक्यया
  बुधमनोज्ञया पुष्करेक्षण ।
विधिकरीरिमा वीर मुह्यतीर्
  अधरसीधुनाप्याययस्व नः ॥८॥

madhurayā girā valgu-vākyayā
  budha-manojñayā puṣkarekṣaṇa |
vidhi-karīr imā vīra muhyatīr
  adhara-sīdhunāpyāyayasva naḥ || 8 ||

तव कथामृतं तप्तजीवनं
  कविभिरीडितं कल्मषापहम् ।
श्रवणमङ्गलं श्रीमदाततं
  भुवि गृणन्ति ये भूरिदा जनाः ॥९॥

tava kathāmṛtaṁ tapta-jīvanaṁ
  kavibhir īḍitaṁ kalmaṣāpaham |
śravaṇa-maṅgalaṁ śrīmad ātataṁ
  bhuvi gṛṇanti ye bhūri-dā janāḥ || 9 ||

प्रहसितं प्रियप्रेमवीक्षणं
  विहरणं च ते ध्यानमङ्गलम् ।
रहसि संविदो या हृदि स्पृशः
  कुहक नो मनः क्षोभयन्ति हि ॥१०॥

prahasitaṁ priya-prema-vīkṣaṇaṁ
  viharaṇaṁ ca te dhyāna-maṅgalam |
rahasi saṁvido yā hṛdi spṛśaḥ
  kuhaka no manaḥ kṣobhayanti hi || 10 ||

चलसि यद् व्रजाच्चारयन् पशून्
  नलिनसुन्दरं नाथ ते पदम् ।
शिलतृणांकुरैः सीदतीति नः
  कलिलतां मनः कान्त गच्छति ॥११॥

calasi yad vrajāc cārayan paśūn
  nalina-sundaraṁ nātha te padam |
śila-tṛṇāṅkuraiḥ sīdatīti naḥ
  kalilatāṁ manaḥ kānta gacchati || 11 ||

दिनपरिक्षये नीलकुन्तलैर्
  वनरुहाननं बिभ्रदावृतम् ।
घनरजस्वलं दर्शयन्मुहुर्
  मनसि नः स्मरं वीर यच्छसि ॥१२॥

dina-parikṣaye nīla-kuntalair
  vana-ruhānanaṁ bibhrad āvṛtam |
ghana-rajasvalaṁ darśayan muhur
  manasi naḥ smaraṁ vīra yacchasi || 12 ||

प्रणतकामदं पद्मजार्चितं
  धरणिमण्डनं ध्येयमापदि ।
चरणपङ्कजं शन्तमं च ते
  रमण नः स्तनेष्वर्पयाधिहन् ॥१३॥

praṇata-kāma-daṁ padmajārcitaṁ
  dharaṇi-maṇḍanaṁ dhyeyam āpadi |
caraṇa-paṅkajaṁ śantamaṁ ca te
  ramaṇa naḥ staneṣv arpayādhi-han || 13 ||

सुरतवर्धनं शोकनाशनं
  स्वरितवेणुना सुष्ठु चुम्बितम् ।
इतररागविस्मारणं नृणां
  वितर वीर नस्तेऽधरामृतम् ॥१४॥

surata-vardhanaṁ śoka-nāśanaṁ
  svarita-veṇunā suṣṭhu cumbitam |
itara-rāga-vismāraṇaṁ nṛṇāṁ
  vitara vīra nas te 'dharāmṛtam || 14 ||

अटति यद् भवानह्नि काननं
  त्रुटि युगायते त्वामपश्यताम् ।
कुटिलकुन्तलं श्रीमुखं च ते
  जड उदीक्षतां पक्ष्मकृद्दृशाम् ॥१५॥

aṭati yad bhavān ahni kānanaṁ
  truṭi yugāyate tvām apśyatām |
kuṭila-kuntalaṁ śrī-mukhaṁ ca te
  jaḍa udīkṣatāṁ pakṣma-kṛd dṛśām || 15 ||

पतिसुतान्वयभ्रातृबान्धवान्
  अतिविलंघ्य तेऽन्त्यच्युतागताः ।
गतिविदस्तवोद्गीतमोहिताः
  कितव योषितः कस्त्यजेन्निशि ॥१६॥

pati-sutānvaya-bhrātṛ-bāndhavān
  ativilaṅghya te 'nty acyutāgatāḥ |
gati-vidas tavodgīta-mohitāḥ
  kitava yoṣitaḥ kas tyajen niśi || 16 ||

रहसि संविदं हृच्छयोदयं
  प्रहसिताननं प्रेमवीक्षणम् ।
बृहदुरः श्रियो वीक्ष्य धाम ते
  मुहुरतिस्पृहा मुह्यते मनः ॥१७॥

rahasi saṁvidaṁ hṛc-chayodayaṁ
  prahasitānanaṁ prema-vīkṣaṇam |
bṛhad-uraḥ śriyo vīkṣya dhāma te
  muhur ati-spṛhā muhyate manaḥ || 17 ||

व्रजवनौकसां व्यक्तिरङ्ग ते
  वृजिनहन्त्र्यलं विश्वमङ्गलम् ।
त्यज मनाक् च नस्त्वत्स्पृहात्मनां
  स्वजनहृद्रुजां यन्निषूदनम् ॥१८॥

vraja-vanaukasāṁ vyaktir aṅga te
  vṛjina-hantry alaṁ viśva-maṅgalam |
tyaja manāk ca nas tvat-spṛhātmanāṁ
  sva-jana-hṛd-rujāṁ yan niṣūdanam || 18 ||

यत्ते सुजातचरणाम्बुरुहं स्तनेषु
  भीताः शनैः प्रिय दधीमहि कर्कशेषु ।
तेनाटवीमटसि तद् व्यथते न किं स्वित्
  कूर्पादिभिर्भ्रमति धीर्भवदायुषां नः ॥१९॥

yat te sujāta-caraṇāmburuhaṁ staneṣu
  bhītāḥ śanaiḥ priya dadhīmahi karkaśeṣu |
tenāṭavīm aṭasi tad vyathate na kiṁ svit
  kūrpādibhir bhramati dhīr bhavad-āyuṣāṁ naḥ || 19 ||

Act Four

Bhāgavata Purāṇa Book 10 Chapter 32

श्रीशुक उवाच
इति गोप्यः प्रगायन्त्यः प्रलपन्त्यश्च चित्रधा ।
रुरुदुः सुस्वरं राजन् कृष्णदर्शनलालसाः ॥१॥

śrī-śuka uvāca
iti gopyaḥ pragāyantyaḥ, pralapantyaś ca citradhā |
ruruduḥ su-svaraṁ rājan, kṛṣṇa-darśana-lālasāḥ || 1 ||

तासामाविरभूच्छौरिः स्मयमानमुखाम्बुजः ।
पीताम्बरधरः स्रग्वी साक्षान्मन्मथमन्मथः ॥२॥

tāsām āvirabhūc chauriḥ, smayamāna-mukhāmbujaḥ |
pītāmbara-dharaḥ sragvī, sākṣān manmatha-manmathaḥ || 2 ||

तं विलोक्यागतं प्रेष्ठं प्रीत्युत्फुल्लदृशोऽबलाः ।
उत्तस्थुर्युगपत्सर्वास्तन्वः प्राणमिवागतम् ॥३॥

taṁ vilokyāgataṁ preṣṭhaṁ, prīty-utphulla-dṛśo 'balāḥ |
uttasthur yugapat sarvās, tanvaḥ prāṇam ivāgatam || 3 ||[1]

काचित्कराम्बुजं शौरेर्जगृहेऽञ्जलिना मुदा ।
काचिद्दधार तद्बाहुमंसे चन्दनभूषितम् ॥४॥

kācit karāmbujaṁ śaurer, jagṛhe 'ñjalinā mudā |
kācid dadhāra tad-bāhum, aṁse candana-bhūṣitam || 4 ||

काचिदञ्जलिनागृह्णात्तन्वी ताम्बूलचर्वितम् ।
एका तदङ्घ्रिकमलं सन्तप्ता स्तनयोरधात् ॥५॥

kācid añjalināgṛhṇāt, tanvī tāmbūla-carvitam |
ekā tad-aṅghri-kamalaṁ, santaptā stanayor adhāt || 5 ||

1. 3a *taṁ vilokyāgataṁ* kṛṣṇaṁ

एका भ्रुकुटिमाबध्य प्रेमसंरम्भविह्वला ।
घ्नन्तीवैक्षत्कटाक्षेपैः सन्दष्टदर्शनच्छदा ॥६॥
ekā bhru-kuṭim ābadhya, prema-saṁrambha-vihvalā |
ghnantīvaikṣat kaṭākṣepaiḥ, sandaṣṭa-darśana-cchadā || 6 ||

अपरानिमिषद्दृग्भ्यां जुषाणा तन्मुखाम्बुजम् ।
आपीतमपि नातृप्यत्सन्तस्तच्चरणं यथा ॥७॥
aparānimiṣad-dṛgbhyāṁ, juṣāṇā tan-mukhāmbhujam |
āpītam api nātṛpyat, santas tac-caraṇaṁ yathā || 7 ||

तं काचिन्नेत्ररन्ध्रेण हृदि कृत्वा निमील्य च ।
पुलकांग्युपगुह्यास्ते योगीवानन्दसम्प्लुता ॥८॥
taṁ kācin netra-randhreṇa, hṛdi kṛtvā nimīlya ca |
pulakāṅgy upaguhyāste, yogīvānanda-samplutā || 8 ||[2]

सर्वास्ताः केशवालोकपरमोत्सवनिर्वृताः ।
जहुर्विरहजं तापं प्राज्ञं प्राप्य यथा जनाः ॥९॥
sarvās tāḥ keśavāloka-, paramotsava-nirvṛtāḥ |
jahur viraha-jaṁ tāpaṁ, prājñaṁ prāpya yathā janāḥ || 9 ||

ताभिर्विधूतशोकाभिर्भगवानच्युतो वृतः ।
व्यरोचताधिकं तात पुरुषः शक्तिभिर्यथा ॥१०॥
tābhir vidhūta-śokābhir, bhagavān acyuto vṛtaḥ |
vyarocatādhikaṁ tāta, puruṣaḥ śaktibhir yathā || 10 ||

ताः समादाय कालिन्द्या निर्विश्य पुलिनं विभुः ।
विकसत्कुन्दमन्दारसुरभ्यनिलषट्पदम् ॥११॥
tāḥ samādāya kālindyā, nirviśya pulinaṁ vibhuḥ |
vikasat-kunda-mandāra-, surabhy-anila-ṣaṭpadam || 11 ||

2. 8d *yogīvānanda*-nirbharā

शरच्चन्द्रांशुसन्दोहध्वस्तदोषातमः शिवम् ।
कृष्णाया हस्ततरलाचितकोमलवालुकम् ॥१२॥

śarac-candrāṁśu-sandoha-, dhvasta-doṣā-tamaḥ śivam |
kṛṣṇāyā hasta-taralā-, cita-komala-vālukam || 12 ||

तद्दर्शनाह्लादविधूतहृद्रुजो
  मनोरथान्तं श्रुतयो यथा ययुः ।
स्वैरुत्तरीयैः कुचकुंकुमाङ्कितैर्
  अचीक्लृपन्नासनमात्मबन्धवे ॥१३॥

tad-darśanāhlāda-vidhūta-hṛd-rujo
  manorathāntaṁ śrutayo yathā yayuḥ |
svair uttarīyaiḥ kuca-kuṅkumāṅkitair
  acīkḷpann āsanam ātma-bandave || 13 ||

तत्रोपविष्टो भगवान् स ईश्वरो
  योगेश्वरान्तर्हृदि कल्पितासनः ।
चकास गोपीपरिषद्गतोऽर्चितस्
  त्रैलोक्यलक्ष्म्येकपदं वपुर्दधत् ॥१४॥

tatropaviṣṭo bhagavān sa īśvaro
  yogeśvarāntar-hṛdi kalpitāsanaḥ |
cakāsa gopī-pariṣad-gato 'rcitas
  trailokya-lakṣmy-eka-padaṁ vapur dadhat || 14 ||

सभाजयित्वा तमनङ्गदीपनं
  सहासलीलेक्षणविभ्रमभ्रुवा ।
संस्पर्शनेनाङ्ककृताङ्घ्रिहस्तयोः
  संस्तुत्य ईषत्कुपिता बभाषिरे ॥१५॥

sabhājayitvā tam anaṅga-dīpanaṁ
  sahāsa-līlekṣaṇa-vibhrama-bhruvā |
saṁsparśanenāṅka-kṛtāṅghri-hastayoḥ
  saṁstutya īṣat kupitā babhāṣire || 15 ||

श्रीगोप्य ऊचुः
भजतोऽनुभजन्त्येक एक एतद्विपर्ययम् ।
नोभयांश्च भजन्त्येक एतन्नो ब्रूहि साधु भोः ॥१६॥

śrī-gopya ūcuḥ
bhajato 'nubhajanty eka, eka etad-viparyayam |
nobhayāṁś ca bhajanty eka, etan no brūhi sādhu bhoḥ || 16 ||

श्रीभगवानुवाच
मिथो भजन्ति ये सख्यः स्वार्थैकान्तोद्यमा हि ते ।
न तत्र सौहृदं धर्मः स्वार्थार्थं तद्धि नान्यथा ॥१७॥

śrī-bhagavān uvāca
mitho bhajanti ye sakhyaḥ, svārthaikāntodyamā hi te |
na tatra sauhṛdaṁ dharmaḥ, svārthārthaṁ tad dhi nānyathā || 17 ||

भजन्त्यभजतो ये वै करुणाः पितरौ यथा ।
धर्मो निरपवादोऽत्र सौहृदं च सुमध्यमाः ॥१८॥

bhajanty abhajato ye vai, karuṇāḥ pitarau yathā |
dharmo nirapavādo 'tra, sauhṛdaṁ ca su-madhyamāḥ || 18 ||

भजतोऽपि न वै केचिद् भजन्त्यभजतः कुतः ।
आत्मारामा ह्याप्तकामा अकृतज्ञा गुरुद्रुहः ॥१९॥

bhajato 'pi na vai kecid, bhajanty abhajataḥ kutaḥ |
ātmārāmā hy āpta-kāmā, akṛta-jñā guru-druhaḥ || 19 ||

नाहं तु सख्यो भजतोऽपि जन्तून्
भजाम्यमीषामनुवृत्तिवृत्तये ।
यथाधनो लब्धधने विनष्टे
तच्चिन्तयान्यन्निभृतो न वेद ॥२०॥

nāhaṁ tu sakhyo bhajato 'pi jantūn
bhajāmy amīṣām anuvṛtti-vṛttaye |
yathādhano labdha-dhane vinaṣṭe
tac-cintayānyan nibhṛto na veda || 20 ||

एवं मदर्थोज्झितलोकवेद-
स्वानां हि वो मय्यनुवृत्तयेऽबलाः ।
मयापरोक्षं भजता तिरोहितं
मासूयितुं मार्हथ तत्प्रियं प्रियाः ॥२१॥

evaṁ mad-arthojjhita-loka-veda-
svānāṁ hi vo mayy anuvṛttaye 'balāḥ |
mayāparokṣaṁ bhajatā tirohitaṁ
māsūyituṁ mārhatha tat priyaṁ priyāḥ || 21 ||

न पारयेऽहं निरवद्यसंयुजां
स्वसाधुकृत्यं विबुधायुषापि वः ।
या माभजन् दुर्जरगेहशृङ्खलाः
संवृश्च्य तद्वः प्रतियातु साधुना ॥२२॥

na pāraye 'haṁ niravadya-saṁyujāṁ
sva-sādhu-kṛtyaṁ vibudhāyuṣāpi vaḥ |
yā mābhajan durjara-geha-śṛṅkhalāḥ
saṁvṛścya tad vaḥ pratiyātu sādhunā || 22 ||

Act Five

Bhāgavata Purāṇa Book 10 Chapter 33

श्रीशुक उवाच
इत्थं भगवतो गोप्यः श्रुत्वा वाचः सुपेशलाः ।
जहुर्विरहजं तापं तदङ्गोपचिताशिषः ॥१॥

śrī-śuka uvāca
itthaṁ bhagavato gopyaḥ, śrutvā vācaḥ su-peśalāḥ |
jahur viraha-jaṁ tāpaṁ, tad-aṅgopacitāśiṣaḥ || 1 ||

तत्रारभत गोविन्दो रासक्रीडामनुव्रतैः ।
स्त्रीरत्नैरन्वितः प्रीतैरन्योन्याबद्धबाहुभिः ॥ २ ॥

tatrārabhata govindo, rāsa-krīḍām anuvrataiḥ |
strī-ratnair anvitaḥ prītair, anyonyābaddha-bāhubhiḥ || 2 ||

रासोत्सवः सम्प्रवृत्तो गोपीमण्डलमण्डितः ।
योगेश्वरेण कृष्णेन तासां मध्ये द्वयोर्द्वयोः ।
प्रविष्टेन गृहीतानां कंठे स्वनिकटं स्त्रियः ॥ ३ ॥

rāsotsavaḥ sampravṛtto, gopī-maṇḍala-maṇḍitaḥ |
yogeśvareṇa kṛṣṇena, tāsāṁ madhye dvayor dvayoḥ |
praviṣṭena gṛhītānāṁ, kaṇṭhe sva-nikaṭaṁ striyaḥ || 3 ||

यं मन्येरन्नभस्तावद्विमानशतसंकुलम् ।
दिवौकसां सदाराणामौत्सुक्यापहृतात्मनाम् ॥ ४ ॥

yaṁ manyeran nabhas tāvad, vimāna-śata-saṅkulam |
divaukasāṁ sa-dārāṇām, autsukyāpahṛtātmanām || 4 ||[1]

ततो दुन्दुभयो नेदुर्निपेतुः पुष्पवृष्टयः ।
जगुर्गन्धर्वपतयः सस्त्रीकास्तद्यशोऽमलम् ॥ ५ ॥

tato dundubhayo nedur, nipetuḥ puṣpa-vṛṣṭayaḥ |
jagur gandharva-patayaḥ, sa-strīkās tad-yaśo 'malam || 5 ||

वलयानां नूपुराणां किङ्किणीनां च योषिताम् ।
सप्रियाणामभूच्छब्दस्तुमुलो रासमण्डले ॥ ६ ॥

valayānāṁ nūpurāṇāṁ, kiṅkiṇīnāṁ ca yoṣitām |
sa-priyāṇām abhūc chabdas, tumulo rāsa-maṇḍale || 6 ||

तत्रातिशुशुभे ताभिर्भगवान् देवकीसुतः ।
मध्ये मणीनां हैमानां महामरकतो यथा ॥ ६ ॥

tatrātiśuśubhe tābhir, bhagavān devakī-sutaḥ |
madhye maṇīnāṁ haimānāṁ, mahā-marakato yathā || 7 ||

1. 4d *autsuky*anibhṛtā*tmanām*

पादन्यासैर्भुजविधुतिभिः सस्मितैर्भ्रूविलासैर्
भज्यन्मध्यैश्चलकुचपटैः कुण्डलैर्गण्डलोलैः ।
स्विद्यन्मुख्यः कवररसनाग्रन्थयः कृष्णवध्वो
गायन्त्यस्तं तडित इव ता मेघचक्रे विरेजुः ॥ ८ ॥

pāda-nyāsair bhuja-vidhutibhiḥ sa-smitair bhrū-vilāsair
bhajyan madhyaiś cala-kuca-paṭaiḥ kuṇḍalair gaṇḍa-lolaiḥ |
svidyan-mukhyaḥ kavara-rasanāgranthayaḥ kṛṣṇa-vadhvo
gāyantyas taṁ taḍita iva tā megha-cakre virejuḥ || 8 ||

उच्चैर्जगुर्नृत्यमाना रक्तकंठ्यो रतिप्रियाः ।
कृष्णाभिमर्शमुदिता यद्गीतेनेदमावृतम् ॥ ९ ॥

uccair jagur nṛtyamānā, rakta-kaṇṭhyo rati-priyāḥ |
kṛṣṇābhimarśa-muditā, yad-gītenedam āvṛtam || 9 ||

काचित्समं मुकुन्देन स्वरजातीरमिश्रिताः ।
उन्निन्ये पूजिता तेन प्रीयता साधु साध्विति ।
तदेव ध्रुवमुन्निन्ये तस्यै मानं च बह्वदात् ॥ १० ॥

kācit samaṁ mukundena, svara-jātīr amiśritāḥ |
unninye pūjitā tena, prīyatā sādhu sādhv iti |
tad eva dhruvam unninye, tasyai mānaṁ ca bahv adāt || 10 ||[2]

काचिद् रासपरिश्रान्ता पार्श्वस्थस्य गदाभृतः ।
जग्राह बाहुना स्कन्धं श्लथद्वलयमल्लिका ॥ ११ ॥

kācid rāsa-pariśrāntā, pārśva-sthasya gadā-bhṛtaḥ |
jagrāha bāhunā skandhaṁ, ślathad-valaya-mallikā || 11 ||

तत्रैकांसगतं बाहुं कृष्णस्योत्पलसौरभम् ।
चन्दनालिप्तमाघ्राय हृष्टरोमा चुचुम्ब ह ॥ १२ ॥

tatraikāṁsa-gataṁ bāhuṁ, kṛṣṇasyotpala-saurabham |
candanāliptam āghrāya, hṛṣṭa-romā cucumba ha || 12 ||

2. 10d prīyamāṇena *sādhv iti*

कस्याश्चिन्नाट्यविक्षिप्तकुण्डलत्विषमण्डितम् ।
गण्डं गण्डे सन्दधत्याः प्रादात्ताम्बूलचर्वितम् ॥१३॥

kasyāścin nāṭya-vikṣipta-, kuṇḍala-tviṣa-maṇḍitam |
gaṇḍaṁ gaṇḍe sandadhatyāḥ, prādāt tāmbūla-carvitam || 13 ||

नृत्यती गायती काचित्कूजन्नूपुरमेखला ।
पार्श्वस्थाच्युतहस्ताब्जं श्रान्ताधात्स्तनयोः शिवम् ॥१४॥

nṛtyatī gāyatī kācit, kūjan nūpura-mekhalā |
pārśva-sthācyuta-hastābjaṁ, śrāntādhāt stanayoḥ śivam || 14 ||

गोप्यो लब्ध्वाच्युतं कान्तं श्रिय एकान्तवल्लभम् ।
गृहीतकंठ्यस्तद्दोर्भ्यां गायन्त्यस्तं विजह्रिरे ॥१५॥

gopyo labdhvācyutaṁ kāntaṁ, śriya ekānta-vallabham |
gṛhīta-kaṇṭhyas tad-dorbhyāṁ, gāyantyas taṁ vijahrire || 15 ||

कर्णोत्पलालकविटङ्ककपोलघर्म-
वक्त्रश्रियो वलयनूपुरघोषवाद्यैः ।
गोप्यः समं भगवता ननृतुः स्वकेश-
स्रस्तस्रजो भ्रमरगायकरासगोष्ठ्याम् ॥१६॥

karṇotpalālaka-viṭaṅka-kapola-gharma-
vaktra-śriyo valaya-nūpura-ghoṣa-vādyaiḥ |
gopyaḥ samaṁ bhagavatā nanṛtuḥ sva-keśa-
srasta-srajo bhramara-gāyaka-rāsa-goṣṭhyām || 16 ||

एवं परिष्वङ्गकराभिमर्श-
स्निग्धेक्षणोद्दामविलासहासैः ।
रेमे रमेशो व्रजसुन्दरीभिर्
यथार्भकः स्वप्रतिबिम्बविभ्रमः ॥१७॥

evaṁ pariṣvaṅga-karābhimarśa-
snigdhekṣaṇoddāma-vilāsa-hāsaiḥ |
reme rameśo vraja-sundarībhir
yathārbhakaḥ sva-pratibimba-vibhramaḥ || 17 ||

तदङ्गसङ्गप्रमुदाकुलेन्द्रियाः
केशान् दुकूलं कुचपट्टिकां वा ।
नाञ्जः प्रतिव्योढुमलं व्रजस्त्रियो
विस्रस्तमालाभरणाः कुरूद्वह ॥१८॥

tad-aṅga-saṅga-pramudākulendriyāḥ
keśān dukūlaṁ kuca-paṭṭikāṁ vā |
nāñjaḥ prativyoḍhum alaṁ vraja-striyo
visrasta-mālābharaṇāḥ kurūdvaha || 18 ||

कृष्णविक्रीडितं वीक्ष्य मुमुहुः खेचरस्त्रियः ।
कामार्दिताः शशाङ्कश्च सगणो विस्मितोऽभवत् ॥१९॥

kṛṣṇa-vikrīḍitaṁ vīkṣya, mumuhuḥ khe-cara-striyaḥ |
kāmārdhitāḥ śaśāṅkaś ca, sa-gaṇo vismito 'bhavat || 19 ||

कृत्वा तावन्तमात्मानं यावतीर्गोपयोषितः ।
रेमे स भगवांस्ताभिरात्मारामोऽपि लीलया ॥२०॥

kṛtvā tāvantam ātmānaṁ, yāvatīr gopa-yoṣitaḥ |
reme sa bhagavāṁs tābhir, ātmārāmo 'pi līlayā || 20 ||

तासां रतिविहारेण श्रान्तानां वदनानि सः ।
प्रामृजत्करुणः प्रेम्णा शन्तमेनाङ्ग पाणिना ॥२१॥

tāsām rati-vihāreṇa, śrāntānāṁ vadanāni saḥ |
prāmṛjat karuṇaḥ premṇā, śantamenāṅga pāṇinā || 21 ||

गोप्यः स्फुरत्पुरटकुण्डलकुन्तलत्विड्-
गण्डश्रिया सुधितहासनिरीक्षणेन ।
मानं दधत्य ऋषभस्य जगुः कृतानि
पुण्यानि तत्कररुहस्पर्शप्रमोदाः ॥२२॥

gopyaḥ sphurat-puraṭa-kuṇḍala-kuntala-tviḍ-
gaṇḍa-śriyā sudhita-hāsa-nirīkṣaṇena |
mānaṁ dadhatya ṛṣabhasya jaguḥ kṛtāni
puṇyāni tat-kara-ruha-sparśa-pramodāḥ || 22 ||

ताभिर्युतः श्रममपोहितुमङ्गसङ्ग-
घृष्टस्रजः स कुचकुंकुमरञ्जितायाः ।
गन्धर्वपालिभिरनुद्रुत आविशद्वाः
श्रान्तो गजीभिरिभराडिव भिन्नसेतुः ॥२३॥

tābhir yutaḥ śramam apohitum aṅga-saṅga-
ghṛṣṭa-srajaḥ sa kuca-kuṅkuma-rañjitāyāḥ |
gandharva-pālibhir anudruta āviśad vāḥ
śrānto gajībhir ibha-rāḍ iva bhinna-setuḥ || 23 ||

सोऽम्भस्यलं युवतिभिः परिषिच्यमानः
प्रेम्णेक्षितः प्रहसतीभिरितस्ततोऽङ्ग ।
वैमानिकैः कुसुमवर्षिभिरीड्यमानो
रेमे स्वयं स्वरतिरत्र गजेन्द्रलीलः ॥२४॥

so 'mbhasy alaṁ yuvatibhiḥ pariṣicyamānaḥ
premṇekṣitaḥ prahasatībhir itas tato 'ṅga |
vaimānikaiḥ kusuma-varṣibhir īḍyamāno
reme svayaṁ sva-ratir atra gajendra-līlaḥ || 24 ||

ततश्च कृष्णोपवने जलस्थल-
प्रसूनगन्धानिलजुष्टदिक्तटे ।
चचार भृङ्गप्रमदागणावृतो
यथा मदच्युद् द्विरदः करेणुभिः ॥२५॥

tataś ca kṛṣṇopavane jala-sthala-
prasūna-gandhānila-juṣṭa-dik-taṭe |
cacāra bhṛṅga-pramadā-gaṇāvṛto
yathā mada-cyud dviradaḥ kareṇubhiḥ || 25 || [3]

3. 25d *yathā* madādho *dviradaḥ kareṇubhiḥ*

एवं शशाङ्कांशुविराजिता निशाः
स सत्यकामोऽनुरताबलागणः ।
सिषेव आत्मन्यवरुद्धसौरतः
सर्वाः शरत्काव्यकथारसाश्रयाः ॥२६॥

evaṁ śaśāṅkāṁśu-virājitā niśāḥ
sa satya-kāmo 'nuratābalā-gaṇaḥ |
siṣeva ātmany avaruddha-saurataḥ
sarvāḥ śarat-kāvya-kathā-rasāśrayāḥ || 26 ||

श्रीपरीक्षिदुवाच
संस्थापनाय धर्मस्य प्रशमायेतरस्य च ।
अवतीर्णो हि भगवानंशेन जगदीश्वरः ॥२७॥

śrī-parīkṣid uvāca
saṁsthāpanāya dharmasya, praśamāyetarasya ca |
avatīrṇo hi bhagavān, aṁśena jagad-īśvaraḥ || 27 ||

स कथं धर्मसेतूनां वक्ता कर्ताभिरक्षिता ।
प्रतीपमाचरद् ब्रह्मन् परदाराभिमर्शनम् ॥२८॥

sa kathaṁ dharma-setūnāṁ, vaktā kartābhirakṣitā |
pratīpam ācarad brahman, para-dārābhimarśanam || 28 ||

आप्तकामो यदुपतिः कृतवान् वै जुगुप्सितम् ।
किमभिप्राय एतन्नः शंशयं छिन्धि सुव्रत ॥२९॥

āpta-kāmo yadu-patiḥ, kṛtavān vai jugupsitam |
kim-abhiprāya etan naḥ, śaṁśayaṁ chindhi su-vrata || 29 ||

श्रीशुक उवाच
धर्मव्यतिक्रमो दृष्ट ईश्वराणां च साहसम् ।
तेजीयसां न दोषाय वह्नेः सर्वभुजो यथा ॥३०॥

śrī-śuka uvāca
dharma-vyatikramo dṛṣṭa, īśvarāṇāṁ ca sāhasam |
tejīyasāṁ na doṣāya, vahneḥ sarva-bhujo yathā || 30 ||

नैतत्समाचरेज्जातु मनसापि ह्यनीश्वरः ।
विनश्यत्याचरन्मौढ्याद्यथारुद्रोऽब्धिजं विषम् ॥ ३१ ॥

naitat samācarej jātu, manasāpi hy anīśvaraḥ |
vinaśyaty ācaran mauḍhyād, yathārudro 'bdhi-jaṁ viṣam || 31 ||

ईश्वराणां वचः सत्यं तथैवाचरितं क्वचित् ।
तेषां यत्स्ववचोयुक्तं बुद्धिमांस्तत्समाचरेत् ॥ ३२ ॥

īśvarāṇāṁ vacaḥ satyaṁ, tathaivācaritaṁ kvacit |
teṣāṁ yat sva-vaco-yuktaṁ, buddhimāṁs tat samācaret || 32 ||

कुशलाचरितेनैषामिह स्वार्थो न विद्यते ।
विपर्ययेण वानर्थो निरहङ्कारिणां प्रभो ॥ ३३ ॥

kuśalācaritenaiṣām, iha svārtho na vidyate |
viparyayeṇa vānartho, nirahaṅkāriṇāṁ prabho || 33 ||

किमुताखिलसत्त्वानां तिर्यङ्मर्त्यदिवौकसाम् ।
ईशितुश्चेशितव्यानां कुशलाकुशलान्वयः ॥ ३४ ॥

kim utākhila-sattvānāṁ, tiryaṅ-martya-divaukasām |
īśituś ceśitavyānāṁ, kuśalākuśalānvayaḥ || 34 ||

यत्पादपङ्कजपरागनिषेवतृप्ता
  योगप्रभावविधुताखिलकर्मबन्धाः ।
स्वैरं चरन्ति मुनयोऽपि न नह्यमानास्
  तस्येच्छयात्तवपुषः कुत एव बन्धः ॥ ३५ ॥

yat-pāda-paṅkaja-parāga-niṣeva-tṛptā
  yoga-prabhāva-vidhutākhila-karma-bandhāḥ |
svairaṁ caranti munayo 'pi na nahyamānās
  tasyecchayātta-vapuṣaḥ kuta eva bandhaḥ || 35 ||

गोपीनां तत्पतीनां च सर्वेषामेव देहिनाम् ।
योऽन्तश्चरति सोऽध्यक्षः क्रीडनेनेह देहभाक् ॥ ३६ ॥

gopīnāṁ tat-patīnāṁ ca, sarveṣām eva dehinām |
yo 'ntaś carati so 'dhyakṣaḥ, krīḍaneneha deha-bhāk || 36 ||[4]

4. 36d *eṣa krīḍana-dehabhāk*

अनुग्रहाय भक्तानां मानुषं देहमास्थितः ।
भजते तादृशीः क्रीडा याः श्रुत्वा तत्परो भवेत् ॥३७॥

anugrahāya bhaktānāṁ, mānuṣaṁ deham āsthitaḥ |
bhajate tādṛśīḥ krīḍā, yāḥ śrutvā tat-paro bhavet || 37 ||

नासूयन् खलु कृष्णाय मोहितास्तस्य मायया ।
मन्यमानाः स्वपार्श्वस्थान् स्वान् स्वान् दारान् व्रजौकसः ॥३८॥

nāsūyan khalu kṛṣṇāya, mohitās tasya māyayā |
manyamānāḥ sva-pārśva-stān, svān svān dārān vrajaukasaḥ || 38 ||

ब्रह्मरात्र उपावृत्ते वासुदेवानुमोदिताः ।
अनिच्छन्त्यो ययुर्गोप्यः स्वगृहान् भगवत्प्रियाः ॥३९॥

brahma-rātra upāvṛtte, vāsudevānumoditāḥ |
anicchantyo yayur gopyaḥ, sva-gṛhān bhagavat-priyāḥ || 39 ||

विक्रीडितं व्रजवधूभिरिदं च विष्णो
श्रद्धान्वितोऽनुशृणुयादथ वर्णयेद्यः ।
भक्तिं परां भगवति प्रतिलभ्य कामं
हृद्रोगमाश्वपहिनोत्यचिरेण धीरः ॥४०॥

vikrīḍitaṁ vraja-vadhūbhir idaṁ ca viṣṇoḥ
śraddhānvito 'nuśṛṇuyād atha varṇayed yaḥ |
bhaktiṁ parāṁ bhagavati pratilabhya kāmaṁ
hṛd-rogam āśv apahinoty acireṇa dhīraḥ || 40 || [5]

5. 40c *bhaktiṁ* harau *bhagavati pratilabhya kāmaṁ*

APPENDIX 1
Note on Translation

Many translations of the Rāsa Līlā story appear within larger translations of the greater *Bhāgavata* text.[1] In the past half century, I know of only two treatments that focus exclusively on the *Bhāgavata*'s Rāsa Līlā text: *Lord of the Autumn Moons* (1957) by Radhakamal Mukerjee, who presents a short introduction and translation of the verses; and *Vallabhācārya on the Love Games of Kṛṣṇa* (1983) by James D. Redington, who presents an introduction to and translation of the Rāsa story, along with a complete translation of Vallabha's commentary. Recently, Dominic Goodall has presented a translation of the five chapters of the Rāsa Līlā as part of an anthology in *Hindu Scriptures* (1996); he also relies on Redington's translation of Vallabha's commentary for his translation. Here, I have tried to give the text itself more scholarly attention than it has formerly received and, additionally, to present dimensions of the Caitanya school's vision of the text, drawn directly from several important commentaries.[2]

For many years I have mined the dramatic and poetic jewels of the Sanskrit verse in the Rāsa Līlā text. Sanskrit is a language in which words find, as a rule, an extraordinary spectrum of meanings, taking in much more of the universe than words are accustomed to doing in English. Connotative sense is more important in English than it is in Sanskrit, since the latter casts a much wider lexical net for words, gathering an enormous range of denotative

1. Some of the better known published and available translations appear within translations of the complete *Bhāgavata* text: one by J. M. Sanyal; an annotated translation by Ganesh Vasudeo Tagare; and another which includes the original Devanagari text, by C. L. Goswami. Particularly noteworthy is a translation published in the West, which includes the Devanagari and English transliteration of the text along with extensive commentary, by Bhaktivedanta Swami and Hridayānanda dāsa Goswami. Their edition presents a verse-by-verse running commentary based on commentaries by the traditional teachers of the Caitanya school. Recently, Edwin F. Bryant has produced an elaborate introduction to and translation of the whole tenth book of the Bhāgavata. See bibliography for the publication details of these works.

2. In addition to scholarly works, performances of the Rāsa Līlā take place in India to this day, and recognition of this great story is increasing in the English-speaking world. Perhaps the earliest modern and religious rendition of the Rāsa Līlā is found in *Kṛṣṇa: The Supreme Personality of Godhead*, by A. C. Bhaktivedanta Swami Prabhupāda, a retelling of Book Ten of the *Bhāgavata*. Popular writing on the passage is also emerging. For example, twenty pages of a book recently written for a wider readership in the West, entitled *Ka: Stories of the Mind and Gods of India,* by Roberto Calasso (New York: Vintage, 1999), has been devoted to Krishna and the Gopīs and understanding their divine relationship.

senses containing many shades of meaning. Context, then, for Sanskrit words is especially critical for understanding the specific, even precise, denotative force of words. This is just one reason why it often takes more than one English word to embody the particular sense of a single Sanskrit word.

Unlike English, Sanskrit prose does not depend on the ordering of words to form sentences; all syntactical information for sentence structure is embedded in the endings of nouns and verbs. That is, Sanskrit is a highly inflected language in which noun stems receive any number of endings that indicate gender, number, and case, and verb stems receive endings as to tense, number, and person. For this reason, as well, a Sanskrit word often requires more than one word in English to communicate its sense.

This syntactical flexibility and its lexical treasures make Sanskrit an ideal language for poetic expression—each verse offers a special kind of music, a unique picture. Conveying even a modicum of these poetic qualities in the Sanskrit through translation would be an achievement. Even more challenging, the epic verse of the Rāsa Līlā contains a blend of deep theological content woven together with subtle eloquent poetic or dramatic elements.

In addition to all the particulars of the Sanskrit-to-English translation challenge, one wrestles with the greater issues that confront any translator whose efforts are more than a mere transfer of information—faithfulness to the original text and its literary values, rendering accurately the deeper cultural content of the text, and faithfulness to the spirit of the language into which the text is translated. These three are not easy to negotiate, and must be weighed constantly throughout the translation process.

I have viewed the translating of the Rāsa Līlā text as something like the task of conducting a symphony orchestra. A poem in its original but inaccessible language is like an orchestral score that does not come alive until it is conducted and performed. The conductor must read the score and the musicians reincarnate the piece of music in performance. Similarly, the translator of poetry must conduct the complex piece, with all its movements and orchestral color, in a new and unique performance according to his or her appreciation and love for the music. Like musicians, the English words play their parts, as they are employed to translate the Rāsa Līlā verse; their instruments of meaning are woven into the orchestral performance of the reincarnated poem.

The epic verse utilized in the Rāsa Līlā drama is highly structured in form and meter (see "Poetic Meters in Sanskrit Text"). Each of the many types of epic verse throughout the text is a quatrain, consisting of rhythmic long and short syllabic patterns within measured verse lines. End-rhyme is not strict, nor is it particularly emphasized, as we often find in English; rather, verse rhythms and patterns of assonance and consonance are a more prominent feature. Furthermore, Sanskrit is especially beautiful, in part because of its rules governing euphonic combination or *sandhi,* whereby endings of words coalesce with the beginnings of following words, creating conjunctions between words that produce a sonorous flow. Sanskrit, then, becomes a particularly enticing language to hear.

It would be impossible in the English language to imitate the tremendous poetic palette found in the Sanskrit. I believe, however, that there are certain epiphanic qualities of the text that can emerge in the process of translation, even while remaining faithful to the original text. I have endeavored to produce a very accurate reading of the Rāsa Līlā, while striving to convey mimetically some of the flow and cadence in the phraseology of the English rendition. Often this phraseology occurs naturally in compound word phrases in the Sanskrit, even phrases consisting of one or more compounds appearing as a unit, that is, a complex compound. This phenomenon that pervades the language is known as *samāsa,* in which words in related phrases merge without inflection, except for the last word of the simple or complex compound. In addition to phraseologies, I also have attempted to respect the order of words in verses. As mentioned above, Sanskrit word order is not important syntactically. But this freedom of word order makes the ordering of words in poetic verse even more crucial, as it allows such ordering to be all the more deliberate and purposeful. Thus the particular revelational quality of each verse depends upon the ordering of its words and, further, the corresponding phrases that they form.

In my translation of verse, utilizing what I call "dedicated free verse translation," I have attempted, whenever possible, to remain at least roughly faithful to the original ordering of words and phrases. Furthermore, for the purpose of conveying the phraseologies of the original, I have endeavored to emulate, as mentioned in the section entitled "The Sanskrit Text," an appearance of the original verse form: thus, the quarter- or half-verse breaks found in the Sanskrit are indicated by, first, a single leading line beginning a verse, under which slightly indented phrases continuing that line appear, many times one on top of another, until the verse arrives at the next quarter line (in the case of all longer verse meters) or the half-verse line (in the case of the *anuṣṭubh* meter, which consists of eight-syllable quarter-verse lines). The indentation and line breaks in the English translation attempt to follow or mirror the half or quarter line structure of the Sanskrit verse.

As stated earlier, the most widely employed purāṇic meter in the Rāsa Līlā text is the *śloka* or *anuṣṭubh* meter. Throughout the translation, verses of this meter type are indicated by only two leading lines, with their respective sets of following indented line or lines. An example of this shortest verse is the following transliterated verse (with quarter-verse divisions marked by commas), and its corresponding format in English translation:

dṛṣṭaṁ vanaṁ kusumitaṁ, rākeśa-kara-rañjitam |
yamunānila-līlaijat, taru-pallava-śobhitam ||

You have seen the forest
filled with flowers,
glowing with the rays
of the full moon;
Made beautiful by leaves of trees,
playfully shimmering
from the gentle breeze
off the river Yamunā.

All other verses, which are of one of several longer varieties found in the Rāsa Līlā, are placed in four sets of leading lines along with their indentations, as I demonstrate in the following verse:

Seeing lotus flowers bloom,	*(dṛṣṭvā kumudvantam)*
the perfect circle of the moon	*(akhaṇḍa-maṇḍalaṁ)*
Beaming like the face of Ramā,	*(ramānanābhaṁ)*
reddish as fresh *kuṅkuma;*	(*nava-kuṅkumāruṇam*)
Seeing the forest colored	(*vanaṁ ca . . . rañjitaṁ*)
by the moon's gentle rays,	(*tat-komala-gobhī*)
He began to make sweet music,	(*jagau kalaṁ*)
melting the hearts of	(*manoharam*)
fair maidens with beautiful eyes.	*(vāma-dṛśāṁ)*

The above is an especially good example of the order of words in the translation closely paralleling that of the original word order. In the transliteration of the verse, I have underlined the repeated assonances and consonances that give the verse its rhyme and rhythm:

dṛṣṭvā kumudvantam akhaṇḍa-maṇḍalaṁ
ramānanābhaṁ nava-kuṅkumāruṇam |
vanaṁ ca tat-komala-gobhī rañjitaṁ
jagau kalaṁ vāmā-dṛśāṁ manoharam ||

It can be seen, then, that the verse lineation and structure in translation is informed by the ordering and rhythms of words, phrases, and ideas within the original source text.

Other approaches I engage include the following: personal or proper names are duplicated as they appear in the transliteration, unaltered; meanings or identifications are provided in footnotes to the translation; and the precise wording of the original is respected, as there is a certain precision to its poetry. Pronouns, therefore, are not substituted for their antecedent personal names or ideas. My conviction is that the poet of the original text places in each verse exactly what the reader needs to know before the narrative and poetic imagery is revealed in the successive verses. Additionally, in the service of the general reader, only a minimal number of Sanskrit words and terms have been retained in the translation. Some more commonly known Sanskrit words are anglicized and not italicized.

Capitalization as we know it in English does not exist in Sanskrit. Although initial letters of proper names and beginnings of sentences are capitalized in the translation of Sanskrit, personal pronouns for the deity are not. Certain words, however, that are associated with the divinity are capitalized, in order to distinguish these superlative senses from their typical usages. For example, in the translation of the phrase *ādi-puruṣa,* which means "original (*ādi-*) person (*-puruṣa*)," I capitalize the initial letter of the word "person" to express the powerful sense of divinity that this word has for the Vaishnava tradition. The word *atman* I translate as "Soul" in order to indicate that the soul spoken of here is different from a mortal soul. This use of capitalization for expressing divine personification can be seen in other instances as well; thus, I have an initial capital for the word "love" when it is directly associated with the deity, as the personification of the supreme Cupid.

APPENDIX 2
Poetic Meters in Sanskrit Text

ACCENT AND SYLLABLE LENGTH: EMPHASIS AND RHYTHM IN SANSKRIT VERSE

The Sanskrit language distinguishes between accent and length of syllables. Syllables within words are spoken in either short or long lengths of time, and there are numerous varieties of poetic meters for many types of verse lengths. Following are basic rules to acquaint the reader with the recitation of Sanskrit verse, so important to the language.

ACCENT

1. The first syllable of all words having two syllables is accented; for example, *bhakti, deva.*
2. The penultimate (second-to-last) syllable of all words having more than two syllables is accented if the syllable contains a long vowel, a diphthong, or a short vowel followed by two consonants: for example, *nirvāna, Gaṇeśa, gṛhastha.*
3. The antepenultimate (third-to-last) syllable is accented in most other cases: for example, *Mahābhārata, Himālaya, Rāmāyana, Upaniṣad.*

SANSKRIT METERS USED IN RĀSA LĪLĀ TEXT

KEY TO SYMBOLS OF SYLLABLE LENGTH IN POETIC METER

˘ = *laghu,* light syllables. These are made up of short vowels that are not followed by any more than one consonant (*anusvāra* "ṁ" and *avagraha* "ḥ" included), either within a word or between words. Light syllables are short, half the length of long syllables; for example, *nama oṁ viṣṇupādāya* (underlined vowels indicate light syllables).

– = *guru,* heavy syllables. These are made up of long vowels or those that are made up of short vowels followed by more than one consonant (*anusvāra* "ṁ" and *avagraha* "ḥ" included), either within a word or between words; for example, *nama oṁ viṣṇupādāya* (underlined vowels indicate heavy syllables).

o = an indication that there is a place in the metrical pattern of a quarter verse that allows for either a "light" or "heavy" syllable.

| = *yati*, caesura, or a point during the recitation of a quarter-verse line in which a natural pause occurs.

Anuṣṭubh (8 syllables in each *pada*)

Verses in the *anuṣṭubh* meter, also known as *śloka*, are the most commonly occuring verses in purāṇic and epic Sanskrit texts. Consequently, it is also the most common verse form in the Rāsa Līlā, occuring 112 times.

The most common form is the following:

o o o o ⏑ – – o (used in first and third *padas*)

Example: *bhagavān api tā rātrīḥ* (RL 1.1a)

o o o o ⏑ – ⏑ o (used in second and fourth *padas*)

Example: *śāradotphulla-mallikāḥ* (RL 1.1b)

Triṣṭubh (11 syllables in each *pada*)

rājahaṁsī ⏑ ⏑ ⏑ – ⏑ – – – ⏑ ⏑ – (also called *vibhūṣaṇā*)

Example: *jayati te'dhikaṁ janmanā vrajaḥ* (RL 3.1a)

indravajrā – – ⏑ – – ⏑ ⏑ – ⏑ – –

Example: *evaṁ pariṣvaṅga-karābhimarśa* (RL 5.17a)

upendravajrā ⏑ – ⏑ – – ⏑ ⏑ – ⏑ – –

Example: *yathādhano labdha-dhane vinaṣṭe* (RL 4.20c)

upajāti o – ⏑ – – ⏑ ⏑ – ⏑ – o (a mixture of *indravajrā* and *upendravajrā*)

Example: *nāhaṁ tu sakhyo bhajato 'pi jantūn (indrarajrā)*
bhajāmy amīṣām anuvṛtti-vṛttaye (upendravajrā) (RL 4.20a–b)

Mātrāchandas (*Ardhasamavṛtta*)

aupacchandasika (11- and 12-syllable *pādas* alternating, less fixed)

Example: *evaṁ mad-arthojjhita-loka-veda-* (11 syllables)
svānāṁ hi vo mayy anuvṛttaye 'balāḥ (12 syllables)
(RL 4.21a–b, the only occurrence in RL)

Jagatī (12 syllables in each *pada*)

indravaṁśā – – ⏑ – – ⏑ ⏑ – ⏑ – ⏑ –

Example: *tad-darśanāhlāda-vidhūta-hṛd-rujo* (RL 4.13a)

vaṁśastha ⏑ – ⏑ – – ⏑ ⏑ – ⏑ – ⏑ – (also called *vaṁśasthavila* or *vaṁstanita*)

Example: *dṛṣṭvā kumudvantam akhaṇḍa-maṇḍalaṁ* (RL 1.3a)

viṣamacatuṣpadī: irregular syllabic pattern (*viṣama*) of quarter-verse lines (*catuṣpadī*); in the Rāsa Līlā, this type of irregular verse is consistently a combination of *indravaṁśā* and *vaṁśastha* quarter-verse lines.

Example: *sahāsa-līleṣaṇa-vibhrama-bhruvā*
saṁsparśanenāṅka-kṛtāṅghri-hastayoḥ (RL 4.15b–c)

ŚAKVARĪ (14 SYLLABLES IN EACH *PADA*)

vasantatilakā – – ᴗ – ᴗ ᴗ ᴗ – ᴗ ᴗ – ᴗ – o

(Also called *vasantatilaka*, or *uddarṣiṇī*, or *siṁhonnatā*)

Example: *vikrīḍitaṁ vraja-vadhūbhir idaṁ ca viṣṇoḥ* (RL 5.40a)

ATYAṢṬI (17 SYLLABLES IN EACH *PADA*)

mandākrāntā – – – – ᴗ ᴗ ᴗ ᴗ ᴗ – – ᴗ – – ᴗ – –

Example: *pāda-nyāsair bhuja-vidhutibhiḥ sa-smitair*
bhrū-vilāsair (RL 5.8a)

STORYLINE AND POETIC METER ANALYSIS

Numbers are to sequential verses; bracketed numbers indicate verse meter.

ACT 1. KRISHNA ATTRACTS THE GOPĪS AND DISAPPEARS (BhP 10.29)

Scene 1. Narrative: Krishna makes flute music and the Gopīs come running to the forest (vv. 1–11)

Description: Krishna witnesses exquisite beauty of Vraja landscape

1 [8]

Description: Reddened moonlit autumn evening dispels sorrow

2 [12] *viṣamacatuṣpadī*

Description: Krishna moved by beauty of surroundings to make music

3 [12] *viṣamacatuṣpadī*

Description: Upon hearing music Gopīs abruptly abandon their homes

4 [12] *viṣamacatuṣpadī*

5–11 [8]

Scene 2. Discourse: On the Gopīs' passionate love for Krishna surpassing knowledge of divinity (vv. 12–16)

Question: King asks how Gopīs can love him as Lover if he is supreme

12 [8]

Response: Sage says that all emotions are perfected when offered to God

13–16 [8]

Scene 3. Dialogue: Krishna urges the Gopīs to return home and the Gopīs plead to stay in the forest (vv. 17–41)

Description: Krishna's words to the Gopīs introduced

17 [8]

Hero's Speech: Krishna warns Gopīs of dangers, urging them to return

18–27 [8]

Description: The Gopīs' words to Krishna introduced

28 [8]

29–30 [14] *vasantatilakā*

Heroines' Speech: The Gopīs beg Krishna to stay with him in forest

31–41 [14] *vasantatilakā*

Scene 4. Narrative: Krishna plays with the Gopīs in the forest and suddenly disappears (vv. 42–48)

Description: Krishna and the Gopīs play in the forest

42 [8]

43 [12] *indravaṁśā*

44–45 [8]

46 [14] *vasantatilakā*

Description: The Gopīs become proud and Krishna disappears

47–48 [8]

ACT 2. THE GOPĪS SEARCH FOR KRISHNA (BHP 10.30)

Scene 1. Narrative: The Gopīs imitate Krishna and inquire from inhabitants of the forest (vv. 1–23)

Description: Gopīs imitate actions of Krishna

1	[8]		
2		[12] *viṣamacatuṣpadī*	
3		[12] *vaṁśastha*	
4		[12] *viṣamacatuṣpadī*	

Heroines' Monologue: Gopīs talk to plants and creatures of the forest

5–8	[8]		
9–12			[14] *vasantatilakā*
13	[8]		

Description: Gopīs imitate Krishna and others in *līlās*

14–23	[8]

Scene 2. Narrative: The Gopīs track footprints and discover special Gopī who has been deserted by Krishna (vv. 24–44)

Description: Gopīs detect footprints of Krishna and special Gopī

24–33	[8]

Description: Special Gopī's painful abandonment by Krishna

34–39	[8]

Description: Gopīs find special Gopī and hear her story

40–44	[8]

ACT 3. SONG OF THE GOPĪS (BHP 10.31)

Scene. Monologue: The Gopīs pray with humility and passion, while longing for Krishna during his absence (vv. 1–19)

1–18	[11] *rājahaṁsī*	
19		[14] *vasantatilakā*

ACT 4. KRISHNA REAPPEARS AND SPEAKS OF LOVE (BHP 10.32)

Scene 1. Narrative: Krishna suddenly reappears and the Gopīs react in various emotional ways (vv. 1–14)

Description: Krishna gallantly reappears before Gopīs

1–2	[8]

Description: Gopīs' emotional reactions to Krishna's reappearance

3–12	[8]	
13–14		[12] *viṣamacatuṣpadī*

Scene 2. Dialogue: Krishna describes three types of love in response to the Gopīs' inquiry; Krishna is grateful for the Gopīs' love (vv. 15–22)

Description: Introduction to dialogue

15		[12] *viṣamacatuṣpadī*

Heroines' Question: Gopīs ask Krishna about the nature of love

16	[8]	

Hero's Response: Krishna affectionately responds to Gopīs' question

17–19	[8]	
20		[11] *upajāti*
21		[11 / 12] *mātrāchandas*
22		[12] *viṣamacatuṣpadī*

ACT 5. The Rāsa Dance (BhP 10.33)

Scene 1: Narrative: The Gopīs form circle for Rāsa dance and Krishna dances with each Gopī simultaneously (vv. 1–20)

Description: Formation of the Rāsa dance and its commencement

1–7	[8]	

Description: How Krishna and Gopīs dance with each other in Rāsa

8		[17] *mandākrāntā*
9–15	[8]	
16		[14] *vasantatilakā*
17		[11] *upajāti*
18		[12] *viṣamacatuṣpadī*
19–20	[8]	

Scene 2. Narrative: Krishna and the Gopīs play after Rāsa dance (vv. 21–26)

Description: Bathing in the river and playing in the forest

21	[8]	
22–24		[14] *vasantatilakā*
25		[12] *vaṁśastha*
26		[12] *viṣamacatuṣpadī*

Scene 3. Discourse: On the ethical question of Krishna's dancing with other men's wives (vv. 27–35)

Question: King asks how Krishna can dance with other men's wives

27–29 [8]

Response: Sage states that Krishna is in hearts of Gopīs and beyond morality

30–34 [8]

35 [14] *vasantatilakā*

Scene 4. Narrative: The special nature of Krishna's divine play is presented; hearing Rāsa Līlā story bestows greatest benediction (vv. 36–40).

Description: Special nature of Krishna's divine play

36–38 [8]

Description: Gopīs return to their homes

39 [8]

Benediction: Hearing Rāsā Līlā bestows highest devotion

40 [14] *vasantatilakā*

VERSE NUMBERING VARIATIONS AND ACTUAL VERSE COUNT

Sanskrit verses are quatrains made of two "lines" or four "feet" (*padas*). In Sanskrit, a vertical line "|" following the last word of a single line indicates the end of a sentence or line, and a double vertical line "||" following the last word of the verse indicates the end of the second sentence or line of a verse. A verse number will often follow this double line enclosed by a second set of double lines.

Providing a total verse count of the RL is not simple, nor is it possible to find a completely consistent verse numbering among various editions of the text. Even traditional commentators do not rely upon the numeric assignments to verses, due to variations in the numeric identification of verses. They identify a verse, instead, by saying, "the verse beginning with the words . . . ," and thus a verse is identified by its first two- or three-word combination. This variation in numbering between editions is due to subtle variation in the methods of verse division and counting in the second and fifth chapters or acts of the story. The second act is often presented as having either 44 or 45 verses, and the fifth act as having either 39 or 40 verses, without reducing or increasing the actual lines within verses or the number of verses themselves. In act two, for example, there are two contiguous verses that are numbered as

2.31, the first verse numbered as 2.31–1 and the second as 2.31–2, which adds an additional verse beyond the normal chapter verse count and numbering.

There are four verses in the text that consist of three, rather than the usual two, sentence lines that form a verse (RL 2.23, 2.31.2, 5.3, and 5.10). I have determined the number of verses in the RL as 176 by counting the total number of half-verse lines, and dividing this total by two, rather than adding the numbers of verses appearing at the end of chapters, which would yield a total of 173.

APPENDIX 3
Synoptic Analysis of the Rāsa Līlā

A simple synoptic analysis of three comparable Krishna-Gopī stories found in the *Harivaṁśa* (HV), *Viṣṇu Purāṇa* (VP), and *Brahma Purāṇa* (BP) texts reveals how the Rāsa Līlā story of the *Bhāgavata Purāṇa* (BhP) appears to utilize commonly shared themes by enhancing them philosophically, dramatically, and poetically. Such an analysis also reveals that the *Bhāgavata* contributes a significant amount of original material. Since the *Viṣṇu* and *Brahma Purāṇa* versions of the story are virtually identical, I will engage only the *Viṣṇu Purāṇa,* without reference to the *Brahma Purāṇa,* for my analysis here.[1]

The most striking differences are worth mentioning first. The HV and VP versions are each portions of a single larger chapter within which the story is situated, whereas the *Bhāgavata*'s story spans five chapters that effectively constitute acts in a drama. Note in the synoptic chart that the VP story begins with verse 14, and the HV, verse 15. In the BhP, the story line is very developed in each of the chapter divisions, clearly delineating thirteen scene-like sections that constitute its five acts or chapters. By contrast, the HV and VP versions appear to be much less refined, even unfinished works. The BhP text is also lengthier than either of the other two versions, consisting of a total of 176 verses.[2] Indeed, the number of verses in the BhP's story constitutes well over eight times that of the HV, which totals twenty-one verses, and over three and a half times that of the VP, which totals forty-nine verses. The significantly greater length of the BhP text immediately tells us that it is a far more elaborate story.

The language and prosody of the HV and VP versions are fairly simple. Both engage the standard epic *anuṣṭubh* or *śloka* verse meter, which possesses a narrative-poetic quality. The BhP, on the other hand, exhibits many of the qualities of classical Indian dramaturgy and, to some extent, Sanskrit poetics. In addition to the epic verse, used in 63 verses, the BhP utilizes five other longer, more elaborate verse meters that embellish and greatly enhance the story line, heightening its emotion and drama.

In the BhP version, several scenes are added that are not found in the VP or HV versions, and motifs of the story are embellished. For example, the BhP's 31st chapter, or act three, known as the Song of the Gopīs, in which the cowherd maidens ardently pray to Krishna during his absence, has no corre-

1. For further discussion on the *Brahma Purāṇa* and its comparison to the BhP and HV texts with regard to all the Gopī narratives, including the RL, see Hardy, *Viraha Bhakti* (Delhi: Oxford University Press, 1983), pp. 86–104.

2. See "Verse Numbering Variations and Actual Verse Count" in appendix 2.

sponding material in either the VP or HV, one of the obvious reasons the BhP version is favored over the others. Furthermore, neither the HV nor the VP texts contains content comparable to that of act one scene 4 of the BhP text, during which Krishna plays with the Gopīs in the forest and suddenly disappears. Altogether, the HV is missing eight of the thirteen scenes that the BhP presents, and the VP, four. Moreover, three scenes found in the BhP version correspond to only one verse in the VP. Significant parts of the story line are also absent from both the VP and HV. In fact, it is only the eleventh verse of the HV that remotely hints at something that could be construed as the Rāsa dance. Additionally, there is no apologia or theological discourse, as there is in the BhP, between the narrator and primary listener. Both the HV and VP possess, however, at least a few elements that can be identified with the first, second, fourth, and fifth chapters of the BhP version.

TABLE 4. SYNOPTIC ANALYSIS OF THE RĀSA LĪLĀ STORY FROM *BHĀGAVATA PURĀṆA*, *VIṢṆU PURĀṆA*, AND *HARIVAṀŚA* TEXTS

BhP Chapters	BhP Verses Book 10, Chs. 29–33	VP Verses Book 5, Ch. 13	HV Verses Ch. 63
Ch. 29 / Act 1			
Scene 1	1–11	14–21	15–18, 24
Scene 2	12–16	22	—
Scene 3	17–41	23	—
Scene 4	42–48	—	—
Ch. 30 / Act 2			
Scene 1	1–23	24–29	26–28
Scene 2	24–44	30–42	—
Ch. 31 / Act 3			
Scene: Gopī Monologue	1–19	—	—
Ch. 32 / Act 4			
Scene 1	1–14	43–46, 48	19–23
Scene 2	15–22	47	—
Ch. 33 / Act 5			
Scene 1	1–22	49–60	25
Scene 2	23–26	—	29–35
Scene 3	27–36	—	—
Scene 4	37–40	61–62	—
Total number of verses	173 [176]	49	21

Glossary

Acyuta.	"The infallible one." A name for Krishna.
Adhokṣaja.	"The Lord who is beyond the perception of the senses." A name for Krishna.
ādi-puruṣa.	"The original Person." An epithet for Krishna. See *puruṣa.*
Arjuna.	One of five righteous Pāṇḍava brothers; the great general in the *Mahābhārata* war who was counseled on the battlefield by Krishna in their dialogue of the *Bhagavad Gītā.*
ātman.	"Soul," "self," "mind"; referring to Krishna as "[supreme] Soul" (also spelled *ātmā*). See *ātmārāma, mahātma, paramātman.*
ātmārāma.	"One who possesses pleasure (*rāma*) within the self (*ātmā*)." This phrase often refers to Krishna or saintly persons.
Bādarāyaṇa.	The father of the sage Śuka, the narrator of the Rāsa Līlā story, and most of the *Bhāgavata* text. Bādarāyaṇa, who is also known as Vyāsa, is the compiler of the ancient Indian sacred texts known as the Vedas. With the exception of the first verse, throughout the story the narrator is referred to by the simple name Śuka, but in some editions of the *Bhāgavata,* the RL story begins with the epithet "son of Bādarāyaṇa," invoking the narrator's authoritative status, in order to specially honor this greatest of divine stories.
Balarāma.	The older brother of Krishna.
Bhagavān.	"The Beloved Lord," or the "one who possesses (*-vān*) all supreme excellences (*bhaga-*) in full." The word means generally "God" or "the divine." Refers to Krishna throughout the episode, meaning the powerful yet intimate and personal "supreme Lord."
bhakta.	Literally, "the devoted," or "the devotee of the Lord."
bhakti.	"Devotional love," "loving devotion to God," or "worship of God."
Brahmā.	The "god of creation" (to be distinguished from Brahman). Often associated with the other primary cosmic divinities of sustenance (Vishnu) and destruction (Śiva). In this episode, Brahmā is also called Vikhanas (see Vikhanas).
Brahman.	"Supreme spirit," "God," or "ultimate reality." The whole of supreme reality, or the nondual monistic dimension of the supreme reality.

Brāhmaṇa. Member of the highest, or priestly, caste (*varṇa*).

cakra. The supernatural disk of Vishnu or Krishna, used for killing demons. Or, any of the seven yogic centers of life energy within the human body, roughly aligned with the spinal cord.

Cedi, king of. Śiśupāla, the king who insulted Krishna in the assembly of great personalities and elders attending the *rājasūya* sacrifice. Krishna granted liberation to him by beheading him with his *cakra.*

Dāmodara. A name for Krishna, meaning "one whose waist has been bound." Krishna's mother, Yaśodā, attempts to bind him with a rope to keep him from stealing butter (see BhP 10.9).

Devakī. The name of Krishna's birth mother, the wife of Vasudeva.

Devī. The Goddess.

dharma. "Duty," "religion," "the laws of goodness," etc. See *svadharma.*

dhīra. A person who is "peaceful and wise." A self-realized soul.

Gandharvas. Plural of Gandharva. The name of a group of celestial singers who also produce the most exquisite divine instrumental music.

Goddess. See Indirā, Lakṣmī, Ramā, Śrī.

Gopa. "One who protects the cows." A cowherd boy or man. More specifically, husband of a Gopī.

Gopī. A married or unmarried cowherdess or milkmaiden. In the RL, the word is used mostly in the plural to refer to Krishna's beloveds. *See* Gopīs. For literal meaning, *see* Gopa.

Gopīs. Plural form of Gopī. The specific group of cowherd maidens from the rural area of Vraja who are viewed as the divine consorts of Krishna. The collective heroines of the RL episode.

Govinda. "One who tends the cows." A proper name for Krishna. Viśvanātha explains that the name Govinda can be used to convey the sense of someone "who utilizes (*vindate*) playful speech (*gāḥ*)."

guṇa. "Underlying forces of nature," the three constituent "qualities" of the natural world as well as the consciousness of the conditioned self, consisting of *sattva, rajas,* and *tamas* (clarity or light, haziness, and darkness of spirit, respectively). See *nirguṇa.*

Hari. "One who steals one's heart" or "one who takes away suffering." A name for Krishna.

Hṛṣīkeśa. "The Lord of the senses." A name for Krishna.

Indirā. A name for the Goddess Lakṣmī, the consort of Nārāyaṇa.

Īśa. "Cosmic controller." In the RL, refers to the god Śiva. The word can also refer to Krishna or Vishnu as "the Lord." See Rudra.

īśvara. "The supreme cosmic controller." A word for God or an epithet of Krishna.

kajjala. A blackish substance, sometimes considered a collyrium, applied to the eyelashes or eyelids as decorative makeup.

Kālindī. Another name for the river Yamunā.

kāma. "Love," "worldly love," "passion" (worldly or divine). The word typically refers to worldly love. Teachers of the Caitanya school engage this word to indicate the intensity of pure love for God.

karnikāra. Golden yellow flowers that hang in bunches from the branches of the Indian Laburnum (*Cassia fistula*) tree. The flowers consist of beautiful delicate blossoms that are primarily ornamental, since they do not produce a scent.

Keśava. "The long-haired one." A name for Krishna.

Krishna. The "dark" one, or "blackish," indicating Krishna's dark "sapphire" color. The most prominent personal name for Bhagavān, or the Supreme Lord, throughout the Rāsa Līlā episode. Krishna as a name of God denotes particularly, for the Caitanya school and other Vaishnava lineages, the original form of God from whom all other divine forms and manifestations come.

kṛṣṇa. Sanskrit transliteration for the name Krishna.

Kṛṣṇā. Another name for the river Yamunā (note the macron, or long mark, over the letter a).

kuṅkuma. A brilliant or deep reddish powder, often described as saffron or vermilion. It is produced from the plant and pollen of the flowers of the botanical *Crocus sativus.* This substance is placed above the forehead in the area of the parted hair by married Indian women.

Lakṣmī. The supreme Goddess, divine consort of Vishnu or Nārāyaṇa.

līlā. "Play" or "divine play." The word can have the sense of "playfulness" as well as the different sense of "drama." It refers to the revelational displays or dramatic manifestations of the various divine events in the life of Krishna.

Mādhava. A name for Krishna, derived from the word *madhu,* which means "honey" or "sweet."

Madhu. The name of the dynasty into which Krishna was born.

Madhupati. "Lord of the Madhu dynasty." An epithet of Krishna.

mahātmanaḥ. "The great Soul." An epithet of Krishna.

mālati. A type of jasmine flower. See *mallikā.*

mallikā. Jasmine flowers with exotically fragrant small star-shaped white or pink blossoms.

Mathurā. The biggest city in the Vraja region, located within about ten miles of Vrindāvana village.

Maya. The personality whose son is the demon Vyomāsura. The episode of Krishna slaying Vyomāsura is found in BhP 10.37.28–33. Maya should be distinguished from the similar word *māyā,* meaning "energy" or "illusion," etc.

māyā. "Power," "energy," "illusion," and can be the shortened form of Yogamāyā (see below).

Mukunda. "One who grants liberation (*mukti*)." An epithet of Krishna.

Murāri. "Enemy of the Mura demon." An epithet of Krishna.

Nanda. The name of Krishna's foster father, the husband of Yaśodā.

nirguṇa. "Without *guṇa,*" or "without being bound by the underlying forces of nature." See *guṇa.*

paramātman. "Supreme Soul." Krishna's special expansive form located in the heart of all beings and at the core of all existences.

parameśvara. "Supreme controller" or "supreme Lord." An epithet of Krishna.

Parīkṣit. The king to whom the Rāsa Līlā and the other stories of the *Bhāgavata Purāṇa* are narrated.

premā. "Love" or "affection." It can mean "pure love" and specifically "love of God."

puruṣa. This word has many senses. It can mean "spirit" in contradistinction to *prakṛti* or "matter." It can also mean "person" or, in relation to God, "the supreme Person." See *ādi-puruṣa.*

Pūtanā. The demonness who tried to kill Krishna as a baby by nursing him from her poisoned breast. The Pūtanā story is found in BhP 10.6.1–44.

Ramā. Name for Lakṣmī, the divine consort of Krishna when he is in his more majestic and powerful form known as Lord Nārāyaṇa. To be distinguished from the incarnation of Vishnu, Rāma (the macron over the first "a" rather than the second). See Śrī.

Rāma. The shortened name for Krishna's brother, Balarāma. (To be distinguished from Nārāyaṇa's consort Ramā—the macron over the second "a" rather than the first). This abbreviated name can also refer to Krishna's incarnation of Rāmacandra found in the *Rāmāyaṇa* by Vālmīki.

rās līlā.	Name of the pilgrimage dramas performed in Vraja that always commence with a reenactment of the Rāsa dance.
rasa.	"Taste." The word can be understood as "the intimate experience or relationship with God," and more broadly, a deep aesthetic appreciation or experience. In order to distinguish *rasa* from *rāsa* (see below), I have presented the latter in nonitalic letters and capitalized: Rāsa.
Rāsa.	A special ancient sophisticated dance form of India, in which a circle of women with interlocking arms is formed, each woman having a male partner who places his arm around her neck. The dance involves singing, as well. Viśvanātha points out that Rāsa also refers to the sum of all *rasa*s or all intimate experiences with the supreme.
rāsa-goṣṭhī.	The "assembly" or "gathering" of the Rāsa dance. Another way of referring to the Rāsa Līlā story.
rāsa-krīḍā.	The "play" of the Rāsa dance. Another way of referring to the Rāsa Līlā story. The related word *vikrīḍitam* appears in RL 5.40. See the synonymn *līlā.*
Rāsa Līlā.	The "play (*līlā*) of the dance (*rāsa*)," or as I have more broadly translated it, "Dance of Divine Love." The most commonly used name to refer to the specific episode within the tenth book of the *Bhāgavata Purāṇa* (versions of which are also found in the *Harivaṁśa* and *Viṣṇu Purāṇa*) which tells the story of how Krishna attracts the cowherd maidens away from their homes, into the forest. Together, in the final fifth chapter, they all dance and sing in the Rāsa dance. This phrase, however, does not appear in the episode or anywhere in the *Bhāgavata* text itself.
Rāsa-*maṇḍala.*	The actual circle (*maṇḍala*) of the Rāsa dance. Another way of referring to the Rāsa Līlā episode, but more specifically to the Rāsa dance.
rāsotsavaḥ.	"Festival (*-utsavaḥ*) of the Rāsa dance."
Rātrī.	"Night." The goddess presiding over the night presented in the *Ṛg Veda.*
Rudra.	A name for the powerful god Śiva, the god of destruction. See Īśa.
Sātvatas.	Sacred to the Satvats or those who worship Krishna; name for the Yādava Dynasty, the Yadus who worship Krishna.
Śauri.	The name of Krishna as the one who appears in the dynasty of Śūra. This name conveys the heroic character of Krishna.
Śiva.	*See* Rudra.

Śrī. A name for the Goddess Lakṣmī, the divine consort of Nārāyaṇa. See Ramā above.

śrutis. The plural form of the word *śruti,* which refers to the revelational scriptures of the Vedas and other closely associated literatures, such as the Upanishads.

Śuka. The narrator of the *Bhāgavata* text to King Parīkṣit. He is the son of Vyāsa, the compiler of the Vedas. See Bādarāyana above.

sva-dharma. "One's own dharma." See dharma.

tad-ātmika. "The self completely absorbed in that [beloved object, Krishna]." A phrase descriptive of the Gopīs.

tan-maya. "One who is filled with that [beloved object, Krishna]." A phrase descriptive of the Gopīs.

tat-parā. "One who is fully dedicated to that [beloved object, Krishna]." A phrase descriptive of the Gopīs.

tulasī. The most sacred plant to Krishna. The green leaves and delicate green and purple blossoms of the plant are offered to Krishna's feet and used in his garlands as well. The purplish flowerets have their own distinct scent. Also, capitalized, the goddess associated with this plant.

Uddhava. The messenger of Krishna to the Gopīs, who possesses a bodily likeness to Krishna. The passage in which Uddhava appears is BhP 10.47, in which the famous Bhramara Gīta is found.

Upanishads. The name of a body of sacred Sanskrit literature, often consisting of recorded dialogues between a master and disciple, which focus on philosophical and mystical themes. The name for this type of sacred text means "sitting down near the feet of a teacher." These texts form the basis for Vedānta philosophy and are regarded as authoritative by most Hindu traditions. Although it is said that there are as many as 108 Upanishads, there are at least ten that are considered the most important, such as the Chāṇḍogya, Bṛhadāranyaka, Taittirīyā, Īśa, Śvetaśvatāra, Kaṭha, and several others.

Urukrama. "The wide-striding one." A name for Krishna, referring to Krishna's incarnation as Vāmana.

Uttamaśloka. Epithetical name for Krishna or Vishnu translated in the Bhramara Gīta as "the most excellent and famous one" or, more literally, "The one whose hymns of praise (*śloka*) are the greatest or highest (*uttama*)." This name for Krishna is used throughout the *Bhāgavata* text, but is not found in the Rāsa Līlā story.

Vaijayantī. "Victory." The name of Krishna's garland of five different-colored flowers strung together.

Varāha. The name of Krishna's incarnation in the form of a divine boar.

Vāsudeva. "Son of Vasudeva [Krishna's father]." A name for Krishna.

Vedas. The Vedas (or Veda) are the foundational sacred Sanskrit texts of India, seen by many Hindu traditions as the basis for and symbol of all knowledge. Acceptance of the authority of the Vedas, on some level, is necessary for validating religious orthodoxy or identity.

Vikhanas. Name for the god of creation, known most often as Brahmā (to be distinguished from the word *brahman,* "the supreme spirit").

Vishnu (Viṣṇu). "The all-pervading one." A name for Krishna in his divine manifestation of power and cosmic majesty.

Vraja. The rural village, synonymous with Vrindāvana; or the greater region in North India in which Krishna and his consorts reside. See Vrindāvana.

Vrindāvana (Vṛndāvana). "The forest (*-vana*) of *tulasī* (*vṛndā-*)." The name of the specific village where Krishna resides, within the Vraja region. See *tulasī* above.

Vṛṣṇis. The people of the Vṛṣṇi Dynasty, the dynasty from which Krishna comes.

Yadus. The people of the Yadu Dynasty, another name for the dynasty from which Krishna comes.

Yamunā. The sacred river that runs through Vraja, famous for being dear to Krishna and the Gopīs. Also known as the Kalindī and the Kṛṣṇā in this episode. *See* Kalindī and Kṛṣṇā.

yoga. "Union" or "connection," connoting the soul's intimate relationship with the divine. The physical and meditative discipline by which mystics can attain perfection as well as many supernatural powers.

Yogamāyā. "Illusive power of yoga." The Goddess, or Devī, the feminine embodiment of "illusive power" who makes arrangements for God's pleasure. This term more connotatively means "the illusive power of God (*māyā*) which creates arrangements for loving union (*yoga*)," and is often abbreviated simply as the word *māyā.* See *māyā*; yoga.

yogeśvara. "Supreme Lord of yoga." A name for Krishna. This name can be associated with the power of Yogamāyā, implied by the presence of the word "yoga" in the name.

yogi. One who practices yoga, the powerful discipline that leads to mastery over the mind and body, producing blissful states of consciousness in relation to the Supreme. *See* yoga above.

Bibliography

BHĀGAVATA PURĀṆA: SANSKRIT EDITIONS AND TRANSLATIONS

Bhāgavata Purāṇa. Sanskrit text; multi-commentary edition, including commentaries by Śrīdhara Svāmin, Sanātana Gosvāmin, Jīva Gosvāmin, Viśvanātha Cakravartin. Allahabad, n.d.

Bhāgavata Purāṇa of Kṛṣṇa Dvaipāyana Vyāsa (with Sanskrit Commentary Bhāvāthabodhinī of Śrīdhara Svāmin), edited by J. L. Shastri. Delhi: Motilal Banarsidass, 1983.

Bhaktivedanta Swami Prabhupada, A.C., and Hridayananda Das Goswami. *Śrīmad Bhāgavatam.* Original Sanskrit Text. Cantos 1–12 in 18 vols. Sanskrit text, translation, and commentary (cantos 1 through 10, part 1 by Prabhupāda; and cantos 10, part 2 through canto 12 by Goswami). Los Angeles: Bhaktivedanta Book Trust, 1993.

———. *KṚṢṆA, The Supreme Personality of Godhead: A Summary Study of Śrīla Vyāsadeva's Śrīmad-Bhāgavata,* Tenth Canto. Vols. 1–3. New York: Bhaktivedanta Book Trust, 1970.

Bryant, Edwin F. *Krishna: The Beautiful Legend of God.* New York: Penguin, 2004.

Goodall, Dominic, ed. "Bhāgavata-Purāṇa Book X (Chapters 29–33)." In *Hindu Scriptures,* edited by Goodall. Berkeley: University of California Press, 1996.

Goswami, C. L. *Śrīmad Bhāgavata Mahāpurāṇa.* Sanskrit text and English translation. Third edition. 2 vols. Parts 1 and 2. Gorakhpur: Gita Press, [1971] 1995.

Mukerjee, Radhakamal. *Lord of the Autumn Moons.* With an introduction and commentary. Bombay: Asia Publishing House, 1957.

Redington, James D., S.J. *Vallabhācārya on the Love Games of Kṛṣṇa.* Delhi: Motilal Banarsidass, 1983.

Sanyal, J. M. *The Srimad-Bhagavatam of Krishna-Dwaipayana Vyasa.* Vols. 1 and 2. English translation. New Delhi: Munshiram Manoharlal, 1970.

Śrīmad-Bhāgavata-Mahāpurāṇam. With the commentaries of various teachers. Ahmedabhad: Śrī Bhāgavata Vidyāpīṭh Nyāsīpariṣad, n.d.

Śrīmad Bhāgavatam. Tenth Book with Viśvanātha Cakravarti commentary in Sanskrit Text in Bengali transliteration. Śrī Māyāpura: Śrī Caitanya Math, n.d.

Śrīmad Bhāgavatam, Sanskrit edition. Volumes 1 and 2. Madras: V. Ramaswamy Sastrulu and Sons, 1937.

Tagare, Ganesh Vasudeo. *The Bhāgavata-Purāna.* Parts 1–5. Introduction, translation, and annotation. Ancient Indian Tradition and Mythology 7–11. J. L. Shastri, series editor. Delhi: Motilal Banarsidass, 1976–78.

RELATED PRIMARY SOURCES IN ORIGINAL LANGUAGES AND IN TRANSLATION

Baladeva Vidyābhūṣana. *Govinda Bhāṣya.* English translation by Major B. D. Basu. Found in *Vedānta-Sūtras of Bādarāyaṇa with the Commentary of Baladeva.* Sacred Books of the Hindus. New York: AMS Press, 1974.

———. *Prameya Ratnāvalī.* Sanskrit text and translation by Major B. D. Basu. Found in *Vedānta-Sūtras of Bādarāyaṇa with the Commentary of Baladeva.* Sacred Books of the Hindus. New York: AMS Press, 1974.

———. *Siddhānta Ratna of Baladeva Vidyābhūṣaṇa.* Edited with introduction by Gopi Nath Kaviraja. Princess of Wales Saraswati Bhavana Texts 10 (Part 1). Benares: Vidya Vilas Press, 1924.

The Bhaktirasāmṛtasindhu of Rūpa Gosvāmin. Translated with introduction and notes by David L. Haberman. New Delhi: Indira Gandhi National Centre for the Arts; and Delhi: Motilal Banarsidass, 2003.

Bilvamaṅgala, Līlāśuka. *The Love of Krishna: The Kṛṣṇakarṇāmṛta of Līlāśuka Bilvamaṅgala,* edited and translated by Frances Wilson. Philadelphia: University of Pennsylvania Press, 1975.

Classical Hindu Mythology: A Reader in the Sanskrit Purāṇas. Edited and translated by Cornelia Dimmitt and J.A.B. van Buitenen. Philadelphia: Temple University Press, 1978.

Dimock, Edward C., Jr. *Caitanya Caritāmṛta of Kṛṣṇadāsa Kavirāja: A Translation and Commentary.* Harvard Oriental Series 56. Cambridge: Harvard University Press, 1999.

Griffith, Ralph T. H., trans. *The Hymns of the Ṛgveda.* Edited by J. L. Shastri. Delhi: Motilal Banarsidass, 1973.

Harivaṁśaḥ. Critical edition by Parashuram Lakshman Vaidya, 2 vols. Poona: Bhandarkar Oriental Research Institute, 1969–71.

Hindu Scriptures. Edited with new translations by Dominic Goodall (based on an anthology by R. C. Zaehner). Berkeley: University of California Press, 1996.

Hume, Robert Ernest, trans. *The Thirteen Principal Upanishads.* Second edition. London: Oxford University Press, 1975.

Jayadeva Gosvāmin. *Love Song of the Dark Lord: Jayadeva's Gītagovinda.* Sanskrit text; edited and translated by Barbara Stoler Miller. New York: Columbia University Press, 1977.

Jīva Gosvāmin. *Bhāgavata-sandarbha: Bhakti-Prīti Sandarbhas.* Sanskrit text in Bengali script. Critical notes by Haridās Śarman. Vrindaban: Pūrīdās, Gaurābda 465 (1951).

———. *Bhāgavata-sandarbha: Tattva, Bhagavata, Paramātma, Kṛṣṇa Sandarbhas.* Sanskrit text in Bengali script. Critical notes by Haridās Śarman. Vrindaban: Pūrīdās, Gaurābda 464 (1950).

———. *Krama-sandarbhaḥ.* Sanskrit text in Bengali script. Critical notes by Haridās Śarman. Vrindaban: Pūrīdās, Gaurābda 466 (1952).

Kavikarṇapūra Goswāmi. *Śrī Śrīmad Ānanda Vṛndāvana Campūḥ.* Sanskrit text in Bengali script. Critical notes by Haridās Śarman. Vrindaban: Pūrīdās, Gaurābda 468 (1954).

Kṛṣṇadāsa Kavirāja Gosvāmī. *Govinda-līlāmṛtam.* Ramañretī, Vṛndābana: Kṛpāsindhu Dasa Bābāji Mahārāja, Caitanyābdaḥ 463 (1949).

———. *Śrī Caitanya-caritāmṛta.* Original Sanskrit and Bengali Text. Translation and Commentary by A. C. Bhaktivedanta Swami Prabhupāda. 9 vols. Los Angeles: Bhaktivedanta Book Trust, [1975] 1996.

———. *Śrī Govinda-līlāmṛtam.* Vols. 1–4. Original Sanskrit text with commentary by Haridāsaśāstrī. Vrindaban: Sri Gadadhara Gaurahari Press, n.d.

———. *Śrī Śrī Caitanya Caritāmṛta.* Amṛta Pravāha-bhaṣya Commentary by Bhaktivinoda Thakura. Calcutta: Gaudiya Mission, Caitanyābda 471 (1957).

Nizami. *The Story of Layla and Majnun.* Translated from the Persian and edited by Dr. Rudolf Gelpke; English version in collaboration with E. Mattin and G. Hill; final chapter translated from the Persian by Zia Inayat Khan and Omid Safi. New Lebanon, N.Y.: Omega Publications, 1977.

Pauwels, Heidi Reika Maria. *Kṛṣṇa's Round Dance Reconsidered: Harirām Vyās's Hindī Rās-pañcādhyāyī.* London: Curzon, 1996.

Prabodhānanda Sarasvatī. *Śrī Śrī Rāsa Pravandhaḥ.* Sanskrit text in Bengali script. Critical notes by Haridās Śarman. In a collection of his works entitled *Śrīla Prabodhānanda Sarasvatī Gosvāmipāda Granthamālā.* Vrindaban: Pūrīdās, Gaurābda 467 (1953).

Radhakrishnan, S., trans. *The Principal Upaniṣads.* New Delhi: INDUS, 1944.

Rūpa Gosvāmin. *Bhakti-rasāmṛta-sindhuḥ.* Sanskrit text in Bengali script. Commentaries of Jiva Gosvāmin, Mukundadas, and Viśvanātha Cakravarti. Navadvīpa: Haribol Kutir, Gaurābdaḥ 462 (1948).

———. *Bhakti-rasāmṛta-sindhuḥ.* Sanskrit text. Commentaries of Jīva Gosvāmin, Durgamasaṁgamanī; Viśvanātha Cakravartti, Bhaktisārapradarśinī; and Śyāmadasa, Harikrpā-bodhinī (in Hindi). Vrindaban: Śyāmalāl Hakīm, n.d.

———. *The Nectar of Instruction (Śrī Upadeśāmṛta).* Sanskrit text. Translation and commentary by A. C. Bhaktivedanta Swami Prabhupāda. Los Angeles: Bhaktivedanta Book Trust, 1975.

———. *Ujjvala-nīlamaṇiḥ.* Sanskrit text in Bengali script. Commentaries by Jīva Gosvāmin and Viśvanātha Cakravarti. Murshidabad edition. Baramapura: Rādhāraman Press, 1341 B.S. (c.1934).

Sanātana Gosvāmin. *Bṛhad-vaiśnava-toṣanī.* Sanskrit text in Bengali script. Critical notes by Haridās Śarman. Vrindaban: Pūrīdās, Gaurābda 465 (1951).

Śāṇḍilya, The One Hundred Aphorisms. The Sacred Books of the Hindus 7, Bhakti Sastra, Part 2. Sanskrit text and translation by Major B. D. Basu. Allahabad: Bhuvaneswari Asrama, 1911.

Schweig, Graham M., trans. *The Bhakti Sūtra: Concise Teachings of Nārada on the Nature of Love.* Translations from the Asian Classics. New York: Columbia University Press, forthcoming.

———. *Bhagavad Gītā: Song of the Beloved Lord.* San Francisco: Harper Collins, forthcoming.

Shri Brahma-Samhita. Sanskrit text and translation by Bhakti Siddhanta Saraswati Goswami. Brahma-saṁhitā-tīkā commentary of Jīva Gosvāmin (Sanskrit text). Second edition. Madras: Sree Gaudiya Math, 1958.

Twelve Essential Upanishads, Vol. 4 (*Svetāsvatara* and *Gopālatāpani Upanishads*). Translated and edited by Bhakti Prajnan Yati. Madras: Gaudiya Math, 1984.

Vedānta-Sūtras of Bādarāyaṇa. Sanskrit text and translation of Vedānta Sūtras; translation of commentary by Baladeva Vidyābhūṣana. Sacred Books of the Hindus. Edited by Major B. D. Basu. New York: AMS Press, 1974.

The Viṣṇu Purāṇa. Translated by H. H. Wilson. 2 vols. Delhi: Nag Publishers, 1980.

Viswanatha. *Vishwanatha's Sahityadarpana.* Sanskrit text. Edited and translated by Kumudranjan Ray. Vol. 1 (Chapters 1–5), vol. 2 (Chapter 6), vol. 3 (Chapters 7–9), vol. 4 (Chapter 10). Calcutta: K. Ray, 1957.

Viśvanātha Cakravartin, *Bhakti-rasāmṛta-sindhu-bindu.* "The Bhaktirasāmṛtasindhubindu of Viśvanātha Cakravartin." Translation and introduction by Klaus Klostermaier. *Journal of the American Oriental Society* 94, No. 1 (January–March 1974).

———. *Śrī-Bhakti-rasāmṛta-sindhu-binduḥ.* Sanskrit text. Vṛndāvana: Śrī-Harināma Press, n.d.

SECONDARY SOURCES

Archer, W. G. *The Loves of Krishna in Indian Painting and Poetry.* New York: Grove, n.d.

Bhandarkar, Sir R. G. *Vaiṣṇavism, Śaivism, and Minor Religious Systems.* Varanasi: Indological Book House, 1965.

Bhattacharya, S. K. *Kṛṣṇa-Cult.* New Delhi: Associated Publishing House, 1978.

Bhaṭṭāchārya, Siddheśvara. *The Philosophy of the Śrīmad-Bhāgavata,* Vols. 1 and 2. Santiniketan: Visva-Bharati, 1960.

Bloch, Ariel, and Chana Bloch, trans. *The Song of Songs: A New Translation.* Berkeley: University of California Press, 1995.

Brown, C. Mackenzie. "The Theology of Rādhā in the Purāṇas." In *The Divine Consort: Rādhā and the Goddesses of India,* edited by John Stratton Hawley and Donna M. Wulff. Berkeley: Berkeley Religious Studies Series, 1982.

Bryant, Edwin F. "The Date and Provenance of the *Bhāgavata Purāṇa* and the Vaikuṇṭha Perumāl Temple." *Journal of Vaishnava Studies* 11, No. 1 (Fall 2002).

Carman, John Braisted. "Bhakti." In *Encyclopedia of Religion,* edited by Mircea Eliade, vol. 2. New York: Macmillan, 1987.

———. "Comments: The Reversal and Rejection of Bhakti." In *The Divine Consort: Rādhā and the Goddesses of India,* edited by John Stratton Hawley and Donna M. Wulff. Berkeley: Berkeley Religious Studies Series, 1982.

———. "Conceiving Hindu 'Bhakti' as Theistic Mysticism." In *Mysticism and Religious Traditions,* edited by Steven Katz. New York: Oxford University Press, 1983.

———. "Hindu Bhakti as a Middle Way." In *The Other Side of God: A Polarity in World Religions,* edited by Peter L. Berger. New York: Anchor Press/Doubleday, 1981.

Carpenter, J. Estlin. *Theism in Medieval India.* New Delhi: Munshiram Manoharlal, 1977.

Chakravarti, Sudhindra Chandra. *Philosophical Foundation of Bengal Vaishnavism.* Delhi: Academic Publishers, 1969.

Clooney, Francis X., S.J. *Seeing through Texts: Doing Theology among the Śrīvaiṣṇavas of South India.* Albany: State University of New York Press, 1996.

Das Gupta, Mrinal. "Śraddhā and Bhakti in Vedic Literature." *Indian Historical Quarterly* 6, no. 2 (June 1930).

Das Gupta, Shashibhusan. *Obscure Religious Cults.* Calcutta: Firma KLM, 1976.

Dasgupta, S. N. *Hindu Mysticism.* New York: Frederick Ungar, 1977.

———. *A History of Indian Philosophy.* 1–5. Cambridge: Cambridge University Press, 1940.

De, S. K. *Ancient Indian Erotics and Erotic Literatue.* Calcutta: Firma K. L. Mukhopadhyay, 1969.

———. *Aspects of Sanskrit Literature.* Calcutta: Firma KLM, 1976.

———. *Early History of the Vaiṣṇava Faith and Movement in Bengal.* Calcutta: Firma K. L. Mukhopadhyay, 1961.

———. *History of Sanskrit Poetics.* Calcutta: Firma KLM, 1976.

Devanandan, Paul David. *The Concept of Māyā: An Essay in Historical Survey of the Hindu Theory of the World, with Special Reference to the Vedānta.* London: Lutterworth, 1950.

Dhavamony, Mariasusai. *Love of God: According to Śaiva Siddhānta.* Oxford: Clarendon Press, 1971.

Dimock, Edward C., Jr. "Doctrine and Practice among the Vaiṣṇavas of Bengal." In *Krishna: Myths, Rites, and Attitudes,* edited by Milton Singer. Chicago: University of Chicago Press, 1966.

———. *The Place of the Hidden Moon: Erotic Mysticism in the Vaiṣṇava-Sahajiyā Cult of Bengal.* Chicago: University of Chicago Press, 1966.

Dimock, Edward C., Jr., and Denise Levertov, trans. *In Praise of Krishna: Songs from the Bengali.* Introduction and Notes by Edward C. Dimock, Jr. Chicago: University of Chicago Press, 1967.

Dimock, Edward C., Jr., Edwin Gerow, C. M. Naim, A. K. Ramanujan, Gordon Roadarmel, and J.A.B. van Buitenen. *The Literatures of India: An Introduction.* Chicago: University of Chicago Press, 1969.

Eck, Diana L. *Encountering God: A Spiritual Journey from Bozeman to Banaras.* Boston: Beacon, 1993.

Eliade, Mircea. *Yoga: Immortality and Freedom.* Princeton: Princeton University Press, 1958.

Entwistle, Alan W. *Braj: Centre of Krishna Pilgrimage.* Groningen: Egbert Forsten, 1987.

Gerow, Edwin. *A Glossary of Indian Figures of Speech.* Paris: Mouton, 1971.

———. *Indian Poetics.* Vol. 4 of *A History of Indian Literature,* edited by Jan Gonda. Wiesbaden: Otto Harrassowitz, 1977.

Goswami, Shrivatsa. "Rādhā: The Play and Perfection of Rasa." In *The Divine Consort: Rādhā and the Goddesses of India,* edited by John Stratton Hawley and Donna M. Wulff. Berkeley: Berkeley Religious Studies Series, 1982.

Green, Deirdre. "Living between the Worlds: Bhakti Poetry and the Carmelite Mystics." In *The Yogi and the Mystic: Studies in Indian and Comparative Mysticism,* edited by Karel Werner. London: Curzon, 1989.

Gupta, Shashibhusan Das. *Obscure Religious Cults.* Calcutta: Firma KLM, 1976.

Haberman, David L. *Acting as a Way of Salvation: A Study of Rāgānugā Bhakti Sādhana.* New York: Oxford University Press, 1988.

———. "Divine Betrayal: Krishna-Gopal of Braj in the Eyes of Outsiders." *Journal of Vaishnava Studies* 3, no. 1 (Winter 1994).

———. *Journey through the Twelve Forests.* New York: Oxford University Press, 1994.

———. "On Trial: The Love of the Sixteen Thousand Gopees." *History of Religions* 33, no. 1 (1993).

Hardy, Friedhelm. *Viraha-bhakti: The Early History of Kṛṣṇa Devotion in South India.* Delhi: Oxford University Press, 1983.

Hawley, John Stratton. *Sūr Dās: Poet, Singer, Saint.* Delhi: Oxford University Press, 1984.

Hawley, John Stratton, in association with Shrivatsa Goswami. *At Play with Krishna: Pilgrimage Dramas from Brindavan.* Princeton: Princeton University Press, 1981.

Hawley, John Stratton, and Mark Juergensmeyer. *Songs of the Saints of India.* New York: Oxford University Press, 1988.

Hawley, John Stratton, and Donna M. Wulff, eds. *The Divine Consort: Rādhā and the Goddesses of India.* Berkeley: Berkeley Religious Studies Series, 1982.

Hein, Norvin J. "Caitanya's Ecstasies and the Theology of the Name." In *Hinduism: New Essays in the History of Religions,* edited by Bardwell L. Smith. Leiden: E. J. Brill, 1976.

———. "Comments: Rādhā and Erotic Community." In *The Divine Consort: Rādhā and the Goddesses of India,* edited by John Stratton Hawley and Donna M. Wulff. Berkeley: Berkeley Religious Studies Series, 1982.

———. *The Miracle Plays of Mathurā.* New Haven: Yale University Press, 1972.

Hopkins, Thomas J. "The Social Teaching of the Bhāgavata Purāṇa." In *Krishna: Myths, Rites, and Attitudes,* edited by Milton Singer. Chicago: University of Chicago Press, 1966.

Hospital, Clifford George. "The Marvellous Acts of God: A Study in the Bhāgavata Purāṇa." Ph.D. dissertation, Harvard University, 1973.

Ingalls, Daniel H. H., trans. *Sanskrit Poetry from Vidyākara's "Treasury."* Cambridge: Belknap Press of Harvard University Press, 1965.

Jarow, E. H. Rick. *Tales for the Dying: The Death Narrative of the Bhāgavata-Purāṇa.* Albany: State University of New York Press, 2003.

John of the Cross. *The Collected Works of Saint John of the Cross.* Translated by Kieran Kavanaugh, O.C.D. and Otilio Rodriguez, O.C.D., with revisions and introductions by Kieran Kavanaugh, O.C.D. Washington: ICS Publications, 1991.

Jung, C. G. *Mandala Symbolism.* Translated by R.F.C. Hull. Collected Works of C. G. Jung, vol. 9, part 1. Princeton: Princeton University Press, 1959.

———. *Memories, Dreams, Reflections.* New York: Vintage Books, [1961] 1965.

Kapoor, O.B.L. *The Philosophy and Religion of Śrī Caitanya.* Delhi: Munshiram Manoharlal, 1976.

Kinsley, David R. *The Divine Player: A Study of Kṛṣṇa Līlā.* Delhi: Motilal Banarsidass, 1979.

———. *Hindu Goddesses: Visions of the Divine Feminine in the Hindu Religious Tradition.* Berkeley: University of California Press, 1988.

———. *The Sword and the Flute: Kālī and Kṛṣṇa, Dark Visions of the Terrible and the Sublime in Hindu Mythology.* Berkeley: University of California Press, 1975.

Klostermaier, Klaus K. "Criteria of Authenticity of Mystical Experience." In *Indian Philosophical Annual* 17. University of Madras: Radhakrishnan Institute for Advanced Study in Philosophy, 1984–85.

———. "Hṛdayavidyā: A Sketch of a Hindu-Christian Theology of Love." *Journal of Ecumenical Studies* (Temple University), 1972.

———. *In the Paradise of Krishna: Hindu and Christian Seekers.* Philadelphia: Westminster, 1969.

———. *A Survey of Hinduism.* Albany: State University of New York Press, 1989.

———. "A Universe of Feelings." In *Shri Krishna Caitanya and the Bhakti Religion,* edited by E. Weber. New York: Verlag Peter Lang, 1988.

Krishna The Divine Lover: Myth and Legend through Indian Art. Edited by Enrico Isacco. New York: C.H.P. Editions, 1982.

Lynch, Owen M., ed. *Divine Passions: The Social Construction of Emotion in India.* Berkeley: University of California Press, 1990.

Majumdar, A. K. *Bhakti Renaissance.* Bombay: Bharatiya Vidya Bhavan, 1979.

———. *Caitanya: His Life and Doctrine.* Bombay: Bharatiya Vidya Bhavan, 1969.

———. *Concise History of Ancient India.* Vol. 1, *Political History.* New Delhi: Munshiram Manoharlal, 1973.

———. *Concise History of Ancient India.* Vol. 2, *Political Theory, Administration, and Economic Life.* New Delhi: Munshiram Manoharlal, 1973.

———. *Concise History of Ancient India.* Vol. 3, Hinduism—Society, Religion, and Philosophy. New Delhi: Munshiram Manoharlal, 1973.

———. *Gauḍīya-Vaiṣṇava Studies.* Calcutta: Jijnasa, 1978.

Marglin, Frederique Apffel. "Refining the Body: Transformative Emotion in Ritual Dance." In *Divine Passions: The Social Construction of Emotion in India,* edited by Owen M. Lynch. Berkeley: University of California Press, 1990.

———. "Types of Sexual Union and Their Implicit Meanings." In *The Divine Consort: Rādhā and the Goddesses of India,* edited by John Stratton Hawley and Donna M. Wulff. Berkeley: Berkeley Religious Studies Series, 1982.

Matchett, Freda. "The Pervasiveness of Bhakti in the Bhāgavata Purāṇa." In *Love Divine: Studies in Bhakti and Devotional Mysticism,* edited by Karel Werner. Durham Indological Series 3. Durham: Curzon, 1993.

McDaniel, June. *The Madness of the Saints: Ecstatic Religion in Bengal.* Chicago: University of Chicago Press, 1989.

Miller, Barbara Stoler. "The Divine Duality of Rādhā and Krishna." In *The Divine Consort: Rādhā and the Goddesses of India,* edited by John Stratton Hawley and Donna M. Wulff. Berkeley: Berkeley Religious Studies Series, 1982.

Mukherji, S. C. *A Study of Vaiṣṇavism in Ancient and Medieval Bengal up to the Advent of Chaitanya.* Calcutta: Punthi Pustak, 1966.

Narang, Sudesh. *The Vaiṣṇava Philosophy According to Baladeva Vidyā Bhūṣaṇa.* Delhi: Nag Publishers, 1984.

Narayanan, Vasudha. *The Way and the Goal: Expressions of Devotion in the Early Śrī Vaiṣṇava Tradition.* Washington, D.C.: Institute for Vaishnava Studies and the Center for the Study of World Religions at Harvard University, 1987.

O'Connell, Joseph Thomas. "Social Implications of the Gauḍīya Vaiṣṇava Movement." Ph.D. dissertation, Harvard University, 1970.

———. "Were Caitanya's Vaiṣṇavas Really Sahajiyās? The Case of Rāmānanda Rāya." In *Shaping Bengali Worlds, Public and Private,* edited by Tony K. Stewart. South Asia Series Occasional Paper 37. East Lansing: Michigan State University, 1989.

Otto, Rudolf. *The Idea of the Holy.* Translated by John W. Harvey. London: Oxford University Press, 1923.

———. *India's Religion of Grace and Christianity Compared and Contrasted.* Translated by Frank Hugh Foster. New York: Macmillan, 1930.

Pope, Marvin H., trans. *Song of Songs: A New Translation with Introduction and Commentary.* New York: Doubleday, 1977.

Sanyal, Nisi Kanta. *The Erotic Principle and Unalloyed Devotion.* Calcutta: Gaudiya Mission, 1941.

Sax, William S., ed. *The Gods at Play: Līlā in South Asia.* New York: Oxford University Press, 1995.

Schweig, Graham M. *Bhagavad Gītā: Comprehensive Sanskrit Concordance and Word Index.* Unpublished manuscript.

———. *A Comprehensive Annotated Bibliography of Secondary Sources on Gaudiya Vaishnavism.* Unpublished manuscript and on-line database. Washington, D.C.: Institute for Vaishnava Studies, 1988.

———. "Dance of Divine Love: The Rāsalīlā of Krishna as a Vision of Selfless Devotion." Doctoral dissertation, Harvard University, 1998.

———. "The Divine Feminine in the Theology of Krishna." In *Sources of the Krishna Tradition,* edited by Edwin F. Bryant. New York: Oxford University Press, forthcoming 2005.

———. "Dying the Good Death: The Transfigurative Power of Bhakti." *Journal of Vaishnava Studies* 11, no. 2 (Spring 2003).

———. "The Five Schools of Vaishnavism." *Hinduism Today,* international edition 12, no. 6, (June 1990).

———. "Humility and Passion: A Caitanyite Vaishnava Ethics of Devotion." *Journal of Religious Ethics* 30, no. 3 (Fall 2002).

———. "Krishna: The Intimate Deity." In *The Hare Krishna Movement: The Post-Charismatic Fate of a Religious Transplant,* edited by Edwin F. Bryant and Maria Ekstrand. New York: Columbia University Press, 2004.

———. "Rādhā and the Rāsalīlā: The Esoteric Vision of Caitanyaite Vaishnavism." *Journal of Vaishnava Studies* 8, no. 2 (Spring 2000).

———. "Rāsalīlā Pañcādhyāya: The Bhāgavata's Ultimate Vision of the Gopīs." *Journal of Vaishnava Studies* 5, no. 4 (Fall 1997).

———. "Sparks from God: A Phenomenological Sketch of Symbol." In *Psychoanalysis and Religion,* edited by Joseph H. Smith and Susan A. Handelman. Baltimore: Johns Hopkins University Press, 1990.

Sen, Dinesh Chandra. *History of Bengali Language and Literature.* Calcutta: University of Calcutta, 1954.

Sen, Sukumar. *History of Bengali Literature.* New Delhi: Sahitya Akademi, 1960.

Shāstri, Surendra Nath. *The Laws and Practice of Sanskrit Drama.* Vol. 1. Varanasi: Chowkhamba Sanskrit Series Office, 1961.

Sheridan, Daniel P. "Devotion in the Bhāgavata Purāna and Christian Love: Bhakti, Agape, Eros." *Horizons* 8, no. 2 (1981).

Sheth, Noel, S. J. *The Divinity of Krishna.* Delhi: Munshiram Manoharlal, 1984.

Siegel, Lee. *Sacred and Profane Dimensions of Love in Indian Traditions as Exemplified in the Gītagovinda of Jayadeva.* Delhi: Oxford University Press, 1974.

Singer, Milton. "The Rādhā-Krishna Bhajanas of Madras City." In *Krishna: Myths, Rites, and Attitudes,* edited by Singer. Chicago: University of Chicago Press, 1966.

Sinha, Jadunath. *Indian Psychology.* Vol. 1, *Cognition.* Calcutta: Sinha Publishing House, 1958.

———. *Indian Psychology.* Vol. 2, *Emotion and Will.* Calcutta: Sinha Publishing House, 1961.

Smith, Wilfred Cantwell. *What Is Scripture? A Comparative Approach.* Minneapolis: Fortress, 1993.

Spink, Walter. *Krishnamandala, A Devotional Theme in Indian Art.* Ann Arbor: Center for South and South East Asian Studies, 1971.

Thielemen, Selina. *Rāsalīlā: A Musical Study of Religious Drama in Vraja.* New Delhi: APH Publishing, 1998.

Tillich, Paul. *Christianity and the Encounter of the World Religions.* New York: Columbia University Press, 1963.

Venkateswaran, T. K. "Rādhā-Krishna Bhajanas of South India: A Phenomenological, Theological, and Philosophical Study." In *Krishna: Myths, Rites, and Attitudes,* edited by Milton Singer. Chicago: University of Chicago Press, 1966.

White, Charles, S.J. *The* Caurāsī Pad *of Śrī Hit Harivaṁś.* Introducton, Translation, Notes, and edited Braj Bhāṣā text. Honolulu: University Press of Hawaii, 1977.

Wulff, Donna M. *Drama as a Mode of Religious Realization: The Vidagdhamādhava of Rūpa Gosvāmī.* Chico: Scholars Press, 1984.

———. "A Sanskrit Portrait: Rādhā in the Plays of Rūpa Gosvāmī." In *The Divine Consort: Rādhā and the Goddesses of India,* edited by John

Stratton Hawley and Donna M. Wulff. Berkeley: Berkeley Religious Studies Series, 1982.

Zimmer, Heinrich. *Myths and Symbols in Indian Art and Civilization.* Edited by Joseph Campbell. Princeton: Princeton University Press, 1946.

Index

Numbers in bold type indicate items on pages of verse.

About the Author

Graham M. Schweig completed his graduate studies at Harvard University and the University of Chicago, and received his doctorate in Comparative Religion from Harvard. Schweig has taught at Duke University and University of North Carolina, and is currently Associate Professor of Philosophy and Religious Studies and Director of the Indic Studies Program at Christopher Newport University, on the Virginia peninsula. He is also Senior Editor of the international periodical, *Journal of Vaishnava Studies.*

From early on, Schweig has been a practitioner of various forms of meditational and devotional yoga under the direct guidance of traditional teachers. His research has taken him to India many times, including a one-year project involving the preservation of rare Vaishnava manuscripts, funded by the Smithsonian Institution. Schweig's work focuses on the devotional theistic traditions of India, forms of love mysticism in world religion, especially Christian and Vaishnava traditions, and the psychology of religion.